PHILADELPHIA

Patricians & Philistines

1900-1950

JOHN LUKACS

FARRAR · STRAUS · GIROUX
NEW YORK

Copyright © 1980, 1981 by John Lukacs
All rights reserved
Printed in the United States of America
Published simultaneously in Canada
by McGraw-Hill Ryerson Ltd., Toronto
Designed by Jeffrey Schaire
First printing, 1981

Abridged versions of the Boies Penrose
and Owen Wister chapters have been
published in American Heritage magazine

Library of Congress Cataloging in Publication Data
Lukacs, John A.
Philadelphia, patricians & philistines, 1900–1950.
Includes bibliographical references and index.
Contents: Philadelphia, 1900—Boies Penrose—
Agnes Repplier—[etc.]
1. Philadelphia (Pa.)—Social life and customs.
2. Philadelphia (Pa.)—Biography.
3. Upper classes—Pennsylvania—Philadelphia.
I. Title.
F158.5.L9   1981   974.8'1104   81–1900   AACR2

TO PAUL

Philadelphian born and bred

CONTENTS

ILLUSTRATIONS

PHILADELPHIA
Patricians & Philistines
1900-1950

PHILADELPHIA
1900

MOST FOREIGN VISITORS in the late nineteenth century, as well as this writer in the twentieth, found Philadelphia to be an unexpected city.[1] This place, in America, was not an exaggerated representation of itself, like New York or Chicago, or like others that would actually become caricatures of themselves. The more one found out about it, the more interesting it became. This was true, too, of certain people who were authentic Philadelphians. Their conventions were complex, and their convictions often paradoxical. The more authentic their character, the more eccentric they were, in the original sense of that adjective, outside the central stream of American life, while they were rooted in Philadelphia.

I have chosen to write about some of them in this book, about Philadelphians who lived and flourished mainly during the first half of this century: a political boss, a magazine mogul, a lady writer, an impetuous diplomatist, a Philadelphia lawyer, a patrician prophet of decline, an art collector, and others. The political boss was perhaps the most monumental politician of his time. The magazine mogul was the most famous embodiment of the American success story in his lifetime. The lady writer, now forgotten, during her lifetime was the dean of American essayists. The diplomatist was the most brilliant of the ambassadors of the Republic during the 1930s. The collector

---

[1] "I distinguish the picturesque and the beautiful, and I add to them . . . a third and distinct character, which I call *unexpectedness*," says one of Thomas Love Peacock's characters in *Headlong Hall*—to be distinguished from *Crotchet Castle*, which had its share of surprises.

was a radical proponent of a fundamental theory of art. They were Philadelphians: often uncelebrated at home, and yet at home in Philadelphia. I have framed their stories by two chapters, descriptions of the city in 1900 and in 1950.

IN 1900 Rudyard Kipling wrote a curious poem about Philadelphia:

> *If you're off to Philadelphia in the morning,*
> *You mustn't take my stories for a guide.*
> *There's little left, indeed, of the city you will read of,*
> *And all the folks I write about have died.*

There follow eight stanzas of uneven length, a total of forty-four longish lines, chockful of arcane information about Philadelphia in the 1790s.[2] Kipling had obviously amassed a large amount of knowledge about Philadelphia. Even more obvious is the fact that he had a sense of affection for the city and for the Pennsylvania country:

> *If you're off to Philadelphia this morning,*
> *And wish to prove the truth of what I say,*
> *I pledge my word that you'll find the pleasant land behind*
> *Unaltered since Red Jacket rode that way.*
> *Still the pine-woods scent the noon; still the catbird sings*
> *his tune;*
> *Still autumn sets the maple-forest blazing;*
> *Still the grape-vine through the dusk flings her soul-*
> *compelling musk;*
> *Still the fire-flies in the corn make night amazing!*
>
> *They are there, there, there with Earth immortal*
> *(Citizens, I give you friendly warning).*
> *The things that truly last when men and times have passed,*
> *They are all in Pennsylvania this morning![3]*

---

[2] Talleyrand, Count Zinzendorf's church, Bob Bicknell's Southern Stages, Toby Hirte, Pharaoh the fiddler, Epply's, "the Buck," Adam Goos, Pastor Meder—names hardly known even by the more assiduous experts of the history of the town.

[3] "Philadelphia," from *Rewards and Fairies. The Definitive Edition of Rudyard Kipling's Verse* (London, 1960), pp. 585–86.

These last two stanzas, and especially the last two lines, used to be quoted by two generations of Philadelphia worthies, Kiplingites as they were, on innumerable occasions: Hunt Breakfasts, Farmers' Clubs, State in Schuylkill lunches. Sometimes they pressed the point unduly. George Wharton Pepper, the prototypical Philadelphian of the first half of the twentieth century, attempted to prove that Kipling's "If" had been "inspired by Washington's character."[4]

Kipling had a special affection for Pennsylvania. When he first crossed the United States in 1889, he came to "Musquash" (Beaver, Pennsylvania). "I arrived at the infinite peace of the tiny township of Musquash on the Monongahela River . . . Imagine a rolling, wooded, English landscape, under softest blue skies, dotted at three-mile intervals with fat little, quiet villages . . ." There follows an Arcadian account of American country life which has hardly an equal anywhere else. And Kipling's frequently waspish *American Notes* end with this sentence: "There are worse things in this world than being 'one of the boys' in Musquash."[5] In more than one sense, he remained one of the boys; or rather, the Pennsylvania boys of 1889 remained Kiplingites through their adult lives. He was the English writer closest to their hearts and to their minds.

They were the patricians of Philadelphia, the aristocracy of the American democracy, of the republic of the Philadelphia that was. Every country—even more, every era—has the aristocracy it deserves. Yet to say "aristocracy," in America, is unsatisfactory. In 1900 in England and in Europe the aristocracies still consisted largely of the nobility, of people with titles, or of people who were about to receive titles. In America the word "aristocracy" has been flung around with abandon; social maniacs like the prissy bachelor who administered the lists of Society in New York, as well as enraged populists in the hinterlands, were obsessed with it; yet aristocracy in America

---

[4] In vain. George Wharton Pepper, *Philadelphia Lawyer* (Philadelphia, 1944), pp. 170–71.
[5] New York, 1930, p. 239.

was largely a fiction. People thought that aristocracy consisted, simply and squarely, of the very rich; that the financial and the social pyramid were one and the same; that distinctions of birth were comparable to distinctions of wealth. There were few exceptions to this national belief. One was the society extant in Philadelphia, where—strange and wonderful condition within the mobile and restless American democracy—in a certain sense everybody knew everybody. This kind of unspoken intimacy, secure and free from suspicion, was something different from the stifling closeness, from the public snooperies, from the lack of privacy within American small towns of the period, from which all kinds of sensitive people fled, including Kipling, who observed "the terrifying intimacy of life" in American country towns, "disturbed by the hatred and troubles and jealousies that vex the minds of all but the gods."[6] Philadelphia was a town of families, where even the *arrivistes* were families, not individuals—a remarkable condition during what was otherwise called the Age of Individualism and of Enterprise. Its social order, with its unwritten laws, had little in common with the traditions or with the composition of aristocracies in Europe or in England. It had something in common with the old patrician societies of early modern Europe, nearer to the middle of the continent, with a social and civic order incarnated by the great merchant families in cities such as Basel, Geneva, Amsterdam, Hamburg, or with the *grands bourgeois* (often Protestant) families in France. It had little in common with Proust's world of the Guermantes; it had many things in common with the world of Buddenbrooks (which Thomas Mann described in 1901). In sum, the scene and its components were patrician rather than aristocratic; solidly bourgeois (in the best sense of that often misused word) and not glitteringly feudal; resting on distinctions of birth, yes, but on distinctions derived from the consanguinity of families with high civic

[6] Cited by Louis Cornell, "The American Venture," in John Gross, ed., *The Age of Kipling* (New York, 1972), p. 75.

reputations and not from noble ancestors; on breeding even more than on blood. The word "aristocrat" suggests an individual self-contained to the point of independence; the word "patrician" suggests a family. And the latter, in the broadest sense, was the ideal of Kipling, too, who had no particular affection—and, what is more important for a poet, no particular feeling—for the aristocracy of England. His dream—and in this he was not alone—was the vision of the English, indeed, of the Anglo-Saxon race, as one large family, responsible for law and order across vast portions of the earth: *the* patrician people of the globe, their privileges being the result of their responsibilities.

The ideals of the Philadelphia patricians corresponded to much of this—because of a condition that to them, in 1900, was obvious to the point of being hardly worth stating. The United States, like Canada and Australia and New Zealand, was predominantly "Anglo-Saxon"—an imprecise term, but no matter. The Channel was wider than the Atlantic. The old Bismarck, shortly before his death, was reputed to have said that the most important fact in the evolving world was that the Americans spoke English; the young Churchill, at the beginning of his career,[7] was already convinced that the alliance, and the prospective confederation, of Great Britain and the United States could be the greatest force for good in the modern world. Now appearances *are* realities, in the celestial world as well as on this earth, but not more and not less than statistical realities, they may be deceiving. In 1900 the American upper class, by which I mean not only the richest but the most influential people in

[7] In December 1900 he spoke in Philadelphia, at the Academy of Music (his honorarium was more than double his usual fee elsewhere in the United States). Half a century later, in 1951, during his last prime ministership, he was invited to Philadelphia again, to give an address at the University of Pennsylvania, at a time when Anglo-American relations were muddled: because of their muted crisis he withdrew. These two dates, 1900 and 1951, mark not only the bright morning and the somber evening of his career; they mark, too, the blossoming and the fading of the prospects of his great lifetime project, the eventual confederation of the English-speaking peoples of the world, resting on the allied might of the United States and Great Britain.

America, the men and women who gave the tone and the direction to public opinion (which, then as now, may have been something different from popular sentiment), were still predominantly the descendants of people who had been natives of the British Isles. Yet by 1900 the majority of the American population were descended from other peoples, a condition pregnant with consequences that Tocqueville, the greatest observer of the American democracy, could not have foreseen. Throughout *Democracy in America* Tocqueville, in describing the institutions and the inclinations and the lives of people, referred to them as Anglo-Americans, which, when he wrote in 1831 and 1832, they indeed were. He was also aware of the fact —seldom noted by his commentators, then and now—that while democracy was becoming a universal phenomenon, the United States was a society with characteristics peculiarly its own. He did not live long enough to contemplate the effects of mass immigration; but he would have, I am sure, agreed that the prosperity and the greatness of the American Republic, the happy mediocrity of American lives and the stability of American institutions, were not only due to the fact that they were founded on democratic principles; they were even more due to the fact that they were Anglo-American. As late as 1900, this Anglo-American element was still dominant; fifty years later, this was no longer so. The Anglo-American element in American life was being overwhelmed; a tremendous event, with enormous consequences.

During the first half of this century, the story of the devolution of Anglo-American Philadelphia is a kind of prism, reflecting subtle and profound changes in the national history of the American Republic. Certain of its characteristics, together with William Penn's legacy of tolerance and broad-mindedness, may have been responsible for the condition that around 1900, when elsewhere the hatred of certain classes of people who felt themselves deprived of the blessings and the welcomes of American democracy was especially bitter, threatening to erupt through the surface, Philadelphia was, as the reformer-journalist Lincoln

Steffens despairingly wrote, "corrupt and contented." There was less radical agitation, less evidence of hatred against the upper classes in Philadelphia than in any comparable city in the United States; just as England, the very country whose aristocracy was socially more influential and widespread than that of any other country in Europe, experienced no revolutions during the nineteenth century, alone among the great nations of the Old World.

Philadelphia, in 1900, was provincial and patrician. Provincial, because, unlike the other great cities of the burgeoning nation, uninterested in sophistication; unlike the older Boston or the newer Chicago, incurious about what was happening in New York. Patrician, because of the close relationship of families composing its principal social and financial institutions; indifferent, rather than hostile, to the rising new rich, even when the latter were ready to make their public contributions to the benefit of the city. Unlike New York or Chicago or even Boston, this had something to do with the long-standing Philadelphian tradition of privacy. Interior life was what counted in Philadelphia, including interior decorousness and the interior decoration of lives. This was true even of the houses of Philadelphia at the peak of the Gilded Age; it was the interior quality, not the exterior appearance of their houses which was impressive, and sometimes surprising.

THIS WAS PHILADELPHIA in 1900, American in its outward appearance, and yet peculiar. The cityscape panoramas taken by photographers from the tower of City Hall, or from another tall building, show a brown sea of houses. Indeed, the predominant color is brown, and there is a sepia undertone even in pictures that are gray or black and white.

Some of the brownness has to do with the soft coal of Pennsylvania, burning in innumerable furnaces of Philadelphia houses. The prospect of this sea of uniform houses is not very inspiring. No matter how you turn the photographs, no matter what the perspective, the impression remains largely the same. There is hardly a single landmark that would be recognizable to people who are not Philadelphians, not one outstanding building, not one particular vista. The solitary exception is City Hall, singular and monumental, with an enormous statue of William Penn topping its tower, 547 feet above the street, into the rim of whose head and hat one may climb, and from whose brow innumerable Kodak pictures have sprung, a Philadelphian Statue of Liberty of sorts, a conception of Franco-American architecture at the peak of the Iron Age.

The statue, constructed by Alexander Milne Calder and his Italian assistant Casani, was raised in 1894, and the big clock was installed underneath it in 1899. For decades City Hall was excoriated by Philadelphia aesthetes and even by some of the formidable machine politicians. "The ignoble . . . Ashbridge ['Stars and Stripes' Sam Ashbridge, the mayor in 1900] who had built City Hall, boasting of the fortune he would take out of the contracts, making good his boast."

> City Hall, symbol of dishonesty and ugliness, squatting over the city's heart, its immense meaningless bulk blocking traffic where it was thickest, wasting space, shutting out sun and air from the gloomy rooms within; great corridors that every day were littered with the refuse of the crowd; ill-ventilated courtrooms, where the fetid air lay heavy over judge and jury, witnesses and accused; imitation marble, velvet plush grown dingy with the grim, meaningless decorations, carving of slaves and Cupids where they could not be seen; fly-specked portraits of forgotten nonentities; gilded Venetian ceilings with checkerboard patterns; a Philadelphia architect's dream, perhaps, of the vanished Tuileries.[8]

It is nonetheless an impressive building. Externally at least, it has stood the test of time rather well.

---

[8] Francis Biddle, *The Llanfair Pattern* (Philadelphia, 1927), p. 233. ". . . that perfected miracle of ugliness and inconvenience, that really remarkable combination of bulk and insignificance, the City Hall." Agnes Repplier, *Agnes Irwin* (Philadelphia, 1934), pp. 41–42.

The principal boulevards are very wide. Broad Street, especially its northern portion, is reminiscent of the *prospekti* of Russian towns, wider than the great boulevards of Paris or the Ringstrassen of Central Europe. There is a kind of Ekaterinburg (or, at that, Indianapolis) atmosphere to North Broad Street, with its endless hardwood porches, devoid of coziness; boulevards of empires whose time runs different but where space is enormous, mid-American or mid-Russian.

Looking now at a photograph of the center of the city,[9] evidently snapped by a crouching photographer (I can imagine him, a little man with a derby), one finds a condition worth observing. The picture is of South Broad Street, a few squares south of City Hall, of the very center of the commercial and business life of Philadelphia, with its principal banks, stores, hotels, institutions, including the Union League, the seat of the powerful Republican Party. The City Hall clock stands at twelve. It is high noon, but there is no crowding of the streets. A horse-drawn carriage is crossing Broad from Walnut. There is the shadow of a trolley car behind. There are fewer than one hundred people in this photo, showing at least one half mile of the principal Philadelphia street in the very heart of the city. It is very different from the 1900 pictures we have of downtown New York or Chicago or London or Berlin. Another photograph shows the same panorama, in 1905, from the same vantage point, with two differences: the new and impressive Bellevue-Stratford Hotel has been erected in the place of the old Lafayette; and a herd of sheep is being driven down Broad Street.

In any event, there are no crowds, and there is nothing of the fierce rhythm of metropolitan life in 1900, at the peak of the Money Age. The impression is of slowness and calm, a kind of provincial calm that withstands the shadows of the ornamented skyscrapers of the period. A decade or so later a Philadelphia woman remembered traveling by horsecar

---

9 Philadelphianisms: "center city" instead of "downtown," "pavements" (paved with "Belgian blocks") and not "sidewalks," "squares" and not "blocks." The first usage is more recent than the rest.

through a busy business section. But there has stayed with me
as my chief impression of the endless street a sense of eternal
calm. No matter how much solid work was being done, no
matter how many fortunes were being made and unmade, it
was always placid on the surface, uneventful and unruffled.
The car, jingling along in leisurely fashion, was the one sign of
animation.[10]

"A wondrous Sunday morning at the edge of a vast vacant
Philadelphia street," Henry James wrote in 1905, "a street not
of Penn's creation and vacant of everything but an immeasur-
able bourgeois blankness . . ." He made much of his observation
that Philadelphia, alone among American cities, wasn't "bristling":

> The absence of the note of the perpetual perpendicular, the
> New York, the Chicago note—and I allude here to the mate-
> rial, the constructional exhibition of it—seemed to symbolize
> exactly the principle of indefinite level extension and to offer,
> refreshingly, a challenge to horizontal, to lateral, to more or
> less tangential, to rotary, or better still, to absolute centrifugal
> motion.[11]

Philadelphia had about 1,300,000 inhabitants in 1900: the
third largest American city, and one of the ten largest cities in
the world, an American metropolis. Why, then, this sense of
spaciousness? One reason for it was the unusually large territory
of the city: about one hundred and thirty square miles, larger
even than London. These municipal boundaries were drawn in
1854, in the so-called Consolidation Act, whereby the county
and the city of Philadelphia became identical. There had been
politics behind this act of course. The result was a very large
area of irregular shape, extending far to the north and to the
northwest of the massed houses, with large tracts of farmland
containing isolated farmsteads and one-string villages with
pleasant names: Fox Chase, Sorrel Horse, Rhawnhurst, Edge

[10] Elizabeth Robins Pennell, *Our Philadelphia* (London, 1914), p. 28.
[11] "Philadelphia," in Henry James, *The American Scene* (Bloomington, Ind.,
1968), p. 286.

Hill, the origin of some of these names having been colonial taverns. People could go fox hunting within the municipal boundaries of the third largest American metropolis. This was different from the more socially conscious, and more restricted, fox-hunting practices of the rich around New York or Boston: in Philadelphia, as in Virginia or the Carolinas, a farmer who was a good horseman would join the hunt as a matter of course.

There was another element to the sedate spaciousness of Philadelphia. The prospect of the town from the top was, as we have seen, depressing because of its monotony. When one contemplates, however, the pictures of many of its streets and serried houses taken from ground level, the prospect becomes different. The dark-red brick houses, with their white mantels and shutters (green shutters on the second floor), with their white marble steps, sand-soaped and scrubbed, suggest that coziness which gave Philadelphia the name of "a city of homes." Before 1900 the opulent French Renaissance or Italianate mansions of the very rich were still few; as late as 1900 the luxurious apartment house, with its hydraulic elevators and marble vestibules, was still largely absent in Philadelphia. The exterior aspect of the town houses of the upper class and the houses of the working class was similar. The differences were mostly interior: because Philadelphia was an interior city, one of the few American places of such character.

Again there was a reason for this. The prices for real estate, for land, for rentals in Philadelphia were low, lower than in most other cities, even during the rise of national prosperity that was transforming the Yankee trader into the Croesus of the Western world. In 1896 a middle-class house containing seven rooms could be rented for $15 a month. In 1900 more people owned their houses in Philadelphia than in any other city in the world.[12] There were few tenements. The houses stood closely pressed against each other; yet the sense of spaciousness pre-

[12] One of the reasons for this was the peculiar Philadelphia institution of ground rents, about which see p. 60.

vailed: in one hundred houses in Philadelphia there lived, on the average, 550 inhabitants; in New York, 1,650, a ratio of one to three. Most of the town houses of the upper class were row houses too. In 1924 George Wharton Pepper invited Magnus Johnson, a Populist Senator from Minnesota, to spend a night at his house. Johnson had thought (and said) that Pepper lived in a palace. When they arrived at the Pepper house on Panama Street, Johnson was astonished. "Is *this* where you live, Senator? My God, Senator, you live in an alley!"[13]

Ugly rows of houses were constructed in West and North Philadelphia after 1885 (between 1886 and 1893, 50,000 houses were built, most of them financed by the 450 neighborhood Savings and Loan Associations); yet there was not much in Philadelphia that resembled the hideous three-deckers built in and around Boston for the more prosperous workingmen's families around 1900. In many parts of the town the houses had gardens, not fronting on the street, but hidden and fenced at the back: an interior city, "the city with a country heart."

Like all American cities, Philadelphia never had walls. There was no distinct separation of city from country. The municipal boundaries were largely invisible, legal fictions. Penn was among the first men in the modern world who planned and laid out a grid pattern for numbered streets; yet he insisted that certain squares be kept clear of houses and planted with trees. And even in 1900, at the peak of the urban era, Philadelphia was more of a town than a city: "of all goodly villages, the very goodliest, probably, in the world; the very largest, and flattest, and smoothest, the most rounded and complete" (wrote the visiting Henry James); a "demure country village . . . which has done the work and earned the money of a big bustling town, the cloistered seclusion with which it enjoys its luxury and hides behind its plain brick fronts" (wrote the native Elizabeth Robins Pennell).[14] For a town of its size Philadelphia had few

---

[13] See, however, pp. 29 ff. The Peppers, too, had a comfortable country house.
[14] James, *op. cit.*, p. 270; Pennell, *op. cit.*, pp. 4–5.

monumental hotels, towering apartment houses, shining thoroughfares, glittering evening vistas, smart cafés, opulent music halls, elegant restaurants, splendiferous shops with foreign wares. (The best of its shops were known for the excellence of their local wares: Dexter's for cakes, Margerum's for beef, Fluke's for dainties, Dreka's for stationery, Sautter's for ice cream, Jones's for oysters, Darlington's and Colladay's and Leary's for books, Bailey's and Caldwell's for silver, glassware, jewelry.) There was in Philadelphia none of the coruscating glitter of the late afternoon of Western civilization in 1900, when London, Paris, Vienna glowed like the night-blooming cereus and when the steel and stone fingers of New York were reaching up to the top of the world. The streets of Philadelphia were empty in the evening, except for a few places here and there. Philadelphia did have an Academy of Music, somewhat nondescript and almost dingy outside, though plushy and acoustically plummy inside. It was baptized "Academy of Music" during the prim 1850s, when the original designation, Philadelphia's Opera House, somehow sounded too racy to the Quaker families who were then mostly in charge of musical culture in Philadelphia. During the nineteenth century, music in Philadelphia was Germanic and somber. The musical excellence of the city was, as yet, far from having been established.[15] The Philadelphia Orchestra gave its first concert in 1900; its conductor was Fritz Scheel, formerly master of an orchestra in an amusement park.[16]

Fine restaurants in Philadelphia were nonexistent. The food and drink in private houses were exceptionally good, resting on long-established traditions, such as those of the old Madeira stocks, about which S. Weir Mitchell would write, sometimes at undue length.[17] The Philadelphian *Miss Leslie's Complete Cookery*, first published in 1837, was still in print in 1900 and

---

[15] Nathaniel Burt (a musician and musicologist): "By the 'nineties Philadelphia was something of a provincial musical backwater." *The Perennial Philadelphians: The Autonomy of an American Aristocracy* (Boston, 1963).

[16] After Scheel came Pohlig (1907), then Leopold Stokowski (1912), under whose reign the opulence of the orchestra began.

[17] *A Madeira Party* (New York, 1895).

widely used—this tells us something about the remarkable continuity in Philadelphian patterns of living. Until about 1890 many of the families, patricians as well as workingmen, dined at four. A unique tradition among the better families was the interest which men took in cooking: often the men marketed for meat, and, curious fact, it was their prerogative to make mayonnaise. Chicken salad and fried oysters (a delicious Philadelphia combination), oyster croquettes, fresh shad and shad roe, soft-shell crabs, Philadelphia ice cream, cream cheese, cinnamon buns, terrapin, snapper soup, and scrapple were staples of the Philadelphia cuisine, most of these items standard for the tables of patricians as well as for the boards of workingmen. (So were certain other habits: in Philadelphia the universal custom was to wash the front steps of the houses on Saturday mornings, when Philadelphia streets from end to end were all mops, rivers, and lakes.) One exception to this uniformity of habit was drink: few of the lower-class families would drink wine (sometimes not even Italians), few of the patricians would descend to beer; there were different tastes in whiskey, and the curious custom, persisting to this day, that while even adults of the lower classes would consume quantities of soft drinks, the patricians would profess a great distaste for them—unlike in the South, where the belles, young or matronly, would guzzle Coca-Cola from morning till the setting of the sun. Another exception to the uniformity of good food in Philadelphia was bread—uniformly poor. After 1890 two of the patrician families got together and imported a Frenchman (an Alsatian, Jules Junker), to provide good French-style bread for Philadelphia.[18] The famous caterer was Augustine, a black man with an impressive establishment on Fifteenth Street. "It was considered vulgar to entertain in a hotel, and you gave a ball at your own house."[19]

[18] He must have been successful. In 1900 he had one of the first automobiles in Philadelphia. An oil painting of Junker's car careening through Fairmount Park hangs in one of the corridors of the Atwater Kent Museum.
[19] Biddle, op. cit., p. 51.

"Philadelphia is a city very peculiar," wrote Lafcadio Hearn,

isolated by custom antique, but having a good solid morality, and much peace. It has its own dry drab newspapers which are not like any other newspapers in the world, and contain nothing not immediately concerning Philadelphia. Consequently no echo from New York enters here—nor any from anywhere else . . . But it's the best old city in the whole world all the same.[20]

There was (and at times there still is) an air of blueness in the evenings, a lightness in color perhaps due to the mists of the Delaware and the New Jersey marshes.

And the Archbishop rode away from my christening supper with the twin lamps on his carriage shining, like jeweled eyes, on the blue shadows of an April night in Philadelphia, when the century was young . . . The dusk came with a soft blue alleviation as if not to blot out the beautiful day in darkness. There were still a few gas lamps on Pine Street, and the lamplighter would come along with his ladder and torch, and the lamps would sizzle and sputter for awhile and then come on brightly. The lamps in the long salon parlors across the street would be lit. Mrs. Windsor had wax candles in the candelabra on the mantel and each candle gleamed with a little flame.[21]

Philadelphia was composed of neighborhoods, and to a considerable extent it still is. In 1900 Southwark and Chestnut Hill, Grays Ferry and Germantown, Kensington and Mount Airy, Port Richmond and Overbrook, Manayunk and South Philadelphia (this list of pairs is far from complete) had less in common than any two component states of the Republic, say, California and Maine. This is why there is something uniformly unsatisfactory in most of the modern histories of Philadelphia. They deal with mayors, elections, civic improvements, institutions, architectural accomplishments that left the lives of most

[20] Elizabeth Bisland, *The Life and Letters of Lafcadio Hearn* (Boston, 1906), p. 452.
[21] Constance O'Hara, *Heaven Was Not Enough* (Philadelphia, 1955), pp. 23, 29.

inhabitants untouched. When it comes to the lives of the people, the authors almost invariably (and let me defend them, almost naturally) write about those—the upper classes and the civic leaders—whose records are largely extant. In the "Elegy Written in a Country Churchyard" Gray wrote of "the short and simple annals of the poor." Yet most Philadelphians were not really poor, and their annals are neither short nor simple. There exist records of all kinds, some of them buried in parish registers, the minutes and scrapbooks of innumerable societies, neighborhood newspapers, almanacs which proliferated around 1900, including all kinds of odd information about trolley lines, burial customs, local habits, worthies and habitations. My ideal history of Philadelphia would consist of a short and brilliant (and necessarily impressionistic) summary, to be followed by a rich and detailed history of each neighborhood. I repeat: many of these neighborhoods had little in common with each other. They communicated very little with each other. There was the patrician quarter: Chestnut, Walnut, Locust, Spruce, and Pine (south of Market and west of Fifteenth Streets); there were thirty or forty other neighborhoods, the rest of the town. In 1900 there were few people in the five boroughs of New York who had never been to Times Square, few people of the working-class suburbs of Boston who had not seen the Common, few people in vast Chicagoland who had not visited the Loop. There were, in 1900 (and even in 1950), many Philadelphians who had never walked in Rittenhouse Square, in spite of the considerable network of trolley lines across Philadelphia (where public transportation was corrupt but sufficiently ample). Many, perhaps most, of the inhabitants were quite uninterested in the people, the buildings, the institutions of another neighborhood, sometimes only a mile or so away. When an Irish Catholic boy from Manayunk married a Polish Catholic girl from Port Richmond, his people spoke of a Mixed Marriage. If his brother, also from Manayunk, a parishioner of St. John the Baptist, married a Polish Catholic girl from St.

Josaphat's, two hundred yards away, people would speak of a
Mixed Marriage. If a Philadelphian from Chestnut Hill married a . . . but he didn't.

Much of this self-imposed separateness was a matter of na-
tionality; some of it a matter of religion; but most of it was,
simply, the result of distance: mental, rather than physical. The
lack of interest of most people in those outside their circle
was as genuine as it was self-willed. It was not the result of
ethnic fears or hatreds; it was, rather, the result of indifference.
They did not know because they did not wish to know.

In Philadelphia in 1900 there was less social mobility than in
any other American (let alone European) town at the same
time. The ubiquitous American restlessness was largely, not
entirely, missing. Fewer people moved from one house to another than in any other city in the Republic. This had something to do with the fact that their houses, with their rents and
costs, were satisfactory to them; it had more to do with the
condition that the social aspirations of most inhabitants were
limited. They wished to rise *within* their communities, not
beyond them.

There was a Southern touch to Philadelphia, even though
in 1900 the city was Republican to the core: its Pennsylvania
hinterland had produced some of the chief radical Republicans,
Simon Cameron and Thaddeus Stevens; much of its financial
and political and even social leadership was concentrated
around the Union League, a legend unto itself, a citadel of
Republicanism with a national reputation. The Quaker, like
the New Englander, had been an Abolitionist, with a capital A.
Yet Philadelphia—in its physical aspect as in its everyday life—
resembled Baltimore much more than it resembled New York,
which is not surprising; what *is* surprising is that it had at least
as much in common with Charleston as with Boston. Some of
this was the result of family connections; certain patrician
families had been married to South Carolinians. Before the
Civil War, too, the commercial connections between Phila-

delphia and Charleston were considerable.[22] There was a Southern element in the often somnolent calm of Philadelphia lives; there was Southern dishes in the Philadelphia diet: crabs, oysters, terrapin, snapper, a Southern way with certain vegetables, the catfish and waffles served in the little white inns along the Wissahickon in Fairmount Park.

Philadelphia was solidly Unionist as well as Abolitionist, but its blacks formed a world of their own; not as in New York or elsewhere in the North, but almost to the point of being hidden. In 1865 there were anti-black riots, resulting in an ordinance forbidding blacks to ride in the horsecars; Jim Crow was not abolished by city ordinances until the 1870s. In his serious work *The Philadelphia Negro* (1897), W. E. B. Du Bois was "disturbed by the slow advance, if not 'actual retrogression,' of the Negro since the Civil War."[23] Their housing differed from the tenements of the Northern cities.

> There were rows of box-houses divided from our yards by a high fence. There the colored people lived, you could see right in their tiny houses. In the spring and fall they lived in their backyards, some of them even planted flowers which sprouted timidly in the midst of the steaming wash boilers and the clothes always hanging on the lines, for women on Waverly Street took in washing for the white folks. In winter they all moved into the kitchens, and the smoke rose thick from the wood stoves. They were poor, but there was no despair on Waverly Street . . .[24]

As late as 1900, the gradual movement of the black population into buildings and blocks of houses abandoned by the whites had hardly begun at all. In Philadelphia the number of

---

[22] Owen Wister: "Philadelphia happens to lie virtually on the border between two colonial parts of the country, distinct from each other; south of the Schuylkill the South may be fairly said to begin, and north of the Delaware the North." He wrote this in his declining years, in his privately printed history of the Philadelphia Club (1934).

[23] Klein and Hogenboom, *A History of Pennsylvania* (New York, 1973), p. 314.

[24] O'Hara, *op. cit.*, p. 26.

blacks was unusually small, about 6 percent of the population in 1900;[25] many of them worked as domestic servants.

The effects of mass immigration, of that largest and most momentous of events in the history of the United States, which reached its peak around 1900, were also less visible in Philadelphia than in other large cities in the East, even though the population of the town had swelled during the preceding decade, increasing by nearly 23 percent, mostly immigrants. Still, the percentage of the foreign-born was lower in Philadelphia than in any of the large American cities—23 percent in 1900, compared to 38 percent in New York and 35 percent in Boston. In 1882—exactly two hundred years after the founding of the city by William Penn—the steamship *Illinois* docked in Philadelphia, unloading 360 Jews from Russia. They were welcomed with curiosity and sympathy, their immigration having been organized by Quakers, who saw them as victims of religious oppression. (The only comparable municipal welcome was that accorded to a few Russian Jews who arrived in Madrid that same year, the first visible return of Jews to Spain after their expulsion.) Thereafter the Jewish population grew rapidly; by 1900 there were more Jews than blacks in Philadelphia. A sizable portion of the town, called at times "Little Russia," was a Russian (and Rumanian) Jewish region, south of Pine Street, around Third and Fifth. The Jews were exceptional in their mobility. They changed their dwellings and moved from neighborhood to neighborhood faster than any other Philadelphian group. By 1900 certain Jewish families had moved into houses on the fashionable streets, and the middle-class Jewish suburbs were beginning to form. Yet this bland summary is but one part of a more complex story. In 1900 the Jews in Philadelphia were in a state of extraordinary flux, and not only because of the quick increase in their numbers and their frequent displacement.

[25] There were 39,371 blacks in 1890, 655,000 in 1970. In 1896, 74 percent of the blacks in the Seventh Ward were engaged in domestic and personal service.

They were divided among themselves. There was, in Philadelphia, a small but impressive, if somewhat scattered, traditional group of Jewish patrician families, going back to colonial times —Madeira, Seixas, Lavino, Rosengarten, Horwitz, Etting, Franks, Levy, Gratz, Hays—many of whom married into other patrician families.[26] At one time Philadelphia was the principal American seat of Sephardic Judaism, including families whose roots went back to medieval or Renaissance Portugal and Spain. By the 1850s they were largely absorbed by the newer, German-speaking Jewish immigrants, many of whom established their middle- or even upper-middle-class status within one generation or two. They were Reformed Jews, Protestant-like in their philosophies and temple habits, and thoroughly Americanized. (Some of them made a mentally easy conversion to the Quaker faith.) Many of the German-Jewish families were exercised and worried by the influx of their uncouth co-religionists from Russia. In his fine humorous account of Jewish life in Philadelphia around 1900 Philip Goodman wrote:

> We quit the Franklin Street house in 1902. In that year almost every old family in the block moved away, many of them, like ourselves, to the new residential quarter in the western part of the town. A blight had hit the Street in the form of a diaspora from the ghetto. With the arrival of the first few families, we Untouchables smiled tolerantly at their *sheitels*, their matted beards, and their Talmudized customs. We treated them distantly and with condescension, and a few of us hoped we might be able to freeze them out. But natural tides are not so averted. Almost before we realized it our *terra sancta* had been invaded by these strange locusts, who affronted our middle-class self-respect . . . To hear us talk and protest, you might have thought that we were Americans by right of our pure Mohawk blood.[27]

[26] ". . . members in good standing of everything Philadelphians should be members of, and are mostly pillars of the right Episcopalian churches. As among the English aristocracy . . . a little touch of Jewishness is almost requisite . . ." Burt, *op. cit.,* p. 65.
[27] *Franklin Street* (New York, 1942), pp. 3–4.

The older families may have been unduly pessimistic about the difficulties in the Americanization of the newer immigrants. Yet in one sense their anxieties proved correct. By 1900 social anti-Semitism had risen to the surface in Philadelphia. The town was spacious enough to accommodate all kinds of new-comers, in the case of the Jews, practically without friction; the rise of the Jews in the professions and in politics was exceptionally fast; but the tacit exclusion of Jews—of all Jews—from certain institutions, certain patrician associations, and certain neighborhoods became an unwritten law during the first half of the twentieth century; it had not been so during the nineteenth.

The German element in Philadelphia was already present in the eighteenth century. The aspiring among them would anglicize their names (Pfeffer: Pepper; Pfannebaker: Pennypacker, etc.), but, unlike other anxious aspirants, they rarely attempted to obscure their origins (except some of them during the anti-German mania of World War I). In this respect, too, Philadelphia was more like Baltimore than like Boston or New York. The German-American population was considerable and it left its mark on the town in *Turnvereine,* German bands, and certain staples of Philadelphia food: cream cheese, cole slaw, scrapple, buns, bock beer. All of the numerous breweries had German names. Few people know that the equestrian statue of George Washington, now in front of the Art Museum—a Philadelphia landmark—was the work of Professor Siemering of Berlin. Statues of Goethe, Schubert, Schiller, and Humboldt were erected by German-American associations in Fairmount Park. There was an unspoken accord between the Quaker and the Protestant and the German virtues of thrift, cleanliness, sentimental honesty. Upon the news of the German victory over the French at Sedan in September 1870, a great torchlight parade wound its way through the center of the city, with many of the civic associations marching, not all of them German-American ones. Yet by 1900 the kind of uneasiness about Germany that had begun to affect the English was beginning to be apparent, especially among the patrician class. While the lower strata of the middle classes had no compunctions about marrying Germans (few of the Irish would object to German in-laws, provided that they were of the same religion), the upper strata of the bourgeoisie, for the first time, began to keep at a distance from the Germans—the early appearance of a pattern that ran through Europe and America during the first half of the twentieth century, when, whether in Bulgaria or in the Argentine, the upper classes were often Anglophile and the lower classes Germanophile. It is difficult to write with precision about the Germans in Philadelphia. By 1900 the possession of a German name in Philadelphia no longer carried the stigma of foreignness or of immigrant status. Politicians with German names abounded both in the machine and in the reform movement. In 1903 the Governor of the Commonwealth of Pennsylvania was Samuel Whitaker Pennypacker, descendant of an old Pennsylvania family of German origin, of which he was inordinately proud. In his *Autobiography of a Pennsylvanian*, one of the queerest books of its kind, he took great pride, among other things, in having instructed his son to keep a record of the number of pages he read each week, as well as to move his bowels regularly every morning. He also took great care to inform the citizenry that when he and his family were moving to the governor's mansion in Harrisburg, he had elected to proceed to Broad Street Station by the Fifteenth Street trolley car, in the course of which passage he addressed the conductor on the virtues of thrift. He saw himself as the embodiment of all that was best in the German and the Pennsylvania traditions. Because, rather than in spite of this, he was a kind of caricature of both.

Even more curious was the fact that the Irish in Philadelphia differed from the national American pattern of their development. They were as numerous in Philadelphia as in the other great cities in the East and the Middle West. Many of them had come to Philadelphia early: the song "I'm Off to Philadelphia in the Morning" was an Irish one. Yet they did not rise to eminence, not even to the kind of civic power and eminence that by 1900 had become their hallmark elsewhere. In New York, politics were dominated by the Irish element, in Boston in 1884, the Irish wrested the mayoralty of the city from the older Bostonians. In Philadelphia, the first Irish mayor was not elected until 1963. The Irish had their share of ward leaders; they were influential in local politics, but seldom above the limitations of their precincts. Unlike New York, Boston, and Chicago, Philadelphia had few Irish *nouveaux riches*. There were few Irish in the professions. In 1900 hardly any Irish family had risen to the level where they could see themselves— not to speak of being seen by others—as belonging to the upper class. One of the reasons for this was the existence, in Philadelphia, of a large lower-class Protestant population: Scotch-Irish and Welsh, Methodists and "low" Presbyterians, who had stepped into city politics after the patrician families had relinquished their municipal responsibilities. Mostly because of these people, there was a reservoir of anti-Catholic prejudice in Philadelphia; it had provoked the ugly riots of the 1840s, when people were killed and Irish Catholic churches burned; but the anti-Irish prejudice was rigid among the patrician families, too (anti-Irish rather than anti-Catholic: there were Catholic converts, and re-converts, among Drexels, Bories, Bullitts, etc., without any particular stigma attached to them). Yet the most important element in the restricted aspirations of the Philadelphia Irish lay in the deep-seated condition that they were as Philadelphian as they were Irish: reticent and tight-lipped and self-consciously satisfied within their parishes and neighborhoods.

What happened to the voluble and rumbustious, to the rebellious and extrovert side of the Irish character in Philadelphia? It must have existed; but it was not much in evidence. Certain groups among the Philadelphia Irish were active in the promotion of revolutionary movements in Ireland; Davitt and Casement had visited Philadelphia; and there were bloody clashes on North Broad Street on Orange Day, when Irish workingmen hurled bricks, bottles, iron bolts at the marching Orangemen. There was, among the Irish, a great deal of bitterness against their established Protestant "betters" in Philadelphia, but it was a suppressed bitterness; it was furnished by few points of friction, since their contacts were infrequent. Again the spaciousness and the neighborhood divisions of the town explain much of this. Their lives were comfortably separated from those of the others. The horizons of their aspirations, too, were comfortably limited. This curious absence of social ambition existed even among the few old and established Irish families.

The Italians—like the Jews and the Poles, the Hungarians and various Slavic groups of people—had begun to arrive in considerable numbers after 1875. In 1900 they were not yet ubiquitous in South Philadelphia, but their presence was beginning to be evident. They ran up against a great deal of prejudice among their lower-class neighbors. The patricians found the Italians' presence unobtrusive and even charming— an echo of the Italophile and aesthetic inclinations of Anglo-Victorianism. There had been a scattering of French families in Philadelphia, going back to the early nineteenth century, most of them with craftsman ancestors, Bouviers, Janviers, Nalles, Vauclains, but there was no such thing as a French neighborhood, and by 1900 the French element had virtually dissolved.

In 1901 one of the more curious Philadelphia customs made its first appearance: the Mummers' Parade on New Year's Day. The parade consists of groups bedecked in fantastic costumes, marching up Broad Street on the first day of the year, clowning and strutting to the plunking and twanging music of string bands, competing for prizes awarded by the City Council. It is a revel sprung from the working-class neighborhoods, where the garish sequined costumes are constructed long weeks, indeed, months before New Year's Day. The earliest Mummers in Philadelphia issued from Southwark and Kensington, neighborhoods that in 1900 were still inhabited by many families of English or Scotch-Irish working-class people. (A portion of

Kensington was called "Little England." The American Line offered cheap weekly sailings from Philadelphia to Liverpool. As late as the 1920s it was possible to sail from Philadelphia to England on the somewhat dingy but sturdy steamers named the *Haverford* and the *Swarthmore*.) "Oxford" and "Girard" were millhands' cricket clubs. The idea of the parade seems to have come from H. B. McHugh, a newspaperman; J. Hampton Moore, secretary to Mayor Ashbridge in 1901, took it up (Moore was later to become mayor of Philadelphia himself). The City Council offered $5,000 in prize money.[28] Within a few years the Mummers' Parade became a major traditional event in Philadelphia.

The Mummers' Play was an English tradition, carried on—often at Christmastime—by the English working class, which shared the English national inclination for dressing up and acting. Yet the word "mummer" is of medieval and German origin; and the Mummers' Parade in Philadelphia gradually acquired certain American characteristics of its own. The bizarre and gaudy panoply of costumes, monsters, dragons came to reflect a kind of medieval tinge, one of the hidden facets of the American character. A "mummer" in England, as defined by the *Oxford English Dictionary*, was "an actor in a dumb show." In Philadelphia the show was neither dumb nor silent: the string bands with the turn-of-the-century tunes, their polka beat gave a Central European, German and Western-Slavic rhythm to the street show from its very beginning.[29] Within a few years

[28] Charles Edgar Welch, Jr., "The Philadelphia Mummers Parade: A Study in History, Folklore, and Popular Traditions" (unpub. Ph.D. dissertation, University of Pennsylvania, 1968).

[29] "Oh, Dem Golden Slippers" was a particular favorite of the working class in England, too, in the 1890s—and of the Sudanese infantry in Lower Egypt. It was written in 1879 by James G. Bland, a black born in Flushing, N.Y., the author of many songs, including "Carry Me Back to Old Virginny." He is buried in Merion, Pa. (See p. 296.) In 1940 Carl Van Vechten told Albert C. Barnes about Bland, who had been buried penniless in Philadelphia. Barnes started a campaign to remove Bland's remains from an unmarked grave. In 1946 the Lions Club of Virginia erected a granite headstone for Bland in Memorial Park in Merion, after considerable trouble with Barnes as well as with the Merion Civic Association.

the principal locus of its participants shifted definitely to South Philadelphia; its clubs[30] and members became predominantly Italian and Polish, with a few Irish groups hanging on; for by 1950 the English working-class neighborhoods had virtually disappeared.

UNTIL ABOUT 1870 some of the patricians kept their positions of civic leadership. After that, few went into politics. More and more they let the machine politicians, lower-class Protestants for the most part, run the city. (The last patrician mayor of Philadelphia had served during the Civil War, that of Boston and New York a generation earlier.) The reform movements of the early 1880s sputtered out, in part because of a general lack of interest. There was between the two classes a tacit division of responsibility; they would not interfere in each other's spheres of interests, standards, way of life. This was not altogether attributable to cynicism. The patricians shied away from politics because they thought it sordid. Around 1900 there were more than three hundred houses of prostitution in Philadelphia, condoned and, on occasion, supported by the politicians. In 1900 there were nearly seven hundred churches in Philadelphia. The politicians and the churches got along very well. A Law and Order Society, composed mostly of Methodist, Baptist, and Presbyterian pastors, supported, among other things, the high price of liquor licenses, an elevation of spiritual enterprises which accorded wonderfully with the politicians' interests. A patrician such as Boies Penrose, who got into politics (as we shall see) because he found it more interesting than the usual avocations of his class, was a rare phenomenon. In turn, the politicians left the patricians alone. The latter were free to devote their attention to their lives, of which their money was an

---

30 Names of the principal Mummers' Clubs *circa* 1905: Silver Crown Club, Elkton Shooters, The George A. Furnival Association, John F. Slater Club, The Katzenjammer Band, White Caps, Old Times, Energetic Hoboes, Mixed Pickles, Ivy Leaf.

essential ingredient, but this did not mean that they were un-
abashed, or even selfish, materialists. Most of them wanted to
keep their family fortunes, rather than to increase them further. "When I was ten years old [1901] and already interested
in history and ancestry," Sturgis Ingersoll wrote, "I asked my
father whether it was not unusual for an American family to
have kept to the front for 200 years. He answered: 'Quite unusual, and the reason lies in the fact that no one generation
made a fortune.' "[31] How different this was from George Baer,
the *nouveau riche* president of the Reading Iron and Coal Company, who in 1902 proclaimed that God had put the owners
in control of the mines, and emphasized to Theodore Roosevelt
that coal mining was a religious business.

The distance between the patricians and politicians corresponded to the increasing distance the former put between
themselves and the city. After 1870, when they were moving
away from politics, they were beginning to move away from
the city as well. In New York, with its high prices for houses,
ground, and rent, it was the middle class that embarked on what
eventually became the great American movement to the suburbs. An aspiring clerk could afford a house in Brooklyn when
he could not afford one in Manhattan. The steel spans of the
bridges across the East River followed as a matter of course, so
did the consolidation of New York City into five boroughs, in
1898. In Philadelphia the movement out of the city began with
the upper classes. Before the last decades of the century, the
patrician families lived in the center of town, and went to work
in places within walking distance of their house. The railroads,
principally the Pennsylvania Railroad, made it possible for
wealthy people to move out into the country (to the so-called
Main Line, from 1874 onward), and a string of wealthy suburbs
came into existence. There was one exception to this: the
suburb of Chestnut Hill within the boundaries of Philadelphia,

---

[31] R. Sturgis Ingersoll, *Recollections of a Philadelphian at Eighty* (privately
printed, 1972), p. 12.

where certain patricians established large estates, and from which they could travel into town by rail. Yet it was a municipal exception, rather than an attitudinal one: the families who lived in Chestnut Hill were in spirit not less removed from the city than those who lived in Merion or Bryn Mawr. Most of them kept their town houses around Rittenhouse Square for the winter. The patrician residential quarter in the lovely, tree-shaded streets was still there, but most of the families would spend less and less time in them each year. Whereas in 1880 their estate in the country was their seasonal and secondary, though often impressive, residence, by 1900 it had become their principal residence, the town house having become, in practice, the seasonal and secondary one.

Much of this had to do with a Philadelphia tradition. William Penn had brought an old English ideal to Philadelphia, the conception of *rus in urbe*: the countryside within the city. Long before 1900 Philadelphia was a city with a country heart. There was Fairmount Park, the largest city park in the entire world, a dark-green valley twelve miles long, which it was tacitly understood that the commissioners could manage without interference by the politicians—in other words, a rare enclave of patrician administration, which lasted well into the twentieth century. A few other small square parks existed in the city, kept and spruced up even during the dreariest of decades. There were the private gardens in the back of the town houses, all attesting to the Philadelphian addiction to greenery. It amounted to an avocation, not to rural sentimentality; it was perhaps one of the unique marks of the Philadelphia spirit. This determination to preserve something of a country atmosphere in the midst of a wholly urban civilization was absent in the great cosmopolitan cities and even in the patrician towns of Europe, certainly by 1900, when rich people had their country houses, but the town was one thing and the country another. Certain streets and houses of London had something of this air during the eighteenth century, when the Thames was ample and the green gardens and terraced lawns, painted, among others, by Canaletto, reached down to the river; but during the nineteenth century the presence of *rus in urbe*, save for the great heath-like public parks, had vanished from London, too, notwithstanding the love of the English for gardens. And in this respect, too, in Philadelphia there echoed the tone of a past age, with its ideals muted rather than sonorous, like the muffled sound of a bell high in the mountain air. There remained something within the third largest city of the youthful North American Republic that was *older* than the ways of the aging mother country—a paradox; but, then, there were English visitors in the 1900s who thought that certain Americans were preternaturally old.

When many of the Philadelphia families invested in a suburban or country estate, this did not mean a radical change in their domestic ideals or preferences. They needed little adjustment. They were instantly at home in the country behind Philadelphia, with their horses, large vegetable plots, icehouses, riotous gardens carefully and, more than often, adventurously tended by the lady of the house. It was the Philadelphian version of English way of life. It rested, even more than in England, on a web of close and interlocking family relationships. Philadelphia in 1900 still contained enough material for a novel of manners. Not for nothing did these Philadelphians read Trollope, even during those two generations when his reputation in England faded. Life was almost idyllic. Visiting Englishmen, men as different as Kipling and John Lord Fisher and Arnold Bennett, who saw Philadelphia during the first decade of the new century, were impressed with it, pronouncing Philadelphia the most English city in the United States: because of its way of life, not because of the ethnicity of its inhabitants. During the nineteenth century Thackeray and Matthew Arnold had said much the same thing. Sarah Bernhardt had not liked it at all.

Cricket clubs and lawn tennis and fox hunting: even during

the damp and hot summers[32] Philadelphia was reminiscent of
something English (or at least Anglo-Indian: perhaps Poona? or
Simla?). As a matter of fact, it was better than England. The
houses were more comfortable than in England, because they
were well heated. The damp chilliness, the cold-water discipline of the English upper classes were different from the
Philadelphia spirit. Among Philadelphians, otherwise so Anglophile in so many ways, children were not extruded from the
home to boarding schools at an early age. (In certain families
the proper seasoning of boys was thought to be promoted by
sending them to ranches owned by relatives or friends in the
West.) The families, their relatives, the generations were closer
to each other than in England. The home atmosphere was
warmer. A sentimentality, richer than in England (perhaps corresponding, in mysterious ways, to the richness of the Pennsylvania land, to the amplitude of the Pennsylvania country),
suffused the climate of their lives by means of a tranquil and
comfortable domesticity. Their food was better than English
food. The heat in the summer could be oppressive, but winter
was often bracing and sharp, not chilly and damp; it provided
brilliant snowy scenes, sleigh rides, uncontrolled laughter. In
sum, in 1900 the lives of the patricians (as also those of many of
the workers) of Philadelphia were less cramped than those of
their English counterparts; they lived better than the English
in almost every way.

They also lived longer. Longevity among the Philadelphian
patrician families was remarkable; but in 1900 the average
inhabitant of Philadelphia, too, could count on at least four

---

[32] Meteorological statistics confirm the impression that during the nineteenth
century summers were hotter and winters colder than after 1900. After 1880
winter skating and summer yachting were gone from the Delaware, probably
because of the increasing pollution of the river. During the last decades of the
century it became *de rigueur* to escape the summer. Certain villages in Maine,
resorts of college professors and well-to-do divines earlier, became enclaves of the
Philadelphia patriciandom by 1900; Northeast Harbor, for example. The Pennsylvania Railroad ran an overnight Pullman train, the Bar Harbor Express,
from Philadelphia to Bar Harbor until 1947.

more years than his or her English counterpart. Before me lies a manuscript study of Catholic women writers of Philadelphia, many of them maiden ladies who flourished about 1900. Of the thirteen listed, eleven lived longer than eighty-one and three lived into their nineties.

There was security and comfort, ample enough; only passion was missing. 1900 was close to the zenith of the American achievement—and also to the zenith of American power in the world, which, notwithstanding its monstrous arsenal of atom and hydrogen bombs, began to decline after 1950. In 1902 Ralph Adams Cram, Henry Adams's close friend, contemplating the vast and impressive development of wealth in America, speculated that the top of the society of the United States may have reached the verge of aristocracy, that some of the millionaires of America were on the verge of becoming the Borgias and Medicis of the Modern Age, that an American Renaissance was about to burst forth from these accumulating riches and from a national quickening of spirit. He was wrong. In any event, his eyes were fixed on New York or Boston, rather than on Philadelphia, where there was no one even vaguely similar to Mrs. "Jack" Gardner. What was best in Philadelphia had nothing to do with the cruel and dangerous spring of a Renaissance. What was best in Philadelphia had, already in 1900, the marks of an autumnal civilization, long ripened rather than newly ripening. In England the Grantchester clock may have stood at ten to three; in Philadelphia it was later than that.

Physically speaking, too, late August, not April, was the cruelest, most dangerous month in the climate of Philadelphia. The worst epidemics in the history of Philadelphia, affecting its people worse than elsewhere, began in late August: yellow fever in 1793, and the influenza epidemic in 1918.

IN 1900 there was still enough space, and land was cheap enough, for some of the newer-rich aspirants to this kind of Anglo-American life to set up in the suburbs, building houses that were sometimes self-conscious, stiff stockbroker Tudor versions of the older mansions and estates.[33] They joined the cricket clubs in droves. They aspired to the status of the modern gentleman, aspirations that were made dependent on solid pretensions of Anglo-Saxon or Anglo-Celtic ancestry. There had been a thin stream of Welsh immigration to Philadelphia and up the Schuylkill to central Pennsylvania during the eighteenth century, lasting into the 1850s. Now, after 1880, when the suburban agglomeration began following the rail lines, the names of all kinds of villages were changed to Welsh place names. Athensville became Ardmore; an entire string of station names on the Main Line was culled from versions of Cwm. The era of the parvenu millionaires, of the *nouveaux très riches,* too, had come to Philadelphia later than to New York; but by 1900 it was in full swing. The Elkinses, the Wideners, the Stotesburys were at the gates of Society, pressing against the doors of the Assembly. Tremendous erections of architecture ensued. Palaces of the Newport-Trianon style of 1900 were rising in the Philadelphia suburbs. "Philadelphia, in my youth," wrote Constance O'Hara fifty years later, "laughed right heartily at Eva Stotesbury, her diamond dog collar and her Rolls-Royce with two men on the box. The Wideners with their mansion at Elkins Park would have been dismissed as utter parvenus . . . No one ever forgot to mention that the Wideners had been butchers."[34] (This is overkill: the latter fact was unmentionable as well as unforgettable.)

Here is a list of some of the suburban palaces of the period, many of them surrounded by formal parks and gardens, built around Philadelphia by the Francophile and neoclassical architect Horace Trumbauer:

> For William W. Harrison in Glenside, 1892 ("Grey Towers").
> For George Widener Elkins, Elkins Park, 1896.
> For William Lukens Elkins, Elkins Park, 1896 ("Elstowe Park").

[33] For an example of what this would do for the institutionalization of a suburb, respondent to the civic badgering of Edward W. Bok, see pp. 173–74.
[34] O'Hara, *op. cit.,* pp. 109–110.

For Peter A. B. Widener, Ashbourne, 1898 ("Lynnewood Hall").
For John B. Gribbel, Wyncote, 1900.
For John M. Colton, Jenkintown, 1900.
For James W. Paul, Jr., Radnor, 1900.
For Joseph B. McCall, 1901.
For C. Hartman Kuhn, Devon, 1904.
For H. M. Nathanson, Rydal, 1907.
For Thomas P. Hunter, Haverford, 1909.
For Robert L. Montgomery, Villanova, 1909.[35]

Other palatial mansions, built around the turn of the century, include "Cedar Lawn," built for John McGlinn in Sharon Hill; "Ingeborg," built for William Simpson, Jr., in Overbrook; "Yorklynne," built for John Gilman in Overbrook; John B. Stetson's palace in Ashbourne; John Wanamaker's "Lindenhurst" in Jenkintown; "Ballytore," built for his rival Isaac H. Clothier, in Wynnewood; Cyrus H. K. Curtis's cathedral of a house in Wyncote; Henry H. Houston's "Drum Moir" in Chestnut Hill; Alexander J. Cassatt's "Cheswold" in Haverford; "Dolobran," built for Clement Acton Griscom in Haverford, etc., etc.

The older families would scoff at these: not without reason. In less than fifty years practically all the owners and their descendants of these palatial houses would be gone from them. Many of these houses were sold within one generation; after 1950 many of them were gutted or torn down.

The high legal tradition of which Philadelphians have been proud begins with the sparkling story of Andrew Hamilton, who in 1735 had the printer Peter Zenger acquitted in New York, a legendary (and somewhat exaggerated) victory for freedom of the press in the Colonies. Yet it was not until the nineteenth century that the reputation of the Philadelphia practice

[35] The dates given are those of the start of the project in Trumbauer's office. He was an excellent architect. His second in the office was Julian Francis Abele, a young black architect of talent (very unusual for the times). James J. Maher, *The Twilight of Splendor: Chronicles of the Age of American Palaces* (Boston, 1975), p. 405. The above list is of course far from complete.

of law became solidly established. It was then that Law in Philadelphia became, as it were, a Sacred Profession.[36] Chew, Coxe, Rawle, Ingersoll, Hopkinson, Reed, Binney, Tilghman, McKean, Dallas: each of these Old Philadelphia families produced more than one lawyer at some time during the nineteenth century. The chancellor of the first Bar Association in America—people have claimed that it was the first in the English-speaking world—was William Rawle ("from the time the first Rawle joined the bar in 1725 till the last legal Rawle died in 1930, there has been a Rawle active in the Philadelphia courts").[37] Founded in 1802 as a library company, it became the Law Association of Philadelphia in 1827, finally changing its name to Bar Association in 1931. Its chancellors were not only men of professional eminence but undisputed leaders of society: Rawle, Duponceau, Sergeant, Binney, Ingersoll, Meredith, Biddle, McMurtrie, Townsend, Bispham. Except for Duponceau and Meredith—the first a brilliant Frenchman who had been at Valley Forge in his youth and was converted to Protestantism and to the American Enlightenment, the second the first president of what at the time was the somewhat *parvenu* Union League—every one of the chancellors was an eminent Philadelphian. It was as if during the nineteenth century the Most Eminent Bostonians had been the successive presidents of Harvard—which they hadn't.

To these Philadelphians this patrician guardianship of the law obviously meant more than honors and titles outside Philadelphia. Yet their reputation was not confined to Philadelphia. Some time after 1850 the term "Philadelphia lawyer" became a national cliché. I have not succeeded in finding the origin of the phrase, though I suspect that it spread out from the theater (to win a case, you had to "bring in a Philadelphia lawyer"), with its tenor of exceptional skillfulness—a kind of

---

[36] ". . . the law is more Solid, medicine more Noble, and since Philadelphia on the whole prefers the solid to the noble, law does perhaps have the edge." Nathaniel Burt, *op. cit.,* p. 102.
[37] *Ibid.,* p. 118.

skillfulness suggesting the intimate knowledge of the intricacies of an arcane system. Tocqueville had already noted this characteristic of Anglo-American jurisprudence in 1831: "A French lawyer is just a man of learning, but an English or an American one is somewhat like the Egyptian priests, being, as they were, the only interpreter of an occult science."[38]

There was more to it than that. "If you ask me," Tocqueville wrote, "where I should put aristocracy in America, I should not hesitate to answer that it is not among the rich, who have no common bond uniting them. It is at the bar or on the bench that the American aristocracy may be found."[39] This notion of a legal aristocracy, together with the impression that the legal profession, in America, served as a kind of corrective, "a counterweight," to unbridled democracy, may have crystallized in his mind during his visit to Philadelphia, where he spent sixteen days in October 1831, after nearly a month in Boston.[40] He and his friend Beaumont had come to study the American prison system, including the then novel method of solitary confinement in the Philadelphia penitentiary; but this kind of research became ancillary to the conversations he had with certain patrician Philadelphia *légistes*, Charles Jared Ingersoll and Judge Charles Sydney Coxe, just as his monumental *Democracy in America* grew beyond the study of the prison system, which had been the original purpose and pretext of Tocqueville's American voyage. Before his visit to Philadelphia a coalition of Old Quakers and Whigs had been defeated in a city election, losing most of their appointments, including the wardenship of the prisons which Tocqueville came to inspect. "The effect of the popular system is so well known," Coxe told Tocqueville, "that to remedy the evil the legislature has given

[38] *Democracy in America* (Mayer ed., New York, 1960), vol. I., p. 246.
[39] *De la démocratie en Amérique* (Paris, 1961), vol. I., p. 280 (my translation).
[40] His Boston notes about law deal predominantly with the American practice of the jury. His Philadelphia impressions eventually led to a chapter in *Democracy in America* ("On the Legal Mind and How It Serves as a Counterweight to Democracy"), wherein it is significant that Tocqueville constantly uses the term *légistes* rather than *avocats*, legal scholars of eminence rather than lawyers.

the nomination of the warden to a commission composed for the most part of judges."[41] Tocqueville saw the meaning of this. "Hidden in the *légistes'* soul," he was to write, "one finds some of the tastes and habits of an aristocracy. They, too, have an instinctive inclination for order and a natural love for formalities; they, too, conceive a great distaste for the behavior of the multitude . . ."[42] "Lawyers," he wrote elsewhere, "like democratic government without sharing its inclinations or imitating its weaknesses, a double cause for their power through it and over it."[43] It is not an exaggerated figure of speech to speak of a legal aristocracy in Philadelphia, surely not during the nineteenth century, and we may detect an element of populist uneasiness in the cliché "Philadelphia lawyer."

In this respect, too, 1900 was a kind of turning point. With the retirement of George Tucker Bispham the succession of Eminent Philadelphians in the chancellorship of the Law Association was interrupted. More significant was the fact that it was then, around 1900, that the cliché changed its meaning. It underwent a devolution: it acquired a cheaper, vaudeville tinge, from a superb practitioner of an arcane art to someone who was selfish, perhaps even slippery: *inter duos litigantes advocatus gaudet.* In another fifty years the term disappeared from American usage: by 1950 "Philadelphia lawyer" was a phrase remembered only by a few.[44]

UNLIKE BOSTON, with its intellectual tradition, and with the drawing card of Cambridge across the river, Philadelphia was

[41] *Tocqueville and Beaumont in America* (Pierson ed., abridged, New York, 1959), p. 298.
[42] *De la démocratie en Amérique,* vol. I., p. 281.
[43] *Democracy in America,* Mayer ed., vol. I., p. 245.
[44] Groucho Marx remembered it. A California woman: "I think when Philadelphia lawyers prepare a brief, their briefs are probably fifty pages long, and a brief that we would make here would be about five pages long." Groucho: "Well, you must remember that Philadelphia has a much colder climate and you need longer briefs there than you do here." *The Secret World of Groucho* (New York, 1976), p. 190.

almost indifferent to intellectual achievement. Intellectual life was somnolent. The University of Pennsylvania, founded by Franklin, played less of a part in the cultural life of Philadelphia during the nineteenth century than Harvard in that of Boston, or than Columbia in the life of New York. Few of the sons of eminent Philadelphians enrolled in it. For one thing, its brownstone buildings were situated in West Philadelphia, a social remove away. During the last twenty years of the century there came a change. The university was revitalized. It graduated 86 students in 1880, in 1900 it graduated 950.[45] Its medical school and its law school had risen to national eminence; so had the standards of the college, especially in English, history, architecture. By 1900 it was no longer unusual for the sons of the patrician families to graduate from the University of Pennsylvania. Its efflorescence lasted for about two generations. After 1950 the social reputation of the university declined. Its intellectual standards decreased apace with the increase of its buildings. Except for certain of its component institutions, again principally the law, medical and business schools, it became the motley conglomerate of a city university. In 1900 the most famous university figure was Dr. J. William White, a patrician physician, athlete, and *literatus*, a quintessential Kiplingite in his appearance, attitudes and preferences;[46] in 1950 it was the surgeon Dr. Isidore S. Ravdin. The name of the palestra of the university bears that of Dr. White; that of Dr. Ravdin is borne by a wing of the university hospital.

With all its respect for persistent performance, Philadelphia in 1900 was hardly the place for the writer, the intellectual, the artist to earn his living by his craft. The principal literary figure, Dr. S. Weir Mitchell, was a physician. Owen Wister had an income of his own, and was something of a recluse. The sole exception to this pattern was Agnes Repplier, a lady of letters whom we shall meet later. She made her living by writing

[45] Edwin Wolf II, *Philadelphia: Portrait of an American City* (Harrisburg, 1975), p. 225.
[46] About him see pp. 119–32.

essays. The greatest American painter at the turn of the century, Thomas Eakins, suffered from lack of local recognition. When Mary Cassatt returned to Philadelphia from Paris on a visit, the Philadelphia *Ledger* contented itself with this item in the social column: "Miss Mary Cassatt, sister of Mr. Cassatt, President of the Pennsylvania Railroad, returned from Europe yesterday. She has been studying painting in Paris and owns the smallest Pekinese dog in the world."[47]

There was something English in this indifference to aesthetic and cultural professionalism, this preference for amateurism in the older sense of the latter term. Few Philadelphians were intellectual, yet many of them were bookish. One of the finest bookshops in the United States, Leary's, was a Philadelphia institution, owned by Edwin S. Stuart, mayor of the city at one time and governor of Pennsylvania at another. We have seen that around 1900 the level of musical interest was rising. The Metropolitan Opera of New York gave a weekly performance at the Academy. There was also a string of fine theaters and, after 1908, the Hammerstein Opera House, an opulent music factory on North Broad Street.

In 1900 the Philadelphia patricians were barely beginning to exercise their cultural leadership. The preservation and the collection of art were still largely a private matter, not a civic one. The art museums were in a deplorable state. The private collections were uninteresting—one exception being that of John G. Johnson, whom we shall meet soon. *Baedeker's* guide to the United States (1909) under "Exhibitions of Art" lists two: "Among the finest private collections of art are those of *Mr. William B. Bement*, 1814 Spring Garden St., and *Mrs. Henry C. Gibson*, 1612 Walnut St., to which properly accredited visitors may obtain entrance." The works of art listed

---

[47] She remained something of a Philadelphian nonetheless. One of her relatives told me the following story: when his father, an amateur painter of fine talent, had visited Paris in his youth, calling on the fascinating Miss Cassatt in her studio, he was somewhat disappointed: it was, he said, not very different from paying a visit to a relative in West Philadelphia.

in these private collections were, almost without exception, uninspiring period pieces of the late nineteenth century (Cot, Meissonier, Bouguereau, etc.); the names of their owners have fallen into nearly total obscurity. We have seen that the lives of the patricians of Philadelphia were less cramped than those of their English counterparts. Were their minds cramped? Some of their descendants would think so, especially in retrospect. "The filthy streets, the disorder and monotony, the sour ugliness were but the outer shell which the spirit within had built," wrote Francis Biddle in 1927. "Pittsburgh might be dirty, New York cruel, Chicago blatant; yet behind their sprawling vitality burned or flickered the flame of aspiration. You could blow on it, and watch it flare to achievement. It didn't so much matter that Philadelphia had no art, no criticism, no newspaper that had wit or influence, put up with a shabby opera and stale plays; but it did matter that her people accepted the second-rate, and lived in the tenuous dream of a moderately thin past, or the lazy acceptance of an over-padded present, without gaiety and without earnestness, mechanical, content, indifferent."[48] Yet this thin, and very self-consciously aesthetic, lawyer was wrong.[49] Within a generation this would change. The public support of the arts became the civic enterprise to which some of the patricians of Philadelphia would devote their principal enthusiasms, with the Philadelphia Museum of Art as the greatest result. The man principally responsible for its founding was the modest and unassuming Eli Kirk Price, whose father, a Quaker worthy, had written *The History of the Consolidation of the City of Philadelphia* in 1873—the not untypical evolution of two successive Philadelphia generations, from the 1870s to the 1920s, from law and civic reform to law and art.

In 1900 the greatest collector of paintings was John G. Johnson, a corporation lawyer of phenomenal talent who had

[48] *Op. cit.*, p. 252.
[49] About him see pp. 261–63.

risen to eminence from near-poverty. This was possible within the practice of the law which, in Philadelphia, had become something like what the Church had been in England: perhaps the only profession where talent could count more than birth or wealth, and where a bright poor boy could make a spectacular career. The excellence of the law school of the University of Pennsylvania was connected with this condition; perhaps even deeper went the legalistic inclinations of the Quaker mind.

This was one of the legacies of William Penn; yet in 1900 the Quaker influence was no longer so pervasive, or so strong, as before.[50] The old Quaker families were no longer ubiquitous. Many of them had become nominal Quakers. The number of orthodox Quakers had dwindled. Many of the nominal Quakers married out of Meeting; indeed, by 1900 some of the prominent, and most of the socially ambitious, Quakers had become Episcopalians. For a while during the nineteenth century it seemed that in Philadelphia there lived, side by side, two groups of patrician families, one mainly formed by Episcopalians, the other by Quakers; and indeed, there were significant differences in the habits and attitudes and preferences of the two groups. For one thing, the Quakers were somberer, thriftier, more civic-minded then the Episcopalians. Between 1864 and 1885 they founded three first-rate colleges in what were then becoming suburbs: Swarthmore, Haverford, Bryn Mawr. By 1900 the two patrician societies had overlapped and merged. A college such as Bryn Mawr, fifteen years after its foundation, was no longer prototypically or even predominantly Quaker in student body, faculty, or spirit; a patrician institution such as the Assembly was no longer overwhelmingly Episcopalian. There were still Quaker institutions, Quaker habits, Quaker summer resorts, but there were no longer Quaker neighborhoods or even

---

[50] Lord Bryce about Philadelphia in the 1880s: ". . . the old Quaker character has died out, or remains perceptible only in a certain air of staid respectability which marks the city as compared with the luxury of New York and the tumultuous rush of Chicago." *The American Commonwealth* (New York, 1893), vol. I., p. 404.

Quaker suburbs.[51] In the interlocking directorates of clubs, of old insurance companies, of banks, of law offices, of manufacturing companies that constituted the financial and civic establishment of Philadelphia, eminent Quakers and eminent Episcopalians sat together.

Deeper than this duality ran the duality of the Philadelphia spirit. "The Philadelphia law of laws," wrote Elizabeth Robins Pennell, "obliged every Philadelphian to do as every other Philadelphian did . . . every Philadelphian was too much occupied in evading what was not the thing in the present to bother to cultivate a sentiment for the past." Yet at the same time and about the same scene Henry James wrote of "the reserves and traditions of the general temperament; those of gallantry, hilarity, social disposability, crowned with the grace of the sporting instinct . . . reminiscent of an 'old order.' "[52] Both of these supersensitive observers exaggerated; yet neither, I think, was altogether wrong. The secure sentiment of a particular past, in Philadelphia, has always coexisted with the conformity to the publicly acceptable standards of the present. The former, in spite (or, perhaps, because) of its traditionalism, was rather broad-minded and generous; the latter, in spite (or, perhaps, because) of its progressivism, was rather narrow-minded and hard. This paradoxical duality has persisted through the centuries. We may, I believe, attribute many of its origins to two different figures of the distant past. Philadelphia —very much including the Quaker tradition within Philadelphia—had, and still has, a split mind. Its character was shaped partly by William Penn, partly by Benjamin Franklin. One was the contemplative humanitarian; the other the utilitarian eager beaver. Penn was the essential English (or, rather, Anglo-Celtic) case of the Rich Young Man Turned Humanist;

[51] Partial exceptions: Cherry Street, east of Twentieth; Powelton in West Philadelphia (about the latter see Philip S. Benjamin, *The Philadelphia Quakers in the Industrial Age, 1865–1920* [Philadelphia, 1976], p. 71); Swarthmore and Haverford in the suburbs, the latter less and less Quaker, year by year.

[52] Pennell, *op. cit.*, pp. 117–18; James, *op. cit.*, p. 302.

Franklin was the more Germanic (and essentially Bostonian) ideal of the Poor Apprentice who became a Famous Scientist. Penn was the founder; Franklin, after all, a newcomer from Boston; but newcomers in Philadelphia do not have a hard row to hoe. It is easy to fancy Franklin addressing the assembled ironmongers in the elephantine vault of the Masonic Temple in 1875, inaugurating the first nickelodeon movie in Philadelphia in 1900, judging the Miss America contest in Atlantic City in 1925, or introducing someone like Buckminster Fuller at the American Philosophical Society in 1975; it is difficult to imagine Penn doing anything of the sort. The shy, the gentle, the introverted, the myrtle-and-brick Philadelphia, where houses were named "Strawberry Mansion" and "Solitude," was that of William Penn. The city of the first utilitarian prison (a failure), of anthropological institutes, of the first national advertising agency (N. W. Ayer, founded in 1901), of the Curtis Publishing Company, was that of Benjamin Franklin. Franklin represented a certain inclination of the Philadelphia mind; Penn gave what was best to the Philadelphia heart. And by 1900 most Americans associated Philadelphia with Franklin as much as, if not more than with Penn: in their minds *The Saturday Evening Post* and the *Ladies' Home Journal* were vaguely but indissolubly connected with images such as Independence Hall. Still within Philadelphia the tolerant spirit of Penn continued to prevail. His peculiar mixture of pallid purposefulness, of deep-seated melancholy hidden behind the beneficent vigor of action has been his mysterious legacy to this day. From the noontime of American bustle one may still sense the cigar smoke, the steamed clams, the cracking jokes, that red-cheeked, sleeve-gartered, democratic touch of easy-handed corruption but also of easy-minded tolerance, the smell of the sea in the oyster houses, the Sunday-evening kindness in the air. 1900 was a Philadelphia world very different from Penn's, and yet in many ways closer to his large tolerant spirit than to the little crackerjack rules of Benjamin Franklin. During the next fifty years the voice of Benjamin Franklin became the Voice of America; but somehow, here and there, the unspoken voice of William Penn still echoed in Philadelphia. It muted the marching music and the clangor of iron at the peak of the Money Age. The ironic comment of the brilliant Thomas Beer, writing about 1900 in his life of Mark Hanna, would have been understood by many people in Philadelphia (had they read him, which they almost certainly did not). "Our historians," Beer wrote in the year of the great stock-market crash, about the end of the American Victorian age, "primly tell us that [people] 'joined in the mad scramble for worldly success.' Perhaps historians may yet discover that success is just a form of amusement, mostly sacred to those who have not brains to attain it."[53]

In any event, worldly success in Philadelphia meant much more than money, it meant social acceptance. And about this there existed a kind of exaggerated consciousness, a sensitive and thin-skinned attitude that would contrast deep down with what superficially seemed the elephantine calm of Philadelphia life and its aspirations. The Assembly has been a Philadelphia institution, an annual dance, first established in 1748, with invitations restricted to members of the patrician families. Membership in the Assembly in Philadelphia was the local equivalent to a European court, to something like the *Erste Gesellschaft* in Vienna, where in 1900 the court still held to the rules of Spanish royal etiquette. It meant an invitation to the social stratosphere. I shall not describe the Assembly in detail, many others have done so. In most of the novels written about Philadelphia, whether by outsiders or insiders, the Assembly (or, more precisely, the invitation to the Assembly)[54] figures as a central event. Mrs. Pennell went so far as to consider the Assembly as *the* bastion of Philadelphia. "When I think how mere wealth is taking possession of 'Chestnut, Walnut,

[53] *Hanna* (New York, 1929), p. 62.
[54] This precious token in 1900 consisted of a card, which was not mailed but delivered in person by a dignified black man, departing on his rounds from the Philadelphia Club. Before 1910 there were two Assemblies each winter.

Spruce, and Pine,' " she wrote in 1914, "how uptown is marrying into it, how the Jew and alien are forcing their way in, I see in loyalty to the traditions of the Assembly the Philadelphian's strongest defense of the social rights which are his by inheritance."[55] (It is pleasant to record that the young Elizabeth Robins had *not* been invited to the Assembly.) There is another, perhaps no less exaggerated episode in the otherwise rebellious insider William Bullitt's novel about Philadelphia.[56] The hero, John Corsey, leaves his wallet in the shop of an old Jewish pawnbroker who has failed to recognize his status. The pawnbroker finds the invitation to the Assembly in the wallet. " 'Oh, Mr. Corsey! You'll excuse me, Mr. Corsey, I'd never have! Oh, Mr. Corsey you'll excuse . . .' "[57] The clannishness which suffuses these reminiscences is cramped. It is reminiscent of what Saki called "the fevered undercurrent of social strivings and snubbings." Yet Saki was a chronicler of the Edwardian Age, and Philadelphia never had an Edwardian Age of its own. As late as 1910, its standards were still Victorian. In 1900 its passage began from the Victorian to the Progressive Age without much of an inner murmur, accompanied by the noise of rivets, steam hammers, and raucous phonograph music.

And it was during this passage, and during the next fifty years, that Philadelphia moved ever further from the focus of American life. By 1950 many of its traditions and habits were no longer quaint but literally eccentric: removed from the mainstream, from the central impetus. This devolution was represented in the lives and in the achievements (and, at times, in the non-achievements) of certain individuals, the description of whose characteristics forms the bulk of this book. Each of them marked by a kind of duality, by an inner contradiction: the immensely talented Boies Penrose, whose great political

[55] *Op. cit.*, p. 158.
[56] About it see pp. 209 ff. The Assembly is the "Concourse" in Bullitt's novel, and the "Patrician Ball" in Owen Wister's unfinished *Monopolis*, about which see pp. 255 ff.
[57] *It's Not Done* (New York, 1926), p. 96.

powers would merely clothe the melancholy despair he felt about the American democracy; the immensely successful Edward Bok, the founder of the modern *Ladies' Home Journal,* the most successful magazine *circa* 1900, the Philadelphia *arriviste,* the modern reincarnation of Franklin who institutionalized much of Philadelphia; the rebellious William Bullitt, who tried to shake the dust of his native town again and again; the quintessential conformist and Philadelphian George Wharton Pepper, whose eccentricity resided in the paradoxical condition of the perfection of his conformism; the solitary lady of letters, Miss Repplier, who remained lonely throughout her life in spite of having been accepted by the best of Philadelphians; Owen Wister, who believed in the natural supremacy of the Anglo-Saxon race *and* in the fatal decline of whatever remained of American civilization; Albert Coombs Barnes, who loved Philadelphia and who hated Philadelphians . . . By 1950 most of them were dead; for all of them their time was gone. Yet all of them represented more than an era. They left a mark on the history of their city and of their country, and on the minds of the oddest kind of people, including this author.

BOIES PENROSE

O R

The Conservative as Gargantua

THE HISTORY OF POLITICS is a history of words. "Boss" is as
American as "Santa Claus," both terms being Dutch in origin.
"Boss," wrote the English captain Thomas Hamilton, was a
peculiar Americanism, a substitute for "master." Hamilton's
famous book, *Men and Manners in America*, was published in
1831, coincident with the beginning of machine politics in the
United States. It was then, too, that "big" became a favorite
Americanism, an adjective suggesting quality as well as quantity; power and prestige, not merely size.[1] Yet it was not until
after the Civil War, when the era of the big bosses was opening,
that "boss" and "bossism" acquired a political significance. Most
of the bosses ruled the swelling cities of the nation; a few of
them perfected their machinery in order to run an entire state.
Most were Democrats; a few were Republicans. Many exercised
a politically disputable, yet practically unchallengeable, power
over their local legislatures; a few were able to extend that
power over their party in the United States Senate. Most had
risen from the lower middle class; a few descended into politics
from the upper classes. Most of them believed that power fol-

[1] " 'Big' [by 1820] had become the favorite adjective of magnitude in the
United States, and at a later date [latest by 1865] also came to signify fine or excellent." H. L. Mencken, *The American Language, Supplement One* (New York,
1945), p. 46, note 2.

lowed money; some of them believed that money followed power. A few, having acquired power, wanted to keep it, instead of parlaying it into something else—very different from the power brokers of today. Among them Boies Penrose stood out. Intellectually as well as physically, he was the biggest boss of his day.

He was a boss on the national scale: one of the few—very few—Philadelphians who achieved national influence in politics during the history of the Republic. He was one of the most powerful, and frequently feared, figures in the Senate of the United States. Yet his power within his native city was limited. He wanted to become mayor of Philadelphia, having accomplished a brilliant ascent in state politics, but he was rejected; twenty years later, in the fullness of his power in Washington and in Harrisburg, he was forced to compromise with the family of machine politicians who ran Philadelphia; and all through those years the best response he could get from proper Philadelphians was a kind of reserved respect. Yet there remained profoundly Philadelphian elements in his character: his disdain of publicity and the melancholy privacy of his inner self.

His public life was an exaggerated representation of his times. He was born five days before Lincoln was elected President; when he died, Wilson already had one foot in the grave. He was handsome and healthy in his youth; later he grew bloated and corpulent, like the Republic. Like the big engines, the big bankers, the gold watch chains, the national heavies, the solid citizens, Presidents such as Taft, who weighed over three hundred pounds, Penrose looked like, and in many ways was, a period piece. In other ways he was not. An exaggerated representation is not necessarily a caricature; and Penrose cared little for his image. He was loath to pay tribute to virtue. This, in an age marked by gross hypocrisy, was one of the more remarkable features of his character.

THE CHILDHOOD PHOTOGRAPHS of Boies Penrose show an extraordinarily beautiful child. Except for his clothes, and for that
inevitable atmosphere which such ambrotypes breathe, there
is little that is Victorian about him. He has a Regency face,
almost porcelain in its fineness: a remarkable forehead, clear
strong eyes, a slightly pouting lower lip, an expression that is
disdainful rather than contemptuous, rather English, and very
different from that later senatorial countenance that had something Prussian about it, and this not only because of his enormous bulk.

He was born an Anglo-American aristocrat. This word has
been grossly misused in recent times, promiscuously attributed
to families who, no matter how clannish, successful, and rich,
have been but one generation removed from the lower middle
classes. The Penrose ancestry was extraordinary. The founder
of the family in America, Bartholomew Penrose, came from a
Cornish family of a certain distinction.[2] His son Thomas became a rich shipowner in colonial Philadelphia. His son James
married Sarah Biddle, the daughter of one of the most powerful
Philadelphian families at the time.[3] Their son Clement Biddle
Penrose married Anna Howard Bingham, who was the grand-
daughter of a younger son of the Duke of Norfolk. Their oldest
son married another Biddle, Valeria, famous for her extraordinary looks, the great-great-granddaughter of one of the original
proprietors of New Jersey. Their son was Boies's father, Dr.
Richard Alexander Fullerton Penrose, who married Sarah
Hannah Boies, whose ancestry was no less distinguished than

---

[2] The name is not uncommon in Cornwall. Bartholomew Penrose was a
Quaker, a fact sometimes obscured in the family genealogies. In spite of the
assiduous efforts of the genealogist Josiah Granville Leach, *History of the Penrose Family of Philadelphia* ("published for private circulation by Drexel
Biddle," Philadelphia, 1903), the date of his birth and his birthplace were not
ascertainable.

[3] She had an interesting life. After James Penrose died she married a John
Shaw, and thereafter (in 1784) a good-looking Swiss officer, Rodolphe Tillier,
who eight years later was one of the Swiss Guards of Louis XVI killed in the defense of the Tuileries (the Penrose genealogy says, wrongly, "on the grand stair-
way of Versailles").

was his own.[4] Two of her ancestors were graduates of the first class of Harvard College in 1642, another ancestor was secretary to Lord Baltimore, yet another a descendant of the Earl of Charteris.

The portraits of Boies's father show a kind, dignified patrician-physician. (He was the founder of the Children's Hospital, and Professor of Obstetrics and Diseases of Women and Children at the University of Pennsylvania.) He was an exemplary gentleman, *integer vitae scelerisque purus*, a Horatian Victorian without the Aristides-like arrogance of the proper Athenians. His wife was lovely, learned, and strong. They were married in 1858, on a beautiful late September day, in Wilmington, Delaware, at that time a quiet provincial town with a Southern touch, by the Bishop of the Episcopal Church, a relative. They were young, handsome, intelligent, successful, and rich. Yet they chose to withdraw from the greater world. Everything about their lives suggests a curious and melancholy reticence, an early withdrawal into a kind of interior life, as if this were the only decent way to live at the time of the booming blossoming of the American democracy. It was the attitude of certain people who were acutely aware of being the descendants of old families; there was something fatalistic about this attitude, about this odd mixture of shyness and pride. They lived at 1339 Spruce Street, in a comfortable house of small dimensions, few ornaments, and no pretensions. In the 1860s this house stood on the outer edge of the fashionable portion of the Eighth Ward of Philadelphia, most of the prominent and rich

[4] From Boies Penrose's history of his family for the Class Record of Harvard in 1881, copied by his sister-in-law Katharine Drexel Penrose in her Commonplace and Household Book: "My mother's family on her parental side came from Barbadoes to this country. They were originally from England. William Woodbridge the first graduate of Harvard College and Nathaniel Hubbard, the third of the same class of 1642, were her ancestors in a direct line. They were Tories and moved to Canada at the end of the Revolutionary War. There my grandfather was born. His family name was Hubbard, but it was changed by act of legislature to Boies, when he was adopted by his uncle Jeremiah Boies of Boston, a graduate of Harvard College in the class of 1783. Almost all my mother's family on her father's side were educated at Harvard . . ."

families having moved further west, across Broad Street. The Penroses did not participate in this social migration. In spite of her great beauty and intelligence and family connections, Dr. Penrose's young wife showed little interest in the society of Philadelphia. She bore him seven sons within ten years. When her seventh son was born she was less than thirty-five years old. She had not twelve more years to live.

She took an untiring interest in the education of her sons. Her two older sons, Boies and Charles Bingham, were educated with the help of private tutors. They graduated from Episcopal Academy with high marks, identical to the difference of one-tenth of a percentage point. They were fifteen months apart in age, but they entered Harvard University together. They lived in a comfortable house in Cambridge, presided over by an aunt. Here the parallel ends. While his brother advanced from honor to honor,[5] Boies Penrose was on the verge of being expelled at the outset of his senior year. His parents were disturbed. Letters passed between Spruce Street and Cambridge. His mother was dying. Whatever his motives, his purposeful character now asserted itself. He rallied, and graduated with honors. He returned from Boston to a house half empty; his mother had died.

Between 1881, when Penrose returned from Harvard, and 1884, when he chose to enter politics, the city of Philadelphia underwent a political revolution in the literal sense of the word: a complete turn of the wheel. Prominent citizens had finally roused themselves in the cause of reform, against the powers of the Gas Ring, which ruled City Hall, over which hovered their odoriferous halo. A Committee of One Hundred raised the banner of reform. In 1881 they succeeded in electing

---

[5] Among other achievements, he won the highest honors in physics in seven years. President Eliot told a visiting Philadelphian that he "never knew such a case in the history of Harvard; that Penrose, in every one of his studies, got a maximum [100]." Letter from W.H. in the Philadelphia *Public Ledger*, 1 July 1881. Like his father, Charles Bingham Penrose chose the career of a professor of medicine. He married Katharine Drexel, an exceptional woman: college-educated, vivacious, widely read, sophisticated, very rich. Charles Bingham Penrose was the only one of seven brothers who had children. See p. 80, note 47.

a reform mayor and a reform receiver of taxes. They did not succeed in reforming either the habits of the municipal bureaucracy or the voting habits of the electorate. In 1883 the voters rejected the reform controller; the next year they turned the amiable reform mayor out of office. The machine was back in power. There were few new faces among the leaders. The wheel had gone full circle; the ring in the hub remained at the center, where it had been before.

Boies Penrose was both witness to and participant in these events. He saw the Gas Ring for what it was: artless and corrupt, shameless and vulgar. He was reading law in a firm whose senior partners, Wayne MacVeagh and George Tucker Bispham, were champions in the struggle for municipal regeneration, as was S. Davis Page, the senior partner of another firm which Penrose would join when he was admitted to the bar. In February 1884 an important municipal election came up. The young Penrose stepped up to the battlements. He stood at the polling places, tall and defiant, sporting a large Reform badge on his overcoat; he held a no less impressive copy of the Voters' Register in his hand. The toughs of the ward leaders growled and, on occasion, snapped around him, but to no avail. There were to be no tricks at the polls that day. In a ward which had been one of the safest for the machine in the past, the candidate of the machine lost three to one.[6] Everyone saw that this was mostly due to Penrose's doing. He had intimidated the intimidators. He was the civic hero of the day.

It was a turning point in his life. The proper people of Philadelphia were impressed. So were the politicians and the ward leaders. There occurred now a marriage of convenience. Penrose was interested in politics; the politicians were interested in Penrose. The ward leaders did not merely take to him; they took to him on his terms, and elected to be his allies. He

---

[6] The reform candidate, with the improbable name of H. La Barre Jayne, eventually receded into obscurity; the loser, a German-American politician by the name of Wencel Hartman, eventually became an influential politician in City Hall.

wanted to be chosen for the state legislature; they nominated and elected him. On a raw January day in 1885 Penrose took the train to Harrisburg. His political career was launched. In 1887 he was elected State Senator, in 1892 he was president of the State Senate, in 1897 Senator of the United States.

People later suggested[7] that this turning point also produced a transformation in his character. Penrose chose a career in low politics at the time when "The Best Men Would Not Go into Politics"—the famous title of a famous chapter in Bryce's *The American Commonwealth*. The young patrician and reformer broke with the traditions of his family: he became voracious, cynical, and impenitent. Penrose threw himself into the muddy pool of politics because he liked low company. This may be too simple an explanation. Within the family there was a precedent. His grandfather, whose career he studied and admired, had been a politician. Charles Bingham Penrose, with his noble brow and his breathtakingly beautiful wife, enjoyed the rude sounds and smells of the political arena.[8] First State Senator, then Speaker of the Senate of Pennsylvania, he was instrumental in electing Simon Cameron, one of the most ruthless and corrupt politicians of the era, to the United States Senate in 1856;[9] he was a close friend of Thaddeus Stevens, another demagogue; he was one of the founders of the Republican

[7] Including Penrose's two biographers, Walter Davenport, *Power and Glory: The Life of Boies Penrose* (New York, 1931); Robert Douglas Bowden, *Boies Penrose: Symbol of an Era* (New York, 1937). Mention must be made of Henry Hart, *The Great One* (New York, 1934), a *roman à clef* about Penrose and some of his associates. Hart, a newspaperman with the old Philadelphia *Record*, had intended to write a biography of Penrose (I found letters from him to Dr. R. A. F. Penrose, Boies's brother) but decided instead on a novel.

[8] In January 1839 members of the Pennsylvania Senate broke into a riot; Charles Bingham Penrose escaped through a window, in the company of Thaddeus Stevens. Sidney George Fisher on 18 July 1838: "One more day of it, and I shall shake the dust of Carlisle from my feet, never I trust to see it again . . . This morning Mr. Penrose, Mr. Watts & Judge Reed called on me; also about a dozen of the students, coarse-looking young men . . ." *The Diary of Sidney George Fisher, 1834–1871*, Wainwright ed. (Philadelphia, 1967).

[9] When a generation later Simon Cameron retired from the Senate in favor of his son, J. Donald Cameron, Boies Penrose was instrumental in the nomination and the election of the latter.

Party in Philadelphia. He was largely indifferent to the opinions of certain proper Philadelphians, who regarded him with considerable distaste. He may have had a taste for low company; he certainly had an appetite for power. His grandson Boies, too, believed in power; he thought in terms of power; this was evident from his statements at a surprisingly early time of his life. The contrast between the young patrician and the corrupt politician, between the brave reformer and the cynical reactionary, between the athletic Achilles and the conservative Gargantua may be intellectually and logically attractive, but it will not stand. At the age of twenty, at Harvard, Boies Penrose delivered an oration on "Martin Van Buren as a Politician." This terse, opinionated, and clear paper dealt with the origins of Bossism; it also contained, *in nuce*, the lifelong political philosophy of Boies Penrose.

"Martin Van Buren," Penrose began, "was the first and the greatest of American politicians; of that class of statesmen who owe their success not so much to their opinions or characters, as to their skill in managing the machinery of party . . ." "He marks the transition in American politics from statesmen like Adams and Webster to the great political bosses and managers of today . . . Adams was the last statesman of the old school who was to occupy the White House, Van Buren was the first politician present." And this was "the inevitable outcome" of the development of the country. The vast mass of the people, "for the most part ignorant and reckless and with little to lose," now held the sovereign power.[10] "The voters of the United States were no longer the same voters who had founded the constitution.[11] In the rivalries of parties the mechanical arts of

[10] "At the same time the foreign born element had been growing larger and larger. In the rivalries of parties the immigrant was invested with all the rights of an American citizen . . . the former happy uniformity in the circumstances of the people no longer existed." Penrose exaggerated this condition: in 1836 the number of foreign-born voters was still very small.

[11] The young Penrose attributed little importance to Jackson. "In the election of Andrew Jackson the sovereign people asserted their power. But in reality, Jackson, the man of the people, was but a puppet in the hands of the politicians. In reality, the majesty of the politicians, not of the people, was

electioneering were soon reduced to a system . . . Political opinions, in fact, were a secondary consideration. All the statesmanship that the times required was the artful adaptation of general propositions to the existing temper and opinions of the masses.

"The present condition of American politics, therefore, is the natural result of the radical democratic development of the country. We can now understand the contempt which the practical politician bestows too often upon the civil service reformer . . ." The preaching "by a certain class of political amateurs" amounts to little. "The exponent of mechanical methods, the manipulator of the machine, the political boss" is the inevitable result of the lowered intellectual character of the electorate, and of "the consequent decay of interest in real political issues, in short [of] the substitution of mechanical for intellectual influences at elections." "The civil reformer," he added, "loves to hold up to our admiration the civil service of England. But in English politics we see daily the more and more pronounced coming of the same tendencies we have seen in American politics . . ."[12] "Cynical attacks," the young Penrose concluded, on the politicians of today "are peculiarly unjust. By management and not by statesmanship are questions generally decided in the Legislatures . . . When management is all that is essential, have we a right to be disappointed if Van

---

asserted . . ." This was an unusually sophisticated and perceptive opinion, written by this young man less than a year before Franklin Roosevelt was born. In 1945, less than a year after the latter had died, another fledgling genius from Harvard, the young Arthur Schlesinger, Jr., established his reputation with a book, *The Age of Jackson,* with the thesis that Jackson had been the true founder of American democracy and a forerunner of Roosevelt's New Deal. The national success of this book was largely due to the fact that Schlesinger's opinion, unlike Penrose's, was in perfect accord with the intellectual climate of his times.

[12] It is interesting to note how this passage coincides with Walter Bagehot's later analysis of the transformation of English politics during the age of Peel: under the coming democratic "constitutional" system "you have excluded the profound thinker; you must be content with what you can obtain—the business gentleman." Walter Bagehot, "The Character of Sir Robert Peel," *Biographical Studies* (London, 1895) , p. 42.

Buren is not Webster?" All of Penrose's political career was
consistent with this conclusion.

The early acuity of his mind was extraordinary. He may have
been a throwback to the eighteenth century, when Hamilton
and Jefferson were accomplished political thinkers and statesmen in their twenties, and Pitt the Younger the Prime Minister
of Great Britain. Penrose was impressively mature at twenty.
At Harvard he began to show some of those tendencies that
eventually became his pronounced characteristics. He was lazy,
even as his mind was quick. In spite (or perhaps because) of his
considerable learning, Penrose developed a quick disdain for
the presentations of the Harvard professorate. He was a vigorous youth, with powerful appetites, physical as well as mental.
His father became ever more withdrawn after the death of
Boies's mother. He also had an exaggerated conviction about
the virtues of diet. The young Boies would go out, night after
night, to oyster houses and steak houses, where he would sit,
solitary and saturnine, downing large quantities of food and
drink. Then he would return to the second floor of the Spruce
Street house and immerse himself in reading, mostly political
and historical stuff. During the day he was that most proper of
Philadelphians, a young lawyer in a city reputed for its legal
aristocracy. Yet he became soon bored with the conventionality
of the law. "My office," he recalled later, "was always full of
visitors. On the one side of the outer waiting room sat my
clients; on the other side sat the politicians. I could not see
them all, so after a careful survey of the characteristics of both
classes of men I decided that ward leaders were less bothersome
than clients, and I gave up the law."[13] He chose a political
career, unusual for a young patrician of his day, but this was
not an abrupt break; it did not entail a drastic transformation
of his already developed convictions.

Penrose wrote two short treatises during his early twenties,
with enough matter in them to establish him as an American

[13] Cited in his obituary, *Public Ledger*, 2 January 1922.

political historian of the first rank. They show Penrose's literary gifts; they reflect, again, the consistency of his political ideas. His history of the city government of Philadelphia remains to this day the most brilliant and concise summary of the topic. He wrote it together with his then law partner Edward P. Allinson; but it carries the marks of Penrose's own style:

> We shall, in these pages, avoid the puerile error of complaining of the wickedness and corruption of professional politicians. It is very common to speak of that class as something outside of and apart from the ordinary citizen . . . The politician, professional or otherwise, follows the stamp of his age; he is just what his age or environment demands or permits, neither better nor worse. The rules of his morality may differ from those of the clergyman or the merchant, but it weighs about as many ounces to the pound, and we are inclined to think that, from his intimate acquaintance with human nature, he gives better weight.[14]

Government must be "founded on experience, making due allowance for the necessary weakness as well as the general integrity of humanity . . . The most potent factors, which the lawgiver must keep always in sight, are the indifference and selfishness of the so-called better class of citizens . . . The practical politician is a useful citizen; he is shrewd, far-sighted, tireless and often honest as this world goes; but practical men as a class never work continually for nothing or simply for abstract patriotism."[15] Penrose and Allinson published another work,

[14] Penrose and Allinson, *History of the City Government of Philadelphia* (Baltimore, 1886). During their research in the vast and disorganized archives of the city, the authors discovered the original charter of Philadelphia, dated 1701.

[15] *Op. cit.* pp. 8–9. The work is succinct, clear, and laced on occasion with wit. Example: "Some cases are curious . . . after the sheriff's commissions are deducted, one Laughlen McClane pays a fine which amounts to £24.5.0 for kissing Osborn's wife—a large sum for those days, which would lead us to infer that kissing was a luxury and women scarce" (p. 23). The work ends with a short and brilliant description of why the reform wave of the mid-1870s failed. It was "by its nature . . . necessarily ephemeral. It could not retain the spoils system and did not attract the workers. Its candidates, when elected, soon betrayed it and went over to the Regulars . . . The people became restive, and refused their support to what jarred on their conservative ideas . . . 'Who made thee a ruler and a judge over us?' They became tired of hearing Aristides called the Just" (p. 63).

Ground Rents in Philadelphia,[16] a dull topic at first sight, at closer reading a masterly exposition. It delineates the legal and financial basis of a matter that Penrose considered most important, the chance given to all kinds of people to own their property. The number of people living in separate houses owned by them was greater in Philadelphia than in any other great city in the world. Boies Penrose, who started his political career when Karl Marx died, recognized very early one of the basic, if not thé basic, failures of the Marxian assumption: the so-called working classes, instead of being the most revolutionary and radical, were in reality the most conservative and property-minded elements of industrialized society, of the mass democratic state.

That was the last of the literary efforts of Boies Penrose. In his account of his family's history for the Harvard Class Record of 1881 he had written that the early Penrose family was "commercial rather than literary."[17] The career he had chosen was neither commercial nor literary. Other people in politics, including certain proper Bostonians, would combine their political career with a literary one. Penrose would not.

LESS THAN THREE YEARS after that frozen January day in 1885 when Penrose had taken the train to Harrisburg, he was elected state senator. In another four years, at the age of thirty-one, he presided over the Pennsylvania Senate. Five years later he was elected to the United States Senate, where he remained, growing ever more powerful, for twenty-four years of his life, a political career that was spectacular at its outset and solid for its entire duration, an impressive combination.

Three generations after these events, we are confronted with the problem of how to describe this career in detail. The career of Boies Penrose may have been impressive; his achievements

16 Publications of the University of Pennsylvania, Political Economy and Public Law Series No. 3 (Philadelphia, 1888), p. 3.
17 See above, note 4.

were not. There was hardly a single piece of significant legislation, whether in the Senate of Pennsylvania or that of the United States, connected with his name. But this is only one part of the problem: for, in this respect, Penrose's career was not that different from that of the political bosses of his period. There is another part of the problem: their machinations and manipulations may have been fascinating to their contemporaries; they are not fascinating to us. They mainly involved manipulations of money. There was something ludicrous in this obsession with money—or, rather, in the deviousness with which the politicians went after it. They penetrated the drawers and the breakfronts of the public till with the most complicated of instruments, replacing the Victorian mahogany veneer after their work was done. The description of their now largely antiquated financial and legal instruments may be of interest to aficionados of accounting, just as the description of ancient chisels may be of interest to specialists in interior woodwork. For others it is not interesting at all.

Boies Penrose had inherited enough money to keep him comfortable throughout his life. In his personal finances he was both cavalier and scrupulous. His secretary would make most of the necessary purchases; for the rest he had to make sure that Penrose had a large wad of pocket money every day. Penrose presided over large secret financial transactions, involving the Republican Party machine; none of his enemies could ever accuse him of taking money for himself. All of this impressed the politicians around him. He was not of their ilk, and not only because of his patrician background and mien. They cared for money. Penrose cared for power. This alone ensured the harmony of their cooperation. When he found that politicians of his party, frenzied for loot, had gone overboard and were thrashing in deep water, Penrose said: "They're damned fools, not criminals." Yet he, who did not suffer fools gladly, would go to considerable lengths to get them out of trouble.

In the manipulation of votes Penrose was less cavalier and

less scrupulous; yet even here his enemies could not pin him
down with evidence of fraud. Here again Penrose proceeded
from the assumption that proper and assiduous management
would ensure that American voters select what is accustomed
and patriotic. One day he was watching a patriotic military
parade march up Broad Street in Philadelphia. A companion,
carried away with enthusiasm, said something about the admirable nature of this spectacle. The spectacle, Penrose said, that
excited *his* unbounded admiration and deepest emotion "is a
well-drilled body of voters marching in perfect and obedient
order to the polls."[18] Yet he was not only a master in getting
out the vote. He understood the importance of manipulating
public opinion. He and his ally Matthew Stanley Quay controlled much of the news reporting in the state; they owned
stock in a number of newspapers. Penrose consorted with reporters, invited them, dropped all kinds of hints to them. In
this respect he was a twentieth-century politician, rather than a
surviving nineteenth-century one.

On the day of his first electoral triumph—and for some
time afterward—the proper people were impressed. He was not
impressed with them. He had concluded his treatise on Philadelphia ground rents with a scathing summary of the failure
of the reform movement in Philadelphia. He read the manuscript before the Historical Society of Pennsylvania: it is not
difficult to imagine the frozen faces of that distinguished audience, many of whom were members of the reform movement
that this young giant—a lion in a den of Daniels—dismissed in
so many words. He had supported the reform charter for Philadelphia, but he was deeply skeptical of its results. The first
mayor elected under the charter was a pious manufacturer, a
pharaoh-bearded rope-maker by the name of Edwin H. Fitler,
of whom Penrose said that he was certain of the church vote
"because he looks like a prosperous apostle."[19] Reformers were

[18] Ann Hawkes Hutton, *The Pennsylvanian. A Biography of Joseph P. Grundy*
(Philadelphia, 1962), p. 153.
[19] Davenport, *op. cit.*, p. 49.

"watery-eyed," "pious fools." Their substance was thin. Many of his political allies feared the reformers; Penrose had only contempt for them. They were hypocrites. They prided themselves on having opinions higher than the common man, which made them feel good. Even more than the corrupt politicians, they depended on the support of the wealthier classes. "To whom did the reformers go when they needed the money to finance their campaigns of blather?" Penrose asked. "To the wage earners? Not by a damn sight. They went to the capitalists, to the great merchants and manufacturers who, as it happened, themselves yearned to be legislators and write laws."[20]

"There is more simplicity," Chesterton wrote, "in a man who eats oysters on impulse than in a man who eats grape-nuts on principle." Penrose, who was a gargantuan devourer of oysters, the bigger the better, would have agreed. Yet his character was not simple. He had no scruples at all in presiding over the briberies doled out by his associates; he approved complicated plots whereby the latter would shortchange and defraud people through legislative legerdemain. His experience at law made him understand that even more important than the letter of the law was the procedure in the courts: he had his minions arrange the fixing of juries, occasionally studding them with reliable veniremen with prison records. He succeeded in halting the proceedings against one of his men who had committed vote fraud. Yet no one could prove that any one of his elections depended on fraud. He would reign over his party in the Senate with the sleepy eyes of a grand vizier who had seen everything. Yet when a piece of legislation came before him, he would spend hours examining it, to make sure that it contained not even the smallest of legal loopholes. He cultivated his contacts with the courthouse politicians, rumpled men with owlish faces who carried their pints of whiskey in brown paper bags. Yet he kept an impeccable staff of secretaries, and turned over his entire senatorial salary to the chief one among them.

[20] *Ibid.*, pp. 95–96.

His mail was enormous; he made sure that every letter addressed to him received a prompt answer; and he declined to use the franking privilege of the Congress on his personal mail. He had, as we have seen, an excellent prose style; yet his speeches are uninteresting to read, and his letters even more so. He wrote nothing that could cause him any kind of embarrassment. He was supposed to have boasted that he never wrote a letter to a woman "that you couldn't chill beer on."[21] He was a super-patriot; yet when his political opponent Robert La Follette was about to be expelled from the Senate because of his opposition to the war against Germany, Penrose made one of his few affectionate gestures. He rose and put his hand on La Follette's shoulder when the latter entered the chamber. Later he pulled wires behind the scenes to quash the motion against La Follette. Both before and after World War I, Penrose was an unreconstructed isolationist; yet during the war he simply and squarely proposed that there ought to be "a dreadnought for every state of the Union." After his freshman year at Harvard his mother took him to Europe; after three weeks he asked to be allowed to return home. He was contemptuous of any kind of American involvement in the Old World; yet he was well versed in the classics. He was a collector of first editions of travel books, of certain manuscripts, an amateur scholar of the history of exploration, and a voracious reader.

He was a genius at getting things done in a way that cost him a minimum of effort. He knew how to delegate authority; he employed secretaries who were tirelessly efficient. He was one of the first politicians to utilize the telephone on a large scale; his telephone bills ran to several thousand dollars a month; he recognized the usefulness of the telephone as an instrument of instant, and unrecorded, contact. In 1914 his secretary persuaded him to purchase an automobile. The large red Winton touring car became his trademark. He found it to be a useful

21 *Ibid.*, p. 200.

vehicle, like the telephone, for the purpose of visiting all the counties of the state.

He sought the companionship of all kinds of people; yet he was essentially lonely. He drew away from close friendships throughout his life; he disdained patricians as much as he disdained plebeians. To his niece and nephew he was the classic uncle: a generous giant who spoke few words and was, perhaps, therefore especially impressive. The invitations of Philadelphia dowagers he refused with a bland toneless formality. On the few occasions when he appeared at a dinner party, he was usually taciturn and bored, a graceless hulk of a man. Henry Adams wrote about Simon Cameron that Pennsylvania apparently liked crude, forceful politicians. Penrose fitted this scheme, his patrician background notwithstanding. He was surely very different from other patricians of his era who had ventured into politics, such as the wiry, wispy Henry Cabot Lodge. It is difficult to imagine Boies Penrose contemplating the châteaux of France in the company of an intellectual wife with the tea-cake name of Nannie.

He never married; he never had a durable relationship with a woman. He was very attractive to women when he was young; even when he had grown enormous, his attraction remained in spite of some of his unpleasant characteristics, since he exuded the smell that attracts women, a smell of virility and power. He frequented brothels at an early age; these were especially numerous in the south end of the Eighth Ward, where he started his political career. His legendary appetites were reputed to be sexual as well as alimentary. Yet during his career there was but a single instance when his enemies could pin the scarlet letter of scandal on his monstrous coattails. In 1894 he wanted to run for mayor of Philadelphia. At the last moment his nomination was withdrawn. The story was that the opposition had produced a photograph of Penrose issuing from a known house of prostitution. It was a grave disappointment for Penrose, perhaps the greatest one of his career. Three years later he went to the Senate, but he had wanted to be mayor of Philadelphia more than anything else. He kept his habit of renting a woman whenever he wanted one. In an all but forgotten novel, *The Great One* by Henry Hart, the protagonist, Penrose thinly disguised under a different name, has a searing and exceptional affair during his Harvard years with a beautiful society girl who flings herself at him because of her bad marriage. The affair is unhappy and results in a deep wound. The carapace of cynicism hardens. The hero will never marry. I find this idea plausible. Yet there is not a shred of evidence, or of family reminiscence, sustaining it. His sentiments about women remain a mystery.

There remains the undoubted evidence of his personal habits; these, too, were full of paradox. Penrose's strength and his height—six foot four—made him a coveted candidate for the college football team. He refused, because he hated any kind of physical contact with other bodies, especially with muddy and sweaty ones, as he himself said. He hated to be touched. People who placed a hand on his arm or shoulder would be pushed away; so would anyone who tried to lean close to whisper something in his ear. In sum, anyone engaged in the business of attracting his confidence had to be careful to keep a proper distance. Instant repulsion would otherwise occur. He had a phobia about germs; yet his huge and hairless hands were often dirty, his fingernails unkempt. He had a fine dark head of hair; yet he, who would make few compromises in his quest for comfort (he would leave his vest unbuttoned even on certain ceremonial occasions), wore large hats on the hottest of days. His suits were made of the best English cloth; they were often spotted with foodstains. His boots were polished; yet at times they were tied with string and, on one occasion, it was said, with a corset string borrowed from a prostitute. He would drink cheap gin and Pennsylvania whiskey in low dives. Did he have what the French call the *nostalgie de la boue,* the desire to wallow in the mud? Perhaps: but there is little evidence that he behaved with indiscretion. He kept his *gravitas* at the low-

est of tables, and, perhaps, in the lowest of beds. Unlike English
or Russian aristocrats of his period, Penrose had not much of
a secret life. He drank himself into a stupor like a Roman, not
like a Russian. He was magnificently coarse. His eating habits
were gigantic: a dozen eggs for breakfast, with six rolls, a quart
of coffee, an inch-thick slab of ham. People saw him consuming
an entire stuffed turkey for lunch. There is the story by J. Washington Logue, a Pennsylvania congressman in whose presence
Penrose had ordered reedbirds for dinner; the waiters brought
a chafing dish containing twenty-six of them, which he proceeded to devour one by one, finishing the wild rice and drinking the gravy out of a cup, all of this after having drunk nine
cocktails and five highballs. Yet Penrose cared little for luxuries. He was no gourmet. His chief drink was Pennsylvania
Highspire whiskey. His table manners were ugly. Toward the
end of his life, he told the manager of the Bellevue-Stratford
Hotel in Philadelphia to put a screen around the table where
he was eating his lunch. Otherwise he did not care. His sloth was
legendary. It would grow with the years; eventually it would be
incarnated in the layers of fat which turned this man into a
hulk so huge as to be nearly immobile. Immobile: but not
helpless. He was bear-like, not elephantine. In his youth he went
hunting in Colorado with his brother, who was badly mauled
by a bear; disregarding the advice of the guides, Boies carried
him on his shoulders through the wilderness. Now he was the
big boss of Pennsylvania, of the Republican Party, in the Senate
of the United States; his friends and enemies called him Big
Grizzly.

He hardly exercised in his later years; yet his strength did
not desert him until the fatal illness at the end. It would be,
I think, a mistake to speculate that his growing immobility,
his sloth, may have been the result of some kind of a hormonal
imbalance, of a faulty metabolism. It was rooted, rather, in
a deep and permanent sense of futility. There lay the tragedy
of Penrose. He had an enormous appetite. He had little appetite for life.

He was born, he lived, he died in the same house. The furnishings were somber. He slept late in the morning, he never engaged a cook, he relied on a minimum of maid service. He would attend the political and testimonial dinners, of which the elaborate menus, bound in leather and often embossed with his initials, survive; the menus and liquors look rich in retrospect, yet there was nothing unusual about them in that sumptuary period. Penrose had no interest in traveling, even within the United States. His protectionist and isolationist preferences in politics were the preferences of his private life, too. In 1915 he let himself be persuaded to buy a yacht, a broad-beamed comfortable boat rebuilt to accommodate his dimensions. Around the *Betty* all kinds of legends sprang up, including one of her anchored out in the swells, with Penrose in the nude surrounded by a party of politicians and floozies. According to others, Penrose never entertained a single woman on his boat. I find the second version as believable as the first.

He was saturnine and sardonic; yet there are few witty remarks by Penrose worth repeating. At times we may record an occasional grunt that is pregnant with meaning, as when a politician was supposed to have told him: "Boies, the people of Pennsylvania are going to demand more of you." "More what?" demanded Penrose.[22]

Were there two Penroses, a public and a private one: the tight-fisted taciturn Senator during the day, and the drunken orgiast at night? No: he was too much of a piece. He cared little for his image; his impassive face eventually congealed into a mask, but, unlike other public personages in this century, it was his face that became the mask, not the public mask that became his face. Even his name suited his character perfectly: the heavy, masculine, boar-like Boies dominating the pink, the English, the euphonious Penrose. In his mother's old family Boies had been but a variation of Powys; but there is a curious mystery to names as they grow to fit the character of their bearer, as, for

[22] *Ibid.*, p. 147.

example, a Bismarck or a Stalin. Powys Penrose may be a fitting name for a major character in Trollope or a minor character in Henry James, not for this man of whom not only the sound but the shape of Boies Penrose was fitting—all of a piece.

FOR A QUARTER OF A CENTURY Penrose was a national figure. He entered politics at a moment when there occurred a change in generations. McClellan, Grant, Arthur, Hancock, Seymour, Tilden, the Presidents and the presidential candidates of the period following the Civil War, died within a year of Penrose's arrival in Harrisburg. He was a contemporary of Theodore Roosevelt and of Woodrow Wilson. He did not like either of them. The first was "a cock-eyed little runt," the second "a schoolmarm." He had no liking for Progressives of whatever stripe. He preferred the older type of boss, such as Matthew Stanley Quay, who helped to construct his career. They had considerable respect for each other. Quay was compulsive about money: "a plum," "to shake the plum tree" were politico-financial metaphors that he brought into the American language.[23] Penrose was reputed to have said that Quay "made it his policy to keep at least one hand on the public purse. Only once in twenty years was there a state treasurer he could not control while he was in power. That state treasurer was Matthew Stanley Quay."[24] Like Penrose, Quay was not a simple

---

[23] Mencken, *op. cit.*, p. 281, note 3: "*Plum* seems to have been launched by Matthew S. Quay, who, on being elected Senator from Pennsylvania in 1887, promised his followers that he would 'shake the plum tree.' " Yet it was in 1898 that the word became current. A John S. Hopkins, cashier of the Peoples' Bank of Philadelphia—founded and controlled by Quay—committed suicide. A telegram was found among his papers: "John Hopkins. If you buy and carry a thousand M.E.T. for me I will shake the plum tree. M. S. Quay." Shaking the plum tree meant making a deposit of state funds in that bank.

[24] Quay was an interesting man. He was proud of the fact that he had a bit of Indian blood—rare at the time. (His ancestor had come from the Isle of Man and married an Indian woman in Canada. Quay was supposed to have been 3⁄64 Indian. Letter from Richard C. Adams to Boies Penrose, 11 January 1905, in Penrose Papers, hereafter PP.)

character: he was a Biblical scholar, he knew much Latin, he impressed Kipling. Like Penrose, he was extremely careless in dress. Like Penrose, he wanted to govern Philadelphia, but he could not do it against the local political machine. Like Penrose, he enjoyed the smoky pleasures of Harrisburg. When he was elected by the Pennsylvania legislature to the United States Senate in 1887, a legendary party at the Lochiel Hotel ensued, lasting two days and two nights, during which Penrose was reputed to have consumed six quarts of whiskey, several turkeys, chickens, and hams. It is paradoxical that both Penrose and Quay played a decisive role in the career of Theodore Roosevelt, who disliked Quay and who had mixed feelings about Penrose. They were behind Roosevelt's nomination to the Vice-Presidency on the McKinley ticket, in order to spite Quay's enemy Mark Hanna, the puissant boss from Ohio.

Penrose's association with corrupt politicians did little harm to his popularity. The secret (then called "Australian") ballot was introduced in Pennsylvania in 1891, with the reformers' intention to abolish voting fraud. Penrose never had much trouble in getting elected. The Pennsylvania legislature chose him for the United States Senate in 1897. Before this nomination Quay and his friends convinced him to take on the front-running candidate, John Wanamaker, the Merchant Prince, with a reputation refulgent with gold, in a primary contest for popularity in Huntingdon County: Penrose beat Wanamaker nearly two to one.[25] In 1913 the Progressives pushed through a constitutional amendment for the direct election of Senators. It did not cause Penrose much trouble. In 1914 he beat his vocal

[25] "The contest was extremely acrimonious and, of course, I apparently had everything against me, having been recently defeated in the Mayoralty contest during which I was savagely abused in the press and by civic organizations. Wanamaker was at the height of his reputation and prestige, and Huntingdon County generally was conceded to be about as unfavorable a place as I could go into . . ." Boies Penrose to H. B. Nesbitt, 17 July 1919 (PP). Nesbitt, a journalist, was preparing notes for a biography of Penrose, which he did not complete.

opponent, the Progressive Gifford Pinchot, two to one again.[26] His popularity was such that in 1915 the Republican organization considered the creation of a new county from Luzerne and Schuylkill Counties, with the name of Penrose. Penrose was not much interested, and the matter was dropped. In the taverns of the Philadelphia tenderloin district, signed photographs of Boies Penrose hung side by side with photographs of John L. Sullivan. The fact that Penrose considered it politic to support the city machine, including the infamous Vare brothers, even when it was proven that they were ripping off the city by awarding all kinds of contracts to high bidders of their choice, charging the taxpayers double, hurt Penrose not at all. So much for the argument that people, especially in the Age of Materialism, vote according to their pocketbook.

Penrose, let me repeat, cared little for money. He left this world with far less money than he had when he entered it—in his age, and in his circumstances, a rare combination. He was not an especially practical capitalist. Yet he believed in the practicality of the capitalist credo. He supported large industries; he believed that they made the United States great, since they provided ample work and high wages for the masses. He knew that much of this condition depended on governmental rules and regulations, foremost among them the walls of high tariffs that protected American industry from foreign competition. Penrose, like most Republicans, did not really believe in free

[26] An editorial in the very first issue of *The New Republic* (7 November 1914), p. 1: "The severest blow which non-partisan progressivism received at the elections came from the apparently successful Senatorial candidacies of Sherman in Illinois, Gallinger in New Hampshire, and Penrose in Pennsylvania. These three gentlemen are all of them machine politicians with unsavory records, who represent everything most obnoxious to an American progressive. They were to a considerable extent opposed by the progressive elements in their own parties. Yet they were all nominated and elected by popular vote, and no adherent of popular government can question their title to their offices. The meaning of the lesson is unmistakable. Direct primaries and the direct popular election of Senators will not contribute much to the triumph of genuine political and social democracy so long as partisan allegiance remains the dominant fact in the voter's mind . . ."

trade or in free competition; he thought that government ought to intervene and support the industrialists. In this sense he was more of a pragmatic populist than a capitalist. He advised Henry Clay Frick not to fight the strikers. "Give 'em a little extra gravy till they settle down, then raise prices or the tariff to pay for it"[27]—an inflationary philosophy of which Richard Nixon would have approved. At times Penrose could summon demagoguery in order to attack imaginary capitalists. He thundered out against the insidious invasion of margarine: "We are not willing that the profits of our domestic animals shall be taken away from their legitimate sources and given to a select syndicate of capitalists, in order that they may become inordinately rich." For the profits of domestic animals, read the Pennsylvania dairy industry, as powerful in 1910 as it is today.

He did not like making speeches; he was often indolent enough to cite speeches by spokesmen for capitalism for his purposes. He approved when in 1912 Elbert Hubbard described the United States of America as "a great joint-stock company." In 1914 the president of a Pennsylvania manufacturers' association went one better: the divine purpose of the United States was, simply, to maintain "the best market on earth."[28] Penrose did not really think of the United States in these terms; but he accepted, and welcomed, this kind of capitalist support as well as the support that had come to his party from the slush funds of small capitalists, from the assessment of saloon-keepers and brewers. His legislative record was not only un-distinguished; it was not moved by any consistent principle. He opposed four constitutional amendments, the income tax, the direct election of Senators, woman suffrage, and prohibition; but he would often change his vote; he would not support causes that had become evidently unpopular. At times he

[27] Bowden, *op. cit.*, p. 138.
[28] *The Chester Times,* 13 May 1914: "Delaware County Manufacturers Come Out For Penrose."

would even propose and support reformist legislation.[29] On occasion he actually led the fight against corruption. The Public Buildings Commission of Pennsylvania was a source of public robbery on an unprecedented scale.[30] When, after long years, it was finally abolished, Penrose wired his crony in Philadelphia, State Senator James P. McNichol, alias Strawberry Jim: SPLENDID BUT WHAT STEPS TAKEN TO COMPEL COMMISSION TO TAKE CITY HALL WITH THEM? He hated Philadelphia City Hall. There is an irony in this. That white-marbled, French-Victorian pile of a building has become increasingly appreciated since, a national monument to the municipal Mansard era, while Penrose Bridge[31] and Penrose Avenue in South Philadelphia have remained the most depressing of thoroughfares, surrounded by dumps and the metallic filth of endless junkyards.

He did not hate reform, but he hated reformers. He would have agreed with Ambrose Bierce's contemporary aphorism that a conservative is a statesman who is enamored of existing evils, as distinguished from a liberal, who wishes to replace them with new ones. Was he a conservative? It is at least arguable that his opponent, the Progressive Pinchot, an early conservationist and a stern upholder of civic virtues, including prohibition, was the true conservative, rather than Penrose. Penrose abhorred what he saw as the dry, the thin, the abstract

[29] This included bills such as "An Act requiring foundries to be provided with toilet room and water closet; regulating the same; and providing a penalty for violation thereof." Penrose was critical of his political ally and friend Grundy when the latter opposed a law restricting child labor. "He was the best fund raiser in the history of politics and the worst politician since Julius Caesar," Penrose said. Hutton, *op. cit.*, p. 156.

[30] An investigation found that the Public Buildings Commission, in charge of the building of the state capitol in Harrisburg, allowed $1,500 for a bootblack stand, $80 for each hat rack, $2,500 for chandeliers. The furnishings were paid for by weight and not by unit: the contractor filled the legs of chairs, door knobs, and railings with lead.

[31] The Penrose Bridge was renamed the George C. Platt Memorial Bridge in 1979 by an act of the General Assembly of Pennsylvania. (Platt was the engineer who constructed the bridge. His family campaigned for the name change.) The City Streets Department opposed the change in vain.

virtues Pinchot represented. "Somebody told me that the man never had a drink in his life. If that's the fact, there's no use arguing with him. The man needs a drink."[32] "You are a liability," Pinchot once wrote Penrose, "the most perfect living representative of the worst type of politics in America." Penrose did not deign to answer but said that "Pin-Shot seems to me about as important as a cheap side show outside the fence of a county fair, like the tattooed man or the cigarette fiend."[33] Penrose would have agreed with Burke's principle that politics must be adjusted not to reason but to human nature, of which reason is an important part but only a part; but Penrose was too much of a cynic to believe in principles; and in the age of democracy and of universal education Boies Penrose had a lower estimate of human nature than had Edmund Burke of the untutored people in the eighteenth century. Burke said that the people must never be regarded as incurable. "The people are all right," Penrose said, "but their tastes are simple: they dearly love hokum."[34] Penrose dearly believed in the efficacy of hokum. In 1919 a group of newspapermen asked Penrose who would be the ideal Republican candidate for the next President. "We shall select a man of lofty ideals," Penrose said. "He shall be a man familiar with world problems. He will be a man who will appeal warmly to the young voter—the young men and women of our country. A man of spotless character, of course . . . A man whose life shall be an inspiration to all of us, to whom we may look as our national hero . . . The man I have in mind is the late Buffalo Bill."

Penrose was a nationalist. He had a contempt for the foreign-born; he pushed through several acts of legislation to forbid or curtail their employment on public projects.[35] He spoke out

---

[32] Davenport, *op. cit.*, p. 210.

[33] M. Nelson McGeary, *Gifford Pinchot: Forester Politician* (Princeton, 1960).

[34] Bowden, *op. cit.*, p. 198. Also: "The people don't know what they want. They have to be told what they want, then we have to lead them to recognize it when they get it." *Ibid.*, p. 215.

[35] In the Pennsylvania legislative session of 1895 he engineered "an Act providing that none but citizens of the United States shall be employed in any

against the Yellow Peril,[36] and introduced a Senate resolution in 1913 to send American troops into Mexico. In one of his rare foreign-policy speeches in 1914, Penrose said that the Mexicans were a bunch of shiftless Indians. The Spaniard was expelled from Mexico because he "had compelled the Indian to work instead of lying comfortably on the ground and letting ripe bananas drop into his mouth, or the fruit of the cactus bush, and in the more rigorous climates of the highlands putting enough grains of corn into holes in the ground made with a stick and then leaving them to the rains and sunshine of Providence to enable him to eke out a precarious and squalid existence between the seasons."[37] He distrusted Europeans, and wanted to keep the United States out of the First World War.[38] Yet by 1917 he realized that Americans were itching for war, and he chose not to swim against the current. After the war he

---

capacity in the erection, enlargement, or improvement of any public building or public work within this Commonwealth." In 1897 he supported a tax on the employment of "foreign born unnaturalized male persons over 21 years of age." In the United States Senate he supported a House joint resolution, known as the "Musicians' Bill," providing that enlisted musicians shall not come into competition with civilian musicians.

[36] As his grim supporters, the directors of the Pennsylvania Protective Union, put it in a pamphlet (*A Record of Service for Pennsylvania and the Nation*, Philadelphia, 1914, pp. 22–23): "The facts brought out by Senator Penrose fully justified the apprehension of laboring men over the threatened invasion of this "country by cheaply paid Chinese Labor . . . The story of the Yellow Peril was frightful to contemplate."

[37] Speech in the Whitehall Baptist Church of Tacony, Pa., 12 April 1914.

[38] In February 1916 the former governor of Pennsylvania, Samuel Whitaker Pennypacker, another pharaoh-bearded figure in Pennsylvania politics, an isolationist and a Germanophile (see about him, p. 24) wrote Penrose, asking him to commit the Republican Party to absolute—meaning pro-German—neutrality. Pennypacker enclosed his article: "What German Success Means to America and the World." Penrose, aware as he was of the large German element in Pennsylvania, deftly avoided the issue. Penrose to Pennypacker, 1 February 1916 (PP). In 1941 his nephew Boies Penrose II broke with the Republican Party because of its isolationism; the son of Governor Pennypacker, Isaac P., a Philadelphia lawyer, served as local chairman of the America First Committee.

Unlike his nephew, Penrose was not an Anglophile. On 30 May 1917 he spoke at the annual athletic carnival of the Ancient Order of Hibernians in Point Breeze Park: he would urge in the Senate that the Wilson Administration "make representations to Great Britain as to the advisability of settling the Irish question." *Public Ledger*, 30 May 1917.

saw the national revulsion from internationalism, of which reaction he approved.[39] "As far as I can ascertain, the League of Nations occupies an obscure place in the political cemetery of dead issues," he said.[40] Disarmament was a "purely idealistic and nebulous theory." He may have been right, though for the wrong reasons. He had no interest in Europe and disapproved of those who had, or who pretended they had. When the Harding Administration came in, one of Penrose's cronies, Cyrus E. Woods, a Pennsylvania politician, yearned to become ambassador to Spain. Penrose supported his nomination. Woods wrote a fulsome thank-you letter, to which Penrose replied:

Dear Woods,
    I have your letter of June 15th, and am glad to hear from you.
    I congratulate you upon your appointment, although I frequently doubted the wisdom of your going abroad.
    I shall hope to see you before you leave.

Yours sincerely, etc.[41]

The Clover Club is an annual dining assembly for politicos and newspapermen in Philadelphia. Talcott Williams, a Philadelphia journalist, delivered a eulogy to Penrose at their dinner in January 1922. His reminiscences were a period piece full of plummy prose and Biblical allusions. Among many other things, he recalled that in November 1919 he had sat with Penrose in the latter's Senate committee room and asked him whether the great keynote of the Republican Party in the next presidential election would be the tariff. "He said, 'No. I wish it was the tariff, but the tariff is beginning to seem like a back number.' There was a truthful utterance that I never expected to hear from Pennsylvania. I said, 'Well, I suppose you will

[39] "The whole of Washington's blind except that old elephant Penrose and that old cat Lodge." From William C. Bullitt's novel, *It's Not Done* (New York, 1926), p. 264.
[40] *The New York Times*, 1 May 1920.
[41] Penrose to Woods, 22 June 1921 (PP).

take off the surtaxes on these big incomes.' 'No,' he said, 'I have sympathy with wealthy men.' I said, 'Penrose, you ought to have sympathy with wealthy men. You have touched them often enough.' (Laughter.) And smiling blandly upon me, he said, 'Talcott, don't be ribald. You are not writing an editorial.' I said, 'Well, what is going to be the keynote?' He replied, looking the Roman Senator, as he turned to me with those wide open eyes which all of us are familiar with when an idea had taken hold of him and he was going to drive it home, he said, 'Americanism.' I said, 'Senator, you are the man I have been looking for. What is Americanism?' He sank back into his chair in his committee room and he said, 'Dam'f I know, but I tell you, Talcott, it is going to be a damn good word with which to carry an election.' "[42]

So it was. Warren G. Harding, representing Americanism and normalcy, was Penrose's find. Penrose, who understood modern public relations, immediately grasped the fact that in the age of photogravure Harding's good looks, together with Harding's conformism and his own public-relations experience, would make Harding an excellent candidate. One day in the late summer of 1919 Penrose asked Harding to come over to his suite in the Willard Hotel. He addressed him point-blank: "Harding, how would you like to be President?"[43] Penrose and his ally Joseph P. Grundy, the chief of the powerful Pennsylvania Manufacturers Association, pushed Harding forward. Grundy presented Harding at an important dinner of the PMA. Harding made a speech, emphasizing his homey Ohio background, including his membership in the local band. Penrose was too sick to attend. His secretary came back to Spruce Street to report on the speech. "He should have talked more about the tariff and not so much about playing the cymbals in the Marion Brass Band," Penrose said. The legend, according to which

[42] Copy of the speech in PP.
[43] Hutton, *op. cit.*, p. 158.

Penrose engineered Harding's nomination, is untrue. Grundy was the field marshal in Chicago; Penrose kept in touch through the telephone (his bill was $7,000 for the month of July 1920). The vice-president of the Pennsylvania Railroad offered him a special car, but his doctors had forbidden him to travel. Between Harding's nomination and the election Penrose had but one piece of advice to the party: "Keep Warren at home."

BY THE AGE OF FIFTY Big Grizzly had become a monster of a man. His enormous body was dominated by a mountain of a belly. His lips bit down in a face that was frozen darkly with severity and contempt. In spite of his English ancestry, in 1915 Penrose bore a resemblance to someone like Field-Marshal Ludendorff in mufti. He was at the peak of his political power, but he was as lonely as ever. This giant of body and of intellect, this most promising son of an extraordinary line of distinguished ancestors; perhaps his cynicism was not merely the result of political experience. To stand for being an aristocrat in a democratic world was so futile as to be ridiculous; but then, in the world of democratic politics, there was the futility of limited aspirations. He was choked with boredom. And now the mysterious symbiosis of mind and body asserted itself. He was progressively ill with cancer, though it took a long time for this fact to be known. In 1919 he collapsed. His convalescence took a long time. On 4 March 1921, Harding arrived at the Capitol for his inauguration. By that time Penrose had to be moved around in a wheelchair. Woodrow Wilson, half paralyzed, arrived at the Capitol. Penrose's secretary rushed to the secret servicemen, offering Penrose's wheelchair to the stricken ex-President. Wilson, whose hatreds burned even more fiercely in sickness than in health, refused it.

By now Penrose's face had changed. It showed the ravages of the fatal disease. He had lost half his weight. His face had become impressive, almost beautiful. With the heavy flesh gone, there appeared a face of extraordinary structure and line, a handsome forehead, an aquiline nose; his eyes were no longer beady but big and luminous.[44] He became almost childish in his desire for approbation;[45] there appeared in his conversation traces of great kindness, even of sentimentality. His black valet, William Underwood, "Old Bill," was a lay preacher. One day he pushed Penrose's wheelchair toward the sun. "See here, William," said Penrose. "See here. I don't want any of your damned lies. How do I look? Am I getting any better? The truth now." "Senator," said William, "I tell the truth. You ain't got long. Amen." He cried, childlike. "All right, William. Pray for me too."[46] He died on the afternoon of the last day of 1921 in the Wardman Park Hotel in Washington, as he was waiting for the visit of his doctor. He was sitting on the edge of his bed. He tried to stand up. He fell back dead.

All his life Boies Penrose had an aversion to funerals. He had given orders for a spartan interment. There were to be no guests, no attendants, not even a clergyman. There was something terrible and solitary about this scene. The gates were kept closed by the police. Five high-wheeled black automobiles, containing fewer than ten people, including Penrose's brothers, drove to Laurel Hill, that most Victorian of all cemeteries, filled during the nineteenth century with the now grayed and yellowed and half-sunken mausoleums of rich ironmasters, progressively deserted and empty. The grave was swept and garnished, the clods of earth were wet and dark. It was a day of cold black rain.

Penrose had left his estate to his three surviving brothers. It amounted to a fraction of what his father had left him. The furnishings of 1339 Spruce Street were appraised at less than $1,700. His brothers found thirteen unworn suits, a dozen overcoats, four dozen new nightshirts, and in the cellar a stock of

---

[44] Bowden, *op. cit.*, pp. 262–63.
[45] *Public Ledger*, 11 January 1922.
[46] Davenport, *op. cit.*, pp. 238–39.

liquor appraised at a quarter of a million dollars, legally theirs, since their brother had bought it before Prohibition became the law of the land. Because of a silly Pennsylvania law the liquor could not be removed from the premises without a special permit of the State Prohibition Director. Dr. R. A. F. Penrose, a geologist, Boies's brother, moved into the house. He made an attempt to write his brother's biography, which he eventually abandoned.[47] He died nine years later, also wifeless and childless, in the Bellevue-Stratford Hotel. In 1934 the house was demolished for a parking lot. A junk dealer paid four dollars for Boies Penrose's giant bathtub.

"It was a privilege to me to have lived in the age of Penrose," said the Hon. Charles L. Brown, president of the Municipal Court of Philadelphia, at the memorial services of the Pennsylvania General Assembly on 1 May 1923. "When he passed, he entered into the company of all the greatest men of this country of ours, far greater, because of the country's extent, than was Pericles who ruled Athens in the Greece of his day." The cult of size, of Bigness, again. In his memorial speech George Wharton Pepper, who had been appointed as Penrose's successor in the United States Senate, said: Penrose "studied Pennsylvania till he entered into the inmost spirit of her people and understood the practical operation of her vast industrial system . . . How well deserved was the immense influence which he exercised here. It was the result of thoroughness, sanity, sincerity, and strength." On the part of Pepper, a self-consciously proper Philadelphian who had very mixed feelings about Penrose, much of this was cant.

In 1927 the Republican majority of the Pennsylvania legisla-

---

47 Of Penrose's seven brothers, one died in childbirth. Two children were born to Charles Bingham Penrose and Katharine Drexel. None of the other five brothers had children. Thus the total issue of seven sons—a large family even in Victorian times—was two. Their grandfather, Charles Bingham Penrose, Sr., had fathered six children and twenty-two grandchildren. Of these twenty-two grandchildren only nine married; only four had children, a total of six great-grandchildren—the decline of an erstwhile great and powerful family.

ture passed a bill providing $20,000 for a statue of Penrose to be placed on the Capitol grounds in Harrisburg. There was a lot of trouble with this statue. The agreement with the sculptor, Samuel Murray of West Philadelphia, was composed with characteristic businessmen's specifications: "The statue shall be composed of U.S. Standard Bronze and shall be approximately nine (9) feet high in addition to the pedestal of approximately eight (8) feet high, resting on an ample and secure foundation of concrete." Three years later—it was 1930, a depression year—the statue was not yet ready. Grundy wanted it dedicated before the Democratic majority arrived in Harrisburg. He called the sculptor and found him in bed. "He *said* that he was sick," Grundy wrote to Penrose's brother. Meanwhile, the pedestal had cracked. "Here again I can see that sinister influence which has thrown every possible impediment in the making and erection of the pedestal and of the statue of Senator Penrose." Besides this pediment impediment, "so many hitches and difficulties have occurred during the last three years . . . that I do not hesitate to believe treachery has inspired them."[48] When the statue was first shown to the committee, there was a gasp. It showed an elegant Penrose holding a monocle. He had never worn a monocle in his life. The sculptor eventually removed it. Throughout his life Penrose's presence and memory had been impressive. The monument to his life and to his memory was not.

During the middle span of Penrose's life, Lincoln Steffens wrote his famous book on American cities, calling Philadelphia "corrupt and contented," a pair of adjectives that applied to Philadelphia politics at large; many people thought that it also applied to Boies Penrose in particular. The truth was more

---

48 Grundy to Dr. R. A. F. Penrose (PP): "I am still further confirmed in this feeling by the fate that befell the portrait of Senator Boies Penrose painted by Albert Rosenthal, which hung in the Capitol in Harrisburg in 1904, but which under some hostile and malicious hand was mutilated, cut from the frame, and cast into an attic . . . where it long lay neglected, until the year 1929 when it was discovered and rebilitated [*sic*]."

complicated than that. Penrose had giant faults, but he was not personally corrupt. He had a giant appetite, but he was not contented. Beneath that gargantuan flesh and behind that sternest of stoic countenances there lay, I think, the desperately solitary sadness of an unbelieving heart.

THREE

AGNES REPPLIER

OR

The Writer in Solitude

AMONG THE SURVIVING PHOTOGRAPHS of Agnes Repplier there is one which is as appropriate for the theme of this book as it is inappropriate for her. There she sits, not very comfortably, fidgeting with her cup, with the looks of a retired schoolmarm, dowdy, thick-ankled, her humorless countenance topped by a black pot of a hat, or one resembling a caricature thereof. The picture is a period piece. It shows a library of a late-Victorian or an early-Edwardian kind: an entire wall constructed of ornate shelves and books, the latter mostly Collected Editions in fine bindings, a heavily sumptuous collection. Tightly framed by the shelves, a portrait of Samuel Johnson hovers over the assembly. A. Edward Newton, the host and noted book collector, is holding Miss Repplier's recently published volume (a collection of essays in praise of tea) in his left hand and a cup of tea in his other hand; he is sporting a large checked tweed suit and the expression of a large and benevolent retriever. His wife and another gentleman complete the human components of the picture. Between them stands a delicate galleried tea table, top heavy with a very elaborate silver tea set, the entire assembly resting on a correspondingly ornate, rich Oriental carpet. By contemplating the atmosphere I can *smell* the fine dust of that carpet. And when was this picture taken? My friends look at the furnishings, the clothes, the library; they say, without much hesitation: "Nineteen-twelve." "Nineteen-oh-nine." "Nineteen-nineteen."

They are wrong. The picture was taken in November 1932. It is a period piece of a certain kind—which tells us something about Philadelphia, but not about the then-celebrated author for whom this depressingly genteel tea party was given. Photographs, like phonographs, can blatantly lie. Agnes Repplier did not teach school, she was not retired, she had a great sense of humor, she was extremely witty, she was tall and long-legged. What is more important, she was not a period piece. The few literati (very few) who remember her name may think so. They are wrong.

SHE CAME INTO THIS WORLD in the year of the Charge of the Light Brigade, and she left it the year after the hydrogen bomb; she preceded Theodore Roosevelt by four years and she survived Franklin Roosevelt by another five. When she was a child steel pens were beginning to replace quill pens, and she lived to see (if that is the word) television beginning to replace what was left of reading; the last of the Brontë sisters died the year she was born, and she outlasted James Joyce by nearly ten years. Her life was solitary, vexatious, and long.

For ninety-five years she lived in Philadelphia, this woman whose tastes and whose learning were as cosmopolitan as anything. She was utterly honest, and assertive without pretense, a rare combination. There were only three instances when she chose to alter her record. In the supreme court of her feminine conscience she decided that she was born a few years after her arrival in this world. That was her own dread decision: she liked the years 1857 and 1858 so much that they occasionally became the years of her birth. She loved France so much that France eventually became the land of her ancestry.[1] Since she was not

---

[1] Her Repplier grandfather was Alsatian. She preferred to think of him as having come from Lorraine. Yet she refused to Frenchify the pronunciation of the family name, which was (and remains) Repplier not Repplié.

merely a Francophile but her mind was in ways thoroughly Gallicized, was this not what counted, after all? She was not *une française malgré soi*; she was that vastly preferable kind of person, *une française à cause de soi*. In the third place (in order, though probably first in importance), she spun a veil over her unhappy childhood. She wrote about it as if it had been sufficiently sunny and reasonably secure: it wasn't so.

Her father was handsome and weak; her mother was plain, strong, and intelligent. Her own qualities were compromised fatally by the fact that Mrs. Repplier, born Agnes Mathias in 1832, was a Thoroughly Modern Woman in more than one way. She hated domestic duties, and she disapproved of children, including her own. Such inclinations, widely current a century later, were luxuries then. The Reppliers were not rich. Rich parents could afford to be uninterested in their children, since they could deputize nannies and governesses and tutors and domestic servants of all kinds for the discharge of those domestic and educational responsibilities for which they themselves had no particular taste. Other children would be permanently maimed by the deliberate withholding of parental affection. Agnes was not.

She got a Spartan taste of life from the start. "My mother," Agnes told her niece many decades later, "was perfectly just, but her justice was untempered by mercy. No one loved or tried to understand me, and I think I was an interesting child, if anyone had cared enough to find out."[2] Her mother tried to force her to read, for a long time in vain. Agnes taught herself how to read at the age of ten. Before her opened a world of unexpected delights. Her reading capacity was extraordinary; it was wedded auspiciously to an astonishing memory. Well before she knew how to read she could recite alarmingly lengthy poems by heart.[3] Throughout her life she could draw on her

[2] Emma Repplier (Mrs. Lightner Witmer), *Agnes Repplier, a Memoir* (1957) (hereafter Emma), p. 17.
[3] "Until I had mastered print, my memory was abnormally retentive. There was nothing to disturb its hold. My mother taught me *viva voce* a quantity of

astonishing memory with astonishing ease. She seemed to have read everything, and forgotten nothing. She would instinctively react to the resonance of words—an unusual inclination, since she was otherwise tone deaf, and her interest in music non-existent.

When she was twelve her mother enrolled her in Eden Hall, the Convent of the Sacred Heart, in Torresdale. Liquidated exactly one hundred years later because of the temporary insanity of worldliness that infected the nuns in charge, Eden Hall was then a singular institution: a Catholic school in America attempting to maintain the traditions of the Sacré Coeur of the Old World. From Eden Hall—a pile of a building in the middle of what was then a country estate[4]—issued generations of unusual American women, not all of them Catholics. Eden Hall was *très Sacré-Coeur*: strictly pious and hierarchical, aristocratic in aspirations and slightly brushed with snobbery, French with touches of the Second Empire, sentimental and disciplinarian, Victorian as well as classical, the regimentation of its days and the corridors of its building decorated by a statuary that was marble-cold. Wealthy parents drove out in their carriages to visit their daughters. "Energetic parents made the trip by street car and train. Mrs. Repplier, who was neither wealthy nor energetic, stayed home."[5]

Agnes Repplier, often called "Minnie" (she despised the name), occasionally "April Fool" (she was born on 1 April), was not a popular child. She was a self-conscious little girl, inde-

---

English verse, sometimes simple as befitted my intelligence, sometimes meaningless, but none the less pleasant to the ear. I regret to say that I was permitted and encouraged to repeat these poems to visitors. Why they ever returned to the house I cannot imagine. Perhaps they never did." Agnes Repplier, *Eight Decades* (1937) (hereafter *8D*), p. 6.

[4] "Possibly because of the recent anti-Catholic riots, it had been constructed mainly after sundown by candlelight, and the pointing wavered in perpetual sympathy with what had been the workmen's unsteady illumination." George Stewart Stokes, *Agnes Repplier* (1949) (hereafter Stokes), p. 20.

[5] *Emma*, p. 23.

pendent and occasionally rebellious. At the end of her second year her parents were told not to bring her back.[6] Her convent days were over. *In Our Convent Days* is the title of the memoir of those two years that she wrote more than thirty years later, dedicated to her closest friend from Eden Hall, the difficult Elizabeth Robins Pennell. It is a small hand-wrought piece, one of the finest of her writings, shot through with silver threads of delicacy and proportion: light and serious, shimmering and somber, a recollection of pieties and impieties, of young girl-hood and enduring childishness, this *bonbonnière* of a book is more than a precious trinket of period recollections; it is a minor masterpiece that ought to rank with that other *fin de siècle* book of a similar milieu, Valéry Larbaud's *Fermina Marquez*. Agnes Repplier had at least as much, if not more, cause for bitterness about her school as the well-known English writers of the succeeding generation; she had a healthy talent for irony, and a reserve capacity of sarcasm; moreover, she had been expelled from school, an achievement of which Maugham, Greene, Orwell, Waugh, *et al.*, could not boast. Nonetheless, she elected to spin the tale of her convent days into a fine lacy book, unweighted by sentimentality and not at all genteel. She simply chose to come to the best possible terms with her memories. She decided that her childhood had not been unhappy; and that was that.

Perhaps she knew that it is more difficult to be happy than to be unhappy, and she must have realized the silliness of Tolstoy's famous first sentence in *Anna Karenina*: "Happy families are all alike; every unhappy family is unhappy in its own way." (She never liked Tolstoy very much.) She would have, I am certain, agreed rather with La Rochefoucauld, whom she admired: "We are seldom as happy or as unhappy as we imagine."

In that year, 1869, Miss Agnes Irwin took over the school of

---

[6] She was supposed to have been caught smoking, but we cannot be sure. She was, in any event, a smoking addict during the next eighty years.

Miss Tazewell, victim of a properly Philadelphian nautical tragedy. (She had drowned on a boating excursion off Mount Desert Island in Maine.) Mrs. Repplier and Miss Irwin were friends. In the latter's West Penn Square Seminary for Young Ladies, Agnes Repplier was now enrolled. There, too, she was not a success. Most of the girls, less interesting than her friends in Eden Hall, snubbed her.[7] Miss Irwin appreciated her intellectual talents.[8] She also considered the consequences of Agnes's rebellious nature, concluding that they were considerable. One afternoon Agnes, confronted with the task of reading a disagreeable book, looked straight at Miss Irwin and threw the book on the floor. That evening she met Miss Irwin on the steps of their house. She had come to visit her friend Mrs. Repplier, a not unusual occurrence. Nothing was said. Agnes retired in peace. As she put on her coat and scarf and cap next morning, her mother stopped her. Where was she going, she asked, with an asymmetrical smile on her dark face. To school, Agnes answered—wide-eyed, serious, a little frightened perhaps. Her mother told her that she was not going to school that morning, or ever again.

There and then began the most difficult years of her life, stunted and scarred and poor. Her mother would scratch her own bitterness with diamond-hard lines on the interior windowpane of her daughter's eye. "Your daughter has strong opinions," said a guest to Mrs. Repplier. "Yes, indeed," replied the mother, "in spite of their being worthless." "One morning at the breakfast table, when Agnes was about fifteen, her mother regarded her critically and observed, 'You look like a leper who has had smallpox.' Agnes burst into tears. Her mother went on

[7] Her niece: "Judging from my own later experience, a new pupil was practically certain to be asked three questions by her classmates, 'Where do you live?,' 'What does your father do?,' 'What church do you go to?' Depending on the answers, you were apt to be graded socially." Emma, pp. 28–29. Agnes's grades were low.

[8] One day Miss Irwin asked her something in class. "I'm sorry," Agnes replied, "I forget." "You have a tenacious memory," Miss Irwin said, "and you have no business forgetting anything." Stokes, p. 35.

to say that it was silly to behave this way because one had a bad complexion. 'Mirabeau was ugly and pockmarked, yet he grew up to become one of the great writers of France.' "[9] This was not the voice of the Modern Woman. It was the voice of a hard Victorian eccentric who knew talent wherever she saw it, including in her children. She turned Agnes to a career of writing, while she nearly crushed her spirit. Mrs. Repplier was not strong enough to avoid the temptations of self-pity, an indulgence the results of which can be more disastrous to those close to us than to ourselves. When she was "beaten down by life and knew she was dying, she asked Agnes' forgiveness for bringing her into so undesirable a world."[10]

It was an undesirable world. Agnes's adversities were oppressive. Her gentle and taciturn father lost most of his money in his business: added to the social handicaps of being German and Catholic, the Reppliers were now impecunious as well. Agnes had to live through that saddest of young experiences, moving away from a house in which many things were close and familiar. From Twentieth and Chestnut, a mildly fashionable and genteel portion of the swelling city, the Reppliers moved to Fortieth and Locust in West Philadelphia.[11] She was no longer a child, but she was deeply affected by the move to this somber portion of the city, with its dusty trees, hardwood porches, Methodist respectabilities, and the waiting in the rain for the horsecars, ramshackle and crowded, nearly an hour away from the lights of central Philadelphia, with its theaters, stores, and badly lit library. What kind of life was this, composed of tiresome duties of the day, the dullness and dampness of the house, even when the sun was shining, when the depressing

---

[9] "My aunt was over eighty when she told me of this incident, but there was no emotion in her voice, neither anger nor resentment. The years had erased all passion, but the words remained fresh and indestructible." *Emma,* p. 35.

[10] *Ibid.*

[11] She was born on North 11th Street. They moved to 2005 Chestnut Street when she was seven or eight, and to 4015 Locust Street when she was twenty-one.

heat lay on West Philadelphia like a beached and breathless whale; with the vulgar decorativeness of the hydrangeas, with the dark green weediness of it all.

When the financial catastrophe overcame John George Repplier, his wife, quite reasonably, decided that her daughters would contribute to keeping the Repplier household afloat.[12] She was an intelligent woman, after all. The younger daughter (Mary) would teach. Mrs. Repplier dismissed the idea, bruited about the family earlier, that Agnes should enter a convent. Agnes should write. Agnes was barely past sixteen, but "from that very moment she was fired with both desire and need, the best of all possible goads for the artist."[13] The best of all possible goads, perhaps; but the worst of all possible circumstances. The chances for an untutored and ungainly girl, plunked down in the dullest portion of dullest Philadelphia, to earn a respectable living by becoming a writer were not minimal; they were virtually nonexistent. Compared to such circumstances, the lives of Agnes's English contemporaries, of Gissing's writers in New Grub Street, struggling at the feet of the moloch of Commerce, were melodrama. Here is this gawky girl, this early caricature of a bluestocking, scratching away with her pen on the second floor of a West Philadelphia house, weighed down by the dreariest conditions of enforced domesticity, without friends, without a swain, without any knowledge of the world. During the most formative years of her life, her imagination is not nourished by any kind of experience. It is no less powerful for that. It is nourished by books, by the best of books.

The American newspaper, then even more than now, had some of the characteristics of a magazine. It needed "fillers": sketches, odd pieces of information, stories of all kinds. Thou-

---

[12] The youngest son, John (for whom his mother seemed to have cherished a, for her, unusual affection), a handsome and preternaturally clever child, perished of the croup at the age of four. Another son, Louis, afflicted by partial paralysis, would remain the burdensome responsibility of his sisters until his death at the age of seventy-five.

[13] Stokes, p. 47.

sands of now forgotten scribblers, housewives and clerks, filled these gaps for a few dollars. Few of them aspired to much more. Agnes did. As her niece wrote eighty years afterward: "She had abandoned many early hopes, only to cling with increasing tenacity to one dominant ambition—to become a writer of distinction."[14] In 1937, when she was more than eighty years old, she wrote about herself in this autobiographical fragment:

> *1877.* I am twenty years old, and I have begun to write. It is the only thing in the world that I can do, and the urge is strong. Naturally I have nothing to say, but I have spent ten years in learning to say that nothing tolerably well. Every sentence is a matter of supreme importance to me. I need hardly confess that I am writing stories—stories for children, stories for adults. They get themselves published somewhere, somehow, and bring in a little money. Otherwise they would have no excuse for being; a depressing circumstance of which I am well aware.[15]

For seven years more she wrote and wrote, for seven years that were as lean as any. Her mother died. She had to take care of her old and sick father and her paralytic brother. She struggled on in the night. She was getting closer and closer to the summit of her talent, though she did not know this. In July 1884 a very important thing happened. She met Father Isaac Hecker, a German-American priest of some renown, a compassionate and cultured man who was the founder of the Paulist order and of *The Catholic World* magazine. He had been publishing some of Agnes Repplier's stories.

> Father Hecker told me that my stories were mechanical, and gave no indication of being transcripts from life. "I fancy," he said, "that you know more about books than you do about life, that you are more a reader than an observer. What author do you read the most?"
>
> I told him "Ruskin," an answer which nine out of ten studious girls would have given at that date.

14 Emma, p. 7.
15 *8D*, p. 9.

"Then," said he, "write me something about Ruskin, and make it brief."

That essay turned my feet into the path which I have trodden laboriously ever since.[16]

This was that rare thing of perfect advice perfectly accepted and carried out. Less than two years later Agnes Repplier reached the summit of her ambitions. *The Atlantic Monthly* would publish her essay.[17] Its editor, Thomas Bailey Aldrich, saw that he was in the presence of a writer of talent. She was invited to Boston to meet the Aeropagus of American intellect, the circle of Lowell, Holmes, *et al.* Against all odds (and what odds!) Agnes Repplier achieved what she wanted. Her talent was now public. The pattern of her future was set.

She was thirty-one years old, tall, with a serious mien, no longer very young. How acutely, how permanently, she was aware of that! In 1937, when she was eighty-two, she recounted her crucial conversation with Father Hecker, an account every word of which rings true. There is, however, one white lie. She wrote that this meeting had taken place in 1877. It occurred in 1884. Add to this the two years that she customarily deducted from her age, as in this account in *Eight Decades,* when she writes about herself as "a girl of twenty" in 1877. The crucial interview with this good Father Hecker happened not when she was twenty but when she was rising thirty, past the twenty-ninth birthday of her life. Even at the age of eighty-two she wanted to direct minds away from the stunting sadness of those struggling solitary years. She wanted to give the impression of a young girl, succeeding in literature not merely through her gifts but with the help of great good luck. She dreaded giving the impression that her eventual success was the result of her perseverance: the world might think that she was married to books because no man had wanted her when she was marriageable and young.

16 Quoted by Stokes, p. 59.
17 April 1886: "Children, Past and Present."

She had been in love with her half-brother,[18] and perhaps also with a cousin. She liked the company of men, she knew how to flirt, she was sensitive to male flattery; while she was not beautiful, she was not in the least unattractive; but the pattern was set; she would remain a maiden woman for the rest of her long life.

The pattern was set: her first publication in *The Atlantic* brought her a kind of renown that would not cease for the next fifty years. Every man and woman of letters in the English-speaking world learned her name. Within four years of her first publication in *The Atlantic*, Gosse and Saintsbury wrote her complimentary letters. Awards, medals, honorary doctorates came to her in succession. She was the dean of American essayists.[19] Even in her own "dull, tepid" Philadelphia she was discovered. She became a cherished friend and the pride of some of the best patrician houses. She was eighty-one when Ellery Sedgwick, then editor of *The Atlantic*, wrote:

> For two full generations Miss Agnes Repplier has not ceased to be a bright and finished ornament of American letters. Who matches her in craftsmanship? Who excels her in discipline, in the honest withholding of praise, or in its just bestowal? She is the inheritor of a more ancient excellence than ours, and

[18] Agnes's father had two sons from his first marriage. At the age of sixteen George Repplier ran away from home, where his stepmother had been cold and hostile to him. He fled to South America. Fifteen years later he returned to Philadelphia. He asked his father to come to his wedding in Savannah, where he was about to marry a divorced woman in a civil ceremony. The plan was torpedoed by his stepmother, and the link between the two families was broken. Thirteen years later Agnes, "immediately after her mother's death, and while still in deep mourning . . . appeared suddenly and without warning in my parents' home in New York. Her purpose was to make peace and offer amity, and the success of her mission brought to me, a little girl of five, the rarest of gifts, her life-long friendship and love." Emma, p. 35.

[19] "The chair of the American Essay is in Philadelphia, on Clinton Street in the old city. It has been gloriously occupied for forty years by Agnes Repplier who is at present denied the title of professor emeritus, even though she were ready for it, since there is no worthy successor." Mary Ellen Chase, "The Dean of American Essayists," *Commonweal*, 18 August 1933.

among Americans she has become a sort of contemporary ancestor, a summation of the best that has gone before . . .[20]

Few American writers received, or deserved, this kind of en-
comium.

The pattern was set, by her talent and by her sense of duty.
She was compelled to live with her older sister and with her half-
paralyzed brother, in modest circumstances, without domestic
help.[21] They took their meals in a small residential hotel in the
neighborhood, including breakfast: perhaps the most depressing
of their meals, as the three of them sat hardly saying a word.
Wilde, whose work she admired, said that he put all his art into
his life. Agnes Repplier, whose wit and learning and whose
appreciation for the finer things in life were comparable to
Wilde's, subordinated her life to her art. Returning from those
silent breakfasts through the dreary emptiness of city streets
(the streets of American cities do not shine in the morning), she
would hasten toward her room. When she was younger she took
refuge in books. Now she would escape to her work. Her cat
would perch on the chair, or on the far edge of her writing table.
She would take up her pen; and in her large, curious, stilted
handwriting the words were beginning to form.[22]

SHE KEPT UP HER WORK for sixty-five years: more than two dozen
books, perhaps as many as four hundred essays. The books are
now difficult to find, not very attractive in their looks: dun little
Quakerish books in gray covers.[23] (A handsome exception is

[20] Stokes, pp. 217–18.

[21] "In different ways, though proud of her achievements, the sister and
brother resented her constant engagements and growing fame. These three ill-
assorted characters . . ." Emma, p. 118. Agnes to Harrison Morris: " 'The
Reppliers,' like the Jameses or the Robinsons, sets my teeth on edge."

[22] To Harrison Morris: "I can only work in the morning and for three or four
hours. Then I grow tired and stupid. The pleasure is gone, and I have to stop.
So I don't accomplish a great deal, try as I may. Neither do I work with ease,
but with infinite painstaking." Stokes, p. 116.

[23] Houghton Mifflin, her first publisher, were uninspired and niggardly with
her first collection of essays (Books and Men: a singularly dull title) in 1888;

Eight Decades, printed in 1937, her own selection of her best, and probably the best introduction to her prose.)

She was a superb craftsman. "Every misused word," she wrote, "revenges itself forever upon a writer's reputation."[24] She knew the value of words: "For every sentence that may be penned or spoken the right words exist."[25] She rose above the not inconsiderable accomplishments of a linguistic precisionist; she was sufficiently strong-minded to improve upon Shelley. ("For the mind in creation is as a fading coal, which some invisible influence, like an inconstant wind, awakens to transitory brightness.") Agnes Repplier: "The substitution of the word 'glow' for 'brightness' would, I think, make this sentence extremely beautiful."[26]

Words are not mere instruments of precision. They ought to convey delight. " 'The race of delight is short, and pleasures have mutable faces.' Such sentences, woven with curious skill from the rich fabric of seventeenth-century English, defy the wreckage of time."[27] The history of mankind is the history of mind; and the history of mind is the history of speech: "How is it that, while Dr. Johnson's sledge-hammer repartees sound like the sonorous echoes of a past age, Voltaire's remarks always appear to have been spoken the day before yesterday?"[28] She was one of those writers who have a special affinity for the mysterious evocative power of names: "It took a great genius to enliven the hideous picture of Dotheboys Hall with the appropriate and

---

Miss Repplier had to pay some of the costs of the first printing. On 2 October 1888 she wrote: "My copies of the essays have just arrived; neat quakerish little books with an air of deprecating modesty about them that forcibly suggests the most remote corner of the bookseller's shelf. I can see them already shrinking bashfully into their appointed nooks and powdering their little gray heads with the dust of the undisturbed." Reprintings followed swiftly. Her diffidence was unwarranted.

24 Agnes Repplier, *Points of Friction* (1920) (hereafter F) , p. 93.
25 Agnes Repplier, *Essays in Idleness* (1893) (hereafter *E/I*), p. 115.
26 *Ibid.*, p. 117.
27 *Ibid.*, p. 116.
28 *Ibid.*, pp. 94–95. "Dr Johnson," she wrote elsewhere, "whose name is a tonic for the morally debilitated . . ." *F*, p. 217.

immortal Fanny, whom we could never have borne to lose. It took a great genius to evolve from nothingness the name 'Morleena Kenwigs.' So perfect a result, achieved from a mere combination of letters, confers distinction on the English alphabet."[29]

Her own descriptions were no mere combinations of adjectives. Besides her *mots justes* there was, often unexpected, evidence of her own preferences. She was Catholic; she loved Spain; but she was no Hispanomaniac. Here is a great phrase: "The Escorial," she writes, "is Philip, it is stamped with his somber, repellent, kingly personality."[30] Three perfect words: compressed and jeweled expressions of a lifetime of historical thinking.

She read everything; indeed, what she reread[31] would be sufficient unto a department of English in our colleges now. One of the most attractive features of her writing is its unpredictability: neither frivolous nor impulsive, it sprang from the independence of her spacious mind. Of the fifty years in English letters that preceded the death of Byron she knew just about everything that is worth knowing. She sometimes regretted that she had not lived during that "happy half-century"[32] of "sun-

---

[29] *F,* pp. 154-55.

[30] Emma, p. 88.

[31] "But of what earthly good or pleasure is a book which is read only once? It is like an acquaintance whom one never meets again, or a picture never seen a second time." *8D,* p. 5.

[32] "For myself, I confess that the last twenty-five years of the eighteenth century and the first twenty-five years of the nineteenth make up my chosen period, and that my motive for so choosing is contemptible. It was not a time distinguished—in England at least—for wit and wisdom, for public virtues or for private charm; but it *was* a time when literary reputations were so cheaply gained that nobody needed to despair of one." Agnes Repplier, *A Happy Half-Century, and Other Essays* (1908) (hereafter *H*), pp. 1-2.

"Like the fabled Caliph who stood by the Sultan's throne, translating the flowers of Persian speech into comprehensible and unflattering truths, so Dr Johnson stands undeceived in this pleasant half-century of pretence, translating its ornate nonsense into language we can too readily understand.

"But how comfortable and how comforting the pretence must have been, and how kindly tolerant all the pretenders were to one another! If, in those happy days, you wrote an essay on 'The Harmony of Numbers and Versification,' you

lit mediocrity"; yet writing about it, she remained as clear-eyed as ever: she took great pleasure in pointing a descriptive, a definite finger on the inane writings and opinions of that period—indeed, of any period.[33] Accepted opinions! *Idées reçues!* They got what they deserved: an impatient but precise sweep of her verbal broom, leaving an elegant pattern on the museum floor, with an upward swirl in accord with the very tone of English speech. In a private letter about Alma-Tadema, whom she met in London: "a kind, self-satisfied man, who told venerable stories all wrong."[34] When in Boston James Russell Lowell descended from upstairs to take her coat, the ladies ooh-ed and aah-ed. She did not. Why, oh why, Lowell asked her, did people in Philadelphia call Whitman the good gray poet. "I dare say," the great Boston panjandrum growled, "nobody calls me the good, gray poet, though I am as gray as Whitman and quite as good—perhaps a trifle better." "He paused," Agnes adds to a friend, "and I was on the point of saying, 'Then there is only the poet to consider,' but I forbore."[35] Yet she was not an indiscriminate admirer of Whitman: "The medium employed by Walt Whitman, at times rhythmic and cadenced, at times ungirt and sagging loosely, enabled him to write passages of sustained beauty, passages grandly conceived and felicitously rendered. It also permitted him a riotous and somewhat monotonous excess."[36] A bearded sage whom she profoundly disliked was Tol-

---

unhesitatingly asked your friends to come and have it read aloud to them; and your friends—instead of leaving town next day—came, and listened, and called it a 'Miltonic evening.'" *H*, pp. 11–12.

[33] Writing about the inane Mrs. Chapone, an English educationist during the "happy half-century": "A firm insistence upon admitted truths, a loving presentation of the obvious, a generous championship of those sweet commonplaces we all deem dignified and safe . . ." *Ibid.*, p. 122. Elsewhere: "Alas for those who succeed, as Montaigne observed, in giving to their harmless opinions a false air of importance." Agnes Repplier, *Points of View* (1891) (hereafter P) , p. 99.

[34] Emma, p. 77.

[35] *Ibid.*, p. 49.

[36] *F*, p. 93. She had gone to Camden with her friend Harrison Morris. Whitman was rather dirty and offered his guests whiskey in a tooth mug. His own diary does not improve upon this impression: "My friend, Harrison Morris, brought Agnes Repplier, a nice young critter, to see me." *Ibid.*, p. 101.

stoy, who, perhaps "with the noblest intentions, made many a light step heavy, and many a gay heart sad." She greatly preferred Wilde, at a time when such preference was not fashionable, especially in America. About Lytton Strachey's principal shortcoming she was unerring: "the amazing and unconcerned inaccuracies of the modern biographer" (and perhaps about Virginia Woolf, too: "thin" and "self-conscious").[37]

She was Catholic: in England she found Canterbury Cathedral "an empty shell inside. The shrine of the Saint has vanished, and his very bones were burned by that brute, Henry VIII. A chattering verger leads scores of scattering tourists over the level marble floor, once the holiest spot in England."[38] Yet she had none of the sentimentalities of the Chesterbelloc type: when she spent a Holy Week in Rome, "the processions were scrubby little affairs."[39]

She saw it her duty to point out the shortcomings of popular idols as well as of popular ideas. "The fact that Miss [Helen] Keller has overcome the heavy disabilities which nature placed in her path, lends interest to her person, but no weight to her opinions, which give evidence of having been adopted wholesale, and of having never filtered through any reasoning process of her own."[40] She saw through the superficialities of Victorian as well as of post-Victorian sentimentalities. "When we permit ourselves to sneer at Victorian hypocrisies," she wrote, "we allude, as a rule, to the superficial observance of religious practices, and to the artificial reticence concerning illicit sexual relations. The former affected life more than it did literature; the latter affected literature more than it did life."[41] She admired

---

37 *Ibid.*, pp. 252, 248.

38 *Ibid.*, p. 146.

39 *8D*, p. 261. Still, on another occasion she wrote that "the Englishman who complained that he could not look out of his window in Rome without seeing the sun, had a legitimate grievance (we all know what it is to sigh for grey skies, and for the unutterable rest they bring); but if we want Rome, we must take her sunshine, along with her fleas and her Church. Accepted philosophically, they need not mar our infinite content."

40 Agnes Repplier, *Counter-currents* (1916) (hereafter C), p. 281.

41 *F*, p. 150.

Thackeray: "The world is not nearly so simple a place as the sexualists seem to consider it. To the author of *Vanity Fair* it was not simple at all." Yet her ire rose when "Trollope unhesitatingly and proudly claimed for himself the quality of harmlessness. 'I do believe,' he said, 'that no girl has risen from the reading of my pages less modest than she was before, and that some girls may have learned from that that modesty is a charm worth possessing.' "

"This," Agnes adds, "is one of the admirable sentiments which should have been left unspoken. It is a true word as far as it goes, but more suggestive of *Little Women,* or *A Summer in Leslie Goldthwaite's Life,* than of those virile, varied and animated novels which make no appeal to immaturity."[42] She had a great admiration for male virtues, including martial ones; she took a romantic delight in beholding certain warriors. She quoted Ruskin: "All healthy men like fighting and like the sense of danger; all brave women like to hear of their fighting and of their facing danger": *but* then she flew at Ruskin, "who has taken upon himself the defense of war in his own irresistibly unconvincing manner."[43] She spared not Carlyle, "whose misdeeds, like those of Browning, are matters of pure volition," and who is "pleased, for our sharper discipline, to write 'like a comet inscribing with his tail.' No man uses words more admirably, or abuses them more shamefully, than Carlyle."[44] Like Carlyle, Meredith could be tiresome. When "he is pleased to tell us that one of his characters 'neighed a laugh,' that another 'tolled her naughty head,' that a third 'stamped: her aspect spat,' and that a fourth was discovered 'pluming a smile upon his succulent mouth,' we cannot smother a dawning suspicion that he is diverting himself at our expense, and pluming a smile of his own, more sapless than succulent, over the naïve simplicity of the

---

[42] *F,* pp. 158–59. She may have meant Dickens: "Readers of Dickens (which ought to mean all men and women who mastered the English alphabet) ." *H,* p. 217.
[43] *E/I,* p. 85.
[44] *Ibid.,* p. 120.

public."[45] Her admirations were never undiscriminating: Sir Walter Scott "always shook hands with his young couples on their wedding-day, and left them to pull through as best they could. Their courtships and their marriages interested him less than other things he wanted to write about—sieges and tournaments, criminal trials, and sour Scottish saints."

The sour Scottish saints of Scott!

"When we read, for instance, of Lady Cathcart being kept a close prisoner by her husband for over twenty years, we look with some complacency on the roving wives of the nineteenth century. When we reflect on the dismal fate of Uriel Freudenberger, condemned by the Canton of Uri to be burnt alive in 1760, for rashly proclaiming his disbelief in the legend of William Tell's apple, we realize the inconveniences attendant on a too early development of the critical faculty." This kind of wit, taken from the first paragraph of her first book, was her hallmark: polished and dry, it has none of the upstaging one-liner characteristics of much of American humor. How many pearly sentences rolled off her pen, to vanish unremarked! They were too fine for many of her readers, as was often the wittiness of her conversation. In Philadelphia, perhaps especially among her fellow Catholics, she suffered often from the reputation of being a "cynic," from the age-old habit of people finding themselves ill at ease in the presence of unaccustomed opinions, dubbing them "cynical" even when, in reality, the speaker is far more of an idealist than are her unwitting listeners. "We can with tranquillity forgive in ourselves the sins of which no one accuses us,"[46] she once wrote. This is emphatically not the voice of a cynic—rather the contrary.

"Wit," she said, "is the salt of conversation, not the food, and few things in the world are more wearying than a sarcastic attitude towards life."[47] A man should live within his wits as well

[45] Agnes Repplier, *Compromises* (1904) (hereafter *COMP*), p. 50.
[46] *H*, p. 176.
[47] *E/I*, p. 181.

as within his income: she liked this Chesterfieldian maxim. Her
wit was never forced. Since it came to her naturally, it had none
of the marks of effect-writing, none of the absurd, surrealis-
tic, oxymoronic verbal juxtapositions so typical of present-day
American humor. Her wit was all intertwined with her learning.
Madame de Montolieu was a, now justly forgotten, French sentimentalist novel writer, the author of *Caroline de Lichtfield*.
Her equally witless English admirer, a Miss Seward, wrote that
"the merits of graces" of Madame de Montolieu's volumes were
due to their author's "transition from incompetence to the comforts of wealth; from the unprotected dependence of waning
virginity to the social pleasures of wedded friendship." "In plain
words," Agnes Repplier adds:

> we are given to understand that a rich and elderly German
> widower read the book, sought an acquaintance with the
> writer, and married her. "Hymen," exclaims Miss Seward,
> "passed by the fane of Cytherea and the shrine of Plutus, to
> light his torch at the altar of genius"—which beautiful burst
> of eloquence makes it painful to add the chilling truth, and say
> that *Caroline de Lichtfield* was written six years after its au-
> thor's marriage with M. de Montolieu, who was a Swiss, and
> her second husband. She espoused the first, M. de Crousaz,
> when she was eighteen, and still comfortably remote from the
> terrors of waning virginity. Accurate information was not,
> however, a distinguishing characteristic of the day. Sir Walter
> Scott, writing some years later of Madame de Montolieu, ig-
> nores both marriages altogether, and calls her Mademoiselle.[48]

She carried her learning as lightly as her wit. "Erudition," she
said, "like a bloodhound, is a charming thing when held firmly
in leash, but it is not so attractive when turned loose upon a

---

[48] *H*, pp. 79–80. I know but one example (a not altogether incontestable one)
in which Miss Agnes allowed herself a touch of earthy humor. She was writing
about the monumentally silly Mrs. Barbauld, another female educationist of
the eighteenth century. "This pregnant sentence . . . occurs in a chapter of
advice to young girls: 'An ass is much better adapted than a horse to show off
a young lady.'" *Ibid.*, 5.

defenseless and unerudite public."[49] What she (like Wilde) held
principally against the Victorians was their deadening seriousness. She asked herself, in 1890, "whether the dismal seriousness
of the present day was going to last forever."[50] "Humor would
at all times have been the poorest excuse to offer to Miss Brontë
for any form of moral dereliction, for it was the one quality she
lacked herself, and failed to tolerate in others."[51] She could not
stomach the Brownings. "It is hard to tell what people really
prize. Heine begged for a button from George Sand's trousers,
and who shall say whether enthusiasm or malice prompted the
request."[52] She admired the essentially aristocratic virtue of
gaiety: "Cheerfulness and melancholy can be, and usually are,
equally odious; but a sad heart and a gay temper hold us in
thrall."[53] She could achieve a felicitous alliance of common
sense with wit: "Poetry weds King Cophetua to a beggar maid,
and smilingly retires from any further contemplation of the catastrophe."[54] She once "saw a small black-and-white kitten playing with a judge who, not unnaturally, conceived that he was
playing with the kitten."[55]

Humor is a mark of maturity: it "is seldom, to the childish
mind, a desirable element of poetry."[56] In national life it "illu-
minates those crowded corners which history leaves obscure."[57]
This view of humor accorded entirely with her *persona*, and
with her style of expression. She was a prose writer, steeped in
the French tradition of letters, and thoroughly urban.

---

[49] In the superb essay "Books That Have Hindered Me." *P*, p. 71. Also: ". . . if
the experience of mankind teaches anything, it is that vital convictions are not
at the mercy of eloquence." *8D*, p. 267.

[50] *P*, p. 1.

[51] *Ibid.*, p. 8.

[52] Agnes Repplier, *Americans and Others* (1912) (hereafter A) , pp. 245–46.

[53] *8D*, pp. 62–63.

[54] *COMP*, p. 55. "The Cardinal de Rohan had all his kitchen utensils of solid
silver, which must have given as much satisfaction to his cooks as did Nero's
golden fishing-hooks to the fish he caught with them." Agnes Repplier, *In the
Dozy Hours, and Other Papers* (1894) (hereafter D), 117.

[55] *8D*, p. 302.

[56] *E/I*, p. 42.

[57] *D*, p. 95.

She was urban, urbane, cosmopolitan in the literal sense of these words. Philadelphia was not much like Dr. Johnson's London; but, like Dr. Johnson—and probably even more like all true Parisians of her own time—she found little of life that was worth living outside a city. In one of her acutest essays, "Town and Suburb," written during the 1920s, she saw clearly what the abandonment of the city meant: the abandonment of civilizational, even more than civic, responsibilities by the very class of citizens upon whose support, and cultivation, urbane life in America had to depend. "Suburbanites are traitors to the city." As in many of her essays, sixty years of distance has not dimmed the acuity of her insights, often prophetic ones. "The present quarrel is not even between Nature and man, between the town and the country. It is between the town and the suburb, that midway habitation which fringes every American city, and which is imposing or squalid according to the incomes of the suburbanites."[58] Much of this was the result of the adolescent national mania for automobiles, and of their sanctimonious spokesman, Henry Ford, for example, whom she could never stand and who has "added the trying role of prophet to his other avocations." Her preferences for city life were not merely those of practical convenience:[59] and she had little time for the pious preachings of nature lovers: ". . . it is hardly worth while to speak of city life as entailing 'spiritual loss,' because it is out of touch with Nature. It is in touch with humanity, and humanity is Nature's heaviest asset."[60] She cited Santayana, her favorite

---

[58] *8D*, p. 106.

[59] Even so, these lines penned more than fifty years ago ring ever more true: "Professional men, doctors and dentists especially, delight in living in the suburbs, so that those who need their services cannot reach them. The doctor escapes from his patients, who may fall ill on Saturday, and die on Sunday, without troubling him. The dentist is happy in that he can play golf all Saturday and Sunday while his patients agonize in town. Only the undertaker, man's final servitor, stands staunchly by his guns." *8D*, 116.

[60] *Ibid.*, p. 105. "They talk with serious fervour about Nature, when the whole of their landed estate is less than one of the back yards in which the town dwellers of my youth grew giant rosebushes that bloomed brilliantly in the mild city air." *Ibid.*, 109.

American philosopher, who also prized "civilization, being bred in towns, and liking to hear and see what new things people are up to."[61]

Her independence of mind, her love of conversation, were as French as they were English. ("It is not what we learn in conversation that enriches us. It is the elation that comes of swift contact with tingling currents of thought. It is the opening of our mental pores, and the stimulus of marshaling our ideas in words, of setting them forth as gallantly and as graciously as we can.")[62] Yet the often endless volubility of Parisian talk was not for her; her love for the English temper of speech defined her prosody as well as her rhetoric: "If everybody floated with the tide of talk, placidity would soon end in stagnation. It is the strong backward stroke which stirs the ripples, and gives animation and variety."[63] She minded not a certain kind of restraint: "a habit of sparing speech, not the muffled stillness of genuine and hopeless incapacity."[64] When Henry James came to Philadelphia in 1904, Agnes Repplier was asked to introduce him. The lecture was a muffled disaster, James mumbling for an hour and shuffling his papers. The introduction was a small triumph: perfectly minted, witty, engaging, modest, and short.[65]

Delighted as she was with the music of words, immense as was her mnemonic genius for verse, she was essentially a prose writer. Her one collection of verse, including her introduction to it,[66] belongs to that very small minority of her writings that has a musty and dated touch, and which is rather late-Victorian

---

[61] *Ibid.*, p. 103. But William Penn said: "The country life is to be preferred, for there we see the works of God, but in cities little else than the works of men." (*Reflexions and maxims*, No. 220).

[62] *COMP*, p. 5.

[63] *Ibid.*, p. 7.

[64] *Ibid.*, p. 6.

[65] James wrote to Gosse that he liked Agnes Repplier for her "bravery and (almost) brilliancy." Around that time she wrote in her essay on conversation: "We realize how far the spirit of lecture had intruded upon the spirit of conversation forty years ago, when Mr Bagehot admitted that, with good modern talkers, 'the effect seems to be produced by that which is stated, and not by the manner in which it is stated'—a reversal of ancient rules." *COMP*, p. 4.

[66] *A Book of Famous Verse* (1892), edited by AR (hereafter *ABV*).

in its limitations. Her inclination for the fine-turned phrase was at least as French as it was English; she liked paradox, and expression that was elegant and sharp, rather than blunt or muted by suggestiveness. "When Voltaire sighed, 'Nothing is so disagreeable as to be obscurely hanged,' he gave utterance to a national sentiment, which is not in the least witty, but profoundly humorous, revealing with charming distinctness a Frenchman's innate aversion to all dull and commonplace surroundings."[67] "It is bad enough to be bad, but to be bad in bad taste is unpardonable."[68] She preferred the qualities of French lyric expression: "The delicacy of the sentiment is unmatched in English song. The Saxon can be profoundly sad, and he can —or at least he could—be ringingly and recklessly gay; but the mood which is neither sad nor gay, which is fed by refined emotions, and tranquilized by time's subduing touch, has been expressed oftener and better in France."[69]

She was a *moraliste* in the French tradition—something different from what "moralist" in English means. She liked Sainte-Beuve ("I always tremble when I see a philosophical idea attached to a novel"); and Sainte-Beuve "was spared by the kindly hand of death from the sight of countless novels attached to philosophical ideas."[70] Philosophical ideas were one thing, the need for discrimination quite another. "There is no measure to the credulity of the average semi-educated man when confronted by a printed page (print carries such authority in his eyes), and with rows of figures, all showing conclusively that two and two make three, and that with economy and good management they can be reduced to one and a half. He has never mastered, and apparently will never master, the exact shade of difference between a statement and a fact."[71] Sentimentalist nonsense, whether in literature or in education, made her angry.

[67] *E/I*, p. 186.
[68] *F*, pp. 73–74.
[69] *COMP*, p. 166.
[70] *P*, p. 117.
[71] *A*, p. 196.

"The assumption that children should never be coerced into self-control, and never confronted with difficulties, makes for failure of nerve . . . The assumption that young people should never be burdened with responsibilities, and never, under any stress of circumstances, be deprived of the pleasures which are no longer a privilege, but their sacred and inalienable right, makes for failure of nerve. The assumption that married women are justified in abandoning their domestic duties, because they cannot stand the strain of home life and housekeeping, makes for failure of nerve . . . The assumption that religion should content itself with persuasiveness, and that morality should be sparing in its demands, makes for failure of nerve."[72]

She was intellectual; but she knew the limitations of the intellect. "The clear-sighted do not rule the world, but they sustain and console it. It is not in human nature to be led by intelligence. An intelligent world would not be what it is today; it would never have been what it has been in every epoch of which we have any knowledge."[73] She—a rarity among women writers, this—had a very strong, a deep knowledge of history. Her *Philadelphia: The Place and the People* (which she wrote in 1898 upon a publisher's suggestion) remains to this day the most readable history of her native city. Her often superbly detached and witty style of writing; her strong, and instinctively intelligent, judgments are complemented by her talented evocation of atmosphere, and by her interest in all kinds of details of social and of everyday life: the *petits faits* dear to Taine and to some of the best historians of the twentieth century. (In this respect, too, Agnes Repplier proved herself to be a "threshold" writer: standing firm on what was best in the standards of the nineteenth as well as of the twentieth century.) The book suffers from a certain lack of proportion: three-fourths of it deals with the eighteenth century, and hardly more than one-eighth of it with the nineteenth; she may have become somewhat bored with her task, even though the writing of the last chapters surely

[72] *C,* pp. 39–40.
[73] *Ibid.,* p. 145.

matches that of the earlier ones.[74] Agnes Repplier belonged to
the tradition that considered history to be the narrated past, a
form of high literature, and her histories are none the worse
for it, to say the least; but she understood history well enough
to know in her bones that history was more than that, too: not
only a form of literature, but also a form of thought.

> The mediæval chroniclers listened rapturously to the
> clamor of battle, and found all else but war too trivial for
> their pens. The modern scholar produces that pitiless array
> of facts known as constitutional history; and labors under the
> strange delusion that acts of Parliament, or acts of Congress,
> reform bills, and political pamphlets represent his country's
> life. If this sordid devotion to the concrete suffers no abate-
> ment, the intelligent reader of the future will be compelled
> to reconstruct the nineteenth century from the pages of *Punch*
> and *Life*,[75] from faded playbills, the records of the race-track,
> and the inextinguishable echo of dead laughter.

She wrote this in 1893. Eighty-seven years later this historian,
after a lifetime of studying the character of modern history and
the requisites of modern history writing, can but lift his imaginary plumed hat and shout: "Brava!"

"The neglect of history," she wrote more than sixty years ago,
"practised by educators who would escape its authority, stands
responsible for much mental confusion." "I used to think that
ignorance of history meant only a lack of cultivation and a loss
of pleasure. Now I am sure that such ignorance impairs our

---

[74] Example: "Judge Peters enjoyed an enviable reputation as a wit, and some of
his pleasantries have come floating down to us in cold unsympathetic print, illustrating, as a captious biographer expresses it, 'the great difference between
hearing a joke and reading one.' The Indians, whose councils he occasionally attended, and who are not a humorous race, christened him the Talking Bird. It
is a pity ever to waste wit upon Indians." Agnes Repplier, *Philadelphia: The
Place and the People* (1898) (hereafter *PPP*), p. 163. She could write with wit
and detachment about the saddest of events in her native city, the anti-Catholic
Know-Nothing riots of the 1840s: "They stretched ropes across the darkening
streets to obstruct the passage of the cavalry. It was picturesque, and exceedingly
like Perugia in the Middle Ages, when the Baglioni and their rivals fought in the
great square of the Cathedral; but it was not at all like Penn's City of Peace,
which he had founded as an asylum of the oppressed, where no sword was to be
drawn, and no man persecuted for his creed." *Ibid.*, p. 353.

[75] *Life:* a literary and humorous magazine, not the picture magazine of the
mid-twentieth century.

judgment by impairing our understanding, by depriving us of standards, or the power to contrast, and the right to estimate."[76] "In the remote years of my childhood," she wrote, "the current events, that most interesting and valuable form of tuition which, nevertheless, is unintelligible without some knowledge of the past, was left out of our limited curriculum. We seldom read the newspapers (which I remember as of an appalling dullness), and we knew little of what was happening in our day. But we did study history, and we knew something of what had happened in other days than ours; we knew and deeply cared."[77]

History is the best fare for one's imagination; it also provides for a thoughtful conservatism whose absence, especially in America,[78] she regretted. "Political conservatism may be a lost cause in modern democracy; but temperamental conservatism dates from the birth of man's reasoning powers, and will survive the clamour and chaos of revolutions."[79] For "innovations to which we are not committed are illuminating things."[80] "The reformer whose heart is in the right place, but whose head is elsewhere, represents a waste of force . . ."[81] "It is well that the past yields some solace to the temperamental conservative, for the present is his only on terms he cannot easily fulfill. His reasonable doubts and his unreasonable prejudices block the path of contentment. He is powerless to believe a thing because it is an eminently desirable thing to believe. He is powerless to deny the existence of facts he does not like. He is powerless to credit new systems with finality. The sanguine assurance that men and nations can be legislated into goodness, that pressure from with-

76 F, pp. 7, 10. "We can know nothing of any nation unless we know its history."
77 "It was not possible for a child who had lived in spirit with Saint Genevieve to be indifferent to the siege of Paris in 1870. It is not possible for a child who has lived in spirit with Jeanne d'Arc to be indifferent to the destruction of Rheims Cathedral in 1914." F, pp. 25-26.
78 ". . . even a conservative American, if such anomaly exists . . ." D, p. 101.
79 F, p. 102.
80 Ibid., p. 99.
81 C, 32. "A moderate knowledge of history—which, though discouraging, is also enlightening—might prove serviceable to all the enthusiasts who are engaged in making over the world. Many of them (in this country, at least) talk and write as if nothing in particular had happened between the Deluge and the Civil War." Ibid., p. 21.

out is equivalent to a moral change within, needs a strong
backing of inexperience. 'The will,' says Francis Thompson, 'is
the lynch-pin of the faculties.' We stand or fall by its strength
or its infirmity."[82]

> To cheat ourselves intellectually that we may save our-
> selves spiritually is unworthy of the creature that man is meant
> to be.
> And to what end! Things are as they are, and no amount of
> self-deception makes them otherwise. The friend who is inca-
> pable of depression depresses us as surely as the friend who is
> incapable of boredom bores us. Somewhere in our hearts is a
> strong, though dimly understood, desire to face realities, and
> to measure consequences, to have done with the fatigue of pre-
> tending. It is not optimism to enjoy the view when one is treed
> by a bull; it is philosophy. The optimist would say that being
> treed was a valuable experience. The disciple of gladness
> would say that it was a pleasurable sensation. The Christian
> Scientist would say there was no bull, though remaining—if
> he were wise—on the treetop. The philosopher would make
> the best of a bad job, and seek what compensation he could
> find. He is of a class apart.[83]

"Human experience," she wrote during the First World War,
"is very, very old. It is our sure monitor, our safest guide. To
ignore it crudely is the error of those ardent but uninstructed
missionaries who have lightly undertaken the re-building of the
social world."[84] She belonged to the rare company of realistic
idealists, whose knowledge of history and whose self-knowledge
go hand in hand—which provided her with the necessary balance in perceiving, and describing, people and places and
scenes to which she would be otherwise sentimentally inclined.
"Touraine," she once wrote, "is full of beauty, and steeped to
the lips in historic crimes."[85] This kind of demanding realism
was part of her religion: "It was Cardinal Newman who first
entered a protest against 'minced' saints, against the pious and

[82] *F*, pp. 97–98.
[83] *Ibid.*, pp. 122–23.
[84] *C*, p. 137. "Great events, however lamentable, must be looked at greatly."
Ibid., p. 105.
[85] *A*, p. 142.

popular custom of chopping up human records into lessons for
the devout. He took exception to the hagiological license which
assigns lofty motives to trivial actions."[86]

She was a *moraliste*, not a Puritan. She believed in the virtues of cultivating human self-discipline; but also in the virtue
of cultivating human pleasure. In 1890 she wrote: "Why should
the word 'pleasure,' when used in connection with literature,
send a cold chill down our strenuous nineteenth century spines?
It is a good and charming word, caressing in sound and softly
exhilarating in sense."[87] Also: "Joy is a delightful, flashing little
word, as brief as is the emotion it conveys."[88] And about an emotion: ". . . when a happy moment, complete and rounded as a
pearl, falls into the tossing ocean of life, it is never wholly lost."[89]
Her taste for pleasure was as fine as it was strong. In her essay on
Horace, she wrote, about his retreat in the country, that it was
"what was then called the simple life; but, as compared with the
crude and elemental thing which goes by that name in this our
land today, it is recognizable as the austere luxury of a very
cultivated poet."[90] She generally despised preaching, especially
Puritan preaching. " 'Christ died for a select company that was
known to Him, by name, from eternity,' wrote the Reverend
Samuel Willard, pastor of the South Church, Boston, and author
of that famous theological folio, *A Compleat Body of Divinity*.
'The bulk of mankind is reserved for burning,' said Jonathan
Edwards genially; and his Northampton congregation took his
word for it. That these gentlemen knew not more about Hell
and its inmates than did Dante is a circumstance which does not
seem to have occurred to anyone. A preacher has some advantage over a poet."[91] And here is a prize:

> Agnes Edwards, in an engaging little volume on Cape Cod,
> quotes a clause from the will of John Bacon of Barnstable, who

[86] *Ibid.*, p. 72.
[87] *P*, p. 139.
[88] *F*, p. 109.
[89] *P*, p. 147.
[90] *8D*, p. 60.
[91] *Ibid.*, p. 75.

bequeathed to his wife for her lifetime the "use and improvement" of a slavewoman, Dinah. "If, at the death of my wife,
Dinah be still living, I desire my executors to sell her, and to
use and improve the money for which she is sold in the purchase of Bibles, and distribute them equally among my said
wife's and my grandchildren."

There are fashions in goodness and badness as in all things
else; but the selling of worn-out women for Bibles goes a step
beyond Mrs. Stowe's most vivid imaginings.[92]

She did not like Mrs. Stowe.[93] She cared little for Bostonians,[94]
including Emerson: "Unlike Emerson, we are glad to be

[92] *Ibid.*, pp. 86–87. About the "painful and precocious" diary of "young Nathaniel Mather, who happily died before reaching manhood, but not before he
had scaled the heights of self-esteem, and sounded the depths of despair. When
a boy, a real human boy, laments and bewails in his journal that he whittled a
stick upon the Sabbath Day, 'and, for fear of being seen, did it behind the door,
a great reproach of God, and a specimen of that atheism I brought into
the world with me'—we recognize the fearful possibilities of untempered
sanctimony." Agnes Repplier, *Varia* (1897) (hereafter V), p. 36.

[93] From "Books That Have Hindered Me": "The last work to injure me seriously as a girl, and to root up the good seed sown in long years of righteous education, was *Uncle Tom's Cabin,* which I read from cover to cover with the innocent credulity of youth; and, when I had finished, the awful conviction forced
itself upon me that the Thirteenth Amendment was a ghastly error, and that the
war had been fought in vain. Slavery, which had seemed to me before undeviat-
ingly wicked, now shone in a new and alluring light. All things must be judged
by their results: and if the result of slavery was to produce a race so infinitely
superior to common humanity; if it bred strong, capable, self-restraining men
like George, beautiful, courageous, tender-hearted women like Eliza, visions of
innocent loveliness like Emmeline; marvels of acute intelligence like Cassy,
children of surpassing precocity and charm like little Harry, mothers and wives
of patient, simple goodness like Aunt Chloe, and, finally, models of all known
chivalry and virtue like Uncle Tom himself—then slavery was the most en-
nobling institution in the world, and we had committed a grievous crime in de-
grading a whole heroic race to our narrower, viler level. It was but too apparent, even to my immature mind, that the negroes whom I knew, or knew
about, were very little better than white people; that they shared in all the
manifold failings of humanity, and were not marked by any higher intelligence
than their Caucasian neighbors. Even in the matters of physical beauty and
mechanical ingenuity there had been plainly some degeneracy, some falling off
from the high standard of old slavery days. Reluctantly I concluded that what
had seemed so right had all been wrong indeed, and that the only people who
stood preeminent for virtue, intellect, and nobility had been destroyed by our
rash act, had sunk under the enervating influence of freedom to a range of lower
feeling, to baser aspirations and content. It was the greatest shock of all, and the
last." *P*, pp. 75–76.

[94] About John Fiske, the greatly respected Boston historian: "He cannot for

amused, only the task of amusing us grows harder day by day."[95]
Her "amusing" was a rapier word with double edges: "It is
amusing to hear Bishop Copleston, writing for that young and
vivacious generation who knew not the seriousness of life, remind them pointedly that 'the task of pleasing is at all times
easier than that of instructing.' It is delightful to think that
there ever was a period when people preferred to be pleased
rather than instructed."[96]

"Any book which serves to lower the sum of human gaiety is
a moral delinquent"[97] (proof that she could be flippant when
she wanted to be). She could be as impatient with the cant of the
modern critic as with that of the ancient Puritan preacher:

> It is the most significant token of our ever-increasing "sense
> of moral responsibility in literature" that we should be always
> trying to graft our own conscientious purposes upon those au-
> thors who, happily for themselves, lived and died before virtue,
> colliding desperately with cakes and ale, had imposed such de-
> pressing obligations.
>
> "*Don Quixote*," says Mr. Shorthouse with unctuous gravity,
> "will come in time to be recognized as one of the saddest books
> ever written"; and if the critics keep on expounding it much
> longer, I truly fear it will.[98]

She herself counted the "obnoxious word 'ethics' six times
repeated in the opening paragraph of one review, and have felt
too deeply disheartened by such an outset to penetrate any further."[99] Her strong heart as well as her appetite found the vague

---

a moment forget how much better he knows; and instead of an indulgent smile
at the delightful follies of our ancestors, we detect here and there through his
very valuable pages something unpleasantly like a sneer." *B*, pp. 58–59. "Longfellow wrote a 'Drinking Song' to water which achieved humour without aspiring
to it, and Dr. Holmes wrote a teetotaler's adaptation of a drinking song, which
aspired to humour without achieving it." *F*, p. 206.

[95] Agnes Repplier, *Books and Men* (1890) (hereafter *B*), p. 119.
[96] *P*, p. 106.
[97] Emma, p. 257.
[98] *P*, p. 3.
[99] *Ibid.*, pp. 118–19.

and bland white sauce of ethical culture repellent. "There is," she wrote, "nothing new about the Seven Deadly Sins. They are as old as humanity. There is nothing mysterious about them. They are easier to understand than the Cardinal Virtues."[100]

She had a compound attitude toward Quakers. She had a genuine feeling for their humaneness. Unlike most people—unlike, alas, many Philadelphians—she much preferred the melancholy Penn over the ambitious Franklin.[101] She had a good deal of respect for "that old-time Quakerism, gentle, silent, tenacious, inflexible, which is now little more than a tradition in the land, yet which has left its impress forever upon the city it founded and sustained."[102] Yet the unimaginative tightness of the Quaker mind grated on her nerves. She admired Elizabeth Drinker for her singularly detailed and disciplined diary of Philadelphia during the Revolution; but she was exasperated with her self-imposed limitations, with that whalebone corseting of a soul. "The most striking characteristic of our Quaker diarist is precisely this clear, cold, unbiased judgment, this sanity of a well-ordered mind. What she lacks, what the journal lacks from beginning to end, is some touch of human and ill-repressed emotion, some word of pleasant folly, some weakness left undisguised and unrepented. The attitude maintained throughout is too judicial, the repose of heart and soul too absolute to be endearing . . ."[103] Because Agnes Repplier could not stomach Puritans, she stood for tolerance; because she was not a Quaker, tolerance could also leave her cold. "The languid indifference

---

[100] *C*, p. 136.

[101] She instinctively understood the connection between the utilitarianism of a Franklin and the sentimentalism of the Brownings, a century later. She cited "the robust statement of Benjamin Franklin: 'I approved, for my part, the amusing one's self now and then with poetry, so far as to improve one's language, but no farther.' What a delicious picture is presented to our fancy of a nineteenth-century Franklin amusing himself and improving his language by an occasional study of 'Sordello'!" *E/I*, p. 127.

[102] *COMP*, p. 128.

[103] *Ibid.*, p. 151.

. . . which we dignify by the name of tolerance, has curtailed our interest in life."[104] (She would have agreed with her contemporary compatriot and potential confrère, the Philadelphia literary gentleman Logan Pearsall Smith, who fled to England from the bosom of Quakerdom: "Only among people who think no evil can Evil monstrously flourish.") "There are always men and women," she wrote, "who prefer the triumph of evil, which is a thing they can forget, to prolonged resistance, which shatters their nerves. But the desire to escape an obligation, while very human, is not generally thought to be humanity's noblest lesson."[105] She was not an abstract moralist; she had, as we have seen, a stern sense of duty. She was impatient with stupidity— and impatience has not been a Quaker or Philadelphian habit. "Sonorous phrases like 'reconstruction of the world's psychology,' and 'creation of a new world atmosphere,' are mental sedatives, drug words, calculated to put to sleep any uneasy apprehensions. They may mean anything, and they do mean nothing, so that it is safe to go on repeating them."[106] "The combination of a sad heart and a gay temper, which is the most charming and the most lovable thing the world has got to show";[107] this was emphatically not a Quaker combination.

Her mind, in many ways, represented the best of combinations: she was a realistic idealist and a tough-minded romantic. I wrote before that she *chose* to regard her childhood as not particularly unhappy: a choice which was conscious, not a subconscious one, for which all Freudian terms such as "sublimation" or "repression" would be woefully insufficient. She, who had no children, thought and knew a good deal about the trials and tribulations of childhood, and she wrote some of her finest essays about children's minds. She detested people who wrote books such as the one "with the somewhat ominous title *Chil-*

104 *8D*, p. 81.
105 *F*, p. 6.
106 *Ibid.*, pp. 75–76.
107 *Ibid.*, p. 115.

dren's Rights."[108] She understood, because she loved, the imagination of children ("... no child can successfully 'make believe,' when he is encumbered on every side by mechanical toys so odiously complete that they leave nothing for the imagination to supply").[109] Because she was not a sentimentalist, she understood how very complex the minds of children (not at all little adults, as Americans are wont to believe, and to treat them) are:

> The merriment of children, of little girls especially, is often unreal and affected. They will toss their heads and stimulate one another to peals of laughter which are a pure make-believe. When they are really absorbed in their play, and astir with delicious excitation, they do not laugh; they give vent to piercing shrieks which sound as if they were being cut in little pieces. These shrieks are the spontaneous expressions of delight; but their sense of absurdity, which implies a sense of humor, is hard to capture before it has become tainted with pretense.[110]

A passage worth an entire library confected by child psychologists.

It was a kind of participant knowledge: neither objective, nor subjective, but personal. So was her understanding of the psychology of nations. "National traits," she wrote, "are, as a matter of fact, as enduring as the mountain-tops. They survive all change of policies, all shifting of boundary lines, all expansion and contraction of dominion."[111] She understood how the struggles of nations are more important and decisive matters than are the struggles of classes; that the sympathies and the antipathies which the images of certain nations inspire are deep-seated and

[108] *D*, p. 50.

[109] *Ibid.*, pp. 53–54. Reminiscing about her convent days: "The very bareness of our surroundings, the absence of all appliances for play, flung us back unreservedly upon the illimitable resources of invention." Agnes Repplier, *In Our Convent Days* (1905) (hereafter *CONV*), p. 148.

[110] Agnes Repplier, *Under Dispute* (1923) (hereafter *DS*), pp. 303–4.

[111] *8D*, p. 253.

weighty matters, more profound than the superficial and current categories of "international relations." She understood that Anglophilia and Francophilia and Germanophilia were not merely the results of ethnic or ancestral memories; that they were more than political preferences. They were cultural preferences, representing certain inclinations of spirit and mind. On the highest level of her own cultural preferences Agnes Repplier aspired to those peaks of sensitivity which were unique for that Anglo-French civilization that, around 1900, may have marked the pinnacle of the Bourgeois Age. The *entente cordiale* between these two great Western European nations existed in her mind decades before their alliance became a reality on the battlefield, and well before it had become a reality in the form of a treaty. This was no coincidence. She, who was not particularly interested in politics, sensed that Germany represented a danger, not only to the British and the French, but to the kind of civilization she cherished. This is why her impatient and, on occasion, insistent, admonitory writings during the First World War should not be considered as if they were odd political excursions during her literary career, which is what some of her critics took them to be. She was convinced that a victory of Germany over France and Britain would be a disaster to the entirety of Western civilization, and she was bitterly impatient with the majority of her countrymen who were unwilling to face this condition, comforting themselves instead with pious sentiments.

How she loved England! "I, without one drop of English, Scotch, Welsh or Irish blood in my veins, have come into the matchless inheritance of the English tongue and of English letters, which have made the happiness of my life."[112] She had no sympathy with the frequently narrow Anglophobia of Irish

---

[112] From her address to the English-Speaking Union. Emma, 116. When she first set foot in England: "After French, Dutch, German, Flemish, to say nothing of American, the mother tongue was made doubly blessed by being so sweetly spoken . . . The charming intonations of the English fill me with wonder and regret. Why can't I speak in that way?" Stokes, 100. Later she would qualify her

Catholics in the United States;[113] she had even less sympathy with the kind of redskin American nationalism which, wishing to fill the Indian land, preferred to turn its broad back on the English heritage. But she met with the same cold and shrouded obstacles with which so many lovers of England had had their chilly encounters: the English were diffident, with gray ice over their faces.[114] She wrote a beautiful essay about the relationship of England and America, "The Estranging Sea." She, who understood the English so well, felt their unwillingness to respond, to the marrow of her bones. It was an unrequited love.

She was sixty years old when, in 1915, she asked her friend Dr. White to take her to France to serve in the American Ambulance Hospital.[115] (He, wisely enough, refused.) She hated the sanctimonious William Jennings Bryan ("a past master of infelicitous argument, and very ugly to boot"). She did not like Germans, and she would have agreed with the wag who said that Wagner's music was better than it sounds; she did not like their

---

unconditional admiration for English speech, and for certain English characteristics: see below, pp. 119, 127. Throughout her life, however, she determined to spell certain words in the English way: "fervour," "harbour," "humour," etc. (She must have had a recurrence of trouble with proofreaders.)

[113] She preferred the English to the Irish people, as she preferred the King James Bible to the Douay. Around 1600 the English tongue "had reached its first splendour, with the tenderness, vigor, and warmth of a language fresh from the mint. If all other English were to be blotted out from the world, the King James Bible would preserve intact its beauty and its power." Emma, 148. (What would she say today?)

[114] She had a fine correspondence with Andrew Lang, the eccentric critic and essayist, whose letters to her were full of unexpected small delights. When she finally met Lang in London she found him "sulky, and irresistibly charming; tall, lean, grey and very handsome." Stokes, 119. He was lean and gray indeed. On one occasion he asked Agnes Repplier to pay for their tea. At the end of her visit he bade her goodbye and never wrote to her again.

[115] In 1914 she composed a pamphlet, together with J. William White, entitled: "Germany and Democracy, the Real Issue, the Views of Two Average Americans, a reply to Doctor Dernburg." (Dr. Dernburg had presented the case for Germany in *The Saturday Evening Post*.) The pamphlet was subsequently republished in England, France, and Holland. "In good truth," she wrote, "*all* German apologists, writing to enlist the sympathy of Americans, should be made to understand the value of an understatement. If they would claim a little less, we could believe a great deal more . . ." Stokes, p. 175.

heaviness;[116] she did not like Schopenhauer, "the great apostle
of pessimism" who made "so much headway in reducing sadness to a science." She could be critical of the faults of the
French, and especially of their talent for egocentricity: "When
Voltaire sneered at the *Inferno*, and thought *Hamlet* the work
of a drunken savage, he at least made a bid for the approbation
of his countrymen, who, as Schlegel wittily observes, were in the
habit of speaking as though Louis XIV had put an end to can-
nibalism in Europe."[117] Her initial sympathies were monarchi-
cal and aristocratic and romantic: when she first visited Paris
she kissed the tattered cassock of Archbishop Darboy (murdered
during the Commune in 1871) "when no one was looking. Republican France held no place in her heart."[118] She changed her
mind about this; she rallied to the cause of the French Republic
before, during, and after the First World War.[119]

---

[116] As early as 1902 she wrote: "There is a power of universal mastery about
the traveling Teuton which affronts our feebler souls. We cannot cope with
him; we stand defeated at every turn by his restless determination to secure the
best. The windows of the railway carriages, the little sunny tables in the hotel
dining-rooms, the back seats—commanding the view—of the Swiss *funiculaires;*
all these strong positions he occupies at once with the strategical genius of a
great military nation. No weak concern for other people's comfort mars the
simple straightforwardness of his plans, nor interferes with their prompt and
masterly execution. Amid the confusion and misery of French and Italian railway stations, he plays a conqueror's part, commanding the services of the
porters, and marching off triumphantly with his innumerable pieces of hand
luggage, while his fellow tourists clamour helplessly for aid. 'The Germans are
a rude, unmannered race, but active and expert where their personal advantages
are concerned,' wrote the observant Froissart many years ago. He could say
neither more nor less were he travelling over the Continent to-day." *COMP*,
pp. 187–88.

But, then, she also wrote: " 'Potter hates Potter, and Poet hates Poet,'—so
runs the wisdom of the ancients—but tourist hates tourist with a cordial
Christian animosity that casts all Pagan prejudices in the shade." *Ibid.*, p. 185.

[117] *B*, p. 139.

[118] Emma, p. 92.

[119] Her then young admirer, Constance O'Hara, told about a Monsignor
Kieran who "preached a fine sermon . . . rich with classical allusions and splendid
imagery that got off the subject only once or twice when he thundered at the
French for their anti-clericalism. He always got that in—despite Agnes Repplier,
the bluestocking, looking at him coldly from her pew, and thinking no doubt
scornful thoughts about Irish Catholics." Constance O'Hara, *Heaven Was Not
Enough* (1955) (hereafter *OH*), pp. 41–42.

During the war she would write scathingly about suffra-
gettes[120] and pacifists. "The Honourable Bertrand Russell," she
wrote, "whose annoyance at England's going to war deepened
into resentment at her winning it (a consummation which, to
speak the truth, he did his best to avert) . . ."[121] She read in the
newspapers about a high-flown American project: a "World
Conference for Promoting Concord between all Divisions of
Mankind," "a title," she added, "that leaves nothing, save gram-
mar, to be desired."[122] After the war she went to a Philadelphia
dinner party with her friends the Pennells. Joseph Pennell[123]
was unkempt and boisterous, wishing to shake the Philadelphia
bourgeois. "Mark my words!" he roared across the table. "You'll
all live to see the day when the German Army and the British
Army march arm in arm down Chestnut Street!"

An impressive silence followed this astounding declaration.
Then, leaning forward ever so slightly in her place, Agnes Repplier spoke up in a voice that was deadly calm. "Oh, dear Mr.
Pennell," she said slowly and distinctly, "do have them come
down Pine Street. Nothing ever happens on Pine Street."[124]

She believed in the uniqueness of Western civilization. She
was neither an American isolationist nor a Pan-Americanist:
". . . friendship and alliance with those European states whose
aspirations and ideals respond to our own aspirations and ideals,

---

[120] "When the news of the Belgian campaign sickened the heart of humanity,
more than one voice was raised to say that England had, by her treatment of
militant suffragists (a treatment so feeble, so wavering, so irascible, and so soft-
hearted that it would not have crushed a rebellious snail), forfeited her right
to protest against the dishonouring of Belgian women." *F*, pp. 141–42. "The only
agreeable thing to be recorded in connection with Europe's sudden and disastrous war is the fact that people stopped talking about women, and began to
talk about men." *C*, p. 98.

[121] *F*, p. 143.

[122] *C*, p. 71.

[123] Husband of Agnes Repplier's childhood friend Elizabeth Robins (about
whom see pp. 45, 46), a painter, engraver, and etcher of considerable talent: a
large and saturnine man, wishing to combine throughout his life the attributes
of artist and aristocrat, with indifferent success.

[124] Stokes, p. 188.

are as consistent with Americanism as are friendship and alliance with the states of South America, which we are now engaged in loving. It is not from Bolivia, or Chile, or Venezuela, or the Argentine that we have drawn our best traditions, our law, language, literature, and art."[125] "You cannot make the word 'freedom' sound in untutored ears as it sounds in the ears of men who have counted the cost by which it has been preserved through the centuries."[126] She was the finest of Americans. Her mind was cosmopolitan in its scope, she was a devoted Anglophile and Francophile; yet she had nothing in common with her contemporary American exiles, whether of the rarefied or of the merely spoiled kind. She knew more about France and the French than a whole slew of American expatriates; yet she would not have retired to a salon-equipped château even if she had all the money in the world. She was more like Willa Cather than she was like Edith Wharton, even as she was unlike any of her contemporaries. She saw in the United States the potentiality for what was best in the world: not the last best hope of mankind, not the seat of world government, but something somberer and greater: the representative and the repository of the heritage of Western civilization.

Therefore, with all the refined qualities of her mind, she detested and feared American vulgarity less than she detested and feared American sentimentalism (she would have agreed with Wilde, who said that sentimentality was the Bank Holiday of cynicism), beneath the superficialities of which she would instantly detect the deeper element of a corruption of purpose:

> We are rising dizzily and fearlessly on the crest of a great wave of sentiment. When the wave breaks, we may find ourselves submerged, and in danger of drowning; but for the present we are full of hope and high resolve. Forty years ago we stood in shallow water, and mocked at the mid-Victorian sen-

[125] *C*, pp. 291–92.
[126] *F*, pp. 24–25.

timent, then ebbing slowly with the tide. We have nothing now in common with that fine, thin, tenacious conception of life and its responsibilities . . . A vague humanity is our theme . . .[127]

she wrote in 1915. "Americans returning from war-stricken Europe in the autumn of 1914 spoke unctuously of their country as 'God's own land,' by which they meant a land where their luggage was unmolested."[128] She, who habitually kept her ironic talent in restraint, let out the reins when it came to evidence of American self-satisfaction. An American critic, a Mr. Haweis, "guided by that dangerous instinct which drives us to unwarranted comparisons,"

> does not hesitate to link the fame of Knickerbocker's *New York* with the fame of *Gulliver's Travels*, greatly to the disadvantage of the latter. "Irving," he gravely declares, "has all the satire of Swift, without his sour coarseness." It would be as reasonable to say, "Apollinaris has all the vivacity of brandy, without its corrosive insalubrity."[129]

"That failure in good sense which comes from too warm a self-satisfaction" raised her ire even at the age of eighty-one, when she recalled the national temper around 1900:

> Those were good days in which to live. Our skirmish with Spain was over, and we talked about it and wrote about it in terms that would have befitted Marathon. Mr. Hennessy is as enthusiastic about our 'histing the flag over the Ph'lippeens' as if he had not just found out that they were islands, and not, as he had previously supposed, canned goods. A sense of well-being permeates Mr. Dooley's pages. The White House cat is named 'Gold Bonds'; mortgages spell security; the price of whisky, 'fifteen cents a slug,' remains immovable in days of peace and war; the 'almighty dollar' has the superb impregnability that once attached itself to Roman citizenship; and de-

---

[127] *C*, p. 1.
[128] *Ibid.*, p. 67.
[129] *D*, p. 105. Apollinaris: a mineral water.

vout men breathe a prayer that Providence may remain under the protection of the American flag.[130]

She read a letter from Walter Hines Page, printed after the First World War: "In all the humanities, we are a thousand years ahead of any people here . . . God has as yet made nothing or nobody equal to the American people; and I don't think He ever will or can." "Which is a trifle fettering to omnipotence," she would add. [131]

She was over seventy when she wrote that "like the little girl who was so good that she knew how good she was, we are too well-informed not to be aware of our preeminence in this field." In the spring of 1925 the American Ambassador to the Court of St. James's delivered himself of a speech before the Pilgrims' Dinner in London. "In it he defined with great precision the attitude of the United States toward her former allies. His remarks, as reported, read like a sermon preached in a reformatory."[132] Her fine indignation carried over into the twenties, and beyond. Her preferences became slightly more conservative;[133] she was concerned with the ultimate effects of admitting an unlimited number and variety of immigrants to the United

[130] Agnes Repplier, *In Pursuit of Laughter* (1936) (hereafter L), p. 180. Twenty years earlier she wrote: "When Mr. Carnegie thanked God (through the medium of the newspapers) that he lived in a brotherhood of nations—'forty-eight nations in one Union,'—he forgot that these forty-eight nations, or at least thirty-eight of them, were not always a brotherhood. Nor was the family tie preserved by moral suasion. What we of the North did was to beat our brothers over the head until they consented to be brotherly. And some three hundred thousand of them died of grievous wounds and fevers rather than love us as they should." *C*, pp. 65–66.

[131] Agnes Repplier, *To Think of Tea!* (1932) (hereafter TE), p. 79.

[132] *8D*, p. 240.

[133] In 1919 she wrote: "If the principles of conservatism are based on firm supports, on a recognition of values, a sense of measure and proportion, a due regard for order—its prejudices are indefensible. The wise conservative does not attempt to defend them; he only clings to them more lovingly under attack. He recognizes triumphant science in the telephone and the talking machine, and his wish to escape these benefactions is but a humble confession of unworthiness. He would be glad if scientists, hitherto occupied with preserving and disseminating sound, would turn their attention to suppressing it, would collect noise as an ashman collects rubbish, and dump it in some only place, thus preserving the sanity of the world." *F*, p. 100.

States, and wrote sharply about this. Yet she kept her irascibility at the American trait of self-congratulation burning with a glow. "It is a bearable misfortune to be called un-American, because the phrase still waits analysis,"[134] she wrote in 1924. In 1927 she spoke about "Success and Ideals." "Every message, every address, every editorial, every sermon had faithfully echoed this chant of triumph over the unparalleled prosperity of 1926 and the magnificent prospects of 1927. We are the super-state and we have been assiduously taught that, to be good and happy and prosperous, is to fulfill the designs of a singularly partial Providence."[135] "It is not efficiency but a well-balanced emotional life which creates an enjoyable world." And the American "lacked the moral and intellectual humility, which would bring him an understanding of tragedies in which he has no share and supremacies in which he sees no significance."[136] Here is Agnes Repplier, the so-called conservative period piece, writing in the twenties. Walter Lippmann and the American liberal and intellectual consensus would agree to all the above. She would, however, lash out at silliness from every quarter, no matter how intellectually fashionable or timely. In 1931, *The New Republic* "says that the United States is a belligerent country. Assuredly not! Bullying, perhaps, but not belligerent."[137] One source of best qualities was her instant contempt for any kind of intellectual opportunism. "The man who never tells an unpalatable truth 'at the wrong time' (the right time has yet to be discovered) is the man whose success in life is fairly well assured,"[138] Agnes Repplier wrote in 1924 a sentence that alone is worth the contents of an, as yet unwritten, volume on the vice of the twentieth century, which is intellectual opportunism.

"Stupidity," she wrote wisely, "is not the prerogative of any

---

[134] *DS*, p. 75.
[135] Emma, p. 159.
[136] *Ibid.*, pp. 158, 157.
[137] Agnes Repplier, *Times and Tendencies* (1931) (hereafter T) , p. 35.
[138] *DS*, p. 83. She admired this quality in others, watching them with a gimlet eye. "Mr Philip Guedalla, whose charm as a historian lies in his happy detachment—for the time—from the prejudices of his day . . ." *T*. p. 39.

one class or creed."[139] She knew that most stupidity is not the result of neuro-cerebral incompetence but that it is self-induced and willful.[140] "What the world asks now are state reforms and social reforms—in other words, the reformation of our neighbors. What the Gospel asks, and has always asked, is the reformation of ourselves—a harassing and importunate demand."[141] Democracy "is not the final word of progress . . . Democracy is rational but not luminous."[142]

She preferred Theodore Roosevelt to Wilson:

> Nothing is easier than to make the world safe for democracy. Democracy is playing her own hand in the game. She has every intention and every opportunity to make the world safe for herself. But democracy may be divorced from freedom, and freedom is the breath of man's nostrils, the strength of his sinews, the sanction of his soul. It is as painful to be tyrannized over by a proletariat as by a tsar or by a corporation, and it is in a measure more disconcerting, because of the greater incohesion of the process. It is as revolting to be robbed by a reformer as by a trust.[143]

She loved her country, and knew all its faults: "a mad welter of lawlessness, idleness, and greed; and, on the other hand, official extravagance, administrative weakness . . . and shameless profiteering. Our equilibrium is lost, and with it our sense of

---

139 *F*, p. 72.

140 1931: "A young Englishman, teaching in an American school, said that what struck him most sharply about American boys was their docility. He did not mean by this their readiness to do what they were told, but their readiness to think as they were told, in other words, to permit him to do their thinking for them." *T*, pp. 305–6.

141 *F*, pp. 78–79.

142 "I do strive to think well of my fellow man, but no amount of striving can give me confidence in the wisdom of a Congressional vote." Emma, p. 160.

143 *F*, pp. 74–75. Thirty years earlier she wrote: "It is an interesting circumstance in the lives of those persons who are called either heretics or reformers, according to the mental attitudes or antecedent prejudices of their critics, that they always begin by hinting their views with equal modesty and moderation. It is only when rubbed sore by friction, when hard driven and half spent, that they venture into the open, and define their positions before the world in all their bald malignity." *P*, 136. In 1892: ". . . the sanguine socialist of to-day, who dreams of preparing for all of us a lifetime of unbroken ennui." *E/I*, p. 167.

proportion. We are Lilliput and Brobdingnag jumbled together, which is worse than anything Gulliver ever encountered."[144] Certain American assertions drove her to despair. "Mr. Rockefeller is responsible for the suggestion that Saint Paul, were he living today, would be a captain of industry. Here again a denial is as valueless as an assertion."[145] Yet she saw, and wished to encourage with every nerve of her being, the finer potentialities of the American mind:

> When we leave the open field of exaggeration, that broad area which is our chosen territory, and seek for subtler qualities in American humour, we find here and there a witticism which, while admittedly our own, has in it an Old-World quality. The epigrammatic remark of a Boston woman that men get and forget, and women give and forgive, shows the fine, sharp finish of Sydney Smith or Sheridan. A Philadelphia woman's conversation, that she knew there could be no marriages in Heaven, because—'Well, women were there no doubt in plenty, and some men; but not a man whom any woman would have,'—is strikingly French. The word of a New York broker, when Mr. Roosevelt sailed for Africa, 'Wall Street expects every lion to do its duty!' equals in brevity and malice the keen-edged satire of Italy.[146]

And of American speech:

> If some Americans can speak superlatively well, why cannot more Americans speak pleasingly? Nature is not altogether to blame for our deficiencies. The fault is at least partly our own. The good American voice is very good indeed. Subtle and sweet inheritances linger in its shaded vowels. Propriety and a sense of distinction control its cadences. It has more animation than the English voice, and a richer emotional range. The American is less embarrassed by his emotions than is the Eng-

---

144 *F*, p. 106.
145 *Ibid.*, p. 241.
146 *A*, pp. 47–48. Her appreciation for American humor was not restricted to such odd samples of *esprit* from the upper classes: "the indolent and luminous genius of Mr Dooley has widened our mental horizon. Mr Dooley is a philosopher, but his is the philosophy of the looker-in, of that genuine unconcern which finds Saint George and the dragon to be both a trifle ridiculous." *Ibid.*, pp. 49–50.

lishman; and when he feels strongly the truth, or the shame, or the sorrow his words convey, his voice grows vibrant and appealing. He senses his mastery over a diction, "nobly robust and tenderly vulnerable." The former and finished utterances of an older civilization entrance his attentive ear.[147]

She would not care for that quintessentially modern American-intellectual type, the social scientist;[148] but she would care even less for the unctuous foreigner who bilks and misleads Americans by offering credit to their worst intellectual vices:

That astute Oriental, Sir Rabindranath Tagore, manifested a wisdom beyond all praise, in his recognition of American audiences. As the hour for his departure drew nigh, he was asked to write, and did write, a "Parting Wish for the Women of America," giving graceful expressions to the sentiments he knew he was expected to feel. The skill with which he modified and popularized an alien point of view revealed the seasoned lecturer. He told his readers that "God has sent woman to love the world," and to build up a "spiritual civilization." He condoled with them because they were "passing through great sufferings in this callous age." His heart bled for them, seeing that their hearts "are broken every day, and victims are snatched from their arms, to be thrown under the car of material progress." The Occidental sentiment which regards man as simply an offspring, and a fatherless offspring at that (no woman, says Olive Schreiner, could look upon a battle-field without thinking, "So many mothers' sons!") came as naturally to Sir Rabindranath as if he had been to the manner born. He was content to see the passion and pain, the sorrow and heroism of men, as reflections mirrored in woman's soul. The ingenious gentlemen who dramatize Biblical narratives for the American stage, and who are hampered at every step by the obtrusive masculinity of the East, might find a sympathetic supporter in this accomplished and accommodating Hindu.[149]

[147] *T*, p. 225.

[148] In a letter to Harrison Morris, 1912: "You know everything and everybody. Please tell me what is the American Social Science Association, of which I have been asked to become a member. It has dues and gives medals. Shall I accept?" She adds a postscript: "I see by looking again at the card, the name of the thing is the National Institute of Social Sciences. What are social sciences?"

[149] *F*, pp. 160–1.

M<small>ISS</small> R<small>EPPLIER</small> was a solitary person. She would have agreed
with the French maxim *"On trouve rarement le bonheur en soi,
jamais ailleurs"*—one finds happiness rarely in oneself, never
elsewhere—but her *bonheur* was seldom, if ever, separable from
the conscious activity of her mind. Her adult work was all of a
piece. Her adult life was all of a piece. Only they existed on different planes. People who did not know Agnes Repplier may
have thought (indeed, they often did) that she was an eccentric
dowager, an aristocrat of sorts, all dove-gray silk, instructing the
world, keeping her impatience and brilliance, like a pair of
greyhounds, on display and on the leash. Agnes Repplier was a
grande dame of letters all right, but her character was not that
of an aristocrat; she was a bourgeoise, which did not bother her
much.[150] She had, as I wrote before, few pretensions. Or, to be
exact, she had a hundred strong convictions for each of her pretensions—an attractive ratio.

She was not happy, because her life was not easy. She had
little money.[151] She earned almost all her income by writing—
writing erudite essays, and hardly ever compromising her high
standards—a truly extraordinary achievement. Around the age
of thirty-two, as we have seen, she reached a high plateau, and
from there on, her essays flowed from her pen during those solitary mornings and she had no trouble publishing anything. Her
main outlet was *The Atlantic,* but for more than twenty-five
years she also wrote for *Life, The Yale Review, Century Magazine, Forum, Harper's,* and so on. The recognition of her work
brought her other benefits. She could travel to Europe. She first
crossed the Atlantic in 1890 with her sister on the steamer *Nor-
mania.* During the next ten years she was able to visit Europe
three more times, for ever longer periods, as the chaperone of

---

[150] She did not, like Edith Sitwell, wear eccentric and Gothic costumes; she
had, however, a predilection for Turkish rings.

[151] "Real biting poverty, which withers lesser evils with its deadly breath . . ."
E/I, p. 144. Fortunately enough, this was not her experience. Her mother left a
small inheritance. As early as the year 1887 she earned by her writings more
than $1,000, a small but respectable sum for a writer in those days.

two accommodating young girls, the Boone sisters from Eden Hall (who were the wards of Cardinal Gibbons of Baltimore). Between the thirty-sixth and seventy-fifth years of her life she visited Europe half a dozen times, usually in the company of friends, the last time as a member of the official American delegation to the Ibero-American World Exhibition in Seville in 1929, a trip which she enjoyed at least as much as (perhaps even more than) her first, and of which she wrote a short and witty account. Knowledgeable, expectant, perceptive, thoroughly aware of her surroundings and of the people, yet always ready for new impressions and experiences, she was an excellent traveler,[152] and an excellent companion, so far as we can tell. She crisscrossed the United States on innumerable occasions, mostly on lecturing engagements. Her public life corresponded to the age of the public lecture, a peculiarly American form of instructional entertainment. She did not like to lecture; she was far less confident at the lectern than at her desk; but lecturing produced an income that she could not afford to relinquish.[153] After most of these trips she returned to Philadelphia bone-tired. Her finances required that she accept lecturing invitations even after she had reached seventy.

She was not a domestic woman. She was thoroughly urban, fond of good food and wines, smoking innumerable cigarettes (and, on occasion, small black cigars). She did not know how to cook. Her domestic life was not comfortable. After ten years of successful writing, she, her sister, and her brother were able to move from West Philadelphia to downtown Philadelphia, rent-

[152] She wrote in the rubric of her passport: "Face, broad; Complexion, sallow; Mouth, too large." Stokes, p. 122. She was unduly conscious of what she considered the inadequacies of her looks. Her mouth was beautifully shaped.

[153] About her trials on the lecturing circuit she wrote to Mrs. Schuyler Warren (see below) in April 1914: "Boston is even more mad about prostitutes than Philadelphia and New York. She talks about little else, tells blood-curdling stories, which bear every evidence of ripe invention, and the Dedham Club at which I lectured had actually had a real live 'white slave' (at least she claimed to be one, but she may have been only bragging) to address them last month. Now how can a respectable old lady like myself compete with such an attraction! . . ." *Ibid.*, p. 172.

ing apartments successively on Spruce,[154] Chestnut, and Pine Streets. In 1921 they moved to 920 Clinton Street, the house which eventually became her trademark; one of those old Philadelphia streets with red brick houses of good proportions and solidity.[155] For the first time in her life she found a house that suited her character, her image, her personality. Yet the perfection of the milieu was external rather than internal. The interior was dusky, Victorian, not particularly distinguished, full of old bibelots.[156] Her surroundings stood still even when her mind did not.

She would receive single visitors in Clinton Street from time to time; she would never entertain there. (Later she would invite friends for lunch at the Acorn Club.)[157] Yet her friends meant the world to her—literally, not merely figuratively speaking. She relished the friendship and the intellectual companionship of men. She was thoroughly at home with them; they, in turn, relished the masculine strength and directness of her mind. She was not a professional intellectual; she belonged to that select minority of strong minds who disdain being considered "intellectual," as if mental refinement were some kind of skill. Yet she came into her own at a time when there was a percepti-

[154] At that time she lived but a few houses away from Penrose, with whom she had very little in common. On Chestnut Street (2035) she lived but a few doors from the house (2005) where she had lived as a child.

[155] In 1931 a college girl asked for an interview with "Miss Repplier of Clinton Street." "Our glance wanders momentarily through the lace-curtained windows. Again there is that feeling of time gone backward. A black carriage, proud with metal trappings, is passing. A coachman, resplendent in white cord breeches, black coat and cockaded top-hat. A fine sleek horse stepping daintily— Clinton Street, perhaps the only thoroughfare in Philadelphia where a horse and carriage is not an anachronism, but a commonplace." J. O'K. in *The Grackle*, the literary magazine of Chestnut Hill College, Fall 1931. The writer probably did not know that Agnes Repplier, who disliked automobiles, was one of the very last Philadelphians to hire a horse-drawn carriage from a livery stable, as late as the early 1930s.

[156] In 1893 she had written: "It is a painful thing, at best, to live up to one's bricabrac if one has any; but to live up to the bricabrac of many lands and of many centuries is a strain which no wise man would dream of inflicting upon his constitution." *D*, p. 113.

[157] "I like the Acorn Club," she said on one occasion. "They never do anything."

ble tendency among men and women who were attracted to the intellectual life to seek some comfort and warmth in each other's company in what was otherwise a very indifferent world. During winter evenings in the late eighties and nineties Agnes Repplier was part of a small Philadelphia circle of such people, of whose limitations she was amiably, rather than condescendingly, aware.[158] Around 1890 she met four patrician gentlemen, each of whom had a great influence in her life. Harrison Morris, later editor of *Lippincott's Magazine*, became her lifelong friend and literary adviser; Horace Howard Furness, the Shakespeare scholar, cherished her friendship and treated her as an ornament at the gatherings in his suburban house "Lindenshade."[159] S. Weir Mitchell, the talented patrician physician and writer, received her at his more formal entertainments with a kind of avuncular deference; J. William White actually became her occasional collaborator. Like Mitchell, White was part of the Philadelphia medical tradition, at the peak of its reputation around the turn of the century. He was an attractive man and an excellent surgeon. He probably saved her life. He diagnosed cancer in her left breast. He removed it in a masterly operation.[160] She was then forty-three years of age. They were close friends for the next two decades, very close during the First World War. Both were thoroughly convinced Francophiles and Anglophiles. They collaborated on political pamphlets. White went off to France in 1915.[161] He died in Philadelphia a year later. Agnes Repplier wrote his short memorial biography.

[158] There was a Browning Society: "We encouraged each other in mediocrity." Yet this society "endeavoured to keep letters alive, which was certainly a noble enterprise, even if in Philadelphia it was much like keeping a selection of corpses moving about." Stokes, p. 101. She was a founding member of the Contemporary Club in 1886.

[159] His "astoundingly prudish wife" was not an asset during their gatherings. Agnes Repplier to A. Edward Newton, 10 May 1930 (ALS in Princeton University Library).

[160] To cover the upper portion of a thin scar Agnes Repplier wore a black, sometimes velvet choker for the rest of her life. It became her very well.

[161] That year she dined with White and Theodore Roosevelt. "Heavenly! There were seven men. I was the only woman." Emma, p. 111.

Her friendships with women were long-lasting and profound. Elizabeth Robins was her oldest friend, from their convent days. She was a complicated woman, consumed by social ambition, a Quakeress with aristocratic aspirations, tending to subordinate her undoubted intelligence to certain pretensions. After she married Pennell, Elizabeth and Agnes drifted a little apart. The former may have resented the fact that the girl who once was Minnie now outshone her in the literary world. Agnes Irwin, who, as we have seen, thought it best to disembarrass herself of little Agnes in her school, recognized her talents nevertheless at an early age; her solid support and affection for the young girl blossomed into the best kind of friendship, with reciprocal affection resting on the solid foundation of mutual respect and esteem. "Miss Agnes" Irwin died suddenly in 1914; her school remains her monument even now; another monument is the fine short biography that Agnes Repplier wrote after her death. Cornelia Frothingham was a New England woman, an in-law of the Brinley family in Philadelphia; in spite of her sometimes tiresome insistence on civic virtues and self-improvement, this neurotic woman[162] and Agnes Repplier became close friends, traveling often to Europe, Nova Scotia, Maine together. Mrs. Schuyler Warren was the mistress of a sort of literary salon in New York *circa* 1905; well-read, exceptionally handsome, and rich. Agnes Repplier took great pleasure in her company. Two close Philadelphia friends were Caroline Sinkler and Cecilia Beaux, the painter. During the last quarter of her life Miss Repplier often appeared in public together with Miss Frances Wister, a formidable Philadelphia patroness of the arts; their friendship was extraordinary perhaps only because of Miss Wister's enthusiasm for music,[163] to which Miss Repplier was, perhaps by nature, indifferent.

---

[162] "Cornelia Frothingham was ill for ten weeks with a nervous collapse, all the more serious because it had no cause." Agnes Repplier to Mrs. Wilson Farrand, Easter Monday 1913 (ALS in Princeton University Library).

[163] If Miss Repplier could be deaf to the unwitting language of music, Miss Wister could on occasion be deaf to the unwitting humor of words. She gave a

There were people who believed that this bluestocking, this lifelong spinster, had, like her contemporary Willa Cather, a secret longing for people of her own sex. I do not believe this to be true. The evidence of a handful of letters to her friends, perhaps especially to Mrs. Warren and to Miss Frothingham,[164] is insufficient, save for those who are hopelessly inclined to the attribution of sexual motives to every expression of human sentiment. The contrary evidences are more impressive. We have seen how thoroughly she enjoyed masculine company and its attentions. Her occasional references about sexual attraction in her writings are sane and healthy compounds of the common-sensical and the Gallic. They are devoid of sentimentality; with a touch of the *femme moyenne sensuelle* they are much closer to Jane Austen than to the Brontës, and much closer to Colette than to George Sand. When President Eliot of Harvard pronounced Becky Sharp a despicable creature, she corrected him impatiently:[165] to the contrary, she said, the heroine of *Vanity Fair* had many admirable qualities. In some of her writing, passages exist that suggest her healthy sensuality, or at least her natural appetite for it. She wrote of a pampered cat, who grew so tired of his dull orderly life that "he ran away with a vagabond acquaintance for one long delicious day of liberty, at the close of which, jaded, spent, starved, and broken, he crept meekly back to bondage and his evening cutlet."[166] At the same

---

sherry party in honor of Marcel Tabuteau, the famous oboist of the Philadelphia Orchestra. She proposed a toast: "For years," she said, "he delighted me every Friday afternoon with his little instrument."

[164] One of the few examples: when visiting Clarens, Switzerland, with Cornelia Frothingham, she wrote (in 1902): "We want to live here together." Stokes, p. 146.

[165] Her friend Agnes Irwin on Eliot of Harvard: "Wherever he is, he lowers the temperature."

[166] Agnes Repplier, *The Fireside Sphinx* (1901) (hereafter S), 301. About the Westminster cats in London: their bad behavior "has given rise to the pleasant legend of a country house whither these rakish animals retire for nights of gay festivity, and whence they return in the early morning, jaded, repentant, and forlorn." *E/I*, p. 23.

time she had a very clear understanding of the virtues of restraint—especially in art:

> In French fiction, as Mr. Lang points out, "love comes after
> marriage punctually enough, but it is always love for another."
> The inevitableness of the issue startles and dismays an English
> reader, accustomed to yawn gently over the innocent pre-
> nuptial dallyings of Saxon man and maid. The French story-
> writer cannot and does not ignore his social code which ur-
> banely limits courtship. When he describes a girl's dawning
> sentiment, he does so often with exquisite grace and delicacy;
> but he reserves his portrayal of the master passion until matur-
> ity gives it strength, and circumstances render it unlawful. His
> conception of his art imposes no scruple which can impede
> analysis. If an English novelist ventures to treat of illicit love,
> the impression he gives is of a blind, almost mechanical force,
> operating against rather than in unison with natural laws:
> those normal but most repellent aspects of the case which the
> Frenchman ignores or rejects. His theory of civilization is built
> up largely—and wisely—on suppression.[167]

She regretted that she never married;[168] and she learned not
to make an issue of it. She was a spinster, and she learned not
to mind it. She was appalled at the crudity with which American
humorists treated spinsters, and wrote a sensible little essay about
spinsterhood. "It is not an easy thing to be happy. It takes all
the brains, all the soul, and all the goodness we possess. We may
fail of our happiness, strive we ever so bravely; but we are less
likely to fail if we measure with judgment our chances and our
capabilities. To glorify spinsterhood is as ridiculous as to decry
it. Intelligent women marry or remain single, because in married or in single life they see their way more clearly to content.
They do not, in either case, quarrel with fate which has mod-
elled them for, and fitted them into, one groove rather than

[167] *COMP,* p. 51.

[168] Her friends "gave her so much, [but] they were not able to give her what
she craved most. Once she said with strong feeling, 'I never have been first with
anyone.'" Emma, p. 107.

another; but follow, consciously or unconsciously, the noble maxim of Marcus Aurelius: 'Love that only which the gods send thee, and which is spun with the thread of thy destiny.' "[169] She admired that stoic Roman ruler. Horace, she wrote on another occasion, was like Marcus Aurelius, "able to be alone; but he was far too wise to make of himself that lopsided thing called a recluse."[170] So was she.

She was impatient with the self-conscious respect and the superficial sentimentalism with which American men treated their women. There were many things wrong with ancient Rome, but "she was far from being a matriarchy like the United States. She was not a nation of husbands, but a nation of men."[171] "The superlative complacency of American women is due largely to the oratorical adulation of American men—an adulation that has no more substance than has the foam on beer."[172] She was an intelligent feminist, who took a long-range view of things. "Since Adam delved and Eve span, life for all of us has been full of labour; but as the sons of Adam no longer exclusively delve, so the daughters of Eve no longer exclusively spin. In fact, delving and spinning, though admirable occupations, do not represent the sum total of earthly needs. There are so many, many other useful things to do, and women's eager fingers-tips burn to essay them all."[173] "Perhaps the time may even come when women, mixing freely in political life, will abandon that injured and aggressive air which distinguishes the present advocate of female suffrage,"[174] she wrote in 1894. The Michigan magistrate who in 1918 "gave orders that a stalwart male angel presiding over the gateway of a cemetery should be recast in feminine mould may have been an erring theologian and doubt-

---

[169] *COMP*, p. 184.
[170] *8D*, p. 59.
[171] *Ibid.*, p. 54.
[172] *F*, p. 192.
[173] *V*, p. 28.
[174] *D*, p. 72.

ful art-critic; but that he was a stout-hearted American no one can deny."[175]

She knew the follies of the exclusively male, as well as the exclusively female, viewpoint. " 'Never,' said Edmond de Goncourt, 'has a virgin, young or old, produced a work of art.' One makes allowance for the Latin point of view. And it is possible that M. de Goncourt never read *Emma*."[176] But "the pitfall of the feminist is the belief that the interests of men and women can ever be severed; that what brings sufferings to the one can leave the other unscathed."[177] "In Mr. St. John Ervine's depressing little drama, *Mixed Marriage*, which the Dublin actors played in New York some years ago, an old woman, presumed to be witty and wise, said to her son's betrothed: 'Sure, I believe the Lord made Eve when he saw Adam could not take care of himself'; and the remark reflected painfully upon the absence of that humorous sense which we used to think was the birthright of Irishmen. The too obvious retort, which nobody uttered, but which must have occurred to everybody's mind, was that if Eve had been designed as a caretaker, she had made a shining failure of her job."[178] "The too obvious retort" of a fine conversationalist. "Whenever Adam's remarks expand too obviously into a sermon, Eve, in the most discreet and wife-like manner, steps softly away, and refreshes herself with slumber.

[175] *F*, p. 167. " '*Qui veut faire l'ange fait la bête*,' said Pascal; and the Michigan angel is a danger signal . . . No sane woman believes that women, as a body, will vote more honestly than men; but no sane man believes that they will vote less honestly. They are neither 'the gateway to hell,' as Tertullian pointed out, nor the builders of Sir Rabindranath Tagore's 'spiritual civilization.' They are neither the repositories of wisdom, nor the final word of folly." *Ibid.*, pp. 201–2. " 'God help women when they have only their rights!' exclaimed a brilliant American lawyer; but it is in the 'only' that all savour lies. Rights and privileges are incompatible. Emancipation implies the sacrifice of immunity, the acceptance of obligation. It heralds the reign of sober and disillusioning experience. Women, as M. Faguet reminds us, are only the equals of men; a truth which was simply phrased in the old Cornish adage, 'Lads are as good as wenches when they are washed.' " *Ibid.*, pp. 202–3.

[176] *F*, p. 82.

[177] *C*, p. 123.

[178] *F*, p. 183.

Indeed, when we come to think of it, conversation between these two must have been difficult at times, because they had nobody to talk about."[179] She had a finely tuned appetite for malicious humor in conversation, including the eternal topic of how and why certain people are attracted to each other, in which she, rightly, saw the essence of sex. She did not take Freud seriously, which was a good thing. In her essay on "Three Famous Old Maids," the Misses Austen, Edgeworth, and Mitford, she described their "serene, cheerful, and successful lives . . . all rounded and completed without that element we are taught to believe is the mainspring and prime motor of existence."[180]

Her fierce independence of mind,[181] as we have seen, rested on the understanding that freedom is not merely the absence of restraints but that, to the contrary, it springs from the restraints one imposes on oneself. Her independence was sustained, rather than compromised, by her religion. She was a Roman Catholic with a very independent mind, a rarity in her country in her times, but no less a Catholic for that. Weaker or more self-indulgent women than Agnes Repplier could find it comforting to turn against the memories of an unhappy childhood that culminated in cold convent days and expulsion, to explain to themselves and to the world that they could sustain no inner nourishment from those rigid pieties whose hypocritical and superstitious nature they claimed to know only too well. At the same time, the majority of Catholics during Agnes Repplier's life, "when respectability stalked unchecked," chose not to think much, if at all, about the deep differences between what they believed and what they professed to believe. Some of the middle-class Catholics in Philadelphia did not like her, and pronounced some of her writings scandalous. She, on her part, disliked many of the German and Irish Catholics, a petulant

179 *E/I*, p. 164.
180 *Emma*, p. 90.
181 She found independence attractive in every sense. It attracted her to cats, about which she wrote (too often for my taste: at least three essays, and an entire book): she liked the dormant savage energy beneath their lazy composure, and their total absence of docile loyalties.

kind of dislike that flared especially high during the First World
War. The vulgarized Americanisms of some of the clergy
haunted her throughout her entire life.[182] Yet even during her
lifetime the Church was a house of many mansions. Not all
American Catholics were parochial.[183] Cardinal Gibbons, many
of the bishops, the heads and the nun-teachers of the small
Catholic academies and colleges welcomed her with eagerness
and affection. Catholic universities awarded their highest honors
to her. The Catholic community of Philadelphia, indeed of the
United States—it was more of a community then than it is now
—eventually took pride in the achievement of this solitary
woman, who was, after all, one of their own. She patronized and
befriended the handsome and civilized priest Henry Drumgoole,
choosing him for her escort to many a gathering. The Mon-
signori Drumgoole,[184] Sigourney Fay, Edward Hawks were

[182] In 1931: "Linguistic idiosyncrasies are social idiosyncrasies. I thought of this
when I heard an American prelate, a man of learning and piety, allude in a
sermon 'to the most important and influential of the saints and martyrs.' It
sounded aggressively modern. 'Powerful' is a word well-fitted to the Church
Triumphant . . . But 'important' has a bustling accent, and an 'influential'
martyr suggests a heavenly banking-house." *T*, pp. 222–23.

[183] "The one Catholic who made me feel better about the situation was Miss
Agnes Repplier. She was Philadelphia—and it was her co-religionists who rejected this witty and wonderful woman, not the inner circle where she was a
feted and sought-after personage. When I was a child she had an apartment with
her brother Louis and her sister Mary at Twenty-first and Pine Streets. She
was a slight woman with keen grey eyes behind nose-glasses that gave her a
Pecksniffian expression and she had then a nervous jerk to her head." OH, p. 110.

[184] In 1919 Archbishop Dougherty removed Mgr. Drumgoole from St. Charles
Seminary to the rectorate of a workingman's parish, St. Gregory's. "The good
and devout people, most of who worked on the Pennsylvania Railroad, were
astounded at their new Rector, and soon indignant. Archbishop Dougherty had
exposed a congregation of hard-working people to one of the most brilliant
men in the Church. They yearned for the comfortable mugginess of the religion
they knew, and Monsignor Drumgoole, with his assistant Father Edward Hawks,
the converted Anglican, made it a dazzling, golden thing. It was perhaps as well
the Monsignor Sigourney Fay, another converted Anglican, died the year before
Monsignor Drumgoole became Rector of St. Gregory's, for Father Fay was
something of an aesthete, a lover of epigrams, and, devoted to Monsignor Drumgoole, would often have been in residence at St. Gregory's. The puritanical
Archbishop would have something to think about, since Monsignor Fay, a
close friend of Cardinal Gibbons, was not sparing with the perfume he used. He
achieved a brief fame as Father Darcy in Scott Fitzgerald's *This Side of Paradise*,
the novel that heralded the arrival of the twenties." OH, p. 132.

priests after her heart (the last two converts from Anglicanism), representing a higher and more elegant and broad-minded Catholicism that was definitely not isolationist; a minority among the clergy, they supported the British and French cause during the entire First World War.

The character of Agnes Repplier was compendious enough to encompass a taste for the baroque as well as for the classical, even though she had a profound distaste for easy enthusiasms. Her philosophy of life was reflected in "The Chill of Enthusiasm," one of her favorite essays. "If we had no spiritual asbestos to protect our souls, we should be consumed to no purpose by every wanton flame," she wrote.

> If our sincere and restful indifference to things which concern us not were shaken by every blast, we should have no available force for things which concern us deeply. If eloquence did not sometimes make us yawn, we should be besotted by oratory. And if we did not approach new acquaintances, new authors, and new points of view with life-saving reluctance, we should never feel that vital regard which, being strong enough to break down our barriers, is strong enough to hold us for life.[185]

Yet, with all her self-restraint, reserve, and irony, she was not a rationalist. "If knowledge alone could save us from sin, the salvation of the world would be easy work."[186] She had a respect for emotions, and the New Englanders' dichotomy of Reason *vs.* Emotion made no sense to her. [187] Her understanding of life —and not only of letters—was spacious enough for her to comprehend the reasons of the heart.

Like Dr. Johnson's, her life was in many ways a triumph of character. Her accomplishment may be summed up in one short sentence: She was the Jane Austen of the essay. That she is not

---

[185] *8D*, p. 265.

[186] *C*, p. 145.

[187] ". . . our great-grandfathers, who were assuredly not a tender-hearted race . . . cried right heartily over poems, and novels, and pictures, and plays, and scenery, and everything, in short, that their great-grandsons would not now consider as worthy of emotion." *B*, p. 113.

so recognized is a great—and one hopes, temporary—loss. Her essays are always lucid, often profound, and worth rereading. Few of them show the marks of her age. In spite of her quickly faded reputation, there is little of her writing that is a period piece.

We must, however, recognize the essence of a certain kind of truth within that epithet, even though we must qualify it. From her first essay, published in *The Atlantic* in 1886, to the last, published there fifty-four years later (in 1940), there is hardly any difference in the style or in the quality of her writing. Agnes Repplier did not grow. She reached a high and exceptional level of expression when she, against extraordinary odds, first earned her national reputation. She kept up this high level, with few exceptions, until the end of her industrious life. To sustain this was achievement enough; and there may have been an internal relationship between the scope of her art and that of her life. She took pleasure in her own writings (during the last years of her life she would, on occasion, request that her nurse read some of them to her aloud, only to ask that the volume be quickly put back on the shelves when the bell rang, announcing a visitor), but she never let herself be carried away by a wave of unwonted self-confidence; she never overestimated her talents.[188] She did not try her hand at a novel, or a play, or even at a compendious work of literary criticism. The small essay remained her genre; she was satisfied with it, just as her social ambitions never bloomed beyond the particular comforts she found in the often dull but always cozy quietude and familiarity of Philadelphia. "My niche may be small, but I made it myself," she would say. Much of the wit and the wisdom in her essays was not grasped even by her closest friends. She knew this. Yet she did not long for wider intellectual or literary companionship. She was content with the genuineness of the affection from her friends whose intellectual sensitivities may have been want-

[188] She said often that she did not expect most of her writings to survive. On 18 October 1930 she wrote to A. Edward Newton about her *Essays in Miniature*. ". . . a horrid little book" (ALS in Princeton University Library).

ing, here and there, but whose personal sensitivities were not. In this respect—and in this respect only—she was like Edith Wharton, who once said about the society of Old New York that it was a bottle now empty but at the bottom of which there still remained a fine kind of lees, an essence of rarefied and unspoken sentiments.

There is another, related, element to consider. Her first books of essays were composed and published when she had passed the age of thirty. From her solitary reading she brought forth an immense accumulation of intellectual capital, upon which, assisted by her prodigious memory, she could draw for the next fifty years, replenishing it with ease. This capital was large enough not to be exhausted. Thus she was unaffected by the disease that affects American native talent: the brilliant early accomplishment unequaled in later years, never again blossoming in maturity. It was not her genius which was precocious; it was her maturity. Perhaps it was because of this precocious maturity—a rare accomplishment, to the point of being an oxymoron—that she remained unaffected by senility even in her eighties.

Because of this maturity she knew the limitations of public recognition. In this Philadelphia was, as usual, wanting—or, rather, slow.[189] (After she made her reputation in Boston, through *The Atlantic*, a certain lady in Philadelphia would occasionally ask her friends whether they knew a "Miss A. Riplear.") Unlike many other Philadelphia artists, she took this without much agitation. There is a passage in her fine little history of Philadelphia which applies very well to herself. "Philadelphia, like Marjorie Fleming's stoical turkey, is 'more than usual calm,' when her sons and daughters win distinction in any field. She takes the matter quietly, as she takes most other matters, preserving with ease her mental balance, and listening unmoved to the plaudits of the outside world.

[189] The first Philadelphia Award, carrying $10,000, established by Edward W. Bok, was accorded to Cornelius McGillicuddy (Connie Mack), the manager of the Philadelphia Athletics baseball team.

This attitude is not wholly wise nor commendable, inasmuch as cities, like men, are often received at their own valuation, and some degree of self-assertion converts many a wavering mind. If the mistaking of geese for swans produces sad confusion, and a lamentable lack of perspective, the mistaking of swans for geese may also be a dangerous error. The birds languish, or fly away to keener air, and something which cannot be replaced is lost. Yet anything is better than having two standards of merit, one for use at home and one for use abroad; *and the sharp discipline of quiet neglect is healthier for a worker than that loud local praise which wakes no echo from the wider world.*"[190] The italics are mine.

Gradually, slowly, the neglect disappeared. After 1900 she was well recognized, well respected, on occasion celebrated.[191] She often said that she enjoyed her years between forty and sixty the most. But after the First World War, which, as we saw, was a searing experience for her mind,[192] she complained more and more often of being tired, especially from her lecturing. Yet her writing remained lively and sharp.[193] She found a certain satisfaction in her Clinton Street house. In her seventy-fifth year she embarked on her official trip to Spain, where she outwalked and outtalked many of the younger members of the American delegation. She was seventy-seven when she saw the Gershwin musical *Of Thee I Sing*, which she enjoyed thoroughly; she was pleased with the fact that her compatriots delighted in seeing "the inglorious nature of their absurdities."[194] As she gave up

[190] *PPP,* pp. 390–91.

[191] She was vexed by the public celebrity of a distant cousin, who had become a society reporter on *The Evening Ledger*: "Agnes Repplier Junior, who often dispensed with the youthful appendage, was a comely, amiable young woman, not particularly intelligent, and as it turned out, not averse to reaping a little advantage from the hazards of mistaken identity." Emma, p. 123. Her marriage eliminated this vexation.

[192] Between 1912 and 1916 she lost many of her closest friends: Furness, Mitchell, the Irwin sisters, and Dr. White.

[193] *Under Dispute* (1924), *Times and Tendencies* (1931) contain some of her best writing, to wit, "The Unconscious Humour of the Movies" in the latter.

[194] *L,* p. 191.

lecturing, she depended only on her writing. It was then, in the last decade of her writing career, that she turned out a number of books in which we can detect, here and there, a certain decline of verve. Between the seventy-fourth and seventy-seventh years of her life she wrote three biographies,[195] as well as a book on cats and a book on tea. They were followed by a book on laughter, which she wrote and had published after her eightieth birthday. The motto under the title read: *"Un gros rire vaut mieux qu'une petite larme."* A big laugh is worth more than a small tear. This is not the motto of a Genteel Lady of Letters.

In Pursuit of Laughter showed some of the marks of tiredness. Miss Repplier was becoming a bit predictable, and on occasion even repetitious. If *In Pursuit of Laughter* was not a potboiler, well, it was a *pot-au-feu*: a *pot-au-feu* put together by someone thoroughly at home with Gallic and American cooking, with the inherent qualities of all kinds of condiments and meat. "Our passionate loyalty to our humourists, our tolerance of the 'comic' in newspapers and cinemas," she wrote of her fellow Americans, "proves our need of laughter; but we are not gay. The appalling grin with which men and women are photographed for the press is as remote from gaiety as from reason."[196]

On her eightieth birthday the Cosmopolitan Club, of which in 1886 she had been a founding member, gave her a dinner (she was, in reality, eighty-two). The book collector A. Edward Newton was the toastmaster; there were many speeches in her honor. That year (1937) Houghton Mifflin published her own selection of her best essays, entitled *Eight Decades*. We encountered it before; there she did a sleight-of-hand about her age. *Eight Decades* begins with a forty-page autobiography. It is sprightly and colorful, amusing and witty, spangled with small particles of glitter that would be characteristic of the ornament of a woman half her years. Yet it tells very little about herself and her life. She was profoundly aware of the limitations of autobiogra-

---

195 *Père Marquette* (1929), *Mère Marie of the Ursulines* (1931), *Junípero Serra* (1933).
196 *L*, p. 221.

phies,[197] and she would not abandon the kind of rectitudinous
reticence that accompanied her through her life. During the
following year she was found to be suffering from acute anemia.
She also feared that her memory was fading, which worried her
far more than anemia. She now retired to her bed. For the first
time in her life she would not go to Mass on Sunday. "No, I
won't. God is a good deal more understanding than relatives."
"I am light-headed and heavy-footed." "All my time is now
wasted. It has no meaning. Work is over."[198] This was an exag-
geration. Her last essay, on the Housmans, was published in
The Atlantic in January 1940. That year she was complimented
and charmed by a young Philadelphia scholar, George Stokes,
who had begun writing a biographical study of her. She received
him in Clinton Street, sometimes staying in bed, puffing on innumerable cigarettes. The scene should remind us for the last
time: she, the contemporary of literary women such as Mrs.
Humphrey Ward and Julia Ward Howe, had nothing in common with them; she had many things in common with her
younger contemporary Colette.

She lived to see her beloved France conquered and humiliated
anew by a Germany much more brutal than that of the Kaiser
or the heavy-footed tourists; she lived to see England alone
against the wall, in its finest hour. But the fires of her anger now
had died down; the awful scenes and issues of the Second World

[197] "The Happiness of Writing an Autobiography": ". . . even the titles of
certain autobiographical works are saturated with self-appreciation. We can see
the august simper with which a great lady in the days of Charles the Second
headed her manuscript: 'A True Relation of the Birth, Breeding and Life of
Margaret Cavendish, Duchess of Newcastle. Written by Herself.' Mr. Theodore
Dreiser's *A Book About Myself* sounds like nothing but a loud human purr.
The intimate wording of *Margot Asquith, an Autobiography* gives the key to
all the cheerful confidences that follow. Never before or since has any book
been so much relished by its author. She makes no foolish pretence of concealing
the pleasure that it gives her; but passes on with radiant satisfaction from
episode to episode, extracting from each in turn its full and flattering significance.
The volumes are as devoid of revelations as of reticence. If at times they re-
semble the dance of the seven veils, the reader is invariably reassured when
the last veil has been whisked aside, and he sees there is nothing behind it." *DS*,
pp. 90–1.
[198] Emma, p. 164.

War flowed on the surface of her mind. Like the aged Hilaire Belloc, the erstwhile fiery Francophile and Germanophobe, everything she had proclaimed about the danger of the Western nations from Germany came true; but she could no longer rouse herself to an indignant passion comparable to hers during the First World War. Unlike Belloc, she was not senile. She was eighty-eight years old when a bequest brought her an increase in comfort. She moved to an apartment in Overbrook. Meals, including breakfast, were brought to her. She had fallen in her bedroom and moved very little. Yet her mind was amazingly sharp. Reporters from the Philadelphia newspapers came to interview her on her birthdays; she waved them away with a kind of petulant charm. She had the pleasure of the company of her intellectual niece; and she lived to see the publication of a biographical study of her by Professor Stokes. She lived to be ninety-five. "Her face was a picture of distinguished intellect, reticence, sensitiveness and tolerance, yet she never seemed old. She did not regret or complain, for a lifetime of stoicism was not easily discarded. She still possessed ardor and contemplation, and when death came to her, he came softly, imperceptibly, hardly distinguishable from his half-brother, sleep."[199]

[199] *Ibid.,* p. 170.

EDWARD W. BOK

O R

Franklin Reincarnate

HERE IS A FAMOUS American story. A young man decides to seek his fortune. He believes in the supreme value of self-education. He goes to Philadelphia. He is a success in publishing. He is a genius at advertising, including self-advertising. He marries his employer's daughter. He becomes first a civic, then a national celebrity. He goes abroad to represent his country. His autobiography is required reading in the schools. This is the American legend, the life of Benjamin Franklin. Even more it is that of his reincarnation: for all of the above is the summary of the life of Edward William Bok, who followed him a century and a half later.

Bok arrived in Philadelphia when he was twenty-five. He was already well known; now he would become successful and rich. He retired when he was fifty-six, and made a formal announcement in the *Ladies' Home Journal*: "A man's nature seeks to play . . . So now I am going to play at this end of my life . . ."[1] This editorial announcement had little relation to reality. Whatever his playful impulses, Bok immediately plunged himself into the composition of his autobiography, *The Americanization of Edward Bok*. Like *Poor Richard's Almanack*, this book was of the kind that had to be believed to be read. It was a great publishing success, because of its author's

---

[1] *Ladies' Home Journal* (hereafter *LHJ*), January 1920.

unerring comprehension of what the American people, at a given time (it was 1920, and they were about to elect Warren Gamaliel Harding for their President), preferred to believe. Bok's story was not merely that of the honest immigrant who had made good; it was that of the honest immigrant who made America better. In 1920, when the vast majority of Americans preferred to put an end to the unrestricted immigration of unruly masses from Europe, this was exactly what they wanted to hear. Opponents of Franklin thought that his *Autobiography* included the Franklinization of Philadelphia, which they regretted. A few carping critics who regretted what Bok had wrought would call his work the Bokization of the United States of America. There was more to this verbal switch than appears at first sight.

We do not know why the family Bok had decided to translate itself to Brooklyn in 1870, at a time when life for middle-class people in Holland was comfortable and secure. Bok's father seems to have failed in his business more than once. In any event, Edward Bok, after he had sprung from poverty, took great care that there should be no recoil. When he, the schoolboy, asked the baker for whom he was working after school for Saturday afternoons off, the following exchange took place:

> "Want to play ball, hey?" said the baker.
> "Yes, I want to play ball," replied the boy [*The Americanization of Edward Bok* is written in the third person singular], but he was not reserving his Saturday afternoon for games . . .[2]

It was summer, and there was an ice cooler at the end of the trolley line, into which descending male passengers could dip a cup and swallow a free drink. (We shall come back to Bok's obsession with drinking cups later.)

> Here was an opening, and Edward decided to fill it. He bought a shining new pail, screwed three hooks on the edge of which he hung three clean shimmering glasses, and one Saturday

[2] Edward Bok, *The Americanization of Edward Bok* (hereafter *AEB*), (New York, 1921), p. 10.

afternoon when a car stopped the boy leaped on, tactfully asked the conductor if he did not want a drink, and then proceeded to sell his water, cooled with ice, at a cent a glass to the passengers. A little experience showed that he exhausted a pail with every two cars, and each pail netted him thirty cents. Of course Sunday was a most profitable day and after going to Sunday-school in the morning, he did a further Sabbath service for the rest of the day by refreshing tired mothers and thirsty children on the Coney Island cars—at a penny a glass![3]

Within a week or so he would progress from ice water to lemonade—three cents a glass, that was. "In fact, a dollar-note I handled as reverently as to-day I would a Rembrandt etching," he wrote fifty years later.[4]

He subordinated his social life to the higher purpose of self-advancement. He attended a party, where "his latent journalistic sense whispered to him that his young hostess might like to see her social affair in print."[5] He wrote out a list of everyone present and took it to the city editor of the *Brooklyn Eagle*, with "the sage observation that every name mentioned in that paragraph represented a buyer of the paper, and that if the editor had enough of these reports he might very advantageously strengthen the circulation of the *Eagle*. The editor was not slow to see the point and offered Edward three dollars a column for such reports. On his way home,

> Edward calculated how many parties he would have to attend a week to furnish a column, and decided that he would organize a corps of private reporters himself. Forthwith, he saw every girl and boy he knew, got each to promise for him an account of each party he or she attended or gave, and laid great stress on a full recital of names.[6]

He was then eleven years old.
Beyond Brooklyn (the Brooklyn Bridge was not yet built)

[3] *Ibid.*, pp. 11–12.
[4] Edward Bok, *Twice Thirty* (hereafter *TT*) (New York, 1924), p. 47.
[5] *AEB*, p. 12.
[6] *Ibid.*

shone the towers of Manhattan. Bok met a young girl whose father was the editor of *The New York Weekly*. He insinuated himself into their parlor. "The daughter," he wrote forty years later, "has long since passed away, and so it cannot hurt her feelings now to acknowledge that for years Edward paid court to her only that he might know her father, and have those talks with him about editorial methods that filled him with ever-increasing ambition . . ."[7]

This ambitious swain was less than twelve years of age. The next year he had a job at Western Union. When he was rising fifteen he started collecting autographs. "With a simple direct-ness characteristic of his Dutch training"[8] he wrote to General Garfield, asking him a question about his boyhood. Garfield answered at once. Pink with pride, Bok showed the letter around. He "began to study the lives of successful men and women" and, then, "with boyish frankness"—"boyish" re-mained one of Bok's favorite adjectives through his life—he asked these famous people to inform him about certain crucial events in their lives. The results surpassed all expectations. General Grant wrote him about Appomattox; King Kalakaua about the Sandwich Islands; Longfellow and Tennyson about their poetic habits; Whittier told the story of "The Barefoot Boy"; the Confederate General Jubal A. Early explained why he had burned Chambersburg. Edward took this letter (without the General's approval, but no matter) and had it published in the *New York Tribune*. Reporters now descended on Brooklyn to interview *him*.

The boy was not barefoot, and he had plenty of cheek. He began to note in the newspapers the list of "distinguished ar-rivals" in the hotels of New York; and "when anyone with whom he had corresponded arrived, Edward would, after business hours, go uptown, pay his respects, and thank him in person for his letters. No person was too high for Edward's boyish ap-

7 *Ibid.*, p. 14.
8 *Ibid.*, p. 17.

proach: President Garfield, General Grant, General Sherman, President Hayes—all were called on, and all received the boy graciously and were interested in the problem of his self-education."[9] One evening Grant gave him a large-size photograph (one would think with the hope of getting rid of him, though one never knows).

> That evening was one that the boy was long to remember. It suddenly came to him that he had read a few days before of Mrs. Abraham Lincoln's arrival in New York at Doctor Holbrook's sanitarium. Thither Edward went; and within half an hour from the time he had been talking with General Grant he was sitting at the bedside of Mrs. Lincoln, showing her the wonderful photograph just presented to him.[10]

The widow of the great President was, alas, *non compos mentis*; but never mind, Bok got her autograph, composed with trembling hand.

> The eventful evening, however, was not yet over. Edward had boarded a Broadway stage to take him to his Brooklyn home when, glancing at the newspaper of a man sitting next to him, he saw the headline: "Jefferson Davis arrives in New York." He read enough to see that the Confederate President was stopping at the Metropolitan Hotel, in lower Broadway, and as he looked out of the stage-window the sign "Metropolitan Hotel" stared him in the face. In a moment he was out of the stage; he wrote a little note, asked the clerk to send it to Mr. Davis, and within five minutes was talking to the Confederate President and telling of his remarkable evening.
>
> Mr. Davis was keenly interested in the coincidence and in the boy before him. He asked about the famous collection, and promised to secure for Edward a letter written by each member of the Confederate Cabinet . . .[11]

So far, so good. He had plenty of autographs; but what about their practical use? "It was," he reminisced, "proving educative to a wonderful degree, but it was, after all, a hobby, and a

---

[9] *Ibid.*, p. 21.
[10] *Ibid.*, p. 25.
[11] *Ibid.*

hobby means expense. His autograph quest cost him stationery, postage, car fare—all outgo."[12] He was an outgoing boy, with his eye fixed on income. He saw a man in a restaurant opening a box of cigarettes, and discarding the picture in the box. Edward picked up the picture from the floor. It was the portrait of an actress, the reverse side of which was blank. Why not have a biography of each picture on the reverse side? "With his passion of self-education," he wrote, "the idea appealed very strongly to him."[13] He sold the idea to the president of the American Lithograph Company, who offered him ten dollars for each biography of one hundred famous Americans. Edward now told his brother (a shadowy wraith in Edward's autobiography) to share the work: he would get five dollars for each. Subsequently he hired other young men for less pay. "It was commercial, if you will," Edward Bok wrote more than forty years later, "but it was a commercial editing that had a distinct educational value to a large public."[14]

He was sixteen when President and Mrs. Hayes invited him to dinner. The story is worth retelling. The *Brooklyn Eagle* had sent him to report a dinner speech by the President. There were wineglasses in front of the reporters. Bok asked the waiter to remove them. He needed more space for transcribing his speech. The trouble was that the President spoke too fast. Edward bounded after him, and asked for a copy. The President, impressed with the Boy's ambition as well as with his abstemiousness, invited him into his carriage. They rumbled up to Columbia Heights, where the President was staying with A. A. Low. He gave Edward the speech. (Those were the days when a President could recite his speech from memory, having left his own handwritten draft at the house!) Then he invited the Boy for dinner next night. We have but Bok's word for this sequence of events[15]; yet it sounds plausible, perhaps alarmingly so.

[12] *Ibid.*
[13] *Ibid.*, p. 27.
[14] *Ibid.*, p. 28.
[15] *Ibid.*, pp. 29–31.

We also have only Bok's word for what was to follow: facts such as that "a small copy of Emerson's essays was always in Edward's pocket on his long stage or horse-car rides to his office or back."[16] He now invaded Boston. He arrived on a Sunday evening; at seven-thirty next morning he had penetrated the sanctum of Oliver Wendell Holmes, who offered him pie ("That is real New England, you know").[17] From the Autocrat at the Breakfast Table, Bok marched straight to Longfellow's luncheon table. The poet asked Bok to say grace in Dutch. Next day Phillips Brooks gave him entire cases of well-solicited advice. Louisa Alcott called Edward "my good boy" and walked him over to Emerson, who was, alas, old, doddering, full of sleep. Bok was not. "I thought, perhaps, Mr. Emerson," he said, "that you might be able to favor me with a letter from Carlyle."[18] Next day it was the turn of William Lloyd Garrison and Lucretia Mott and Charles Francis Adams, whom he "enjoined to give the boy autograph letters from his two presidential forebears."[19]

Some of this was too good to last. The boy was a growing boy. He was attracted to the theater. One evening the editor of the *Eagle* sent him to cover the appearance of the actress Rose Coghlan in the Brooklyn Grand Opera House. "It so happened that Edward had made another appointment for that evening which he considered more important"—now, what could *that* have been?—"and yet not wishing to disappoint his editor he accepted the assignment."[20] He did disappoint him all right. Bok wrote his account of the great event, unaware of the fact that Miss Coghlan, who had been taken ill, had not performed that night. The career of the budding journalist was over— almost, but not quite. His interest in the theater was not over at all. In his own words, "he noticed the restlessness of the

16 *Ibid.*, p. 34.
17 *Ibid.*, p. 35.
18 *Ibid.*, p. 56.
19 *Ibid.*, p. 60.
20 *Ibid.*, p. 61.

women in the audience between the acts."[21] He concluded that
what they needed was some reading matter: a theater program
crammed with interesting advertisements. His subsequent endeavor in publicity was an instant success. In 1881 the words
"publicity" and "public relations" did not yet exist: but Bok
knew exactly what they meant before they were invented. And
now once more the scarlet theater world pulled Edward toward
its shadow. The perfumed shade of a Miss Fanny Davenport, an
actress, crept over that otherwise so edifying scene of the life
of Bok. He persuaded Miss Davenport to engage him as her
"assistant manager"—in reality, her publicity director. She was
willing to give him a considerable salary. Bok rushed home to
show the contract to his mother. His mother was grim. His
expectations of approval were dashed. Bok now importuned the
Actress to negotiate with the Mother. Their exchange must
have been somber. All the Boy recalls is that Miss Fanny
Davenport "came away from the interview a wiser if a sadder
woman."[22] When, a few months later, he was offered his important job in Philadelphia, he again consulted his mother, who
advised him to stay in New York, a counsel that Bok—wisely,
as he records—did not heed. He, whose entire career depended
on giving convincing, though unsolicited, advice to millions
knew what to do with advice that he had solicited but thought
unconvincing.

Meanwhile, he had a run on religion.[23] Early in his life
Benjamin Franklin professed great admiration for the works of
Cotton Mather, from which issued Franklin's publication of
Mather's *Essays to Do Good*. At the age of twenty Edward Bok
developed an admiration for the works of the Reverend Henry
Ward Beecher. Unlike the relationship of Drs. Mather and
Franklin (there is reason to believe that the former would not

21 *Ibid.*, p. 62.
22 *Ibid.*, p. 151.
23 He also had a run on Wall Street, under the tutelage of Jay Gould: but
"the closer his contact with Jay Gould the more doubtful he became of the
wisdom of such an association and perhaps of its unconscious influence upon his
own life in its formative period." *Ibid.*, p. 73.

have admired certain features in the career of the latter, had he lived to witness them), the admiration that Bok and Beecher had for each other was instantaneous and mutual. Bok knew that the rewards of publicity may be enhanced by a judicious admixture of piety; Beecher knew that piety without publicity was literally not worth speaking about. Beecher's contributions now progressed from *The Plymouth Pulpit* to *The Brooklyn Magazine* and to *The American Magazine*, journals progressively renamed by Bok. The mass production of standardized piety was just around the corner. So Bok decided to "syndicate" Beecher—meaning that the latter's sermons and writings would be reproduced in hundreds of newspapers athwart the vast lands of the Republic. "I don't believe in it, boys," said the Reverend Beecher to Edward and his partner. "No one yet ever made a cent out of my supposed literary work."[24] They offered the Reverend $250 weekly. Two weeks later he stood in their office watching the syndication checks being extracted from the mail. He now believed every word of it. "Bok," said Beecher afterward, "is the only man who ever seemed to make my literary work go and get money out of it." He promised Bok his autobiography after he finished his *Life of Christ*, which would now be speeded up. This kind of history would repeat itself: twenty years later Bok sent a cable to the Reverend Lyman Abbott requesting for the Christmas number of the *Ladies' Home Journal* "a short and snappy life of Christ."

Bok was just about to move on from religion to women when there was another bit of trouble. The Bok syndicate had addressed a redoubtable question to the divines and to the profound thinkers of the Republic: "Should Clergymen Smoke?" One of the contributors to the symposium was the Reverend Richard S. Storrs, a Brooklyn clergyman who combined a moderate liking for tobacco with a violent dislike for the Reverend Beecher. It now transpired that Storrs's contribution was fabricated by the Bok syndicate without the Reverend having

[24] *Ibid.*, p. 80.

written his own bit on the subject. He accused Bok in public. He threatened to sue. The New York newspapers perked up. Bok was much perturbed. He went to the Reverends Beecher and Talmage for advice. "Remember, boy," they told him, "silence is never so golden as when you are under fire."[25] The boy—he was now twenty-two—remained quiet as a mouse. He Who Believes in Publicity Must Need Know When to Shut Up Tight. Eventually Dr. Storrs's "din"—Bok's term for the unfortunate complication—died out. Bok was not brought to court; he was indeed grateful. Yet he persisted in his practice of fabricating contributions. He collected contributions and subscriptions for an anniversary volume for Beecher; but the volume was not yet completed when the celebrated dominie passed away. Bok "felt that the tributes already received were too wonderful to be lost to the world."[26] He published the collection nonetheless—including contributions that were nonexistent. "I received your Beecher Memorial today," Eastman Johnson wrote Bok,

> and was most painfully shocked to see what a senseless article is there attributed to me. What I wrote to you was excusing myself for *not* writing anything about Mr. Beecher, and was not of course for publication. I have no record of what I said but I *know* I could not have written anything as stupid as this: "I am glad enough to add my name to the great and heroic things that Mr. Beecher has done," etc.[27]

Another journalist, who was writing a biography of Beecher, accused Bok of "making money out of Henry Ward Beecher's dead body"[28]—a statement which, all of its malicious character notwithstanding, was not entirely devoid of the truth.

Still, from the thin lips of Edward Bok this cup, too, would pass. In America, he would write, "the possession of sheer merit

[25] *Ibid.*, p. 132.
[26] *Ibid.*, p. 133.
[27] Eastman Johnson to Bok, 28 June 1887 (Gratz collection of MSS. in the Historical Society of Pennsylvania); see also Johnson to Bok, 18 July and 19 July, in the same collection.
[28] *AEB*, p. 134.

was the only real factor that actually counted." This kind of
merit, no matter how sheer, had to be publicly thickened, to
become known. Jowett of Oxford once said that in this world
it was important to be pushing, but that it was even more
important not to seem so. The first part of this maxim accorded
entirely with Bok's view of life; the second did not. "Bok," he
wrote about himself, "had not only tried always to fill the particular job set for him, but had made it a rule at the same time
to study the position just ahead, to see what it was like, what it
demanded, and then as the opportunity presented itself, do a
part of that job in addition to his own."[29] He would ascend even
dizzier heights of self-satisfaction. "Bok," he wrote, "worked,
fully convinced that his play-time would come later. Where
others shirked, he assumed. Where others lagged, he accelerated
his pace. Where others were indifferent to things around them,
he observed and put away the results for possible use later."
"He used every rung in the ladder as a rung to the one above."[30]
In 1889 he mounted another rung of the ladder. He would
now address himself to the profitable reformation of American
women, in Philadelphia.

THE FIRST SUCCESSFUL women's magazine was started by a son
of immigrant parents, in Philadelphia, who developed an early
talent for syndication, that is, for the reprinting of material
taken from others. He was Louis Antoine Godey, the son
of French parents, born in New York, who started his *Lady's
Book* in 1830 from clippings gleaned from English publications,
often without acknowledging the origin of his material. Soon
he merged his magazine with that of Sarah Hale, who had
pioneered a women's magazine in Boston with indifferent
results. *Godey's Lady's Book* was a success for more than thirty
years, when another Philadelphia publication, *Peterson's Maga-*

29 *Ibid.*, p. 121.
30 *Ibid.*, p. 122.

zine, surpassed its circulation. By 1880 both of these magazines had declined. It was at that time that a third women's magazine appeared, again in Philadelphia. Cyrus Hermann Kotzschmar Curtis, his guttural middle names notwithstanding, was a Maine Yankee, whose main passions were music and money, not necessarily in that order.[31] His wife, Louisa Knapp, was a solid German woman from Boston, with considerable common sense. She convinced her husband to adopt the name *Ladies' Home Journal* for the women's magazine that Curtis started in 1883; as a matter of fact, she was its first editor, using her maiden name. It did fairly well, with its circulation rising to 400,000. Six years later Curtis interviewed Bok, and offered him the job as editor. Seven years later Bok married Mary Louise, the Curtises' only child. By that time the *Ladies' Home Journal* was prosperous enough for Curtis to expand his empire. He bought the nearly defunct *Saturday Evening Post* for $1,000—in 1897.

Before coming to Philadelphia Bok was already a successful promotion man, whose syndications included a Woman's Page. On the other hand, he knew little about women, a fact of which he was inordinately proud. He wrote about his boyhood as "too full of poverty and struggle to permit him to mingle with the opposite sex . . . Nor had he the slightest desire even as an editor to know [women] better."[32] None of this would disqualify him from his self-appointed task: "the promotion of virtues and moral influences which constitute woman's mission."[33] His predecessor Benjamin Franklin had taken up the cudgels for the education of women even before he came to

---

[31] In 1923 Bok wrote a biography of Curtis, *A Man from Maine:* "Compare the picture of a boy without twenty-five cents to go and see a monitor lying in Portland Harbor and, with a dog, climbing on a log and paddling his way out to the ship until the crew lifted him aboard, with the picture of the same boy some years later, sailing into the same harbor on his own yacht: one of the largest pleasure-vessels in the United States. What is this if it is not romance? . . . And yet there are folks who say there is no romance in business."

[32] *AEB,* p. 168.

[33] *Ibid.,* p. 160.

Philadelphia. His friend in Boston John Collins thought that the idea was not worth bruiting about. "I took the contrary side," Franklin wrote in his *Autobiography*, "perhaps a little for dispute's sake." He wrote a little treatise on the subject which was then read by his father. Here the similarity ends. Where Franklin liked to dispute, Bok preferred to promote. He was an Editor.

His promotional talents did not at first endear him to Philadelphians. In spite of his brashness, he immediately recognized the initial snubs; he scaled down his social ambitions. For the first few years in Philadelphia he lived in a hotel. Then he noticed that the indifference of Philadelphia worked both ways: if it was reticent in matters that were private, it was also tolerant of public success—of all kinds of public success. Throughout his life in the city Bok was vexed by the reserve of patrician Philadelphia; but he also knew how to take advantage of its philistine conformism, the kind of conformism which is unwilling to take a stand against whatever seems to be publicly recognized and popular. Slowly, gradually, Philadelphians accustomed themselves to the Curtis publishing empire and to the *Ladies' Home Journal*.

"Edward Bok's biographical reading," he wrote about his editorship, "had taught him that the American public loved a personality; that it was always ready to recognize and follow a leader." His concept of leadership was simple. Bok "always kept 'a huckleberry or two' ahead of his readers . . . [The public] always expects of its leaders that they shall keep a notch above or a step ahead."[34] Probably he never read Stendhal, who once wrote that the public is always ready to follow men who are but a step ahead; if they are more than two steps ahead, they give the public an intolerable headache. Bok disliked Wilde, who once said that there are writers (and, presumably, editors) who pursue the obvious with the enthusiasm of a shortsighted

[34] *Ibid.*, pp. 162–63.

detective. It was in the pursuit of the obvious that Bok made his fortune. Witin five years he doubled the circulation of the *Ladies' Home Journal*. In 1903 the magazine reached a circulation of one million. Bok's salary was one hundred thousand dollars a year. An editor (Tom Masson) of the old *Life* magazine wrote:

> *I am Bok, of the* Ladies' Home Journal
> *And a nice young man am I.*
> *My methods are purely supernal;*
> *My job is easy as pie.*
> *The element religious,*
> *With a finesse quite prodigious,*
> *Is the only affectation I pursue;*
> *But I do it with persistence,*
> *That admits no resistance,*
> *With a cash accumulation held in view.*[35]

Even before he assumed the editorship universal literacy, public education, living standards had been rising fast. There was a new generation of American women of all classes, a new and untapped reservoir of potential readers of a magazine that would be addressed to them, a magazine that was educational without being intellectual, direct rather than genteel, elevating and yet standardizing, class-conscious and classless at the same time. Respectability and Americanism were the two main threads woven through the *Ladies' Home Journal* for many decades, even after Bok retired. There were millions of American women desirous of the kind of respectability which the *Journal* publicized, and at which Bok was hammering away.

There was something else about these millions of readers that Bok instinctively understood. Universal education may have put an end to illiteracy, but it also produced millions of people whose imaginations were even more pictorial than they were verbal. He changed the format of the *Ladies' Home Journal*,

[35] *Life*, 4 July 1901.

making it unusually vivid and colorful. It was the first magazine whose cover designs would change from month to month.
He was the first to run a story in the front and continue it
in the back. Print (except for headlines and slogans) could be
broken up; pictorial pages could not. The photograph of a
famous personality was as important as—if not more than—
what he had to say in print.[36] The pictorial quality of the
Ladies' Home Journal soon surpassed that of all other magazines. Bok would reproduce a portfolio of beautiful paintings.
He wanted to get these reproductions into thousands of American homes.[37] He thought that his educational pictorialization
("Good Taste and Bad Taste") changed completely "the physical appearance of domestic furniture in the stores" of the
country.[38] His campaign in reforming American domestic
architecture deserves credit. He started a portfolio, complete
with pictures and designs, of *Ladies' Home Journal* houses,
available within the reach of the budgets of millions. He may
have contributed powerfully to the standardization and to the
suburbanization of the American dream; but the architectural
standards of many of these houses were good, and some of their
designs are pleasant in retrospect.

His urge for self-congratulation prevailed:

[36] Bok to Owen Wister, 1 July 1903 (Wister collection, Library of Congress):
". . . We have a very good photographer in Boston, a good artist and a gentleman whom we could send down [to you] . . ." "Suggestions for photographs of
Mr Wister: Mr Wister and his two crows. Mr Wister on horseback. Mr Wister
at any sport or form of exercise in which he indulges. Mr and Mrs (?) Wister
in garden or any picturesque spot. But be sure *not* to photograph Mrs Wister
unless with her and his consent. Exterior of house. Mr Wister writing in his
study (only one view) showing him at work. Any 'unconscious' or 'unposed'
photograph . . ."
[37] The elevator of taste and the promoter of circulation were, of course, the
same Bok. "Bok," he would write about himself, "determined to work through
the churches. He selected the fifty best pictures, made them into a set and
offered two hundred and fifty sets to churches to sell at their fairs. The managers
were to promise to erect a *Ladies' Home Journal* booth, which Bok knew, of
course, would be most effective advertising, and the pictures were to sell at
twenty-five and fifty cents each." *AEB*, p. 247.
[38] *Ibid.*, pp. 244–45.

Bok had begun with the exterior of the small American house and made an impression upon it. He had brought the love of flowers into the hearts of thousands of small householders who had never thought they could have an artistic garden within a small area; he had changed the lines of furniture, and he had put better art on the walls of these homes. He had conceived a full-rounded scheme, and he had carried it out.[39]

He was among the first editors to use a magazine to mount national campaigns of self-improvement. These included some of his aversions. During the two decades before World War I he organized campaigns against a series of American evils: football on Thanksgiving Day; the interior decoration of Pullman cars; dirty cities; the selling of fireworks on the Fourth of July; improper dances; smoking women; certain women's clubs; Paris fashions; the cult of aigrettes; the public drinking cup. He led national crusades for the licensing and belling of cats, and also for sex education, notwithstanding his own admission of knowing little or nothing about women. About sex education he published a series of articles and pamphlets entitled, simply and squarely, *The Edward Bok Books of Self-Knowledge.* "The root of all kinds of evils"—including venereal disease— lay in the reticence of parents with children "about the mystery of life." Some of his editors said that the topic was "controversial" and "unsavory." Bok didn't think so. "It is the most beautiful story of life." He did not propose to "tell the actual story of the beginning of life—that was the prerogative of the parents." But he would instruct them how to tell their children "the story of life."[40] In the May 1913 number of the *Ladies' Home Journal* he wrote: "Seven years ago the idea of sex education was a tabooed subject . . . today sex knowledge and sex hygiene form a discussable topic in the home."[41] He thought that here, too, he had succeeded, as in his campaign against the unsanitary drinking cup, when, "within a year, one of the

[39] *Ibid.*, p. 249. The chapter is entitled: "A Signal Piece of Constructive Work."
[40] *Ibid.*, p. 346.
[41] *Ibid.*, p. 350.

worst menaces to American life had been wiped out by public sentiment."[42] In 1914 Bok, ahead of the armies of the Kaiser by a huckleberry or two, fired his salvo at Paris:

> The strangling hold which the Paris couturiers had secured on the American woman in their absolute dictation as to her fashions in dress, had interested Edward Bok for some time. As he studied the question, he was constantly amazed at the audacity with which these French dressmakers and milliners, often themselves with little taste and scant morals, cracked the whip, and the docility with which the American woman blindly and unintelligently danced to their measure . . . It was inconceivable that the American woman should submit to what was being imposed upon her if she knew the facts. He determined that she should. The process of Americanization going on within him decided him to expose the Paris conditions and advocate and present American-designed fashions for women.[43]

Unlike his campaigns, which were not always successful—he got into trouble with certain women's clubs—the features he introduced in the *Ladies' Home Journal* almost always ran well. Like his predecessor Godey, who had convinced his main competitor (Mrs. Hale) to join him, Bok took the principal woman columnist of the 1880s (Mrs. Isabel Mallon: "Bab") for his advice columnist, under the name of "Ruth Ashmore." Next Bok started a series: "Unknown Wives of Well-Known Men" (Mrs. Beecher: "Mr. Beecher As I Knew Him"), followed by "Clever Daughters of Clever Men," including an entire issue of contributions by the dutiful daughters of Dickens, Hawthorne, Benjamin Harrison, Greeley, Thackeray, Howells, Sherman, Jefferson Davis, and others. Bok believed in the profitabil-

---

42 Bok's method was to make enough noise to raise bored politicians, recumbent in various state capitols, to the proposition of legislation that would be unreservedly popular. His Great Aigrette Crusade could be called heronism, with a vengeance. His campaign resulted in several state legislatures interrupting their weighty deliberations to pass bills that made it a misdemeanor to import, sell, purchase, or wear aigrettes. Entire shipments of aigrettes, one valued at $160,000, were destroyed. Bok was pleased to recall that "he had not saved the lives of the mother-birds, but, at least, he had prevented hundreds of American women from wearing the hallmarks of torture."

43 *AEH*, p. 327.

ity of personal reminiscence. Jane Addams wrote "My Fifteen Years at Hull House," Lyman Abbott "My Fifty Years as a Minister," and Gene Stratton Porter "What I Have Done with Birds." Bok became sufficiently indulgent to allow reminiscences from the legitimate theater; he commissioned articles by the journalist Ray Rockway on "Playing Tennis with Sarah Bernhardt" and, somewhat unaccountably, one with the title "My Days with Maude Adams in the Desert." He paid Howells $10,000 for his autobiography; his father-in-law Curtis spent $50,000 on advertising it. When Bok crossed over to the Old World, certain complications arose. He descended on the Gladstones in Hawarden Hall. He offered Gladstone $15,000 for twelve articles. The aged statesman, chilly before a fire in his baronial hall, declined, but Bok eventually secured Mrs. Gladstone's promise to commit herself to a series of reminiscences, "From a Mother's Life." Bok proceeded to Oxford in order to corral Lewis Carroll: a futile endeavor, for in the art of springing Bok, Carroll proved himself a master. Florence Nightingale refused to receive him, sending word that she was not well and in the care of a nurse. Uninvited, though armed with the draft of a contract, Bok penetrated the house of Kate Greenaway. Her sister, opening the door, told Bok that Miss Greenaway was not at home. Bok, as his account tells us, remained undeterred:

> "But, pardon me, has not Miss Greenaway returned? Is not that she?" asked Bok, as he indicated a figure just coming down the stairs. And as the sister turned to see, Bok stepped into the hall. At least he was inside! Bok had never seen a photograph of Miss Greenaway, he did not know that the figure coming downstairs was the artist; but his instinct had led him right, and good fortune was with him.[44]

Good fortune almost deserted him in Paris. He called on Dumas, to whom he had offered a contract for an article with

44 *Ibid.*, p. 198.

the title "How I Came to Write *Camille*." Dumas's mood was saturnine, acerbic, and dark. He said that American publishers "were robbers by instinct. All of this distinctly nettled Bok's Americanism." He let Dumas know that he was prepared to give him an envelope, with the pay in French banknotes, in prompt exchange for the manuscript, and that was that. Dumas took the envelope. There was a moment of silence. How about the manuscript? Bok asked. "After I count it," Dumas said.

With all his success as a magazine editor, Bok had the fatal talent of bringing out the worst in people. During the half century of his public life, he amassed an enormous correspondence. The letters that otherwise thoughtful public figures addressed to him were often cloyingly sentimental. He once sent a shipment of Philadelphia scrapple to Kipling, whose thank-you letter was a glorifying paean of pig meat. One of the oddities of their correspondence was Kipling's insistence (*circa* 1900) that Bok comprehend the mystical beauty of the symbol of the swastika ("to rhyme with 'car's sticker,' " Kipling wrote him). He sent Bok a brass swastika door knocker for his new house, a suburban mansion, complete with seven bathrooms, which Bok had erected in Merion, Pennsylvania, and which he named "Swastika." (Years later Bok selected the swastika for the symbol of his Girls' Club, another promotion of the *Ladies' Home Journal*.) Bok's gratitude to Kipling was abundant but not boundless. Since Bok believed that "in the interest of the thousands of young people who read his magazine . . . it would be better to minimize all incidents portraying alcoholic drinking," he suggested that if Kipling "could moderate some of these scenes, it would be more in line with the policy of the magazine."[45] In "William the Conqueror" Kipling wrote of two men who were sufficiently overjoyed on one occasion to order a bottle of champagne, while a third companion called for a whiskey and soda. Bok asked Kipling to change this. Kipling

[45] *Ibid.*, p. 220.

said that a bottle of milk might be substituted. ("When the story was reprinted in book form, the drinks of the characters were restored.")[46]

Bok was aware of the profit latent in Presidents. Women, he thought, were not yet quite prepared "to exercise the privilege of the ballot. Bok determined to supply the deficiency of his readers, and concluded to put under contract the President of the United States, Benjamin Harrison, the moment he left office, to write a series of articles explaining the United States."[47] In 1906 Bok went to see Theodore Roosevelt, suggesting that the President write a column for the *Ladies' Home Journal*. Roosevelt said that he had practically no free time. All right, Bok said, let the column be written by a journalist who would interview Roosevelt while the latter was shaving. An editorial announced: "A Department in which will be presented the attitude of the President on those national questions which affect the vital interests of the home, by a writer intimately acquainted and in close touch with him."[48] (We are left to speculate whether "close touch" had something to do with the President shaving.) Twelve years later Bok called on Roosevelt again, with a brilliant idea. He, Bok, "wanted to invest twenty-five thousand dollars a year in American boyhood." Colonel Roosevelt should assume the leadership of the National Boy Scouts of America; Bok would pay this sum as his salary. "By Jove!" Bok quoted Roosevelt, "it would be wonderful to rally a million boys for real Americanism, as you say."[49] But he declined nevertheless. In 1914 Bok prevailed upon Taft to write an article on the Presidency. Woodrow Wilson followed with an article entitled "The Lonely Man in the White House: Why the President Can Have No Intimates."[50] This was just before Wilson fell for the ample charms of Edith Bolling. Around that

[46] Joseph Jackson, *Literary Landmarks of Philadelphia* (Philadelphia, 1939), p. 24.
[47] *AEH*, p. 191.
[48] *Ibid.*, p. 270.
[49] *Ibid.*, p. 283.
[50] *LHJ*, March 1914.

time Wilson wrote a personal letter to Bok, asking him to do a favor for a woman friend "who has now fallen upon hard times."

> Among other things that she really knows, she really does thoroughly know old furniture and all kinds of china worth knowing.
>
> Pardon me if I have been guilty of an indiscretion in sending this direct to you. I am throwing myself upon your indulgence in my desire to help a splendid woman.
>
> She has a great collection of recipes which housekeepers would like to have. Does a serial cook-book sound like nonsense?[51]

Wilson knew what Bok knew: that the latter was now a power in the land. His influence was enhanced by the insistent campaign of the *Ladies' Home Journal* for Americanism. In 1914 and in 1915 Bok's editorials took pride from those superior values of American civilization that kept America out of the bloody wars of Europe; less than two years later the editorials extolled the virtues of American intervention in order to set right the wrongs of the world. Bok saw no discrepancy in this: "Americanism" was the slogan that covered it all. He, the champion of private enterprise, would recall with satisfaction how, by 1917, the *Ladies' Home Journal* had "practically become the semi-official mouthpiece of all the various government war bureaus and war-work bodies."[52] He himself had become the State Chairman of the YMCA War Work Council. When in 1918 he made a tour of the Western Front, he cited what "an American officer of high rank" told him at Chaumont headquarters: "The mind cannot take in what the war would have been without the 'Y.' "[53] Meanwhile, the *Ladies' Home Journal* published articles such as that by J. Ogden Armour, president of the famous meat-packing company ("Unless women realize the task that confronts them, Hunger and National Defeat

[51] *AEH*, pp. 381–82.
[52] *Ibid.*, p. 391.
[53] *Ibid.*, p. 403.

are ahead of us.").[54] Bernard Baruch, not generally noted for austere habits, wrote in the September 1918 number about "Just What Is Wartime Thrift." Another article bore the sumptuary title: "Dining with the Hoovers: What a Guest Eats at the Table of the Food Administrator."[55] Bok enlisted the prose of the Secretary of War, Newton D. Baker, who wrote in 1918 that "if all the women in America were to stop doing the things that they are doing . . . we should have to withdraw from the war." Bok's own editorials were simple: "It is a time for every woman to be an American." "Housekeeping has been transformed from a daily round to a science and a business," he added.[56] In the June 1918 issue he delivered himself of a profound prophecy: "The most startling single factor that is coming out of the war is woman."[57]

When the war was over, the *Ladies' Home Journal,* in the words of its editor, "began to point the way to the problems which would face women during the reconstruction period. Bok scanned the rather crowded field of thought very carefully, and selected for discussion in the magazine such questions as seemed to him most important for the public to understand in order to face and solve its impending problem. The outstanding question he saw which would immediately face men and women of the country was the problem of Americanization." He committed the Secretary of the Interior (in whose department a government Bureau of Americanization was flourishing at the time) to publish a series of articles on Practical Americanization. It was his last editorial campaign. In 1919 the circulation of the *Ladies' Home Journal* went over two million, the largest of any magazine of its kind. He now retired from the editorial chair. The *Ladies' Home Journal* went on. He made sure that his version of Americanism would be carried on by the maga-

[54] *LHJ,* July 1917.
[55] *Ibid.,* March 1918.
[56] *Ibid.,* March 1918.
[57] *Ibid.,* June 1918.

zine after his retirement. As an editorial in the August 1923 number put it: "There is only one first-class civilization in the world today. It is right here in the United States and the Dominion of Canada. Europe's is hardly second-class, and Asia's is about fourth- to sixth-class." That year Bok himself wrote in a book: "The fact is that never in the history of American business has there prevailed a higher standard of honesty or more inflexible rules of integrity. When one compares the loose method practiced in business only a decade ago with the scientific basis of business to-day, and when the volume of business is taken into consideration where the million is to-day a current figure instead of the thousand of the past, the change is to the everlasting credit of the American business man. American business is to-day a synonym for integrity the world over. You never hear an honest successful business man complain of dishonesty in business. He does not know it, for, not practicing it himself, it is never practiced upon him, or when it is, rarely repeated. The crier of dishonesty in business will always bear watching."[58] It was the year of the Teapot Dome and other scandals.

By that time—the early twenties—the *Ladies' Home Journal* and *The Saturday Evening Post* had become institutions in Philadelphia—institutions in Philadelphia, rather than Philadelphian institutions. Institutions in Philadelphia, because there were now millions of Americans in whose minds these magazines were associated with Philadelphia as much as, if not more than, Independence Hall (which, in any event, was now literally overshadowed by the gigantic skyscraper of the Curtis Publishing Company). Philadelphian institutions: yes and no. Their successive editors were not Philadelphians. George H. Lorimer, the first and most successful editor of *The Saturday Evening Post*, came from New England, where his father had been a preacher. The last successful editors of the *Ladies' Home*

---

[58] *The Man from Maine* (New York, 1923), p. 62.

Journal were the Goulds, a couple who originated in Iowa and made their home in a smart house in Princeton, New Jersey. More and more *The Saturday Evening Post,* definitely Republican, addressed itself to the cheerful mentality of small-town businessmen of the Midwestern kind, while the *Ladies' Home Journal* attempted, not very gracefully, to conform to whatever seemed to be national trends of fashion and opinion.[59] After the bland suburban Eisenhower years, they went downhill. What remained of the *Ladies' Home Journal* (the two words *Ladies'* and *Home* were gradually diminished until they disappeared from the masthead altogether) left Philadelphia for New York. The Curtis Publishing Company, for all practical purposes, ceased to exist in the early 1960s. Yet even during the triumphant years of the Curtis enterprise, there were certain Philadelphians who cared little for the House that Curtis and Bok Had Built. In 1920 Agnes Repplier wrote that the *Ladies' Home Journal* was a disaster, as it bounded from number to number, "triumphantly presenting a non-existent world to unobservant readers. Henry Adams said that the magazine-made female has not a feature that would have been recognized by Adam, but our first father's experience, while intimate and conclusive, was necessarily narrow. We have evolved a magazine-made universe, unfamiliar to the eyes of the earth-dweller, and unrelated to his soul."[60] When Johan Huizinga, perhaps the finest historian in this century, visited the United States in 1926, he wrote: "It would be the triumph of commercial culture if, sometime in the future, advertising swallowed up literature, and praising the good, preaching of

[59] Example: In 1957 a novel by James Gould Cozzens, *By Love Possessed,* a best seller, was being touted as the long-awaited Great American Novel. This dreadful book contained lengthy and heavy passages describing the sexual act; it was the first national best seller including the word "fuck." Following in the wake of *Time*'s cover story on Cozzens, the ever-smiling crisp women columnists of the *Ladies' Home Journal* praised Cozzens's literary accomplishment to the skies, recommending him to their readers. So much for the belief that the New Obscenity was the result of the radicalism of the sixties.

[60] *Under Dispute* (New York, 1924), p. 60.

morality, and satisfaction of fantasy all merged into one. Just look for once through an entire number of the *Ladies' Home Journal* with attention. It will make clear to you what I have in mind."[61]

WHEN EDWARD W. BOK gave up his editorship of the *Ladies' Home Journal*, he was fifty-six years old. He announced, as we have seen, that he was now "going to play" for the rest of his life. We have also seen that this was not true. Bok was not a man who could let well enough alone. The success of his *Americanization* inspired him to turn out several other books, including another autobiography going over the same story, entitled *Twice Thirty: Some Short and Simple Annals of the Road*.[62] Yet he was not at all a simple man. He wished to become something of a Philadelphia institution himself, a patrician among patricians. This was not easy. Some of the older patricians of Philadelphia, a slow and private breed, had not especially appreciated him. He courted their attention and their approval.[63] This was probably one of the reasons why Bok became more and more involved in what he would call his "Adventure in Civics." He became a philanthropist on a gigantic scale.

Well before his retirement, he pronounced the high civilizational merits of suburban life. He founded the Merion Civic

[61] *America: A Dutch Historian's Vision, From Afar and Near* (New York, 1972), p. 250.

[62] A list of Bok's books is as follows: *Successward* (1890). *Before He Is Twenty* (1892). *The Young Man in Business* (1900). *Her Brother's Letters* (1906). *The Edward Bok Books of Self-Knowledge* (1912). *Why I believe in Poverty* (1915). *The Americanization of Edward Bok* (1920.) *Two Persons* (1922). *A Man from Maine* (1923). *Twice Thirty* (1924). His dreadful poem, *God's Hand*, was set to music by Josef Hoffman and published in 1916. In 1923 he edited a volume entitled *Great Hollanders*.

[63] Example: the abject tone of his letters to Owen Wister (30 September 1903, 10 December 1908, and many others) in the Wister Collection of the Library of Congress, cited above.

Association, which, under his guidance, adopted the motto: "To be nation right, and State right, we must first be community right." The motto may have been grammatically indifferent, but the achievements of the Association were not:

The police force was increased from one officer at night and none in the day, to three at night and two during the day, and to this the Association added two special night officers of its own. Private detectives were intermittently brought in to "check up" and see that the service was vigilant. A fire hydrant was placed within seven hundred feet of every house, with the insurance rates reduced from twelve and one-half to thirty per cent; the services of three fire-engine companies was arranged for. Fire-gongs were introduced into the community to guard against danger from interruption of telephone service. The water supply was chemically analyzed each month and the milk supply carefully scrutinized. One hundred and fifty new electric-light posts specially designed, and pronounced by experts as the most beautiful and practical road lamps ever introduced into any community, were erected, making Merion the best-lighted community in the vicinity.

At every corner was erected an artistically designed cast-iron road sign; instead of the unsightly wooden ones, cast-iron automobile warnings were placed at every dangerous spot; community bulletin-boards, preventing the display of notices on trees and poles, were placed at the railroad station; litter-cans were distributed over the entire community; a new railroad station and post-office were secured; the station grounds were laid out as a garden by a landscape architect; new roads of permanent construction, from curb to curb, were laid down; uniform tree-planting along the roads was introduced; bird-houses were made and sold, so as to attract bird-life to the community; toll-gates were abolished along the two main arteries of travel; the removal of all telegraph and telephone poles was begun, an efficient Boy Scout troop was organized, and an American Legion post; the automobile speed limit was reduced from twenty-four to fifteen miles as a protection to children; roads were regularly swept, cleaned, and oiled, and uniform sidewalks advocated and secured.[64]

[64] *AEB*, pp. 361–62.

There are four more paragraphs of this in *The Americaniza-tion of Edward Bok*.

He was enormously proud of his civic endeavors. After his retirement he established award after award: to heroic firemen, to brave policemen, to Fairmount Park Guards, a Harvard Advertising Award for advertisements of elevated character, and a Philadelphia Award ($10,000 per annum) to the man or woman in Philadelphia who proved to be the best citizen during the calendar year. He established the Philadelphia Forum for outstanding lecturers and performers. In 1923 he announced the American Peace Award, offering a prize of $100,000 "to the American who should devise the best practical plan for co-operation of the United States with other nations in attaining and preserving world peace."[65] The terms of this award showed how much Edward Bok, the definite Republican, had in common with Woodrow Wilson.[66] We shall see, later in this book, another example of this duality of Republicanism and Wilsonianism, in the thinking of George Wharton Pepper,[67] one of those eminent Philadelphians who did not mind working together with Bok.

Bok's most meritorious philanthropic act was his support of the Philadelphia Orchestra at a difficult stage of its development. Its deficit ran to more than $50,000, in 1916, when Bok called on the young Leopold Stokowski in the latter's dressing room. For peculiar reasons the orchestra was not permitted to

---

[65] In Bok's words, *TT*, p. 460: "It recorded the sixtieth serious and weighty proposal for organized peace in 617 years of the world's history—going back to the days of Dante, Erasmus, William Penn, Kant, and Benjamin Franklin." More than twenty-two thousand plans were submitted for the prize of $100,000. "Thousands of plans showed a deep aspiration to have the United States take the lead in a common agreement to brand war, in every truth, an 'outlaw.'" The winner of the plan was a Dr. Charles Herbert Levermore. His plan was submitted to the American people in a Bok-organized "referendum," in which 615,000 people (87.5 percent) voted in favor of it.

[66] Bok wrote that he looked very much like Wilson, and that he was often mistaken for the President. *Ibid.*, pp. 336–37.

[67] See below, pp. 226–28.

rehearse on the stage of the Academy; its rehearsals were confined to another room. Bok guaranteed the deficit as an anonymous donor; he organized a drive for a two-million-dollar endowment fund; Stokowski was allowed one public rehearsal on the stage. Stokowski was supposed to have said, "We would not have had the great Philadelphia Orchestra without Mr. Bok."[68] Subsequently Bok became President of the Board of the Philadelphia Orchestra. Interesting—though not untypical[69] —is the fact that unlike his wife, Bok had little, if any, liking for symphonic music.

Anonymity was not something that would appeal to him for long. In 1920 he revealed, and explained, the story of his contribution to the orchestra in his *Americanization*; he would return to it again in *Twice Thirty*. This was perhaps the least attractive feature of his character, his relentless self-advertisement, which made many Old Philadelphians uneasy with him. In *The Americanization of Edward Bok* he inserted many photographs of himself, including a full-page one, sitting at his desk, with the caption: "Pronounced by architects to be one of the most successfully beautiful offices in America."[70] Successful was beautiful, and beautiful was successful. It was Bok's improvement over Keats.

What a complex man he was! He was an advertising genius, who had no clear idea of separating what was private from what was public, even though he said that he attempted to do so. In *The Americanization* he recalled that before 1890 editorship in the United States "was distinctly vague and prohibitively impersonal. The public knew the name of scarcely a single editor of a magazine: there was no personality that stood out in the mind: the accepted editorial expression was the indefinite 'we'; no one ventured to use the first person singular and talk

68 Orville H. Bullitt to Cary Bok, letter cited in *Overtones,* Curtis Institute of Music (Philadelphia, 1974) p. 78. The citation does not show clearly whether Stokowski's phrase was cited by Bullitt or by Bok.
69 A subsequent president of the Board of the Philadelphia Orchestra, John Frederick Lewis, Jr., was tone-deaf.
70 P. 259.

intimately to the reader."[71] In his autobiography he used the third person singular and talked upliftingly about himself.

Here was a man whose private character was absorbed by his public image. Early in life he realized that it was no longer necessary for vice to pay tribute to virtue, since the payment of public tribute to virtue could be immensely profitable. One knows very little about the private Bok. Unlike the earlier prototype of the Victorian hypocrite, Bok did not wear a mask in public. His face was handsome and motionless, clean-shaven, marked by large ears, presenting a determinedly benevolent, thin-lipped smile. He was abstemious in his eating and drinking habits. Yet he spent much money on his clothes. He was a *Homo americanus* of a newer breed: a man who was not only, like Barnum, successful in making and raking in the profits of the publicity of his enterprises but in the enterprise of having made a public success of himself.[72] He would have understood— though perhaps not sympathized with—the wag who, later in this century, would say that a celebrity is someone who is famous for being well known.

In his second autobiography (*Twice Thirty*) Bok wrote that there were two Edward Boks, the public editor and the private citizen, and that he had attempted to keep the two spheres of his life separate. Yet whatever he elected to tell his readers about the private Bok was so little as to be unconvincing. There were many oddities in his revelations of himself. In *Twice Thirty* he wrote that the Boks were "a Dutch family of posi- tion"[73] and that "Bismarck was a friend of my father."[74] He claimed that he sat on Bismarck's lap at a dinner party in their house when he, Edward, was twenty months old. Bismarck was supposed to have said to Bok's father: "Never have I been so minutely and critically scrutinized. I wonder what can be the

[71] *Ibid.*, p. 162.
[72] "Bok was really happiest in that part of his work which concerned itself with the writing of advertisements." *Ibid.*, p. 153.
[73] P. 22.
[74] *Ibid.*, p. 31.

child's thoughts."[75] Yet Bismarck did not visit Holland in 1865.[76] Other than this, Bok made few references to his father in his autobiographies. His father seems to have been a ne'er-do-well, as was his brother Willie, who married a large florid woman with the appropriate name of Flora; he also settled in Philadelphia, but saw little of his brother there.

Edward Bok's private relationship to women remains obscure. He dedicated *The Americanization of Edward Bok* "To The American Woman I Owe Much But To Two Women I Owe More, MY MOTHER And MY WIFE, And To Them I Dedicate This Account Of The Boy To Whom One Gave Birth And Brought To Manhood And The Other Blessed With All That A Home And A Family May Mean." Yet in the same book he would write: "Edward Bok's instinctive attitude toward women was that of avoidance. He did not dislike women, but it could not be said that he liked them. They had never interested him."[77] He repeatedly declared his love and his affection for his mother; there was ample evidence for that. He repeatedly declared his love for his wife; but there is not much evidence for their mutual affection. Mary Louise Curtis Bok was a strong-minded woman, not very pretty, who spoke little but who knew what she meant. In their early married years she and Edward lived with her parents. When Bok had "Swastika" built, he insisted that his mother live with them when she was not visiting Holland. What Mary Louise thought of this arrangement we do not know. When Bok had planted hundreds of tulips in front of "Swastika" and erected above them a brass sign, PROTECTED BY THE PUBLIC, she was not amused. People who knew her thought that she did not like her husband. In any event, she had a genuine talent and love for music. In 1924 she founded the Curtis Institute, soon to become a premier school for musical training in the United States. Bok bought her the

[75] *Ibid.*, p. 32.
[76] My suspicions to this effect were confirmed by the courteous and patient research of Professor Fritz Stern of Columbia University.
[77] *AEB*, p. 168.

mansion on the corner of Rittenhouse Square and Locust Street. She lived now often separated from him, closely attached to a woman friend. Within three years she advanced her contribution to the Curtis Institute from five million to twelve million dollars, an astronomical sum in those years. She was sixty-six when she married Efrem Zimbalist, a Russian Jewish violinist of considerable talent and *joie de vivre*, a merry gnome of a man. She survived Bok by more than forty years. They had two sons: Cary, an unhappy man, alcoholic, who spent most of his life in Maine; and Curtis, a glacial, liberal jurist with a considerable reputation and a fair writing style. The turgid academic style of the latter's son Derek eventually led to his candidacy for the presidency of Harvard University, which position he now occupies. The Curtis publishing empire may have disappeared, but the names of the Curtis Institute and of the Bok family live on.

In his books Edward Bok often congratulated himself on the excellence of his health, the result of his judicious and moderate habits.[78] Yet throughout most of his life he (as did his father-in-law, Curtis) suffered from severe stomach pains. They became worse and worse. He died in 1930. He was buried in Florida under a carillon tower that bears his name. His last years were not happy at all.

It was during the twenties that D. H. Lawrence, feverishly fretting under the New Mexico sun, wrote his thoughtful and intemperate diatribe against Benjamin Franklin, in *Classics of American Literature*. "Oh, but Benjamin," he wrote, "fenced a little tract that he called the soul of man, and proceeded to get it into cultivation . . . He made himself a list of virtues, which he trotted inside like a grey nag in a paddock . . . Moral America! Most moral Benjamin! Sound, satisfied Ben! . . . Why then did Benjamin set up this dummy of a perfect citizen as a pat-

[78] His advice to a doughboy, reprinted in *TT*, pp. 319–21: "I would be mighty wary, in those play hours, of the wines of France. A man never needs alcohol in his being, and he never needs it so little as when he is up against the 'trick' that you and your fellows are going to 'out over' in France . . ."

tern to America? . . . in Philadelphia, setting up this unlovely, snuff-colored little ideal, or automaton, of a pattern American." That virtuous circle: it was one of the things that Franklin and Bok had in common. Yet there was a human dimension to Franklin that is not easily perceptible in Bok. The former, as his *Autobiography* shows, could on occasion laugh at himself; the latter could not. Toward the close of his life Franklin slipped in the esteem of his countrymen, who thought him a wee bit frivolous, though he seems to have enjoyed himself till the end. The great English wit Sydney Smith once said to his brother that they were "exceptions to the laws of nature. You have risen by your gravity, and I have sunk by my levity." I can, with a little effort, imagine Franklin chuckling over this, as he reads it to Bok, who has come to pester him in quest of an autobiography or an article, in whatever circles they may now reside.

WILLIAM CHRISTIAN BULLITT

O R

The Rebel Philadelphian

WILLIAM CHRISTIAN BULLITT was a rarity: a cosmopolitan who remained American to the core. When an American becomes a cosmopolite, his rise in the world often develops together with the—almost always self-conscious—decline of his American mores, standards, beliefs. This is why Henry James's minutely drawn portraits of cosmopolitan Americans are, almost always, caricatures of a certain kind. Perhaps the Transatlantic Master himself could not quite come to terms with this phenomenon; he may not have understood sufficiently the difference between illusion on the one hand and pretense on the other. He may not have known what to do (but, then, in this he was by no means alone) with someone like Bullitt, whose character was the very obverse of the compound of James's cosmopolitan American subjects.

Bullitt's illusions were many. His pretenses were few. His judgments were self-centered and impulsive. These are not the qualities of a good diplomatist. Wholly impervious to Talleyrand's famous warning—*surtout pas de zèle*—William Christian Bullitt had, throughout his career, *trop de zèle*, springing from a surfeit of energy. He is remembered principally as an American ambassador of a now bygone age. Yet he spent less than seven years of a long life in his two ambassadorial posts. His accomplishments were multifarious; his talents were extraordinary. He was a journalist, an agent of high statecraft, a novelist, a psychologist, an ambassador. During various periods of his life he was esteemed by Woodrow Wilson, befriended by Franklin Roosevelt, appreciated by Winston Churchill; Lenin trusted him, Stalin embraced him, Charles de Gaulle welcomed him, Chiang Kai-shek as well as Sigmund Freud solicited his advice and his assistance.

His life was interesting from the very beginning. During his formative years he often traveled in Europe with his parents.[1] When Austria declared war on Serbia in July 1914, Bullitt and his mother found themselves in a hotel room in Moscow—the same room that would be allotted to him twenty years later when he arrived there as the first American ambassador to the Soviet Union. Like the young Winston Churchill, he was attracted to the international affairs of the great nations of the world through journalism: a participant observer who, by describing events and their connections, could perhaps influence them. This was the Golden Age of the Press.[2] He became a principal correspondent for the Philadelphia *Public Ledger*. After a surprisingly short time—especially for Philadelphia— he was appointed associate editor of the newspaper. In 1915 he accompanied Henry Ford and the motley crowd that sailed with Henry Ford on the *Oscar II*, Ford's Peace Ship; Bullitt's articles about the trip were impatient, realistic, and often very funny. In 1916 he undertook a fascinating journey into the heartland of the Central Powers—Germany, Austria, Hungary

[1] They were cultivated people, with international connections. Yet Bullitt's father, who died in 1914, "expressed the hope" in his will that his children would not live abroad. Orville H. Bullitt, *For the President: Personal and Secret Correspondence between Franklin D. Roosevelt and William C. Bullitt* (Boston, 1972), p. 159.

[2] Lord Salisbury in 1901: "The diplomacy of nations is now conducted as much in the letters of special correspondents as in the dispatches of the Foreign Office." Churchill about Balfour *circa* 1902: "An age when almost the only robustly assertive institution in our society was the Press."

—less than a year before the United States was to go to war with them. His experiences included flying in a German airplane over the Russian lines, where he "got shot at and had all sorts of a good time."[3] More important was the fact that the twenty-five-year-old Bullitt and his beautiful wife were received by royal personages and prime ministers; the *gratin* of society and the governors of enormous war machines called at their hotel and left their cards on the morrow of their arrival. It was the rise of the American Century. These people recognized what this young American journalist and his charming wife represented: unofficial, and yet influential envoys of the richest, and the most powerful, state in the world.

Bullitt was an idealist and a realist—among his generation of Americans a rare combination. After the United States had entered the war, he was one of that group to whom President Wilson and Colonel House and Secretary of State Lansing gave the task of researching and preparing the detailed design of an American peace settlement. In Paris, after the Armistice, he was entrusted with the significant job of preparing intelligence summaries; he had been made a member of the somewhat oddly entitled American Commission to Negotiate Peace. Bullitt was fascinated with Russia. He had much sympathy for revolutionary causes, though not necessarily for Communism. He was an idealist, not an illusionist; a realist, not a sentimentalist. He realized that the Bolshevik government in Moscow, pressed and under attack from many quarters in early 1919, might be willing to agree to far-reaching compromises, in exchange for its *de facto* recognition. Lansing and Lloyd George allowed Bullitt to go to Moscow. His negotiations with Lenin, Trotsky, Chicherin remain, to this day, one of the most remarkable episodes in the history of Soviet diplomacy. They treated this young American as their accomplished equal. After Bullitt returned to Paris, with Soviet proposals in his hand that were nothing if

[3] Ernesta Drinker Bullitt, *An Uncensored Diary from the Central Empires* (New York, 1917), p. 160.

not sensational, he was disavowed by Lloyd George and shunned by Wilson. Bullitt was now convinced of two matters, the perfidiousness of the British and the character weakness of Wilson, two convictions that he would not abandon for the rest of his life.

Six weeks before the signing of the Treaty of Versailles, Bullitt resigned from the American delegation in Paris and inaugurated a public attack against Wilson. His letter accused Wilson of ignorance and lack of faith. The last sentence read: "I am sorry that you did not fight our fight to the finish and that you had so little faith in the millions of men like myself, in every nation who had faith in you." "The repercussion of this letter was great," Bullitt later wrote, "out of all proportion to the importance of the person who had written it."[4]

The consequences of this brief and dramatic chapter were considerable in his own mind. He was now a political outcast. He took a certain pride, and perhaps even internal sustenance, from the fact that he had been misunderstood and perhaps even cheated. He was enough of an egoist to recognize the rare and individual savor in the otherwise bitter taste of self-chosen exile. Yet his mind was restless enough not to seek solace in the stoic temper of resignation. He wrote a novel, *It's Not Done*, about Philadelphia, which resulted in successive printings and muffled repercussions, to which we shall return. Bullitt was much interested in psychology, perhaps especially in the psychology of the sexes: in his novel he demonstrated a considerable, and occasionally surprising, comprehension of complex and delicate matters. He developed an early admiration for Sigmund Freud's theories. He saw in them a scientific confirmation of his own disdain for hyprocrisy, and for the reluctance of people to look at certain fundamental matters of human nature. Out of his meetings with the Viennese savant came the singular and surprising book *Thomas Woodrow Wilson: A Psycho-*

---

[4] Sigmund Freud and William C. Bullitt, *Thomas Woodrow Wilson: A Psychological Study* (Cambridge, 1967), p. 272.

logical Study—begun in 1930, completed in 1939, and not published until 1966, written by Bullitt and Freud together. The very history of the conception and the composition of the work has been misjudged and misinterpreted. Ernest Jones, Freud's earnest and premier Welsh biographer, wrote in *The Life and Work of Sigmund Freud* (1957): "It was during [Freud's stay in Berlin in 1930] that the American Ambassador, W. C. Bullitt, persuaded Freud to cooperate with him in writing a psychoanalytic study of President Wilson." There are at least three mistakes in this single sentence. When Freud and Bullitt met in Berlin, the latter was not an ambassador: far from it. The book, as their authors emphatically state, is not a psychoanalysis but a psychological study of Wilson. Most important, the relation of the two authors was the exact opposite of Jones's statement. It was Freud who asked and persuaded Bullitt to work on this book with him, and not the reverse.[5]

---

[5] From Bullitt's Foreword: "[Freud] and I had been friends for some years before we decided to collaborate in writing this volume. He was in Berlin for a small operation. I called on him and found him depressed. Somberly he said that he had not long to live and that his death would be unimportant to him or to anyone else, because he had written everything he wished to write and his mind was emptied.

"He asked what I was doing, and I told him I was working on a book about the Treaty of Versailles which would contain studies of Clemenceau, Orlando, Lloyd George, Lenin, and Woodrow Wilson—all of whom I happened to know personally.

"Freud's eyes brightened and he became very much alive. Rapidly he asked me a number of questions, which I answered. Then he astonished me by saying he would like to collaborate with me in writing the Wilson chapter of my book.

"I laughed and remarked that the idea was delightful but bizarre. My book would interest specialists in the field of foreign affairs. A study of Wilson by him might possess the permanent interest of an analysis of Plato by Aristotle. Every educated man would wish to read it. To bury Freud on Wilson in a chapter of my book would be to produce an impossible monstrosity; the part would be greater than the whole.

"Freud persisted, saying that I might consider his proposal comic, but it was intended to be serious. To collaborate with me would compel him to start writing again. That would give him new life. Moreover, he was dissatisfied by his studies of Leonardo da Vinci and of the Moses statue by Michelangelo because he had been obliged to draw large conclusions from few facts, and he had long wished to make a psychological study of a contemporary with regard to whom thousands of facts could be ascertained. He had been interested in

Bullitt's experience with Wilson helped to crystallize his own convictions. He would represent and incarnate a philosophy of American internationalism that was the very opposite of what Wilson bequeathed to America, including Herbert Hoover, whose respect and admiration for Wilson remained constant. In 1932 Bullitt returned to high politics. One of Franklin Roosevelt's close advisors brought Roosevelt and Bullitt together.

Franklin Roosevelt was the last patrician President of the United States. His ideological frame of mind was standard, bland, American-liberal. Yet a certain kind of patrician self-confidence was an important part of his character. He was at ease with people of his class; he could easily and implicitly trust them. He would appoint certain men among them to high diplomatic posts at a time when the American Republic, after fifteen years of self-righteous isolationism, was about to assume her leading role in world affairs again. There was, in the early thirties, this small and attractive reservoir of amateur talent, composed of certain wealthy and well-established Americans not yet beyond middle age, an easygoing and yet responsible, a sophisticated and yet democratic assortment of Easterners on whom Roosevelt could draw, men such as Bullitt, Biddle, Bohlen, Harriman, Lane.[6] They became representatives of the

---

Wilson ever since he had discovered that they were both born in 1856. He could not do the research for an analysis of Wilson's character; but I could do it easily since I had worked with Wilson and knew all his close friends and associates. He hoped I would accept his proposal.

"I replied that I should be delighted to consider it seriously but felt certain that a psychological study of Wilson could not be compressed into a chapter. To accept it would abandon my book. Two days later I again called on Freud, and after a long talk we agreed to collaborate." *Ibid.*, pp. v–vi.

[6] Bullitt, Biddle, Bohlen were Philadelphians. Pennsylvania produced but one weak President, and few Cabinet members worthy of note. The principal Secretaries of State have come from New England and New York backgrounds. Yet Philadelphia produced some of the best diplomats who served the United States in two hundred years. They came from all kinds of classes: they included men such as the self-appointed Franklin, the quiet Quaker Richard Rush, bluff Irishmen such as Maurice Egan, rumbustious men such as George Earle, the suave and serious Anthony Drexel Biddle, and, of course, Bullitt.

greatest power in the capital of the globe. Their accomplishments compare favorably with those of the American ambassadors of the previous generation, including the First World
War; and, compared to the generation following them, to the
bureaucrats and foundation intellectuals staffing the enormous
American international machine, they shine like modern
Galahads in the photographic age. They were debonair, generous, confident of American power and of human progress. Once
it seemed that these shining prototypes of what was best in
American manhood were the early proconsuls of the *Pax
Americana* of the twentieth century. In reality they were the
last representatives of a certain breed.

Between Roosevelt and Bullitt a warm and exceptional kind
of friendship flowered quickly. Roosevelt told Bullitt to contact
certain people and to report to him from Europe, a confidential
mission that produced silly reverberations in the American
press, especially from Republican isolationists. After Roosevelt
won his impressive mandate from the American people, his
first important diplomatic move was the long overdue *de jure*
recognition of the Soviet Union. Bullitt was included in these
negotiations; and Roosevelt named him the first American ambassador to the Soviet Union.

Bullitt arrived in Moscow in the freezing winter of 1933. It
was the Ice Age of Stalin. Yet the atmosphere of his reception
was that of an extraordinary hothouse in Siberia. Stalin was
much worried about the prospect of a Japanese invasion of the
Soviet Far East. Friendship with the United States was, therefore, the first item on his international agenda. At a great Soviet
banquet, floating on rivers of vodka and Russian sentiment,
Stalin promised Bullitt everything that the latter could have
wanted. He kissed Bullitt twice on the cheek. Bullitt was impressed; yet he saw Stalin for what he was: "a wiry Gipsy with
roots and emotions beyond my experience."[7] He was soon

[7] From his letter to Roosevelt, 1 January 1934, cited by Orville Bullitt, *op. cit.*,
p. 66.

aware that between Soviet promise and Soviet deeds there were unbridgeable chasms, unbridgeable because of the Oriental substance within the Russian character, and perhaps especially within Stalin's. During Bullitt's ambassadorship the American embassy was a glistening enclave in the Muscovite night. He gave the best party in Moscow since the Revolution. He and his young friends introduced the Red Army to polo. They played American jazz music themselves. At the same time, they developed first-class habits of staff work, making the American embassy in Moscow one of the best informed in that vast prison of a city—a more than considerable achievement. Bullitt's staff thought highly of him, they liked working for him—the surest indication of a good ambassador. During the first year of Bullitt's stay in Moscow, Stalin began to transform the muddy jailhouse of the Soviet Union into a maximum-security prison. He wished to isolate his country from the rest of the world even more than before. As early as 1935, Bullitt saw the possibility of an agreement between Stalin and Hitler.[8] When the dangerous prospect of a Japanese invasion was fading, Stalin needed to pay less heed to the few precise requests of the Americans. Bullitt concluded that his efforts to establish, if not a unique, then at least a mutually profitable, relationship between the two largest republics of the globe, would fail because of Stalin and the Russians themselves. He asked to be relieved of his post.

Roosevelt now posted Bullitt to Paris. This was an excellent appointment. Bullitt spoke French well; he was thoroughly versed in the culture and in the civilized manners of France; he had a superb cellar and kept a fine table, and for his residence he rented a splendid château. Even more, Bullitt had *esprit* and

[8] His dispatch of 7 April 1935, cited by Orville Bullitt, *op. cit.*, p. 107: "My own feeling is that the Soviet Government will make the mutual assistance pact with the French and then begin to flirt with Germany as well as France and succeed in getting Germany and France bidding against one another for Soviet support, and that the only country which will derive any real benefit from the present maneuvers will be the Soviet Union." This was unusually perceptive, an assessment virtually without equal at that time.

panache, at a time when the French, desperately fearful of the approaching tornado of a second world war, admired the United States more than perhaps ever before (or since). In the Parisian firmament Bullitt shone like an exceptional star, a supernova. He seemed to incarnate all the best American virtues: directness, dispatch, and a kind of warmhearted courage. His friendships encompassed *tout Paris,* and practically all colors of the complicated French spectrum.[9] Much of this was due to the prestige of the United States at the time, but it was Bullitt who incarnated and vitalized these tendencies. He was later accused of having promised American support to the French against Hitler at a time when such support had been, as yet, far from forthcoming. The diplomatic record does not bear out these accusations. For once Bullitt acted and spoke with discretion as well as with dispatch, the best of possible combinations. Among a line of American envoys to France, including Franklin, Jefferson, Washburn, and Herrick, Bullitt may have cut the finest figure. His finest hour came at a tragic time. He had to witness, and to accompany, the fall of France. On 14 June 1940, when Paris, shining and sad, lay open to the Germans, not like the proverbial victim of rape in tatters, but rather like a beautiful middle-aged woman in her summer clothes, deserted, William Bullitt, in the best and bravest American tradition, disregarding the advice from Washington, chose to stay in Paris and face the Germans. They approached the American embassy with calculated and self-conscious courtesies, to which Bullitt responded with all the tact and reserve of a great envoy of classical stamp.

Two weeks later he elected to follow the errant French

[9] The day after Roosevelt's triumphant reelection in 1936, Léon Blum called on Bullitt. "He entered the front door, flung his broad-brimmed black hat to the butler, his coat to the footman, leaped the three steps to the point where I was standing, seized me and kissed me violently. I staggered slightly; but having been kissed by Stalin, I am now immune to any form of osculation, and I listened without batting an eye to as genuine an outpouring of enthusiasm as I have ever heard." Letter to Roosevelt, 8 November 1936, in Orville Bullitt, *op. cit.,* p. 178.

government of Marshal Pétain on its sorry hegira to Vichy.
Again his contemporary letters and dispatches stand well the
test of time. Behind them loomed the greater issue from which
he did not swerve. The United States had to commit itself to the
great cause, to the defeat of the Third Reich. He returned to
the United States in style, spoke with the President, and acted
accordingly. Among the many Americans who spoke during
that crucial year in favor of an American commitment against
the cause of Hitler, Bullitt stood out: his speeches—especially
the one he gave in Independence Square in Philadelphia in
August 1940—were admirably strong and clear.

Yet his unique relationship with Roosevelt began to change.
In March 1940 Roosevelt considered offering Bullitt the high
post of Secretary of the Navy. This would have elevated Bullitt
to a position comparable to Churchill's in the Chamberlain war
cabinet: the inclusion of an interventionist, and a fighter.
Eventually Roosevelt thought it better to strengthen his Cabinet
by offering the post to Frank Knox, an internationalist Republican, both for domestic and international reasons. In
August 1940 Bullitt's single-minded admiration of his friend
was still great enough to write Roosevelt: "So here you are—
Washington and Lincoln rolled into one, with a touch of the
Lord." A gradual devolution of their relationship was, however,
in the making. In November 1940 Roosevelt appointed Ad-
miral Leahy ambassador to Vichy-France, without consulting
Bullitt or informing him in advance. Bullitt was increasingly
exercised by what he saw as bureaucratic insensitivity and incompetence among the yes-men who surrounded the President.
There was the painful issue of Sumner Welles. Welles was a
knowledgeable diplomat and patriot whose character was
marred by his occasional homosexual escapades, under the influence of alcohol. Bullitt disliked Welles; more important, he
regarded Welles's condition as a grave danger to national security, for this Under Secretary of State was a potential target for
all kinds of blackmail. With his characteristic impatience Bul-

litt drove the issue home by confronting the President directly. Roosevelt, who found the matter painful and one that put him in an awkward position, viewed Bullitt's raising it as an indecent personal vendetta and resented it accordingly. Eventually Welles resigned: but by that time the relations between Roosevelt and Bullitt had deteriorated further.

Here we come to the most important factor in their estrangement. To the men who formed Roosevelt's close circle during the war, Bullitt was a stranger. They were people whose background as well as ideas were quite different from those of William Bullitt. They flattered the President, who, in turn, was more and more dependent on them, and whose physical health and mental agility had begun to decline. On one particular issue—an issue of the highest importance—their ideas concerning the American alliance with Stalin and Soviet Russia were the very contrary of Bullitt's. Bullitt believed that there was a limit to which Stalin could be trusted, and that it behooved the United States to give considerable thought to establishing the acceptable limits of Soviet expansion in Europe toward the end of the war.[10] Roosevelt and his circle believed that Stalin could be trusted, and that the postwar maintenance of Soviet-American friendship was the most important issue in the world. These differences of opinion—and, more important, of judgment—were unbridgeable. On Bullitt's side it was aggravated by his impolitic character.[11] Compromises had few attractions for

[10] On this important matter Bullitt's memoranda and letters to the President were, again, full of excellent points; they have also stood well the passage of time. During one of their last personal arguments, in 1943, Bullitt told Roosevelt about Stalin: ". . . the man with whom he dealt was not the Duke of Norfolk but a Caucasian bandit." Orville Bullitt, *op. cit.*, p. 554.

[11] See the 9 June 1943 entry in Felix Frankfurter's (carefully edited and abridged) diaries, with its patronizing tone: "Had luncheon at William Clayton's (Commerce Department) for Dick Law and John Maud of the British Food Mission. Lord Halifax, Jesse Jones, Billy Bullitt, Nelson Rockefeller, were some of the others present. Billy brought me back to the Court and I told him that when I have time I would like to talk with him at length about a matter that greatly disturbed me. He wanted to know what it was and I told him of the anti-Semitic talk attributed to him. He, of course, said it was sheer nonsense.

him. Yet his loyalty to Roosevelt was so deep-seated and long-lasting that it acted as a kind of brake on his habitually impetuous nature. His disillusionment with the President was gradual, albeit not a whit less—perhaps even more—tragic for that. Still, by 1943 he knew that Roosevelt's esteem for him was largely gone.[12] He, in turn, considered Roosevelt's course dead wrong.

Roosevelt gave Bullitt certain assignments; he sent him to Cairo and London as his personal observer in 1942, and for a while considered offering him the post of Under Secretary of the Navy. In 1943 there was some talk about having Bullitt run for governor of Pennsylvania; eventually he ran for mayor of Philadelphia, with Roosevelt's approval: a hopeless undertaking because of the grip of the Republican machine on the city of Philadelphia, where no Democrat had been elected mayor for sixty years. He asked to join the Army. The Pentagon refused. He then asked General de Gaulle for a military assignment with the forces of Free France. He entered Marseilles and Paris with the Free French, a bright and happy episode in the life of this fighting man, who was thus not only a witness but an actual combatant in the liberation of France. But his political career had come to an end.

Bullitt was fifty-three years old when Roosevelt died and the war ended. He was now free to express his world-political convictions. He wrote a short book and a few articles, mostly in *Life* magazine, about the Soviet danger and about the course that he thought the United States should set as the leader of the free world. Presidents Truman and Eisenhower may have re-

---

I said if I did not think so I wouldn't be talking to him at all, but while I didn't want to talk about it now because there was not time, I will talk later, because though I assume he does not entertain anti-Semitism himself, his tongue, sometimes in anger or hastily, may give expression to things that may encourage anti-Semitism in others." *The Felix Frankfurter Diaries*. Lasch, ed. (New York, 1967), p. 253.

[12] Largely, but not entirely. As late as 29 October 1943 Roosevelt sent an open letter to the publisher of the Philadelphia *Record*, defending Bullitt from accusations that the latter had remained in Paris to witness the entry of the Germans: "This attack on Bullitt is another piece of dirty political falsification."

spected Bullitt, but they did not call on his talents; they did not follow whatever advice he may have had to offer. He was, again, something of an exile. There remained now little of that savor of honorable defeat, even though events proved him to have been right, more right than many others who now held positions of prestige and power. For the next twenty-two years he lived beyond the edge of world politics. Obsessed with the danger of the Communist Soviet Union, he would tender advice to second-rate politicians in Washington and, on occasion, to Far Eastern governments, far from the center of events. He spent much of the last years of his life in Paris, where he was liked by many people, in his small pied-à-terre apartment in the rue de Ponthieu, where he died in 1967.

WILLIAM BULLITT was a Philadelphian: an eccentric Philadelphian, a self-exiled Philadelphian, a rebel Philadelphian, but a Philadelphian nonetheless. And this chapter is not a biography of a diplomatist; it is, principally, a study of character.

In one important sense the Bullitts were not prototypical Philadelphians. They were among the earliest, and most distinguished, settlers of Louisville, Kentucky, where descendants of the ancestral branch of the family even now reside.[13] William Bullitt's grandfather, a lawyer, John Christian Bullitt, came to Philadelphia before the Civil War, on banking business; he liked Philadelphia, with its talented lawyers and odd Southern touches, and elected to stay there. The Bullitts were originally French Huguenots. The French ancestry may have had something to do with William's temperament; and perhaps also with his mind. He was not only impatient; he was extraordinarily quick-witted. Early in his life he developed a distaste for the English, whom he often regarded as so selfish as to be

---

[13] In "Oxmoor," their ancestral estate. The name is also preserved by the estate of Orville Bullitt, outside Philadelphia.

perfidious, and at times so slow-witted as to be nearly degenerate. His experience with rich American Anglomaniacs, with
their acquired English relatives, and with English statesmen
during the First World War and after crystallized these prejudices. The English retaliated in kind. The files of the Foreign
Office include a scattering of extremely critical (and, on occasion, imprecise and unfair) notations about Bullitt. His prejudices were strong, but they were not blind. During the crucial
year of 1940 and after, he believed, and said, that an American
alliance with Britain was inevitable, and that the salvation of
Western civilization depended on it.

His grandfather, a Democrat, had added to his wealth in
Philadelphia. He became a leading citizen, who drafted the
Philadelphia city charter, which was then presented to the
legislature by his son.[14] William Christian Bullitt, Sr., was a
quiet gentleman, a civic-minded businessman of wide judgment and reputation.[15] His wife was a woman of great intellect,
charm, and distinction. William Christian Bullitt, Jr., was born
in 1891, trained to follow in his father's footsteps. His early
career was full of promise, including his active years at Yale,
where he was voted the most brilliant member of his class; he
was editor of the *Yale News,* and elected to Phi Beta Kappa. He
entered Harvard Law School, but he found that he was not attracted to the law.

He had a great deal of masculine charm. He was not tall, and
he lost his hair early in life, yet his male energy was attractive,
his directness of speech and his intelligence were extraordinarily appealing. In sum, this short, hazel-eyed, bald, pink-
skinned man shone with vitality as if it had been sluiced over
him with a pail. All through his life women found him charming; he, in turn, had a fine eye for female beauty. In 1916 he
married Ernesta Drinker, the daughter of a distinguished

[14] See p. 54 on the charter and Penrose.
[15] He was, among other things, vice-president of the Norfolk & Western
Railroad.

Quaker family of Philadelphia, famous for her looks. Their marriage had plenty of promise. Yet it rode into disaster. Their tastes were not unsimilar; their temperaments were incompatible. Surely their ancestries had much to do with this. The Bullitts and the Drinkers were both distinguished Philadelphians; yet they were as different as the sun and the moon. The Bullitts preserved something of their Kentucky, near-Southern ancestry throughout their lives in staid, somber Philadelphia: Bill Bullitt was hot-tempered, warm-blooded, impulsive, often to excess. The Drinkers, who had come to Philadelphia more than a century before the Bullitts, had a New England streak in their character, all of their Philadelphia traditions notwithstanding: scientific, legal, intellectual, essentially cold. (We have seen, in an earlier chapter, Agnes Repplier's complaints about the cold preciseness of the otherwise valuable character of Elizabeth Drinker, who wrote her diary during the American Revolution;[16] it is surely not accidental that the biographies by Elizabeth's descendant Catherine Drinker Bowen, Ernesta's younger sister, dealt principally with Bostonians: Holmes, Adams, *et al.*)[17]

William Bullitt and Ernesta Drinker were married in the chapel of Lehigh University, of which the father of the bride, a kind and decent man, was president; it was a fine wedding, with an Episcopal bishop at the altar. To some extent both groom and bride were exceptions in their families: the brilliant impetuosity of Bill remained without peer among the Bullitts, while Ernesta stood out among Drinkers, not only because of her great beauty, but also because of her sophisticated worldliness. Her breezy and often perceptive diary of the fascinating journey they undertook in the middle of Europe in 1916 attests

16 See pp. 115–16. Not that William Bullitt and Agnes Repplier had much sympathy for each other: see p. 212.

17 Two of their brothers made their careers as scientists at Harvard, another as a rock-ribbed Republican lawyer in Philadelphia. Their avocations, traits of their mind and face, their very looks have been New England, until this day.

not only to her perceptiveness[18] but also to her early affection
for her young husband. Even then one may glimpse, here and
there, a faintly patronizing (and, as yet, faintly amused) attitude
toward "Billy," running and bounding with energy.[19] She saw
him, as most of her family saw him, and as indeed many Philadelphians saw him, in the way his name rang: "Bill" Bullitt,
that strong-willed, bullet-headed Bullitt, so often like a bull in
so many a china shop. He, in turn, took pride in her serenity,
in her sense of proportion and of taste, in the perfection of her
decorativeness, in her savoir-faire, which glowed—glowed,
rather than glistened—at the stateliest dinners in Versailles or
in great country houses in England. But he found her somewhat selfish detachment very difficult. They did not have
children. Bullitt wanted children very much. After six years
their marriage broke up.

And now we come to the essential paradox in the rhythm of
William Bullitt's life. We have seen that his public career was
not only exceptionally interesting and full of dramatic episodes
but that it was as well the career of a strong and rebellious man.
It had two phases: the early, promising, though rapidly frustrated, rise of Bullitt during the last years of the First World
War; and his new career, under Roosevelt, on a high and po-
tentially more important level, in the years before and during
the Second World War, ending again in failure, in part because
of his rebellious character. These two phases were separated
by thirteen years of self-imposed exile from public affairs. Yet
it was during these thirteen years that his private life, full of

18 Example: Count Széchenyi, the Austro-Hungarian minister to Denmark:
"I played tennis with him this afternoon at the club, he in his suspenders and
monocle, and I in street clothes, with a pair of borrowed tennis shoes two inches
too long on my feet, and a racket like a spoon, as a means of defense, in my
hand." *Op. cit.*, p. 11. A vignette of a certain period.

19 Example: A picture exhibition in Berlin, June 1916: "There was one picture of the fall of Maubeuge which Billy insisted he was going to buy. It was at
least twelve by fifteen feet and I had the most dreadful time persuading him
that proud Frenchmen in red trousers and relentless, strong-looking Germans
wouldn't do in full size in a private house." *Ibid.*, p. 31.

turmoil, was as interesting and creative as ever, that he was, true to himself, as much a rebel as at any other time during his life, perhaps even more so. And by private life I mean not so much family affairs or sexual adventures but something that is, at the same time, more evident and also more profound: the life of a man's mind.

Bullitt, I repeat, was an idealist of sorts—a rebel idealist who thoroughly disliked intellectual dishonesty, stiffness, social rigidity, financial greed, pretense.[20] He, who was at ease in all kinds of society, disliked the fearful hypocrisies and the grim rigidities of an age and place where distinctions of wealth had grown dominant over distinctions of birth. He had a very cavalier attitude toward money, of which he had plenty, though less than his enemies attributed to him. He despised the narrow-mindedness and selfishness of the rich.[21] This may have been the main reason for the interest Bullitt had in certain Communists. We have seen that he had few illusions about the Soviet Russian regime, and that even these illusions he dropped years, and even decades, before American statesmen of great and durable reputation would do so. Yet he had a sympathy for certain rebels, for young people who maintained an idealistic interest in the early Communist experiment, for men and women who, somewhat like himself, saw through the hypocrisies and superficialities of a society of materialists. He liked John Reed, even though Bullitt was, from the very beginning, much more skeptical of the Bolsheviks' virtues than Reed in

---

[20] He wrote to Judge Moore from Moscow in 1936: "You will, I think, understand me without further explanation, as you know me thoroughly. The appeal that an ambassadorship has for most Americans leaves me completely cold. I had so much international social life as a child and young man that I know its emptiness as well as any American concerned with politics. It is perhaps a weakness not to care about prestige and position but I simply do not. The work to be done is the thing that counts." 8 April 1936, Orville Bullitt, *op. cit.*, p. 158.

[21] Letter to Roosevelt from Paris, 24 October 1936: "The aristocracy and the upper bourgeoisie are just as dumb here as their opposite numbers in the United States." Orville Bullitt, *op. cit.*, p. 73.

his *Ten Days That Shook the World.* He was a wiser man than Reed (even though Reed was the older man by a few years), but he also saw in Reed a fellow rebel, a wide-eyed and youthful fellow American.[22]

In 1923—three years after Reed's death, and a year after Bullitt's divorce—Bullitt married John Reed's widow. This marriage, unlike his first one, was not at all promising: it was bound to end in disaster.

Conventional as her upbringing and family may have been, Ernesta Drinker was not a conventionally typical person of her class. Louise Bryant, I am sorry to say, was. She was an American bohemian: a type that was beginning to surface in the United States around 1912.[23] An early divorcée, a pioneer of Modern Womanhood in the shallowly rooted society of the West Coast, with some Irish blood in her veins, Louise Bryant was a Modern Intellectual, a believer in Free Love, Female Suffrage, Artistic Movements, Abstract Painting, and Radical Bohemianism, it matters not which: an attractive female in a somewhat common way, with her large glistening eyes; an early denizen of Greenwich Village, of Mabel Dodge's circle, of the *Masses* magazine, of the Provincetown Players (she had an affair with Eugene O'Neill *circa* 1915, at the same time as her more tempestuous affair with John Reed): the kind of social intellectual who believes that she is beyond conventions and traditional classes, belonging not to a class of birth or of wealth but of opinion, taking self-conscious satisfaction in having acquired ideas that are different from those of the common herd of men and women—in short, a conventional type, running true to form. But this William Bullitt did not then know.

Her rebellious side appealed to him. Conversely, the unconventional side of Bullitt appealed to Louise Bryant: she saw in

---

[22] He put flowers on Reed's grave even when he returned to Moscow as the anti-Stalinist ambassador. He had to go to some trouble to arrange this. It is recorded that on the occasion his eyes filmed over with tears.

[23] A date designated by certain American intellectual historians as that of the Little Renaissance. It was very little indeed.

him not only a worldly man but a potential bohemian, in which she was wrong. Their marriage endured for a while: there were bonds of attraction. Physically, Louise Bryant was an earthy woman; the sensuous charm of her sometimes slatternly appearance was probably very attractive after the classic toilettes of his first wife. For a year they lived an exquisitely romantic existence on the Bosporus. There was the scent of Turkish cigarettes; of roses in wild profusion; of her flowing cambric gowns. Throughout her life she had an appetite for men younger than she; Bullitt was four years her junior, which she of course denied. There was the bond of their child, Anne, born in the first year of their marriage. Bullitt may have been poor material for a husband, but he was an extremely devoted father. It was probably a mark of his then still strong devotion to his wife that Anne's middle name was Moën, after Louise's father.[24] In 1925 he settled down to write, of all things, a novel, to which we shall return: it was simply and clearly "dedicated to Louise Bryant, my wife." Yet they separated the year of the novel's publication. Louise drank more and more; she was no longer slatternly on occasion, she was becoming unkempt. Ernesta was a woman habitually, and perhaps unduly, careful of her appearances; Louise was habitually, and surely unduly, careless of her disappearances. There were ugly scenes. Bullitt, with all his rebel character, had grown impatient and weary of the pretensions and the cultivated naïvetés of the bohemian-intellectual world. It had not taken him long to see through John Reed's friends; it did not take him long to see through those of John Reed's widow. He, who could see the crude and hard realities of Stalin's people long before other men had done so, soon saw the weak and insubstantial realities of Greenwich Village people. Some people, including the shallow biographer of Louise Bryant,[25] described Bullitt as "cold." This was far from the truth. He was, simply, not a man who would fool him-

[24] His name, in reality, was Mohan.
[25] Barbara Gelb, *So Short a Time* (New York, 1973).

self for long. Louise was evidently unhappy with their life. In 1930 they were divorced.[26] He asked for, and received, custody of their daughter: a fact which suggests something about his, as well as her, relationship to their only child.[27] He would never marry again; no matter how vibrant and exceptional was his desire for fatherhood, he had no other child.

It was providential that this extremely sordid and painful ending of Bullitt's second marriage was soon to be followed by his second great opportunity to enter the service of his country in its relations with some of the great powers of the world. He had brief affairs with a number of women, having little trouble attracting them with his magnetic personality. One of his mistresses, the wife of a painter, he took along to Moscow, where her official function was to be governess of the ambassador's daughter. There are many photographs from the Moscow-embassy years showing father and daughter together; the mistress-governess appears in none of the pictures, at least in none that I have seen. Whatever amatory experiences Bullitt may have had in Paris were tactful and discreet: the social and aesthetic, not to speak of the culinary and oenologic, record of his Paris embassy compares favorably with that of most of the great British ambassadors on the Faubourg St.-Honoré, a walk away. He was a brilliant and considerate host, whether in Moscow or in Paris or in Philadelphia or on his farm in Massachusetts.

In the finely wrought introduction to the Bullitt-Roosevelt correspondence, George Kennan, who knew William Bullitt intimately, wrote:

---

[26] Even Gelb writes (p. 291) that Bullitt "had been so humiliated by Louise's behavior that he had insisted that the papers in the divorce case be sealed."

[27] Louise sank deeper and deeper, ending her life virtually in the gutter, in Paris, at the age of forty-nine, having destroyed her health by drink and drugs. This happened but a few months before her former husband was to arrive in Paris at the outset of the finest chapter in his career. She remained proud of the large sapphire ring from which she would never part, a relic from a Bullitt grandmother.

· *William Christian Bullitt* ·

I see Bill Bullitt, in retrospect, as a member of that remarkable group of young Americans, born just before the turn of
the century (it included such people as Cole Porter, Ernest
Hemingway, John Reed, and Jim Forrestal—many of them his
friends) for whom the First World War was the great electri-
fying experience of life. They were a striking generation, full
of talent and exuberance, determined—if one may put it so—
to make life come alive. The mark they made on American
culture will be there when many other marks have faded. But
in most of them there seems to have been a touch of the fate,
if not the person, of the Great Gatsby. Like Edna Millay, they
burned their candles at both ends. The civilization of the
1930's and 1940's was not strong enough to support their
weight. They knew achievement more often than they knew
fulfillment; and their ends, like those of Bullitt himself, tended
to be frustrating, disappointing, and sometimes tragic.[28]

There is a great deal of truth in this assessment. Yet Bullitt's
energy was extraordinary. We have seen that in 1932, when he
was more than forty years old, with the wreckage of many ambitions, of two marriages, of an ephemeral literary career behind him, he re-entered public life, accepting the high assignment given him by Roosevelt with zest and enthusiasm, a
dynamism and optimism characteristic of youth. The record
of his achievements and of his mental abilities during those
Rooseveltian years is eloquent proof that Bullitt remained
healthily unaffected by the great American disease of a promising and celebrated early career that burns out fast. His mind
as well as his energies were still at their peak when he was fifty
years old. He wrote some of the best, and most enduring, as-
sessments of world affairs in his memoranda at that time.

His candle may have been a fast-burning one; it certainly
gave out much heat as well as light. All through his life he
allowed himself to be propelled by his own illusions, which he
would not hide under a bushel. He idolized Roosevelt. Eventually he turned away from him, though not until Roosevelt had

28 Orville Bullitt, *op. cit.*, p. xvi.

disappointed him, personally as well as politically. He had much less in common with Wilson. Then the swing from idealization to disillusionment was shorter and more violent. Yet his mind was both strong and restless enough to seek an explanation for his disillusionment. He sought for a reason, for some kind of deep-seated flaw in Wilson's character, which would explain the weakness of that President.

A comparison of Bullitt's and Freud's contributions to their book on Wilson may be of interest here. It took them nine years to complete the book, for many reasons, including their disagreements.[29] In 1938, after Hitler had conquered Austria, Bullitt was instrumental in helping Freud leave Vienna. The Ambassador came to welcome Freud at the Gare de l'Est in Paris. Thereafter he went to see him twice in London. It is perhaps significant that most of their disagreements involved additional passages to the text written by Freud, not by Bullitt. Now the aged Freud, in the last year of his life, consented to eliminate many of these additions.

When, almost thirty years later, the book was finally published, most critics suggested that it was all too much Bullitt and all too little Freud. This was untrue in one sense; and yet true in another. It was untrue, because each chapter of the book[30] had been carefully read and worked over by both authors; each of them wished to attest to this fact by signing each chapter individually and jointly. It was true because the structure and the very style of the book reflects much more of Bullitt than of Freud. It has nothing in common with Freud's

[29] "Both Freud and I were stubborn, and our beliefs were dissimilar. He was a Jew who had become an agnostic. I have always been a believing Christian. We often disagreed but we never quarreled. On the contrary, the more we worked together, the closer friends we became. In the spring of 1932, however, when our manuscript was ready to be typed in final form, Freud made several textual changes and wrote a number of passages to which I objected. After several arguments we decided to forget the book for three weeks, and to attempt then to agree. When we met, we continued to disagree." *Ibid.*, p. viii.

[30] Except for the first—and crucially important—thirty-page chapter, rather modestly entitled "Digest of Data [it is far more than that] on the Childhood and Youth of Thomas Woodrow Wilson," signed by William C. Bullitt.

celebrated studies of Leonardo and Michelangelo, even though the analysis and treatment of Wilson's inner life in this book is essentially unabashedly Freudian. The terms "libido," "super-ego," "repression," "father complex," etc., occur throughout the text, the principal thesis of which is that Thomas Woodrow Wilson throughout his life was dominated by the image of his father: a classic and categorical case of the so-called Oedipus complex.

Notwithstanding Bullitt's acceptance of the Freudian categories—and notwithstanding their shared dislike of Wilson[31]— Bullitt's own thinking was very different from Freud's. Freud was principally interested in Wilson's psyche. Bullitt was principally interested in Wilson's character. "Character" is a word that Freud eschewed during his career. Yet it is no less a reality for that. A man is not only what he is; a man is also what he becomes. He is not only a product of his psychic past, but also a more-or-less conscious creator of his *persona*. By employing the tool of Freudian categories, Bullitt thought that he probed deeper than had others, finding thereby some of the roots of Wilson's incomplete manhood and of his subsequent tragedy. Yet what Bullitt considered as the profound essence of this book is, in reality, its superficial element: its superstructure, so to speak. Bullitt's citations of Wilson's words, his descriptions of some of Wilson's actions and personal traits are illustrations of his own sharp insights into Wilson's character. They are illustrations which do not merely underline a thesis: their selection and their presentation and their juxtaposition are more telling, and more important, than the thesis itself. It is like a painting whose value lies mainly in those features that came to the

---

[31] From the introduction by Freud: "I must . . . commence my contribution to the psychological study of Thomas Woodrow Wilson with the confession that the figure of the American President, as it rose above the horizon of Europeans, was from the beginning unsympathetic to me, and that this aversion increased in the course of years the more I learned about him and the more severely we suffered from the consequences of his intrusion into our destiny." *Ibid.*, p. xi. Bullitt and Wilson: their characters, their physiognomies, their temperaments, their backgrounds, their appetites, their inclinations were not only divergent but also wholly antithetical.

painter with natural ease, and that have little to do with the kind of technique that the painter wished to emphasize.

Where Bullitt succeeded, he succeeded in spite of, rather than because of, the Freudian categories which—as he erroneously thought—furnished the basic structure of his own thinking. While on the one hand he found it necessary, again and again, to point at the evidence of certain deep complexes within Wilson, his way of stating the evidence is something quite different from the cramped prose of psychoanalysts and psychohistorians. Bullitt accumulated fifteen hundred pages of typed notes by 1932. Yet the book contains no footnotes, and it is devoid of jargon. Most of Bullitt's evidence consists of Wilson's own words. There are no hypothetical data or facts of the kind that habitually disfigure the lucubrations of psychohistorians. Moreover, in spite of his avowed emphasis on the importance of the unconscious mind, Bullitt was very much aware of the influences in the formation of the conscious mind —as, for example, when he wrote about the kind of nonconformist mental atmosphere that was decisive in Wilson's case, and which Freud, who did not know enough about Americans, would neither know nor understand. For instance, Bullitt wrote that Wilson's nature "was admirably fitted to the civilization and class into which he was born." "He was fortunate to have been born [among people who were] protected from reality during the nineteenth century by inherited devotion to the ideals of Wyclif, Calvin, and Wesley."[32] "In all his recorded words there is no sign that he understood French, German, or Italian civilization, to say nothing of the classic Greek . . . Woodrow Wilson excluded Jefferson entirely from a *Calendar of Great Americans* which he drew up in 1894, on the ground that 'Jefferson was not a thorough American because of the strain of French philosophy in his thought.' . . . He found France, Italy, and Germany so distasteful when he ventured onto the continent for the first time in 1903, that he fled home

[32] Freud and Bullitt, *op. cit.*, pp. 70–71.

after a few weeks. He did not return to the continent until 1919, when he arrived to rearrange Europe. His conscious mind remained all his life the mind of a North British Presbyterian Minister."[33] *His conscious mind*: the matter about which Bullitt thought and wrote best. And when we add to all of this the evidence of Bullitt's clear and manly style,[34] we ought to conclude that the book, far from being worthless, is in reality indispensable for anyone who wants to know something about Wilson—even though it must be read with discernment and caution.

Its avowed "method" may be of little worth. Yet Bullitt's prose reflects more than a method: it reflects Bullitt's wide knowledge of his subject, as well as his powers of insight and expression. It was published merely a year or so before the truly worthless and pretentious fad of "psychohistory" attracted the attention of American academics and publishers on the make. Its writing and its conception preceded the psychological biographizing of American Presidents by more than thirty years. It is what its title says: "a psychological study" of Wilson. In this respect, too, Bullitt was ahead of his time. But he had to pay, again and again, the price of intellectual independence. He was a lonely man.

There was one personal attachment that lightened the burdens of his existence during the last thirty-two years of his life. Shortly after his arrival in Moscow he wrote to the Department of State: "Send me a secretary who can stand me and can stand Russia." At first sight Carmel Offie was an unlikely candidate, the son of poor Italian immigrants from a mining district in Pennsylvania. He turned out to be one of the greatest assets that a restless and dynamic man could acquire: competent, highly intelligent, versatile, tactful, and utterly loyal. Within a few

---

[33] *Ibid.*, pp. 107–8.

[34] Examples of vintage Bullitt: About 1919: "The propaganda [Wilson] had loosed on America through his friend George Creel had had its effect. The American people had been whipped into a hatred of Germany and Russia. The dowagers were mewing for blood" (p. 246). At least Clemenceau "did not smear the demands of France with British moral marmalade" (p. 276).

months after his arrival in Moscow, Offie had become a secretary, a confidant, and a friend; Bullitt put him in charge of his finances, which was not an easy thing, to say the least. Within a year of his arrival in Paris, Offie was one of the favorite companions of the Duchess of Windsor at the bridge table.[35] Certain people, including British diplomats, resented him. To William Bullitt, he was a blessing.

Offie eased many of the burdens of this restless man even after the Second World War, when Bullitt, for the second time in his life, was an exile from politics and world affairs, a Cassandra not only deeply frustrated in his ambitions but also powerless in face of what he saw as the decline in the power and glory of his country and of the entire civilization of the Western world. There were other public anti-Communists who acted as if they had been vindicated by the belated turn of the American government in the direction of anti-Communism a few years after the war. Bullitt found no satisfaction in this. He had buried his ambitions. He had laid down his pen. Yet what a book he could have written! A great American autobiography, on the level of Henry Adams or of the first volume of the *Memoirs* of George Kennan, with a touch of Hemingway. For, among other things, this self-centered man was a writer. By this I do not only mean that, on occasion, books written by Bullitt were bought by commercial publishers and printed for the public,[36] and not only that his writing—exemplified, among others, in his diplomatic dispatches, memoranda, and letters to Roosevelt—was marked by a style that was direct, muscular, and clear: *le style, c'est l'homme même*, after all. More impor-

---

[35] Bullitt's letter to Judge Moore, 5 October 1936: "You will be pleased to learn that last night Offie was the guest of honor at Maxim's at a dinner given by the Marquise and Marquis de Polignac, who are the greatest snobs in France. Inasmuch as the Polignacs habitually ignore everyone from this Embassy, including the Ambassadors, I think you will agree with me that our child is already going fast and far. The Marquise herself drove him home at midnight." Orville Bullitt, *op. cit.*, pp. 171–72.

[36] They include: *The Bullitt Mission to Russia* (New York, 1919); *It's Not Done* (New York, 1926); *Report to the American People* (Boston, 1940); *The Great Globe Itself* (New York, 1946).

tant is the condition that, at times, William Bullitt wanted to be a writer; he wanted to excel as a writer; and in this endeavor he seems to have been propelled less by vanity than by the conviction that he had certain things to say, certain things that he had seen that were worth seeing and telling about. Within Bullitt the rebel, there was at least a touch of Bullitt the artist. He had a contempt for all kinds of opportunism, perhaps especially for that manifested by the deadening conventionalities of certain habits of mind.

And there was *It's Not Done.*

IT'S NOT DONE is an extraordinary document, for at least two reasons. Like most novels, and especially like first novels by beginning writers, it is thoroughly self-centered and auto-biographical, suffused with all kinds of clues to its author's likes and dislikes, to his mental life; in sum, to his character. The second reason—surely for the purposes of this book—may be more important than the first. The novel is about Philadelphia; and it is a novel of manners.

We shall see that the number of novels written about Philadelphia is astonishingly small.[37] Now, this is an extraordinary fact, since Philadelphia is one of the very few places in the United States where an established, interior, private, and mannered society has existed, with its own conventions and idiosyncrasies, a society composed principally of families, in some ways comparable to the patrician and bourgeois societies whose existence, in England and Europe, was a precondition for the emergence and the flourishing of the literary form of the novel. For the modern novel differs from the epic not only because it is composed in prose and not in poetry; it is a form of narrative that is inseparable from the existence of a certain society; its subject is always the relationship of certain men and women, not only to each other, but also to the framework of society; the modern novel is, inevitably, a kind of sociography; the modern

[37] See pp. 66, 208, 255–56.

novel is a novel of manners. *It's Not Done* could be the title of most of the great novels of two centuries, from Goethe and Jane Austen to Lampedusa and Proust. *It's Not Done*: Bullitt's very title—again we encounter the Bullitt bull among the china cups and saucers—expresses this with a blunt, American, sloganeering fury.

For a Philadelphian, no matter how much of a rebel, to write a novel—worse, a *roman à clef*—about Philadelphians, it wasn't done. Bullitt did it. It is the only considerable novel of manners about Philadelphia.[38] It is considerable not so much because of its literary qualities (they exist, even though they are very uneven) but because of its documentary essence, written by someone who knew how to express himself (even though the talent of self-expression, contrary to current beliefs, is not the equivalent of literature), and who knew what he was writing about: a novel by a self-exiled rebel, but nonetheless one by an insider.

John Corsey, the son of an old Philadelphia family, preternaturally proud of (and a trifle too self-conscious about) the Corsey ancestry: people of high gentlefolk, of Franco-Norman-English origins (Corsey/Courcey) who have never bowed to anyone, including kings. The Corceys live on Rittenhouse Square (they have a large estate in the suburbs). *Everyone* lives on Rittenhouse Square. (In one sense, the book *is* about Rittenhouse Square.)[39] The usual thing happens.[40] John Corsey falls

---

[38] With the partial exception of *Kitty Foyle,* by Christopher Morley (1929). Two Biddles followed Bullitt: the *Llanfair Pattern* (1927) by Francis Biddle, and three novels written by his nephew, Livingston Biddle, Jr., in the 1950s. Their thesis— young love and art thwarted by conventional society—is similar to Bullitt's; their documentary quality is not.

[39] The Bullitt mansion, where William Christian Bullitt, Jr., was born, stood on Rittenhouse Square, on the southwest corner of Nineteenth and Locust Streets. Two apartment houses have replaced it. During his absences from Philadelphia, Bullitt kept his Philadelphia address as that of the Rittenhouse Club (1811 Walnut Street). His opponents used this fact against him in the 1943 election.

[40] Usual, that is, in most of the above-mentioned Philadelphia novels. The hero falls in love with a beautiful girl from the lower classes, that is, outside the bounds of social respectability. In the end they will not marry. Love will occur, even in Philadelphia, but triumph it will not. *Philadelphia vincit amor.*

in love with Nina, the daughter of a French painter, urchin, bohemian, unconventional, artistic, and proud. Yet he marries Mildred, a proper Philadelphian. They have a son. The *nouveaux riches* appear. John Corsey decides to go into the newspaper business. The old families begin selling out to the *nouveaux riches*. Everybody knows everybody. It is all like Guermantes and Verdurins, at times even better. Mildred Corsey is a cold woman. John Corsey is ardent. Love within marriage dies. Their son, a volunteer, dies a hero's death in France (as it appears later, almost despite himself). Corsey goes to Washington, where the plot is enlivened by his affair with a titian-haired woman who turns out to be (or whose maid turns out to be) a German spy. He finds Nina in Paris, after all those years (she had refused to accept his secret remittances). He finds that they have a son, Raoul, an attractive young Frenchman, now an idealistic Communist. Raoul comes to Philadelphia, where he is beaten and arrested by the police. John Corsey succeeds in springing him from jail. He meets Nina, who is still beautiful, but who refuses to marry him. He sells his newspaper. He returns to his wife, a broken man. He accepts an appointment as ambassador to Rome. They leave Philadelphia, the Square, their house. It is 1921.

The cold wife, the fiery devotion to their only child, the contempt for the new rich and for their greedy conventions, the attraction to a woman who is an artist, half-French, proud and individual, the sympathy for a young radical (who turns out to be a natural son), the dislike of American Anglomaniacs, of the British, of Wilson, of certain pushy Jews, the life story of an aristocratic rebel who is burnt out, defeated, acquiescing in the end (he is not yet beyond middle age) in the restoration of a lifeless marriage and in an honorable appointment without much meaning, of a man who leaves Rittenhouse Square and Philadelphia behind, perhaps forever—it is all Bill Bullitt, his personality, the story of his mind, almost to the last jot and tittle, including his intuitive, often incisive, and, for his place and period, extraordinary intelligence about sexual matters.

It's Not Done is outspoken about such matters, without lapsing
into explicit descriptions or crude verbiage: the sexual conflicts
are drawn with strong lines, including a finely rendered scene
of a temporary sexual fiasco, and yet within the proportions of
taste: a not inconsiderable achievement. But *It's Not Done* is
also a document about the society of Philadelphia. It is a classic
roman à clef. Philadelphia is "Chesterbridge." "Roediger" is
John Wanamaker. "Leather" is Widener. "General Bluck" is
Tasker Bliss. "Miss Tarrington" is Agnes Repplier. "Bobby"
is William's younger brother, Orville, etc., etc. Early in the
book the young Nina asks the young John Corsey:

> "What on earth can you like in Chesterbridge?"
> "Everything. It's certainly the only place to live in America."
> "Why live in America?"
> "Oh, come on, Nina, don't be silly. There's no place else to
> live but England. And Chesterbridge has everything that the
> best life in England has. Fine hunting. Loads of nice, well-
> bred people. And I have a position here that I couldn't have
> in England unless my father were the Duke of Norfolk. I don't
> want to throw away . . ."[41]

Twenty years later—it is Philadelphia, 1921—he writes his
brother, Theodore Lord Corsey, in England (whom he had
earlier excoriated for having renounced his Americanship)[42]:

> Chesterbridge had changed, and I don't like the changes.
> Half the people I have respected and liked have moved into
> Hillcrest Cemetery, and I don't like the people who have taken

---

41 *It's Not Done,* p. 88.
42 Theodore: "But I've established myself in England."
       "Do you really like it here, Ted? Do you really
like being an expatriate?"
       "I put it the other way," Theodore smiled tolerantly.
"I've come home after a sojourn in the Colonies."
       "A damned long sojourn: three hundred years. And
do they really accept you here?"
       "Of course."
       "When are you going to get a title?"
       "When the King is gracious enough to—"
  Ibid., p. 236.

their places. I suppose you know that John Collingwood[43] died last week. (A funeral like the Concourse[44] before 1900. Everyone here, eight tenants from his country place bearing the coffin and weeping as if their hearts were broken . . .) He's dead and the town is being run by Leather, Roediger, Yenks, Lowden, *et al* . . .[45]

It is a story of defeat, of resignation, of self-chosen exile. Before him looms the rest of his life, formal and cold. Mildred would be a proper hostess at the embassy. Both Mildred and John Corsey are burnt out, even though their carriage is still erect. Their limousine leaves the Square for the station. It "passed the marble portico of Aunt Gertrude Carrollton's house, the marble steps of Fulke Greville's, the granite of the Club." Suddenly Mildred remembers something that their chief butler told them the day before: there is a large leak developing on the roof:

> "Oh well, let it go," he said. "We'll probably never come back here anyway."
> Children were skating between the trim beds of hyacinths and tulips, and the shadow of the apartment house was creeping slowly across the Square.

This is the last sentence of the book, toward the end of which that creeping shadow is part of the story, and not only a symbol.[46]

It's Not Done, long forgotten now, is a novel by an amateur. At the time of its appearance it was something of a *succès de scandale*; it had at least seventeen printings in two years. Cer-

---

43 John Cadwalader.
44 The Assembly.
45 *It's Not Done*, p. 306.
46 In the novel, the apartment-house skyscraper—the first on Rittenhouse Square—while being erected progressively, reduces the light from the front of the Corseys' house, including John Corsey's bathroom, where he has the habit of shaving naked each morning. One day he receives a letter from a Jewish financier-speculator, "Strauss," the owner of the apartment house, informing Corsey that one of their tenants is shocked as he is confronted with the sight of an unclothed man.

tain Philadelphians went around trying to buy up copies. Surely it contributed to Bullitt's reputation: unsteady, willful, rebellious, indiscreet; in sum: un-Philadelphian.[47] The novel passed out of the stream of the literary traffic as well as from the consciousness of people a few years after its publication. I read it twice, nearly a quarter of a century apart. It does not improve by rereading. Yet I was charmed by some of its contents. It is, I repeat, an extraordinary document.

The course of lives is, almost always, stranger than is the course of fiction. Bullitt wrote his novel *nel mezzo del cammin*, at midpoint of his first chapter of self-chosen exile, in his mid-thirties, when his second, impulsively contracted, marriage was about to crumble. In *It's Not Done* the girl artist, who gave him a son in secret, refuses to go away with the hero or to marry him. Bullitt married the bohemian woman who had come into his life; he dedicated a book to her. The hero of *It's Not Done* resigns himself to an empty marriage and to an ambassadorship of no further promise; his eyes gaze upon the prospect of chilling years down the line of a cold marble corridor. We have seen that the opposite happened. Six years after his novel he was given an ambassadorship which he accepted with eagerness. Yet the fatal disharmony between the rhythm of his private life and of his public career was to prevail.

His potential services to his country, and to his city, remained great. Yet he was heading straight toward obscurity. "Burke," said Fox, "is a wise man; but he is wise too soon." This apothegm applies to William Bullitt. He was wise too soon; and he was not content with his own wisdom. He wanted people to see what he saw. At his worst, he could be insufferably self-centered, to the extent of vengefulness; at his best, he would not temper his views to the prevailing winds of publicity, or to the political climate of the day. When the opportunity arose

---

[47] His brother wrote him a decade or so later, after *The New Yorker* had published a rather superficial profile of William Bullitt by "Genêt": "The only thing left for you is to stand at Broad and Chestnut Streets and brush your teeth in public." Orville Bullitt, *op. cit.*, p. xliv.

for him to point at the record of his own statements and say, "I told you so," he chose not to do it—whether because of pride or of weariness, we cannot tell. In Philadelphia *It's Not Done* haunted Bullitt's reputation for many years. During his race for the mayoralty in 1943 it was held against him by conservatives as well as by liberals. Certain passages were lifted out of context, slyly and falsely suggesting, among other things, that Bullitt was anti-Semitic. His program for Philadelphia was wise and far-seeing: many of its items were to figure in the program of the reform Democrats seven or eight years later.

Bullitt lived to see the global application of the philosophy of Wilsonianism, which has marked so much of the foreign policy of this Republic during the last sixty-five years with regrettable and often disastrous consequence. He chose not to publish the Wilson book while Mrs. Wilson was still alive. It was published in 1966, twenty-seven years after the death of Bullitt's famous collaborator. It was buried in ignominy. Unlike *It's Not Done*, it was dismissed by critics immediately after its publication, and not only in Philadelphia. Less than two months after its publication, William Christian Bullitt was dead.

To many Philadelphians he remained an embarrassment throughout his life. He was, by temperament, an aristocrat as much as a patrician. He was an individualist. He may have done a few things that were not done; he certainly said many things that were not being said. Yet he wanted to come back to Philadelphia, indeed to the Square. He was buried in 1967 from Holy Trinity Church, in that brownstone Episcopalian edifice still standing on the corner of a transformed Rittenhouse Square and Walnut. Many Old Philadelphians were there at the burial. He wanted to be laid next to his father in Woodlands Cemetery. His brother took great care to conform to his wishes. Even after the burial he had to deal with a contretemps. An article appeared in a Philadelphia newspaper, informing the public that William Christian Bullitt had become a convert and entered the Roman Catholic Church shortly before his death.

It mentioned a Father Guthrie to this effect. It is true that during the last twenty years of his life Bullitt found many illuminating things in the Roman Catholic Church, and perhaps especially in its teachings about unchanging human nature. Yet the article about his conversion was untrue. Orville Bullitt insisted that the newspaper print a retraction by Father Guthrie, corresponding in space and position to the place of the original news item. This was done.[48]

William Bullitt was one of the last representatives of a certain breed. George Kennan wrote about him in his *Memoirs*, at a time when Bullitt was still living: "His was outstandingly a buoyant disposition. He resolutely refused to permit the life around him to degenerate into dullness and dreariness. All of us who lived in his entourage were the beneficiaries of this blitheness of spirit, this insistence that life be at all times animated and interesting and moving ahead." Bullitt and some of his friends may have burned their candles on both ends; but, in any event, the great American tragedy remains that of waste: the waste of great assets, of gifts, including personal talent. Much of that is wasted not by the actual possessors but by the potential recipients. The people of his native city rejected William Bullitt: eventually they would chose men such as Frank Rizzo for their mayor. Presidents and powerful men in Washington preferred to spurn Bullitt's advice and not to employ his talents: eventually their successors would put forth such men as Kissinger for the premier American statesman of an age. Yet it was men such as Bullitt who carried within themselves both the vision and the force of the age, of the *Pax Americana* of the twentieth century. Now that the dream has dissolved, we may contemplate the wreckage and the waste: the wreckage of great American opportunities and the waste of great American talent.

[48] *The Catholic Standard and Times*, the Philadelphia archdiocesan newspaper, refused to print a denial, since it would have meant the public repudiation of a priest.

SIX

GEORGE WHARTON PEPPER

OR

The Patrician as Pharisee

G. PEPPER *of Penn. is a model for men;*
  A bulwark in peace or in war,
With character rounded and solidly founded
  On learning and logic and law.
When Senators bicker of tariff and liquor,
  As Senators will now and then,
The speediest stepper is certainly Pepper,
  George Wharton Pepper of Penn.

Let me further explain that in spite of his brain
  He's an athlete, as every one knows,
And if questions logistic evolve toward the fistic
  He's always right there on his toes.
With multiple talents of brain power and Balance
  Who is there, I ask, in the Sen.
Who can stack up with Pepper, the mental Mazeppa,
  George Wharton Pepper, of Penn.!

THIS DOGGEREL, written by George S. Chappell, appeared in the old *Life* magazine in 1925, beneath a sketch by Robert James Malone, and a fair representation of George Wharton Pepper that sketch is. It shows a vigorous worthy, of the fortunate breed to whom the adjective "of middle age" does not truly apply since it is simply a continuation of his youth. (In 1925 he was fifty-

eight years old.) The drawing is that of a paragon of energy. His
mustache is trimmed, and so is his hair; his pipe is sturdily
clenched between his undoubtedly strong and healthy teeth.
It could be the drawing of a British brigadier in mufti, were it
not for the typically American marks of Pepper: his stovepipe
flannels, so tight as to be wrinkled around his columnar legs;
his button-down shirt; his saddle shoes, those shoes which he
sported, day after day, in the solemn, cavernous halls of the
United States Senate. The sketch (and the poem) express the
principal characteristics of his personality. They are Pennsylvanian; and they are collegiate.

He was an embodiment of his name: the old-Philadelphian
bourdon sound of Wharton and the speedily stepping Pepper,
his name fitting into his time with a recognizable click, "Pep"
having been a Theodore-Roosevelt-period word, more Eastern
and chronologically fixable than "zip." (The Oxford English
Dictionary dates its appearance as 1915:"U.S. Vigour, energy,
'go.'") In 1915 Pepper volunteered for the Plattsburg Camp,
for that paradigmatic institution of Rooseveltian Pep, in the
service of National Preparedness. He wired his friend Henry
Stimson, whose reply came back in a zip, in peppy period prose:
"Bully for you! You are a thoroughbred." There exists a photograph of Pepper, twenty-five years later, from the Republican
National Convention of 1940, printed in Pepper's autobiography with the caption: "Putting Pep Into It." That, too, is a
period picture: there is George Wharton Pepper, with his white
mustache, his face glowing as he lets out a shout, cheered and
clapped on by the smiling men and attractive women of the
Philadelphia suburban wards. He is whooping it up, the Republican patrician in the role of the politician, in the heat of
the convention hall at night, whirling his coat jacket above his
head, his trousers suspended by his thin Brooks Brothers braces,
the circus-like multiple parade badges of the Republican delegate affixed to his white shirt and the Phi Beta Kappa key in a
definite little loop out of his watch pocket, over a stomach whose

circumference is remarkably spare for a man of seventy-three.

His life was unbroken, a story of steady accomplishments, recognitions, success. George Wharton Pepper was born at 1215 Walnut Street, in 1867, at the very center of what was then prosperous and social Philadelphia. When his father died his mother took him to live in a small house on South Sixteenth Street with his grandmother. He entered the University of Pennsylvania, with which his Pepper family connections were exceptionally close. The Class Prophecy "predicted that he would be the John Wanamaker and the George W. Childs of his day, the Mayor of Philadelphia and a writer of books."[1]

He was very collegiate, "Bowl Man" (most popular) of his class. He founded *The Pennsylvanian* newspaper for the campus, and was its first editor in chief. At the age of twenty-six he was made Professor of Law. In 1900, at the age of thirty-three, he was listed in the national *Who's Who*. He married respectably, and he earned a great deal of money. He was not yet forty when he began to be named to the boards of one respectable Philadelphia institution after another. In 1922 Governor Sproul appointed him to finish out the dead Penrose's term in the United States Senate. He was elected the next year, though not in 1926. After that he no longer chose to seek national office; he was satisfied in being elected president of the Pennsylvania Bar Association, and subsequently of the Philadelphia Bar Association. He was seventy-seven when he wrote *Philadelphia Lawyer*, his autobiography; the title, the style, the illustrations, the publisher (Philadelphia's Lippincott), the very print and the very binding (in somber blue, with a typeface even more somber) perfect reflections of the man. By that time, as Nathaniel Burt later wrote, "Pepper was by common consent

---

[1] Reinhardt, Box 4 of the George Wharton Pepper papers (subsequently PP), in the Rare Book Room of the University of Pennsylvania. Several of these boxes contain the near-complete manuscript of a biography of Pepper, commissioned and paid for by himself and carrying some of his marginal notations, written by Charles Gilbert Reinhardt, a newspaperman and Pepper's legislative secretary in Washington. The work stopped in 1932–33 and was never completed.

unquestionably Old Philadelphia's Grandest Old Man."[2] *Unquestionably*; and *by common consent*. He kept up his scull rowing on the Schuylkill, a still vigorous ornament of the university boathouse. In his seventies he cut large lots of firewood in the winter. During the last years of his life, the strong features of his face softened, his countenance was gentle and grandfatherly, he was restricted to a wheelchair. He died in 1961, when he was ninety-four.

Throughout most of his life he was trim and handsome. There was perhaps one hidden flaw in his countenance. That impressive face contained an oral machicolation. When he laughed there emerged a row of small and energetic front teeth, with serried gaps between them—a slightly feral touch, which was seldom apparent: for George Wharton Pepper, with all his carefully cultivated sense of humor, was not a man of the great belly laugh. Of all of the photographs in his files, *his* favorite picture was a photo taken in his early fifties, a very collegiate one: Pepper in a shaggy crew-neck sweater, his handsome face shining and glowing. That picture shows him at his most attractive: well-bred and astonishingly youthful. It suggests something else, too: a Man Who Is Playing the Game.[3]

"MY CAST OF MIND," he wrote in his autobiography, "is essentially judicial." "I never dove into the political stream. At the outset I merely waded in—when the water was still. Later, when I went off the deep end, it was as the result of a friendly push."[4]

---

2 *The Perennial Philadelphians* (Boston, 1963), p. 138. In his bibliography Burt, whose portrait of Pepper is very fair, sums up Pepper's autobiography as "a candid and graceful self-portrait." It is not very candid, and not particularly graceful.

3 "And it's not for the sake of a ribboned coat / Or the selfish hope of a season's fame / But his captain's hand on his shoulder smote / 'Play up! Play up! and play the game!' " Henry Newbolt, the British imperialist poet, *circa* 1900. "[His] verses echo always, if not among the players, at least among the umpires" (James Morris).

4 *Philadelphia Lawyer* (Philadelphia, 1944) (subsequently *PL*), p. 77.

True: but somehow not true enough. His cast of mind was essentially judicial; yet his judgment was essentially politic—politic in the old, broad sense of that adjective, meaning "civic-minded," but politic also in the newer, narrower sense, meaning party-minded. If he was "unquestionably Philadelphia's Grand Old Man," he was also the Grand Old Man of the Grand Old Party in Philadelphia, a Philadelphia Republican, Compleat.

In one sense he was a Republican convert. On his father's side the Peppers were Republicans; but on his mother's side the Whartons were survivors of the old, states' rights Democratic Party, as were some of the old Philadelphia families during the Civil War, Ingersolls and Biddles; not merely because they had Southern connections, but because they were repelled by the radical and often rapacious streak of the Republican new rich. Pepper's own account is telling: his mother's influence, he wrote, "had led me to classify myself as a Democrat." So was his mentor, George W. Biddle, with whom he started his career at law. His subsequent departures from the Biddle office and from the Democratic affiliation were contemporaneous. "My political ideas underwent a change . . . It is hard to give an accurate account of the process . . . I had the impression that the Republicans of my acquaintance were in general the Doers and the Democrats the Talkers. I was young and eager for effective action. Moreover the community in which I lived depended for its prosperity upon the tariff . . ."[5] Thereafter his conformity to the Republican Party was undeviating and complete. His Republicanism was a matter of faith—and of propriety and behavior, not unsimilar to his attachment to the Episcopal Church.

He was something of a mugwump in the beginning—as behooved a Philadelphia gentleman of his background. Unlike Penrose, who abandoned his sentiments for Reform Republicanism after one good hard look around, Pepper's conversion

[5] *Ibid.*

was slow. In 1905 a reform group called the City Party challenged the corrupt Republican machine in Philadelphia. "I must have been taking myself rather seriously at the time for I wrote and published a long letter explaining my position and justifying what later came to be known as 'taking a walk.' "[6] This habit of taking a walk or, rather, of moving with caution, was characteristic of Pepper. Five years later he was in the center of national attention because of the then famous Ballinger-Pinchot case. The first was Secretary of Interior under President Taft; the second was the head of the Forest Service, Theodore Roosevelt's prime ally in the then novel cause of conservation. Ballinger was beholden to industry and manufacture; the matter of conservation interested him not a whit. A congressional committee was appointed to investigate Pinchot's charges against Ballinger. Underneath it all lay the first rumblings of the coming break between Roosevelt and Taft. Henry Stimson asked Pepper to accept the job of Pinchot's attorney. After his customary hesitation, Pepper accepted. Pepper and Pinchot: two substantial mugwumpish Pennsylvania gentlemen, committed to fair play and honesty in government. Yet there was one big difference. Pinchot believed in a cause; Pepper believed in politic judiciousness. In his autobiography Pepper claims— and with some reason—that his cool judicial way of proceeding, as distinct from the publicity tempest that Pinchot attempted to arouse, was the only proper way to proceed. Yet one has the feeling (and not only after reading the Pinchotists' version of the case) that Pepper protested too much. We are back at the essential condition: that famous judicial cast of mind was essentially politic.

Before the Ballinger case Taft had offered Pepper a judgeship on the United States Circuit Court of Appeals. After some hesitation Pepper declined. After the Ballinger case Taft considered appointing Pepper to the Supreme Court. Pepper would

[6] *Ibid.*, p. 80.

have accepted that; but the offer was not forthcoming, Pepper thought, because Penrose opposed it.[7] Pepper was loyal to Taft and to the regulars; in 1912 he supported Taft against Roosevelt. In 1915 (and again in 1919) Pepper did not respond to a strong draft movement that wanted him to run for mayor of Philadelphia. Yet, at the same time (1915) he delivered a civic admonition against civic indifference:

> There are many people in this town who think of themselves as representatives of "old Philadelphia" and who have very little community of interest with the masses of citizens. They constitute a little city within a big city and they take very little interest in the body as a whole. This spirit of aloofness or indifference manifests itself not only in politics but in other spheres of activity. Various suggestions have been made as to why this is so. I suppose the reasons are to be sought in the social and economic conditions that are peculiar to this community, because my impression is that there is no other American city in which this indifference exists to so marked a degree.[8]

Guardedness marked his brief career in the Senate. In 1926 he was the "middle" candidate, between the corrupt Vare and the puritan Pinchot. Vare was a Wet, Pinchot a determined Prohibitionist, Pepper a cautious Prohibitionist. (Pinchot said that Pepper was a "damp," not a dry.) He carried sixty-two of the sixty-seven counties of the state, but the Vare machine stole the election in Philadelphia. Vare was later barred from the Senate because of corrupt campaign practices. Yet Pepper's forces had spent much more on the election than had Vare. Presently Pepper accepted Vare's offer to be a chief delegate to the Republican National Convention.

Pepper was now a public figure of undisputed eminence. People would raise their hats to him on Chestnut Street. In

---

[7] "He never forgave me for my appearance before the Senate Committee in opposition to Quay's claim to a seat in the Senate." *Ibid.*, p. 89. Was this the only reason? Pepper's legalisms never appealed to Penrose, Quay or not.

[8] PP, Box 3.

Philadelphia he was the representative interpreter of matters just and right. When Edward Bok established the Philadelphia Forum, a cultural and musical series of public performances, he was glad to announce that Senator George Wharton Pepper would "supply the monthly explanation of current events."[9] Yet Pepper's view of current events was often badly flawed. As late as in 1944 he thought that Coolidge "will . . . be denied by posterity the rank of Pitt, but he may in time be recognized as the Palmerston of our political history"[10]—a peculiar judgment, not only of Coolidge, but of British statesmanship. His occasional articles in *The Saturday Evening Post*[11] were predictable, Republican, sermonizing and bland. His acute cognition of the juridical technicalities and of the parochial realities of state politics was insufficient when it came to the greater currents of world events, and specifically of the American role in the world.

Within the ideology of this cautious and guarded man there was a combative streak—a streak so self-righteous as to be almost vulgar—something that was typical of many American Kiplingites, though not of Kipling himself, who had a profound streak of humane sadness underneath the cadences of his virile music. "The people of a nation that is fighting," Pepper wrote in 1915, may be "living closer to God than the people of a nation that is not fighting."[12] In March 1916 he addressed the Pennsylvania Branch of the Navy League: "I deny that it is un-Christian to fight." Often a tawdry note would creep into his prose, as when in April 1916 he advised some of his Republican cohorts: "Some such slogans as 'Peace with Preparedness';

[9] Bok, *Twice Thirty*, p. 428.

[10] *PL*, p. 209. A photograph surviving from the twenties shows: "Howard Heinz and Senator George Wharton Pepper at the White House to invite President Coolidge [the American Palmerston] to attend the 54th anniversary of the Heinz Pickle Works."

[11] In 1930: "Men Wanted!" "Two Presidents" (Harding and Coolidge), "Principle and Politics."

[12] Letter to Thomas Raeburn White, 1 November 1915, PP, Box 3.

[13] PP. Box 3.

'Plenty from Protection'; and 'Power through Patriotism' would certainly have the right ring."[13] In 1918 his nephew and close friend Franklin Pepper ("dear to me as a son")[14] died a hero's death in France. Pepper was deeply moved by this tragedy. It contributed to his conversion from internationalism to isolationism, but it did not cause it.

As a good Republican he attacked Woodrow Wilson whenever the occasion presented itself. Some of these occasions were unsavory. His doggerel " 'Twas Woodrow" was printed in Horatio Bottomley's *John Bull* in May 1919, the doggerel befitting the publication, a rabid sheet owned by a jingo British journalist who was soon to be convicted of fraud. Other occasions were more respectable. On 20 February 1919 Pepper addressed the American Bankers' Union in New York, perorating against the American entry into the League of Nations. "What good reason is there why the United States should surrender her moral leadership of the world by agreeing to act as directed by the international voting trust?" Yet he shared Wilson's moralistic and legalistic inclination of thinking in terms of an international order based on International Law. He enjoyed the honors as he attended the meetings of international legal associations; in 1923 he wrote an amendment to the Covenant of the League of Nations (he was proud enough of it twenty-one years later to make it the only appendix to his autobiography); in 1945 he was a member of the committee which wanted to make Philadelphia the headquarters of the United Nations.

Like other American Republicans and Kiplingites, Pepper had ambivalent feelings toward the Germans, especially after the First World War; he disliked the French (Kipling was a Francophile through most of his life). Before the Second World War, he reminisced in 1944, certain Americans, "rightly or wrongly, did not consider Hitler and his gang a lasting menace to civilization in general or to the United States in particular and hoped that we could be kept out of what was essentially a

[14] *PL*, p. 121.

European War. In this group there were many who, like me, had close affiliation and warm sympathy for England *but who realized that there were, relatively, so few Americans who felt this kinship that it ought not to be translated into a national policy.*"[15]

The Politic Isolationist; and the Cautious Anglo-Saxon: Pepper had a great admiration for Neville Chamberlain, whom he resembled in more than one way. Then came 1940. Hitler, triumphant over Europe, arrived at the English Channel, threatening Britain. Before France fell, Pepper was still a convinced isolationist.[16] In June the Republican National Convention met in Philadelphia the day that the French capitulated to Hitler. Pepper began by cheering on Governor James, the favorite-son candidate of the PMA and of the Pew family; then he swung his vote to Wendell Willkie, whom he learned to admire. His second conversion, that to Republican Internationalism, had begun.

In his autobiography he wrote that the bombing of Britain had relieved him of his doubts. He wrote that his blood had begun to tell. "I began to feel as if my own home were being bombed . . . I gave myself up to the luxury of unrestrained emotion. I said, 'These people deserve to win; and we must

[15] *Ibid.*, p. 268. My italics. He was a member and officer of the English-Speaking Union—perhaps because, rather than in spite of, his German ancestors, about whom see p. 236.

[16] In March 1940 his friend Thomas Stokes gave a dinner at the Radnor Hunt for Sir Samuel Turner, an Old China Hand Englishman, full of bluster, badgering his American hosts to move against Germany and Japan. Pepper wrote Turner: "I begin with a caution and a confession . . . like multitudes of others whose traditions are English and whose sympathies are pro-Ally, I have completely reversed the international philosophy which was mine in 1914 . . . I am thinking in terms of national interest now." (To Sir S. Turner, 25 March 1940. PP, Box 3) On 23 May 1940, the day before the Dunkirk drama was to open, when France was crumbling, he wrote to a friend in Boston: "I feel at least as strongly sympathetic with the British . . . I have no liking for the French—who will take all that you will give them and then bite your hand. I'd rather see Hitler defeated than victorious . . . I am an Isolationist in the sense that (first) I wish to take maximum advantage of our geographical position, and (second) I wish the United States to maintain strict neutrality in any war except one declared against us . . ." (To Mrs. Eliot Wadsworth, 23 May 1940, PP, Box 3) .

help them to do it.' "[17] Yet his Republicanism continued unrestrained. In October 1940 he wrote in a private letter: "If Mr. Roosevelt is reelected the possibilities of aid for Britain will be immensely reduced. If Mr. Willkie is elected new hope and increased productivity will quickly speed up help to Britain and build up our defense"[18]—a compound of partisanship and wishful thinking. The night before Pearl Harbor the Peppers were dining in the house of his Republican friends the John Hamiltons, with Mr. and Mrs. Herbert Hoover. Like many other Republicans, Pepper during the Second World War felt stronger against Japan than against Germany. There was something of a feral note in his feelings toward Japan. He believed that "the Japs are more formidable than the Germans."[19] "Of course my feeling is most intense when casualties happen to our boys," he wrote in 1944.

> But it all haunts me in the case of our Allies and (strange as it may seem) when I read of the death of some young German soldier. I cannot stifle the thought that in every such case somewhere there is a broken-hearted parent or wife or sweetheart. As to the Japs I feel it to be quite different, in spite of the time and money I have spent to lead them to adopt the standards of conduct which we profess. I know that each individual Jap is as much an object of divine care and compassion as I am; but if it became my duty to kill *somebody* I am sure that I should put a Jap at the top of my priority list. It is not exactly hatred. It is rather a feeling that there is not room enough on earth for both of us in view of our opposing conceptions of life and conduct. Of course this feeling will spend itself by and by. We cannot afford to let it dominate us for all time. But at the moment I cannot but confess that I am what I am.[20]

His opinions of Presidents and of the development of world affairs continued awry. "Much as Franklin Roosevelt did to destroy the America which you and I believe in, I am inclined to think that in a more subtle way Harry Truman is doing more.

[17] *PL*, p. 273.
[18] To Ernest Muehlech, PP, Box 3.
[19] *PL*, p. 276.
[20] *Ibid.*, p. 280.

Truman is essentially the typical 'common man.' "[21] In 1948 he wrote: "The communist ideology is simple, compact and compelling. It has acquired more momentum than Napoleon's manifest destiny concept ever did and nothing but Waterloo is likely to stop it."[22] In April 1951 he wrote to a friend that MacArthur was of course right and Truman deadly wrong: the United States should hit China, for the key to the world situation lay there: to defeat Communism in China was more important than was Europe.[23]

WHAT WERE THE SOURCES of these persistent misjudgments of the world in the mind of this learned, judicious, good-natured, and temperate man? They lay, I believe, within the inadequacies—inadequacies steadily cultivated by himself—of his view of human nature. "The process of getting to know a man is quite simple," he said at the dedication of the Franklin Memorial in 1938. "It has three phases. We make ourselves familiar with his countenance and bearing; we listen to what he has to say to us; and we watch him as he goes about his daily work and note the sort of things in which he is interested."[24] Simple enough to figure as an early-twentieth-century version of Poor Richard. In his address "Benjamin Franklin, the Apostle of Unity," he said: "It has always seemed to me that the only thing that can give coherence and continuity to life—either in wartime or in peace—is the willingness of everybody to address himself with conviction to 'OUR FATHER WHO ART IN HEAVEN.' I am not thinking merely in terms of prayer but in terms of unification of thought."[25] Unification of thought, for him, meant not the existential unity of mankind but the unification

[21] To H. W. Prentis, Jr., 12 August 1949, PP, Box 10.
[22] To Edward Hopkinson, Jr., 2 March 1948, PP, Box 10.
[23] To Mrs. Stanley Walker, 23 April 1951, PP, Box 10.
[24] 19 May 1938. PP, Box 3.
[25] Address given before the Franklin Institute when Pepper received the honorary award of Life Membership. *The General Magazine and Historical Chronicle,* January 1943.

of public purpose. He believed in the benefits of piety for the purposes of this world.

Not for nothing would some of the younger, and less patient, scions of Old Philadelphia families call him Pious George behind his back. Yet he was not a true hypocrite, not the kind of man whose public statements and private conventions are shamefully divergent. He was, rather, a man whose very prudence was the source of his pride, a kind of American pharisee in the sense of Good Works, a sense of which Calvin Coolidge approved, though Jesus Christ might not. One Sunday, as Pepper saw fit to record in his autobiography, he and Mrs. Pepper had attended church with President and Mrs. Coolidge. At lunch Coolidge asked Pepper what he thought of the sermon, the theme of which was gratitude, in which the pastor cited Christ's parable of the one humble man among the ten healed, the only one who was thankful. ("Were there not ten cleansed? but where are the nine? There are not found that returned to give glory to God, save this stranger.") Coolidge said: "I'm not at all sure that the man who came back and prostrated himself was a bit more grateful than the nine who went about their business. When I appoint a man to office I don't want him to thank me. I want him to go and make good."[26] Pepper thought that the sermon was commendable; but he also said that so was Coolidge's reaction to it.

He was a great believer in Service. His notion of service was very Protestant-American. It accorded perfectly with his notion of Athletic Christianity. In 1896 Caspar Whitney, in *Harper's Weekly*, attacked college football summer training as savoring of professionalism. Pepper sprang to football's defense; it was healthy in a moral sense, he wrote. Well before the First World War he thought that in times of peace, too, young men ought to have compulsory military training.[27] He found this to

26 *PL,* p. 202.
27 This was not as unusual as it may seem in retrospect. In 1895 the Pennsylvania legislature debated in earnest a bill for compulsory military training in the public schools of the commonwealth.

be quite in accord with Spiritual Training. "The colleges and universities give food for body and mind," he wrote in a newspaper article in the *Public Ledger* before the war, "but they starve the spiritual . . . By religion I mean Christianity, and by Christianity I mean the recognition of Jesus Christ as the master of the race . . . Many universities and colleges number among their faculty and instructors men who are notable non-Christians. It is a sin deserving of the millstone to allow a student merely for lack of light to perceive the obstacles placed in his path by such instructors." In spite (or, perhaps, because) of his collegiate ancestry and attachments and spirit, he had an academic view of academic freedom: in 1915, as a trustee of the University of Pennsylvania, he stood for denying tenure to Scott Nearing, who, then an assistant professor of economics, made repeated, and somewhat strident, criticisms of some of the features of capitalism. Thirty years later Pepper recalled the episode as a tempest in a teapot, which it undoubtedly was; undoubtedly, too, he knew not what Jane Austen had said— that if you happen to live in a teapot, a tempest may be a very uncomfortable thing indeed. By that time his perspectives of Athletic Christianity had softened somewhat. To his credit, a few years after the First World War he recommended to Harding that prisoners who had been arrested for "sedition" be pardoned; and in 1951 he opposed a stupid bill before the Pennsylvania legislature requiring teachers throughout the state to take loyalty oaths.

During the First World War one Fullerton L. Waldo, of the *Public Ledger*, inquired of Pepper in an interview: "If a young man came to you seeking advice, what would you give him as the first rule of success?" "Your question is not an easy one to answer," Pepper said. "A young man will make the most of his life and in this sense attain success if he regards each piece of work as an opportunity to render a friendly service to the fellowman who will be benefitted if the work is well done."[28] Address-

[28] PP, Box 3.

ing the Congress of Constructive Patriotism in 1917, he came out again for universal training and service, so that the young American will "develop a conception of authority which he can use at his will in the educational sphere and so keep himself from degenerating into helpless speculation in the one and from passing into hopeless individualism in the other." Notwithstanding his professed belief in free enterprise and his condemnation of socialism, Pepper's trust in individualism was not unlimited. He maintained his belief that Americanism and Christianity were just about identical. "It seems to me," he wrote in November 1940, "that effective emphasis on the Religion of the Republic is essential if we are to keep on proclaiming the American Way of Life—which, in the last analysis, is the Christian Way."[29]

In the last analysis . . . In the last sentence of the short foreword of his autobiography he wrote, in 1944: "Perhaps it is only wishful thinking, but my belief is that as America goes so will the world"—a curious article of belief by a self-professed conservative and isolationist, a statement that I have quoted often, on different occasions, in order to suggest that when you scratch the American Isolationist you may well find the American Internationalist (as well as the reverse). It also suggests how the radicalism of the enlightened scoutmaster may break through the patrician surface, how much of the Philadelphian tradition, incarnated by men such as Pepper, had been marked by the spirit of Franklin.

DID PEPPER BELIEVE what he was saying? (Did Franklin?) I do not doubt that Pepper did. What may be doubted is whether he thought his thoughts through. The life and character of George Wharton Pepper are marked by unity, by what seems to be an undeviating set of beliefs; yet we have seen that these beliefs were often contradictory. He, who could find the smallest

[29] To Mrs. Wendell Willkie, 6 November 1940, PP, Box 3.

of loopholes in a legal document, who could detect the smallest chinks in the armor of certain persons, seems to have been un-willing—unwilling, rather than unable—to face the contradictions of his own beliefs.

About his inner beliefs his religious statements are of little help. He was a believing Christian, he certainly believed himself to be a believing Christian, and yet Christian as he was, he was even more the Essential Churchman. His moderation was there in his religion: he took good care to announce that he was a middle Episcopalian. He shied away from High Anglicanism throughout his life. There was a preachy, middling-Protestant touch in his predications, as well as in some of his churchmanly functions: Lyman Beecher Lecturer on Preaching in the Yale Divinity School, Representative of the Protestant Episcopal Church of the United States in the World Conference of Faith and Order (he was also Master Mason of the Grand Lodge of Pennsylvania). In his autobiography there is little about the private Pepper, in spite of the many pages devoted to his family, including lengthy accounts of the daily routine of his life. Like his favorite photograph of himself, it is an account of a man who has excelled in Playing the Game, and was content with it.[30]

He was emphatically not a coward. How else could you Play the Game? But he was excessively careful in committing himself. He took a great deal of pride in what he regarded as his ability to see both sides of the question. He was careful about his prejudices, too. In 1936 a friend wrote him an enraged let-

---

[30] In 1934 he wrote: "It goes without saying that I, like you, look with something like dismay at the passing of the old order . . . The fundamental vice of what is happening in Washington is its exclusive emphasis on externals. What we need is not a New Deal but a regeneration of the people who are playing the game . . ." (Letter to John Spargo, 10 April 1934. PP, Box 3). Reminiscing about his work in the Senate: "Most anything that anybody can say in criticism of the American method of tariff making is abundantly justified. And yet the criticism is hardly worth while because nobody, as far as I know, can suggest a better way. Compromise, bargaining, trading, double-crossing and log-rolling in all its forms—all seem to have a place in the game." PL, p. 152. Is this what he meant by the American Way of Life being, in the last analysis, the Christian Way? (supra, p. 233). I am certain that he did not.

ter about Roosevelt's appointments. Pepper's answer, composed in his precise, level handwriting, which hardly changed in seventy years, may be worth quoting at length:

> Speaking generally, I try to remind myself that my ideas of English liberty must (if my estimate of them is sound) be strong enough to dominate the oriental conception of the pursuit of happiness. For this reason I not only do not fear expression of the views with which I disagree but I welcome them. I think Mr. Justice Brandeis and Mr. Justice Cardozo have a useful and important place upon the Court. I admire them while differing from them in many things. The same thing is true of Felix Frankfurter—altho' in lesser degree. I was one of those who recommended him for appointment to the Supreme Court of the United States while Brandeis and Cardozo are there— but I think he would be a fitting successor to either. You will recall, of course, that Brandeis was appointed by Prest. Wilson and Cardozo by Prest. Hoover. Neither Wilson nor Hoover can be suspected of communistic leanings. I feel as you do about a great many of the individuals named in yr. enclosure—including the lady who calls herself Miss Perkins. Again we must remember, however, that for years and years we welcomed immigration and deliberately shared our heritage with newcomers. We cannot consistently object to their characteristic views—but we must do our utmost to convert them to what we believe to be the more excellent way . . .[31]

What a fence-sitter he was, in how many instances! We have seen his cautious behavior in politics, in the Ballinger-Pinchot case, in the split between Taft and Roosevelt, in the three-cornered primary contest in 1926. Before the Republican convention of 1952 he wrote: "I am for Taft as first choice and Stassen as second." But he also wrote in the same letter: "We are fortunate for having in the Republican Party so many fine aspirants for the Presidency. I personally am for Taft but it

---

[31] Letter to Mrs. Harrold E. Gillingham, 5 January 1936, MSS. in the library of the Historical Society of Pennsylvania. In his autobiography he cited Oliver Wendell Holmes, who said that Cardozo was "a beautiful spirit." "As a common law judge I had for him a great admiration. In the field of constitutional law I found it difficult to follow him. I surmise that men of his type never would themselves have evolved any constitution whatever." *PL*, p. 254.

goes without saying that I have the highest possible regard for Eisenhower."[32]

One need not quote Freudian mechanisms of the unconscious to see in his eternal prudence and moderation a kind of uncertainty—not, of course, allowed to appear on the surface. It may have had something to do with his childhood and his ancestry. The Peppers were German in origin, not Anglo-Saxon or Celtic. Johann Heinrich Pfeffer, with his wife Katherina, had arrived in Philadelphia in the 1760s, wherefrom they moved to Schaefferstown in Lebanon County; his descendants became successful brewers in Lycoming County. Their descendant George Wharton Pepper preferred to claim, on occasion, that they had been descendants of an Irish and Protestant (an important qualification, this) Pepper, or perhaps Peppard, who had emigrated from Ireland to Alsace—a most unlikely emigration.[33] His grandfather's brother (born 1808) bore the middle name of Seckel. None of this is mentioned in the long line of "begats" with which he began his autobiography. Nor is the fact that his maternal grandmother insisted that George Mifflin Wharton be baptized from Quakerdom before she would marry him, a fact which would suggest that George Wharton Pepper's ancestral Episcopalianism was relatively recent. There is another curious element of reluctance in his writing about his childhood. His father died when he was young; thereafter his mother took him to live in a modest house, with his grandmother Mrs. George Mifflin Wharton. When he was ten his mother married again, a Mr. Ernest Zantzinger, a very honorable man. About Zant-

[32] To Edward M. Harris, Jr., 7 January 1952, PP, Box 55.

[33] In 1931 Henry Drinker, a respected Philadelphia Quaker lawyer and colleague, wrote Pepper that while looking up his Drinker ancestors in East Anglia he found a George and Ann Pepper in the parish register of Boxted, Essex, *circa* 1630. Pepper wrote Drinker: "Many thanks for the reference in the entry in the Boxted record. I wish I knew whether George and Ann were ancestors of mine." Letter to Henry Drinker, 5 March 1931, PP, Box 3. He must have known that this was quite unlikely. Box 12 of the Pepper MSS. contains a manifest of the ship *Nancy Pepper* from Bristol in 1799, with the captain's name, Daniel Pepper.

zinger he wrote a single paragraph in his autobiography. There
is almost nothing about him in the manuscript of the long biography composed by Charles Reinhardt, his former legislative
assistant, which Pepper commissioned around 1930, and in
which there are long chapters about his childhood. "During
Senator Pepper's boyhood," Reinhardt wrote in that respectful
manuscript, so respectful as to be almost obsequious, his family
"was in comparatively poor circumstances." At this point the
manuscript contains George Wharton Pepper's marginal note:
"Modify."

There was, after all, a certain amount of insecurity within
this perfectly self-composed man—some kind of emanation from
a partially difficult childhood, a fear of poverty, perhaps—together with an awareness that his ancestry, at least on one side,
was not as impeccably Anglo-Saxon as he would have wished it
to be: matters that, contrary to Freudian theories, were not
buried deeply in his subconscious but somewhere at the back of
his conscious mind. That mind was sharp, acute, and when it
was narrow, it was narrow not by nature but by choice. Its contradictions and its occasional lack of insight were not the result
of some kind of innate inability but of an acquired unwillingness to think, not beneath a certain level but rather beyond a
certain point: a frequent American predicament and perhaps
especially characteristic of men during Pepper's lifetime, a ra-
tionalizing inclination that was legalistic and moralistic, that is,
abstract and mental without being particularly intellectual, and
not at all aesthetic. Proud of his physical fitness, extremely conscious of his appearance, George Wharton Pepper had a limited
interest in art, pictures, sculpture, music. His tastes in literature,
music, poetry were essentially late-Victorian. He was a Gilbert-
and-Sullivan aficionado. His favorite poet was of course Kipling.
His mnemonic talents allowed him to retain alarmingly large
chunks of verse, and he would compose fair *vers d'occasion*. At
the age of seventy-one he took up painting, giving some small
canvases to friends. Like many of his legal briefs, they showed

remarkable sklll without much imagination: mostly seascapes, or scenes of his favorite rocky Maine, fair like his eye, cold and blue.

There was, however, a twinkle in that eye. He had a sense of humor, and a warmhearted feeling for his family and friends. His correspondence with his favorite nephew, Franklin, and with the latter's widow, Rebecca, shows an extraordinary mutual devotion and dependence. He was deeply attached to his daughter Charlotte Eleanor, who died prematurely. He was an excellent *pater familias*. His marriage was respectable and solid. He also had a mistress, a large, good-looking woman whose ample charms were different from those of Mrs. Pepper, who was a New England professor's daughter. Oddly enough, George Wharton Pepper, otherwise forever guarded and forever discreet, would promote this woman to all kinds of respectable public functions, to chairman of committees during the First World War, or to other committees after the war.[34] Or perhaps not so oddly: this was the Pepper who wanted to eat his cake and have it too. Yet there was little that was greedy in that choice. He refused to think that other people among the proper Philadelphians knew of the nature of his relationship: he did not believe what he did not want to believe. He was a public person in a private city. There must not be too large a gap between private convictions and public appearances, between private ideas and public expressions. When he was in his eighties he was taken to lunch at the Midday Club (a businessmen's luncheon club, now defunct), and "the entire body of lunchers stood up in respect."[35] It was a reverence paid to a public Philadelphian—to a man, in turn, whose consciousness of being a proper Philadelphian was so determined as to be almost eccen-

[34] 1922: "In the judgement of all of us Mrs. . . . is eminently qualified for this important responsibility and moreover a logical person to select in view of the high position in the councils of the party to which she has been elected by the Republican Organization of the State." PP, Box 3.

[35] Burt, *op. cit.*, p. 129.

tric: almost . . . but not quite. He represented justice, decency, propriety, in moderate terms. The English jib of Moderation in Everything, Including Moderation, would have made little sense to George Wharton Pepper. Here lies the paradox of his personality: his cultivation of moderation was so nearly complete as to be almost eccentric. Almost: but not quite.

SEVEN

OWEN WISTER

O R

The Decline of the West

WE THINK OF THE COWBOY and the open range as part and parcel of the American legend that spread eastward from the West during the nineteenth century. Yet the legend did not become national until the early twentieth century, and its principal literary architect was an Easterner to the core. The crucial event in its popular dissemination was *The Virginian*, a novel written by Owen Wister, published in 1902. Its success was instantaneous, large-scale, and enduring. Starting out in April, it sold 50,000 copies within four months and 100,000 in a little more than a year; it was reprinted fifteen times within seven months and nineteen times within the following eight years. Fifteen more reprintings followed within a quarter of a century. Such different men as Theodore Roosevelt and Henry James praised it. In 1904 *The Virginian* was made into a play; in 1920 into a silent movie; in 1929 into a talking movie, with the then largely unknown Gary Cooper as the hero and Walter Huston as the villain; the movie launched Gary Cooper on his starry career.

The Virginian was, thus, an event in the history of American literature; but, even more, an event in the history of American imagination. It fixed the framework of the Western story for good, certainly for the better part of the twentieth century, for it was within this frame that most of the Western stories, whether in print, on screen, or on television, were to be set again and again and again.

The story of *The Virginian* is simple, and it may be summed up as follows: At the very outset the narrator (obviously Wister himself) in Wyoming meets "a slim young giant, more beautiful than pictures." He is a "cow-boy" from "old Virginia" (except for one passing instance, we never learn his name), sent to meet the narrator at the railroad and to accompany him to the ranch of the latter's friend Judge Henry. Immediately he impresses the narrator with his bearing, with his manner of speech, and with his courage. There are various incidents demonstrating these characteristics of the Virginian, including—again very early in the story—his first encounter with the villain, Trampas, at the poker table. The Virginian is slow calling a bet. "Your bet, you son-of-a——" Trampas says. "The Virginian's pistol came out, and his hand lay on the table, holding it unaimed." (In the 1929 movie Cooper pushed it into the stomach of the villain.) The Virginian drawls the famous phrase: "When you call me that, *smile!*" Trampas is silent. Then and there their mutual hatred begins. They confront each other several times during the hundreds of pages to follow. (*The Virginian* is a long book, running over five hundred pages in its popular edition.) All of their confrontations are verbal, or they are restricted to certain gestures, until the near-end of the book. Meanwhile, the narrator is amazed, again and again, by evidences of the Virginian's abilities and character. Early, too, in the story the person of Molly Wood appears. She is a pert, independent, and intelligent schoolteacher from Bennington, Vermont, who arrives to teach school in Bear Creek, Wyoming. Love occurs, though for a while she keeps the Virginian at bay. In an early episode the Virginian rescues Molly from drowning; in a later episode she rescues him as he lies wounded in the desert. They are about to be married when the last dramatic encounter with Trampas develops suddenly. There is a saloon scene. Trampas, "courageous with whiskey," tells the Virginian: "I'll give you till sundown to leave town." The Virginian says goodbye to his beloved. He steps out from the hotel. All the town is watching. The sun goes down in the moment when Trampas's gun flashes. He misses, and the Virginian shoots him dead. Molly flies into his arms. Next day they are married by a bishop; they ride toward the mountains in a sunset; they return to find that Judge Henry has made the Virginian his partner. No happier ending may be imagined.

There are all kinds of oddities in this story. For one thing, there is not a single scene in *The Virginian* of cowboys actually herding cattle. Also, when Wister wrote about the West, the open range was already gone. As the judicious Wallace Stegner put it in his preface to the letters exchanged between Wister and Frederic Remington, Wister "acknowledged history in his novel by letting the Virginian take up land, marry, and settle down to the tamed routines of stock-farming. After the last brief flare-up of . . . wildness and killing, it is Molly Wood, and all she stands for, who wins . . . [But] the tame ending that Wister gave him does not, in fact, 'take.' In the reader's imagination the Virginian remains what he was before Molly threw a loop over him. He is as timeless and unchanging as Remington pictured him . . . and he is so because the national myth-making urge that obscurely guided Wister's creation demanded that he be so."[1]

Yet none of these oddities compares to those of the writer who produced them. He who wrote this heroic and optimistic American tale, with its happy ending, was an inveterate pessimist, a melancholy Philadelphia gentleman, brooding endlessly about the inevitable decline of the American nation. His vision was intimately involved with the gestation of *The Virginian*; but his character, and his life, accorded with the Western saga not at all.

[1] *My Dear Wister: The Frederic Remington–Owen Wister Letters.* Ben Merchant Vorpahl, ed. Preface by Wallace Stegner (Palo Alto, 1972), pp. viii–ix.

OWEN WISTER (he never liked his first name: those close to him called him "Dan," his friend Oliver Wendell Holmes called him "Whiskers") came from an old Philadelphia family. The dominant influence in his early life was that of his grandmother Fanny Kemble, the actress and writer, whom no less discriminating a man than George Saintsbury called the most beautiful and wisest woman of her time.[2] He was a strange, withdrawn, talented boy, somehow "lacking in animal spirits," his grandmother once said.[3] He had been to boarding school in Switzerland at an early age; he learned to speak faultless French. At fifteen he composed an opera together with his grandmother. He grew into a very handsome young man. He earned his Phi Beta Kappa at Harvard, majoring in music, graduating *summa cum laude*. He returned to Europe, with a pocketful of introductions. At the age of twenty-two he was in Bayreuth, where he was received by Richard Wagner and Franz Liszt. He played one of his compositions to Liszt, who stood behind the young American, making suggestions as the piece tinkled on, and then sat down to write a letter to Fanny Kemble: her grandson had *un talent prononce*, a definite talent.

Surely this was auspicious; but trouble was bound to arise. His father was not pleased with Owen's proposed career. Reluctantly he agreed to the latter's declaration that he would make music his profession; but soon the son, affected by his father's evident unhappiness, relented.[4] He took up a deadly job, arranged by his relatives: computing interest on the balances of depositors, buried in the vaults of the Union Safe Deposit Company in Boston. Two years later he suffered a nervous collapse. He had returned to Philadelphia, where he was fortunate enough to be put under the care of Dr. S. Weir

[2] *A Letter Book* (London, 1922), p. 275.

[3] Fanny Kemble Wister, *Owen Wister Out West* (Chicago, 1958), p. 7.

[4] Earlier he wrote his father (25 October 1882): "This letter is to tell you that I have decided fully and finally, to make music my profession." The long letter ends: "Goodbye—You understand me perfectly well and you know that I am not a fool." *That I May Tell You*. Journals and Letters of the Owen Wister family. Edited by Fanny Kemble Wister (Wayne, Pa., 1979), pp. 115–16.

Mitchell, the physician and family friend and man of letters who often gave intimate and excellent advice to men and women of the closely knit families of Philadelphia.[5]

Mitchell advised the young Wister to go West for a month or so. This was not as radical or daring a piece of advice as it might seem. During the mid-eighties a number of Easterners, usually the sons of wealthy families, were either sent West by their families or themselves chose to take a sporting trip thereabouts—Theodore Roosevelt, Penrose, Remington, and Eakins, for example, all contemporaries of Wister. (Penrose and Wister were born in the same year, 1860; they first went West in the same year, 1885.) Nor was Wister's traveling particularly adventurous. Unlike Roosevelt or Penrose, he traveled with two Philadelphia ladies, the Misses Irwin, redoubtable spinsters, the founders of a private girls' school;[6] arriving in Wyoming, they were lodged at first in the Cheyenne Club, a well-appointed establishment created by two rich Harvard graduates who had invested in land and livestock in the surrounding country. Mitchell had given Wister an introduction to Amos W. Barber (the "Judge Henry" of some of Wister's later stories, including *The Virginian*), the former governor of the Wyoming Territory and owner of a large ranch in the Big Horn basin.

Like Roosevelt—Wister's lifelong friend, notwithstanding the greatest possible differences in their temperaments—once Wister breathed the clear thin Western air, he was immediately intoxicated with it. "This existence is heavenly in its monotony and sweetness . . . I'm beginning to be able to feel something of an animal and not a stinking brain alone," he wrote in his diary.[7] He had a sentimental attraction to a certain kind of virility, of the kind which a generation later would reappear in the thinking and writing of Ernest Hemingway. Another entry in Wister's early diary reads: "Killed today the first deer

[5] *Ibid.*, p. 16.
[6] About the Irwin sisters see above, pp. 89–90, and p. 133.
[7] 8 July 1885. *Owen Wister Out West*, p. 32.

I ever shot at. Hit it plumb in the shoulder and broke its heart."[8] Unlike Hemingway, whose adolescent desire to demonstrate his physical abilities accompanied him throughout his life, Wister was aware of being, and of remaining, an amateur with a gun, an eternal tenderfoot. One of the agreeable things in *The Virginian*, which is written in the first person singular, is the recounting of occasions when the Virginian is compelled to take care of Wister, who failed to tether his horse correctly or left his English shotgun thoughtlessly behind on the ground.

In any event, the Western air, besides sharpening his appetites, crystallized the ambition of his life. He would become a writer. He was thirty-one in 1891, when, in the company of a friend in the dark-paneled dining room of the Philadelphia Club, the fusion of imagination and of purpose occurred. Recalling that evening, he wrote: "Why wasn't some Kipling saving the sage-brush for American literature, before the sage-brush and all that it signified went the way of the California forty-niner, went the way of the Mississippi steam-boat, went the way of everything? Roosevelt had seen the sage-brush true, had felt its poetry; and also Remington, who illustrated his articles so well. But what was fiction doing, the only thing that has always outlived the fact? Must it be perpetual tea-cups? The claret had been excellent. 'Walter, I'm going to try it myself!' I exclaimed to Walter Furness. 'I'm going to start this minute.' "[9] He wrote his first Western story, *Hank's Woman*, in the library of the Philadelphia Club that night.

Hank's Woman was not the first Western story; but it was the first cowboy story on a certain literary level. Five years before its publication a popular writer, Prentiss Ingraham, started his cowboy stories. At that time the very word "cowboy" was relatively new; as late as in the 1870s cowboys in the West were called simply "herders." In 1882 Ingraham's attention was attracted by a cowboy named (not inappropriately) Buck Taylor,

[8] 19 July 1885. *Ibid.*, p. 36.
[9] Owen Wister, *Roosevelt: The Story of a Friendship* (New York, 1930), cited in *Owen Wister Out West*, p. 12.

at the first Wild West show in North Platte, Nebraska. "Beginning in 1887," Wallace Stegner wrote, "Ingraham immortalized
this rodeo cowboy, first in a fictitious biography and then in a
series of dime novels. He devised for him some colorful semi-
Mexican garb that made him picturesque, and he endowed him
with all the skill, courage, and masculine grace that have marked
every heroic expression of the folk mind from Leatherstocking
to Superman."[10] This picturesque factor was, of course, an
essential element in the popular crystallization of the image. It
was not only that in the 1890s the American public was ready
for a new folk hero. The evolution of photography, manifest in
the reproduction of pictures and drawings in the popular newspapers and magazines, the novel popularity of comic strips (and
soon that of moving pictures) showed that the American popular imagination was beginning to depend on the pictorial, even
more than on the literary, element. Therefore the meeting of
Owen Wister with Frederic Remington was providential. Remington was as much an Easterner as was Wister; as a matter of
fact, Remington must have looked very odd on a horse—he was
an urban character, immensely fat, pale, and bald. Wister and
Remington met in 1892 in a comfortable inn in Yellowstone
Park. Their collaboration and their friendship began then
and there. In the historical evolution of the Western legend
their creations are inseparable.

They were different human types, and eventually their
friendship would wane (the difficult person in their relationship was Wister); their interests, too, were focused differently
—Remington was interested in realistic particulars, Wister was
interested in types of character. Yet they shared something that
was very important. Both had a vision, not merely of the West,
but of the American role in the evolving history of the world.
In this respect Wister's and Remington's vision accorded perfectly with Theodore Roosevelt's at the time. It was the vision
that propagated the legend and not the reverse. In his first sig-

[10] *My Dear Wister*, p. viii.

nificant article, "Horses of the Plains," in the magazine *Century* in 1889, Remington drew the American bronco, "the barb," explaining (at the risk of certain historical and biological inaccuracies) that "barb" had come from Barbary with the Spanish conquistadores. In 1894 Theodore Roosevelt wrote his first essay on "Americanism" in *Forum* magazine, the gist of which was that an American type had arisen which was national not cosmopolitan. In 1895 Wister wrote that such an American type was "no product of the frontier, but just the original kernel of the nut with the shell broken. This bottom bond of race unified the divers young men, who came riding from various points of the compass, speaking university and gutter English simultaneously, and as the Knights of Camelot prized their armor and were particular about their swords, so these dusty successors had an extreme pride of equipment, and put aside their jeans and New York suits for the tribal dress."[11] Seven years later he would write at the outset of *The Virginian*, immediately after his first encounter with the latter: "Here in flesh and blood was a truth which I had long believed in words, but never met before. The creature we call a *gentleman* lies deep in the hearts of thousands that arrive born without a chance to master the outward graces of the type."[12]

"To survive in the clean cattle country," Wister wrote in that 1895 article, "The Evolution of the Cow-Puncher" (his earlier title was "The Course of Empire"),

> requires spirit of adventure, courage, and self-sufficiency; you will not find many Poles or Huns or Russian Jews in that district; it stands as yet untainted by the benevolence of Baron Hirsch. Even in the cattle country the respectable Swedes settle chiefly to farming, and are seldom horsemen. The community of which the aristocrat appropriately made one speaks English. The Frenchman to-day is seen at his best inside a house; he can paint and he can play comedy, but he seldom climbs a new mountain. The Italian has forgotten Columbus, and sells fruit.

11 "The Evolution of the Cow-Puncher," *Harper's*, July 1895.
12 *The Virginian* (New York, 1911), p. 9.

Among the Spaniards and the Portuguese no Cortez or Magellan is found to-day. Except in Prussia the Teuton is too often a tame, slippered animal, with his pedantic mind swaddled in a dressing-gown. But the Anglo-Saxon is still forever homesick for out-of-doors.[13]

Wister saw in the cowboy a revival of a specimen from the Middle Ages, and of the Anglo-Saxon race. His vision was a racial vision of the Anglo-Saxon hero, for his cowboy was not merely a picaresque character, he had the stuff of the hero. In the late nineteenth-century, Wister wrote, the frontier gave the Anglo-Saxon race a last chance: "The race was once again subjected to battles and darkness, rain and shine, to the fierceness and the generosity of the desert. Destiny tried her latest experiment upon the Saxon, and plucking him from the library, the haystack and the gutter, set him upon his horse; then it was that, face to face with the eternal simplicity of death, his modern guise fell away and showed again the medieval man."[14] This hankering after the Middle Ages was one of the rare clear examples of something that few people recognize: the medieval facet of the American heart. Perhaps it is significant that Wister was thinking and writing this when Henry Adams was turning toward Mont-St.-Michel and Chartres.[15] The Knight of the Round Table was the ancestor of the cowpuncher: "From the tournament to the round-up! Deprive the Saxon of his horse, and put him to forest-clearing or in a counting-house for a couple of generations and you may pass him without even seeing that his legs are designed for the gripping of saddles . . . So upon land had the horseman his foster-brother, his ally, his playfellow, from the tournament of Camelot to the round-up of Abilene, where he learned quickly what the Mexican vaquero had to teach him."[16]

13 "The Evolution of the Cow-Puncher"; see also *My Dear Wister*, pp. 80–81.
14 *Ibid.*
15 He did write a dreadful medieval "romance," *The Dragon of Wantley* (1892).
16 "The Evolution of the Cow-Puncher," *supra.*

This was "the gist of the matter," Wister wrote, and it was the gist of his vision at that time of his life. The Cowboy was the Last Cavalier. Remington drew the picture that Wister had put into words. "The Last Cavalier," illustrating "The Evolution of the Cow-Puncher" in *Harper's*, shows an American cowboy, tall and lanky, with a bronzed Anglo-Saxon face, with a drooping mustache, emerging to the left of a misty tableau of assembled ancient halberdiers, Templars, Crusaders, Knights of the Roses, with a seventeenth-century Cavalier wistfully looking back at the American horseman. It is a historical drawing, and yet a period piece: it belongs squarely in the middle of the 1890s, with the Anglo-Saxon visions of Kipling and Roosevelt (Wister visited Kipling during the latter's short and pathetic American sojourn in Vermont, before Kipling was widely known in the United States), and by now little more than a remnant of a passing phase in the evolving imagination of American destiny. It is the precise pictorialization of the vision Owen Wister possessed, and an exemplar of the idea which he would incarnate in *The Virginian*. The vision may have been inaccurate (for one thing, as late as in the 1880s one out of three cowboys out West was either black or Mexican); still, the legend of the cowboy and of the open West, with its rough, fair, male idea of justice, would live on till this day.

ONE MONTH BEFORE that heady dinner in the Philadelphia Club, Wister wrote his mother: "I look forward to the winter with unmixed dislike . . . there are a few people I care to see who care to see me, but Philadelphia is not the place I should choose either for any friends or myself if I could help it."[17] Yet with all of his avocation to the rough life and the scintillating air, he could not shake the dust of Philadelphia from his feet; he was to return to it, wearily, earlier than he had imagined. At first he seemed utterly relieved when literary success came to

17 11 September 1891. *Owen Wister Out West*, p. 130.

him, when his first two Western stories were accepted by
Harper's and the check arrived at his desk in the law office of
his friend Francis Rawle, "where I worked at fiction for twenty-
five years and at the law nevermore."[18] He was not a great
novelist. In a diary note in 1891 he wrote: "Can I apply acid to
my English, tell nothing till the sharp cutting metal is left?"[19]
He couldn't. With all his love for outdoor manliness, with all
his contempt for "stinking brain," he was obsessed by ideas,
which hopelessly affected his style: it was not enough for him
to suggest; he had to illustrate, and to explain. Like Hemingway, there was a deep pessimistic undercurrent beneath his
celebration of the manly virtues; unlike Hemingway, this was
amalgamated with his historical vision, with a preternatural
nostalgia—nostalgia, rather than homesickness—for what was
old. In this respect his vision was both more historical and
more melancholy than the Rooseveltian or even than the Kip-
lingian one. "There ought to be music for The Last Cavalier,"
he wrote Remington, ". . . the Last Cavalier will haunt me
forever. He inhabits a Past into which I withdraw and
mourn."[20] On the one hand, Wister cheered on the new American, the Western hero, shining with the wind and the sun:
"Our first hundred years," he wrote, "will grow to be only the
mythological beginnings in the time to come . . . it won't be a
century before the West is simply the true America, with
thought, type, and life of its own kind."[21] On the other hand,
the prospects for this new gallant aristocracy were dark indeed:
"No rood of modern ground is more debased and mongrel with
its hordes of encroaching alien vermin, that turn our cities to
Babels and our citizenship to a hybrid farce, who degrade our
commonwealth from a nation into something half pawn-shop,
half broker's office."[22]

[18] *That I May Tell You*, p. 19.
[19] *Owen Wister Out West*, p. 125.
[20] *Ibid.*, pp. 181–83.
[21] Diary, 10 July 1885, *ibid.*, pp. 32–33.
[22] *Owen Wister Out West*, p. 182.

This duality marked his mind for many years. Ten years after the first publication of *The Virginian* he wrote in a new preface (dedicated to Theodore Roosevelt, "to the greatest benefactor we people have known since Lincoln"): "After nigh half-a-century of shirking and evasion, Americans are beginning to look at themselves and their institutions straight . . . If this book be anything more than an American story, it is an expression of American faith." In reality, by the time he finished *The Virginian* his vision had faded, and the success of the book meant little to him. He also broke off from Remington. The portion of *The Virginian* that was printed in *The Saturday Evening Post* before the publication of the book included the chapter "Superstition Trail"—in it appeared the last picture Remington sketched for a Wister piece. A year later Wister wrote in a private letter about Remington: "He is the most uneven artist I know . . ."[23] And Wister's mind had moved away from the West (and the future) to the Old South (and the past). Whereas in 1895 he had written: "Americans! There are few of them so far in our history. Every man, woman, and cowboy I see from the East—*and generally from New England, thank goodness.*" [My italics.][24] By 1902 his Western hero was a Virginian; he began his most ambitious novel, *Lady Baltimore,* that year; and in *Lady Baltimore* he wrote: "When I walk about in the North, I merely meet members of trusts or unions—according to the length of the individual's purse; when I walk about in Kings Port I meet *Americans.*"[25] It was now in Kings Port (Charleston) that he would find the remnants of what was heroic and old:

> I have never, in this country, seen any churchyard comparable to this one; happy, serene dead, to sleep amid such blossoms and consecration! Good taste prevailed here; distinguished men lay beneath memorial stones that came no higher than your waist or shoulder; there was a total absence of obscure

23 *My Dear Wister,* p. 304.
24 *Owen Wister Out West,* p. 32.
25 His italics. *Lady Baltimore* (New York, 1906), p. 67.

grocers reposing under gigantic obelisks; to earn a monument here you must win a battle, or do, at any rate, something more than adulterate sugar and oil . . .[26]

There's nothing united about these States any more, except Standard Oil and discontent. We're no longer a small people living and dying for a great idea; we're a big people living and dying for money . . .[27]

This Kings Port, this little city of oblivion, held shut in with its lavender and pressed-rose memories, a handful of people who were like that great society of the world, the high society of distinguished men and women who exist no more, but who touched history with a light hand, and left their mark upon it in a host of memoirs and letters that we read to-day with a starved and homesick longing in the midst of our sullen welter of democracy . . .[28]

Wister was enough of a Northerner to say that he saw in Charleston "the doom of a civilization founded upon a crime." But the Fifteenth Amendment was a "sudden sweeping folly"; and, coming upon the Negro quarter suddenly,

. . . narrow lanes and recesses which teem and swarm with negroes. As cracks will run through fine porcelain, so do these black rifts of Africa lurk almost invisible among the gardens and the houses. The picture that these places offered, tropic, squalid, and fecund, often caused me to walk through them and watch the basking population; the intricate, broken wooden galleries, the rickety outside staircases, the red and yellow splashes of color on the clothes lines, the agglomerate rags that stuffed holes in decaying roofs or hung nakedly on human frames, the small, choked dwellings, bursting open at doors and windows with black round-eyed babies as an over-ripe melon bursts with seeds, the children playing marbles in the court, the parents playing cards in the room, the grandparents smoking pipes on the porch, and the great-grandparents upstairs gazing out at you like creatures from the Old Testament or the jungle. From the jungle we had stolen them, North

26 *Ibid.*, pp. 57–59.
27 *Ibid.*, p. 65.
28 *Ibid.*, p. 50.

and South had stolen them together, long ago, to be slaves, not to be citizens, and here they were, the fruits of our theft; and for some reason . . . that passage from the Book of Exodus came into my head: "For I the Lord thy God am a jealous God, visiting the iniquity of the fathers upon the children."[29]

I know of no other American writer, not Poe, not Melville, not Adams, not any of the moderns, who was thus obsessed with the idea of perdition and decline. Next to Wister's view of history, Oswald Spengler was an optimist. The real reactionary was Wister, not the stoic Penrose, who did not mind the thoughtless progress of mechanized industry; the real nationalist was Wister, not the amiable Pepper, who was pleased with the prospect of seeing the world become like the United States. Nor did he possess the consolations of religion. He was a Wagnerian pantheist.[30] In *Lady Baltimore* his Charleston friend and he come upon a crucifix: "So you believe everything still?" "As he looked at me, I suppose he read negation in my eyes . . ." There was merely "a permanent something, which has created all the religions all over the earth from the beginning, and of which Christianity itself is merely one of the present temples."[31]

He was an only child. He was handsome but not healthy. Severe and undiagnosed illnesses, mental and physical, accompanied him throughout his life. He was not made to be happy. He married his second cousin in 1898, and bought a house in Philadelphia, on a block on Pine Street which was no longer very fashionable. After *Lady Baltimore* (it was published in 1906) he wrote less and less. Except for one or two family

---

[29] *Ibid.*, pp. 175–77.

[30] He saw the Western landscape in Wagnerian terms. Letter to his mother, 11 August 1891: "The place is at once romantic, exquisite, and wholly sublime . . . you can easily expect to see the Gods stretch a rainbow somewhere and march across to Walhalla. I am reminded of certain of the most beautiful passages in Wagner's trilogy—those moments when the whole orchestra seems to break into silver fragments of magic . . . If you can recall the song of the Rhine Daughters—or the last few moments of *Die Walküre* when Brunhilde falls to sleep among the rocks—those passages are inspired by the same thing which vibrates in this cañon . . ." *That I May Tell You*, pp. 18–19.

[31] *Lady Baltimore*, p. 108.

trips he no longer went West. He kept up his friendships, visited Theodore Roosevelt in the White House.[32] In 1907 he decided to run for councilman in the Seventh Ward, on a reform ticket; he lost. The next year the Wisters moved into his grandmother's Butler Place. There his health broke down again. In 1912 he plunged into politics for the last time: he supported Roosevelt on the Bull Moose ticket. There was a rally in the Hammerstein Opera House on North Broad Street. The Wister family drove up "in the family brougham drawn by the fat bay team, Parsifal and Siegfried, who had belonged to our grandmother."[33] Mrs. Wister was not well. She died the next year, leaving Wister with six children.

Around that time he began a novel about Philadelphia. The four chapters of *Monopolis* preserved among the Wister papers in the Library of Congress are a compound of sarcasm and nostalgia, of bitterness together with an exaltation of the other aristocratic virtues. "Where there is no vision, the people perish; with this one Monopolis began." "We keep on the Safe Side." "Shrewdness was to be plainly observed, but where was imagination? Hardness was there, but where was daring?" "Out of moderation's very excess had been created—too much moderation."[34] "Mediocrity's the only thing we recognize." "Our

---

[32] Of this visit his daughter left us a cameo. "In 1908 my parents took us to lunch at the White House with President and Mrs. Theodore Roosevelt. My father had known him well since going to college with him. Though we were two boys and two girls from nine to four in age, we all had dark hair to our shoulders and white piqué suits and dresses. We were greeted at the door by Major Archie Butt, the President's bodyguard, who took his pistol out of its holster and showed it to us. We slid back and forth on the polished floor of the East Room and sat down to lunch with the Roosevelt family. The table was laid with a white tablecloth, and President and Mrs. Roosevelt sat at the middle of the table opposite each other. We had lamb chops with paper frills, and rice for lunch followed by whole shiny raw apples for dessert; but I was too young to peel mine. The surprise and disappointment in the dessert was received in silence by the little Wisters. As Victorian children, we had eaten many a Charlotte Russe at better parties than this." *Owen Wister Out West*, pp. xiii–iv.

[33] *Ibid.*, p. xiv. Owen Wister in the *Monopolis* ms., also in 1912: "[Their livery was] almost the last of its kind in Monopolis."

[34] I found this a month or two after I wrote the last sentences of the previous chapter (p. 239). The *Monopolis* ms. in Box 83. Wister MSS. in the Library of Congress, pp. 21 *et seq.*

climate is a fact. Haven't we humidity and heat enough to take the starch out of many ideals?" "Then you admit we're limp."[35] As in many of his other, non-Western novels, Wister's heroine is an older aristocratic woman. "Aunt Carola comes undiluted from the old New York families of the Hudson River, and when she chooses she can call a spade a spade just as nakedly as if Queen Victoria had never lived."[36] He abandoned the writing of his Philadelphia novel within a year.

On the first day of the year 1914 he wrote in his diary: "The strange feeling came over me that to-day I had begun the final volume of my life."[37] He had twenty-five more years to live. During the First World War he was stirred, as was Roosevelt, and argued ferociously for war against Germany; he pleaded, in an eloquent little book (*The Pentecost of Calamity*), for her exemplary punishment. Then the last stage of his disillusionment set in. Like other fine-spun Americans and idealists of the prewar years (his friend John Jay Chapman comes to mind) he brooded endlessly about how immigration was destroying the nation. All his life he thought about race; now he became a racist of sorts. He would still go to Europe, he kept up his correspondence with old friends, such as Chapman and Holmes, he recognized the talent of the young Hemingway (once he sent Hemingway a check for $500), he served on the Board of Overseers of Harvard for a dozen years, he wrote a commemoration of his friendship with Theodore Roosevelt[38] and snatches of operetta on occasion, but his depression deepened. He had described himself as the narrator in *Lady Baltimore*, and again in his unfinished *Monopolis* and in another unfinished novel, *The Star-Gazers*, as "Augustus," a world-weary young man, with

---

[35] *Ibid.*

[36] *Ibid.*, p. 2. A Mrs. Cuthbert rhapsodically exclaims over the landscaping that the Pennsylvania Railroad had laid out around the suburban station of "Ap Thomas" (Bryn Mawr): " 'So like the lawn of an English vicarage!' Aunt Carola said: 'The woman's an ass!' "

[37] *That I May Tell You*, p. 229.

[38] *Roosevelt: The Story of a Friendship* (New York, 1930).

all passion spent;[39] yet his hatreds remained as strong as ever.[40] He kept referring to himself as a man who had long learned the wisdom of resignation; yet he was not at peace with himself. He settled into the routine of an Old Philadelphian, accepting the directorships of venerable barnacled Philadelphia institutions, including the chairmanship of the Green Tree—the Mutual Assurance Company for Insuring Houses from Loss by Fire, the second-oldest insurance company in America. ("Why the very insurance companies are a barometer of the time," he had written in *Monopolis* in 1912. "They register the economic destruction of the old American family, and the invasion of the Hun, the Vandal, the Croat and all the rest of the steerage.") He accepted the presidency of the Philadelphia Club, whose centennial history he wrote in 1934.[41] He ended his career as he had begun it: a Philadelphia patrician, serious, thoughtful, and withdrawn. There remains an unfinished manuscript on which this author of *The Virginian*, the creator of the cowboy legend, worked before his death (he died in 1938). It was to be a book about French wines.

[39] "Augustus" at the age of thirty-five: "Dear Aunt, I've been dead for a number of years but I didn't wish it generally known." Wister MSS., Box 83.

[40] See his bitter poem "To Woodrow Wilson, On 22 February 1916," printed in the Philadelphia *Public Ledger* on Washington's birthday. As late as 1924, Wister refused to contribute to General Allen's fund for starving women and children in Germany.

[41] The handsome volume, ribbed, with leather corners, of which 510 copies were privately printed, contains a curious notice imprinted with faint type on the inside of the frontispiece: "The Club printed a book shortly after the reception given to celebrate its one hundredth anniversary. This book proved to be inadequate, as there were many errors and omissions. The Library Committee now issues this amplified and corrected edition. The first printing has been recalled."

EIGHT

ALBERT COOMBS BARNES

OR

The Methodist as Aesthete

AT THE BEGINNING of the twentieth century Ralph Adams Cram speculated that the American Renaissance might be around the corner, with some of America's millionaires becoming the new Borgias and Medicis—well, it didn't quite happen that way, certainly not in Philadelphia. Yet in 1928 *The New Yorker* ran a profile, by A. H. Shaw, with the title "Dr. Medici in Merion." "In the midst of a twelve-acre park in Merion, a suburb of Philadelphia," it began, "remote from the beaten path of art museums and galleries, stands a French Renaissance palace of buff limestone, which houses the finest collection of modern paintings in the world, with the one possible exception of a museum in Moscow."[1] In 1928—a year before the Museum of Modern Art was established in New York—this building contained more than one thousand paintings. During the twenty-two years which followed, its holdings increased further, finally including more than two hundred paintings by Renoir, nearly one hundred Cézannes, about sixty-five Matisses, about thirty-

---

[1] 22 September 1928. (Shaw was wrong about that possible museum in Moscow.)

five early Picassos, many Old Masters, including El Grecos, Dutch, Venetians, Italian primitives, and a large collection of modern American painters, as well as pieces of Negro, African, Oriental art, displayed together in two dozen well-designed rooms, most of which are not large enough to avoid the impression, on the occasional visitor, of an *embarras de richesses*, a surfeit. It is an amazing collection; and no less amazing is the fact that at the time of this writing, fifty-two years after 1928, relatively few people, including people in Philadelphia, are aware of its existence. Those who are refer to it as the "Barnes," a kind of monument to the erstwhile owner.

The story of this monument, and of its singular creator, fits into the history of the United States in one important sense. The vast bulk of the great art collections in the United States were accumulated during the first half of the twentieth century, when the United States was the greatest and most prosperous power in the world. We may be even more precise: the two dates marking the end of the beginning and the beginning of the end of this period are 1895 and 1955. They coincide with the beginning and the end of the rise of the American empire. Between 1895 and 1955 the great transatlantic migration of paintings, of sculptures, on occasion of entire buildings, of libraries, of artists, of musicians, of scientists, took place. It would be simplistic and crude to explain the motives and the purposes of this great movement in materialistic terms alone, to attribute them to the then almighty dollar. Many of the American collectors had sophisticated tastes, and their enthusiastic and generous purchases and donations often sprang from a tangible and vitalizing element of American idealism.

There was, in Philadelphia, an old and respectable tradition of painting, beginning with Benjamin West and Charles Willson Peale, well before the Revolution, and leading to such fine painters as Thomas Eakins and Mary Cassatt around 1900. Yet we have seen in the first chapter of this book that in 1900 the Philadelphia museums were in a deplorable state, and the private collections not much better. Soon, however, Philadelphians would begin to make their own contributions to the American tresorification of art.

In Philadelphia the three greatest collectors were Johnson, Widener, and Barnes. John G. Johnson built one of the finest collections in the United States. He loved pictures and hung them in every nook and corner in his large unpretentious house.[2] He bequeathed his marvelous pictures to the city of Philadelphia on the condition that the city erect a suitable gallery for them in, or adjacent to, his house. Through an adroit maneuver of legal legerdemain (never so admitted by Philadelphians) in 1933 his trustees succeeded in transferring the Johnson Collection to the Philadelphia Museum of Art.

In 1900 Johnson was probably the most respected lawyer in the United States. The story of his life does not properly belong within the chronological scope of this book (he was born in 1841 and died in 1917). What belongs to this history is that his interest in art grew apace with his disillusionment with the law; for such a disillusionment would reappear in the lives of such eminent Philadelphians as Boies Penrose, Eli Kirk Price, Owen Wister, Francis Biddle, Sturgis Ingersoll, even though, except for Penrose and Wister, they continued their law practice till the end of their lives.[3] Johnson's father was a blacksmith who also doubled as a butcher (he married the daughter of a butcher); his friend P. A. B. Widener was the son of a butcher; Johnson, like Widener, made a lot of money. There the parallel ends. Widener had a baronial mansion built for himself; Johnson cared not for such things. Widener learned to course race horses; Johnson liked baseball. Widener had himself painted

2 "Francis Biddle has a nice story of Johnson's asking the maid to run upstairs and fetch the Botticelli leaning on the bathtub." Nathaniel Burt, *The Perennial Philadelphians* (Boston, 1963), p. 349. The story must be apocryphal (as my wife put it: "It's not the propriety; it's the humidity"). The legal as well as the literary record of Francis Biddle (Attorney General of the United States during the last two Roosevelt Presidencies, and hanging judge at Nuremberg) suggest his avocation to justice, at the expense of truth if need be.

3 About the decline of the legal aristocracy in Philadelphia, see pp. 35–38 and below, pp. 312–18.

by Sargent: the portrait is prototypical Sargent, elegantly
elongated, an Edwardian piece of flattery. Johnson's portrait
by the little-known Haeseler shows a strong, beady-eyed countenance; it is a marvelous rendition of cranial character. Throughout his life Widener was guided by social ambitions; Johnson
cared little for them. It was because of his legal achievements—
and perhaps also because of his evident indifference to social
climbing[4]—that Johnson was respected by the Philadelphia
families; he belonged to the Philadelphia Club, to membership
in which Widener aspired in vain. *The New York Times*
wrote, in his obituary, that Johnson "fairly basked in obscurity."[5] During the last twenty years of his life, Johnson grew
more and more contemptuous of the legal profession. He had
few lawyer friends. He took no interest in the Bar Association.
He would curse some of the most respected lawyers and judges
in private, and sometimes say unthinkable (if not unprintable)
things about the legal profession in public. My father-in-law,
then a student in the law school of the University of Pennsylvania and winner of the coveted Sharswood Prize, once cajoled
Johnson into giving a talk. He heard Johnson say that "the
law sharpens the mind only to narrow it." He was so convinced
that this was true Johnson, that I argued in vain that he had
taken it from Burke. He also remembered Johnson talking to
law students about art: "Start buying what you like. But don't
ever talk of a picture as 'growing on you.' A picture is a picture,
not a sort of fungus." Evidently Johnson was as impatient with
art jargon as he was with legal jargon.

So was Albert Coombs Barnes, who had many things in
common with Johnson. He was the son of a butcher. They were
students in Central High School, the public school in Philadelphia with a long tradition and high standards. Johnson
grew impatient with the law; Barnes gave up, early in life, his

[4] He *had* married a Philadelphia woman of old and respectable lineage. But
so had Widener.
[5] Cited in George and Mary Roberts, *Triumph on Fairmount: Fiske Kimball
and the Philadelphia Museum of Art* (Philadelphia, 1959), p. 133.

practice of medicine.[6] Both knew what they wanted. They were sardonic, self-centered, childless. They were individualists, their collections depended on their own convictions and tastes, they (unlike Widener and many others) depended not on the discernment of dealers and critics, of Berensons and Duveens. Both were at home in Paris, where they were respected by painters and dealers alike. There *that* parallel ends. Johnson fitted into the society of Philadelphia. Barnes did not.

HE WAS BORN in 1872, in Kensington, a respectable working-class neighborhood in Philadelphia, then inhabited mostly by American workingmen of English, Scotch-Irish, or Irish stock. His father lost his right arm after a wound he had suffered in the Battle of Cold Harbor in 1864; he had his ups and downs; he was a butcher for a while and thereafter held a variety of jobs. His mother was a strong woman of Pennsylvania-German origin who seems to have kept the family together; she was a devout Methodist; Barnes admired her and talked about her throughout his life.[7] The Barnes family moved often. When the Barnes family fortunes began to improve, they moved to 1331 Tasker Street, in a row house next to that of the bookish Edwin S. Stuart, the owner of Leary's famous bookstore, who later became mayor of Philadelphia and governor of the Commonwealth.

The childhood of Albert Coombs Barnes was hard. For years he had to get up to deliver the *Public Ledger* (where his father had gotten a job) at four in the morning. Later he would claim that he played semi-professional baseball and that he was a pugilist. The first of these claims seems to have a measure of truth; the second is more doubtful. His father depended on his son's strength; his mother recognized, early in life, his

---

[6] There is some evidence that, early in life, Barnes wanted to be a lawyer, not a doctor. Henry Hart, *Dr. Barnes of Merion: An Appreciation* (New York, 1963), p. 50.

[7] His original idea was to name the Barnes Foundation after his mother.

abilities. He was admitted to Central High School, a considerable achievement at the time. Thereafter, spurred and helped
by his mother, he went on to the University of Pennsylvania
and then to its medical school. He was a brilliant student and
finished his work in record time: he had his M.D. degree at
twenty. He took his internship at the State Hospital for the
Insane in Warren, Pennsylvania, a small upstate town ruled
by a few rich families.[8] He left Warren after a year, having
saved enough money to take a summer trip to England. He
started to practice medicine—he was barely twenty-one—in his
father's house. After two years he gave it up. "Most of the ills I
treated were imaginary," he said, "or would have cured themselves, and I didn't like bluffing my way through the hard ones.
Besides, I wanted to go to Europe again."[9]

He thought that his main interest was science. He had saved
enough money to cross the Atlantic again, now to Germany,
where he eked out a living in various ways: they included the
selling of American stoves and the singing of Negro spirituals
in beer gardens.[10] When he came back to Philadelphia, he gave
up his medical practice altogether; he would earn his money
by a double job, working as a chemical consultant and as a
writer of medical advertisements. Then he crossed to Germany
again, studying pharmacology, philosophy, chemistry, in an
intermittent way. In 1900 he returned to America. During a

[8] "His experiences there," wrote his thoughtful biographer and friend Henry
Hart (who had dedicated his novel about Penrose, about which see p. 66, to
Barnes), "bred a lifelong interest in psychiatry and psychology, and also, I believe, led to the first formulation of the ideas which became the warp and woof
of his personality and intellectual being." P. 34.

[9] *Ibid.* The expression is similar to Penrose's abandonment of a career at
law; see p. 58.

[10] His lifelong attraction to Negro spirituals came from his early experiences
when he accompanied his mother to Methodist camp meetings. According to
one of his biographers, he had bought his first pictures, small genre oils, in
Germany. "From what he said forty years later he was dead broke after a year
and a half and had to solicit the help of the American consul in Antwerp to
get home. He was given a job on the tanker *Charleroi* sailing from Rotterdam,
but after he had sung Negro spirituals the first night, the captain invited him
to dinner every night thereafter." William Schack, *Art and Argyrol* (New York,
1960), p. 40.

visit in the Poconos to one of his cousins, a doctor, he met Miss Laura Leggett from Brooklyn, the daughter of a respectable family of wholesale grocers, a quiet small blond woman whose self-effacement covered her unstinting reserves of inner strength. They were married the next year. Barnes had earned enough to take his bride on a honeymoon to Europe.

He was now twenty-nine years old, and poised for the leap that would make his fortune. He had been experimenting with silver compounds whose antiseptic qualities would be strong while their caustic qualities would be weak (the very opposite of his personal characteristics), so that they could be made into a solution that would not harm certain tissues. During his honeymoon journey he stopped at Heidelberg again. He had acquired a friend there, a German by the name of Herman Hille, who was good at laboratory work. He proposed to Hille that the latter translate himself to the United States and work with Barnes on their experiments with silver vitellin. Barnes had a group of famous physicians (in Philadelphia as well as in Berlin) test the results. The tests were successful. He called his compound Argyrol—a name that Barnes registered, though he would not patent it, since that would make the ingredients public; besides, the patent would expire after twenty years.

He was an inventive chemist; he knew, too, the advantages of publicity. He sent thousands of circulars to physicians, not to pharmacists (this was a relatively new practice at the time), including the endorsements of famous doctors in the United States and Germany. In 1903 he traveled to London, Dublin, Berlin, giving doctors test samples; he had offices set up in London and even in Sydney. The response was rapid. Within a few months Barnes and Hille had to move their laboratory to a large loft. Within two years Barnes was a rich man. He had started out with a capital of $1,600; the partners made $100,000 during the second year of their operations.[11]

---

11 His detractors often suggested that the inventor of the compound was Hille, not Barnes; and/or that Barnes tricked Hille out of the profits. This is

There is little to indicate that at that time of his life Barnes's interests and ambitions differed substantially from those of other self-made Americans or Philadelphians whose efforts had made them respectable and rich. He seemed to follow the pattern of the successful Philadelphia *nouveau riche.* In 1905 he built a granite, twelve-room, Scottish-style castle of a house in Merion, not far from Bok's house. He named it "Lauraston," after his wife. Like other *nouveaux riches,* he was conscious of his origins and attempted to follow some of the paths of society: he took riding lessons and joined the Rose Tree Hunt.

He also bought a few pictures. The first oil painting he bought, in 1905, was a Corot, for "Lauraston." A few years later he met some of his former classmates at Central High School, including the painter William Glackens. A lifelong friendship developed between the two men.[12] Barnes bought some of his paintings, as well as some painted by Glackens's friends, Maurice Prendergast, John Sloan, Charles Demuth. In 1912 Glackens went to Paris. Barnes gave him twenty thousand dollars to buy paintings; Barnes had studied the catalogues and marked the prices he was willing to pay. Glackens returned with a Renoir (for $1,400), Van Goghs, and the first Matisse (for $50). The money soon ran out. Barnes now followed Glackens to Paris. He went on buying. His life as an art collector had begun. He read a great deal; and he quickly developed a liking for the moderns. This was the year before the famous Armory Show in New York. When the Armory Show opened, Barnes saw pictures with which he was not familiar; but the Armory Show taught him nothing that he had not already learned.

During the next four or five years—they were the years of

---

not true. Hille was a difficult German. In 1907 their partnership was dissolved. Hille received a very large sum, and lived to preside over his own laboratory in Chicago to the age of ninety. The price of Argyrol remained unchanged for fifty years.

[12] Painters who were alumni of Central High in Barnes's time included Sloan, Eakins, Preston.

the First World War in Europe—Barnes's interest in art blossomed to the extent that he would write, and see published, his first articles on the subject of painting, to which we shall return. He was becoming an intellectual as much as an aesthete. He supported *The New Republic*, founded in 1914, and he would, on occasion, contribute to its pages; for a while he supported the radical *New Masses*; he supported the then famous Provincetown Players (he respected Eugene O'Neill's writing but not his character, and he thought John Reed was a "publicity-seeking opportunist"[13]). He discovered the writings of John Dewey, who became his lifelong friend. Barnes was inspired by Dewey's *Democracy and Education* (a book composed in a heavy and difficult style) to the extent that in 1917–18 he enrolled in Dewey's seminar at Columbia University, traveling to New York twice a week for that purpose. By 1919 Barnes was so well known and respected in intellectual circles in New York that Herbert Croly asked him to give a course in psychology at the New School for Social Research, an invitation which Barnes declined. He was ready to go to Europe again.

Immediately after the Armistice, Barnes resumed his Paris buying. The purchases included an El Greco, many more Renoirs, and many moderns: Derain, Pascin, Soutine, Modigliani, Marie Laurencin, de Chirico (who painted Barnes's portrait, gratis), Lipchitz, *et al.* (Barnes turned against the last, whom he came to regard as an opportunist.) His Paris sojourns were as interesting as they must have been wearisome. He stayed in comfortable small hotels, not at the Ritz or the Crillon, where other rich American patrons would set up. With a retinue of friends, critics, dealers he would course from museum to museum, gallery to gallery, talking, lecturing,[14] arguing, buying.

He was a big, raw-boned man, with a determined face (shown better in the photograph taken by Carl Van Vechten than in

[13]Hart, *op. cit.*, p. 69.
[14] John Dewey fell asleep in the Prado while Barnes was berating Raphael. Dewey's excuse was that he had heard that lecture before in the Louvre.

the portrait painted by de Chirico), "the face of a dentist," Aline
B. Saarinen wrote, wrongly; it was, rather, the face of a first-
rate president (*rara avis*) of a second-rate university. Beneath
his eternally wrinkled brows and behind his rimless glasses his
eyes glared strong and clear. His preferences were singular; his
hatreds were puissant; he was impatient, immoderate in temper
and speech, and, more than often, uncompromising—habits
that were rather un-Philadelphian. Until about the age of fifty
his social ambitions were strong but obscure. He was fifty-one
when his disillusionment with the elite of Philadelphia first
resulted in an explosion. After that, his war with Philadelphians
would flare up year after year, making news because of his
strange addiction to publicity. His reputation became that of a
vulgarian, flaunting his collection acquired by a large and
perhaps inexhaustible checkbook: a ham-handed boor, a rich
Don Quixote who, unlike the tattered Spanish comic hero, lived
in his own windmill laden with riches, who was largely unap-
proachable, unspeakable, and unthinkable, even though the
trouble was that on occasion he had to be thought about.

The stories of Barnes's battles are well known, repeated by
his enemies as well as by his two principal biographers. Their
details are often complicated; in some instances there are two
or more sides to the same story. I shall sum up the principal
ones among them for the sole reason that they cast a light on
Barnes's character.

Around 1920, perhaps for the first time in the history of
Philadelphia, a group of cosmopolitan lovers of art began to
gather. "Philadelphia, or at least a charming and delightful
part of Philadelphia," R. Sturgis Ingersoll later wrote, met at
Friday-night parties where "the painters, the musicians, the
Museum people, and amateurs of one sort or another, mixed
in a cheerful belief that something was happening."[15] Barnes's

---

[15] Cited by Schack, p. 127, without reference. In his privately printed memoir
of the painter Henry McCarter, whose bibulous company he often enjoyed,
Ingersoll gave a glimpse of the origins of such a group: ". . . on a 'Friday afternoon at four,' Langdon Mitchell introduced us at Ostendorf's beer saloon on

collection, by this time, was the talk of Philadelphia, certainly among the painters, many of whom he had befriended, and among "the Museum people," many of whom he had attempted to befriend. In December 1922 Barnes established his Foundation as an "educational institution." In January 1923 the Paris dealer Paul Guillaume arranged a show consisting solely of Barnes's modernist acquisitions. Henry McCarter and Arthur Carles, teaching at the Pennsylvania Academy of the Fine Arts, prevailed on Barnes to arrange a show of the modernists in the Academy (the Philadelphia Museum of Art had not yet been built), the same exhibition Guillaume had mounted in Paris.

Philadelphia was not ready for it. The "public"—consisting mostly of society people—looked at the Soutines, Pascins, Modiglianis, etc., with self-conscious embarrassment, and left the show muttering. A respected local psychiatrist said that the painters were degenerates. The newspapers were worse: in the age-old Philadelphian way they tut-tutted, they would not say anything contrary to the accepted opinions of the day. Their reviewers were unsympathetic and patronizing; they suggested that this rich collector was somehow deficient in his artistic knowledge and taste.[16]

Barnes's antipathy for the Philadelphia elite now crystallized. Yet in Philadelphia he would stay. He had Paul Cret[17] build the fine French neo-Renaissance building for his foundation, which was completed in 1925, before the Philadelphia Museum of Art. Thereafter the Foundation and the Museum were two

---

Market Street. George Howe, Francis Biddle, Arthur Carles, Leopold Stokowski, Beauveau Borie, and Paul Cret were of the group. [Two painters, two aesthetes, two architects, one musician, one man-about town.] We drank, by Mac's description, 'excellent, full-taste German beer,' and repeated on successive Fridays, and then came war and we lost touch—to be renewed on a spring day in 1920 on my dropping in at Child's for lunch and joining Mac at his breakfast. Turgenev was on his mind. We talked of *Smoke* and parted on an overtone in *Fathers and Children*." R. Sturgis Ingersoll, *Henry McCarter* (Philadelphia, 1944), p. 3.

16 In Barnes's later words: "All that happened was old ladies from the Main Line called us degenerates for showing such things and a psychiatrist named Dercum said he was certain the artists were insane." Hart, *op. cit.*, p. 22.

17 About him see above, n. 15; and p. 319.

inimical castles five miles apart, like medieval forts of hostile Highland chiefs out of Walter Scott. The Museum rose on a hillock; the Foundation stood on the suburban plain. The Museum was visible from many angles; the Foundation was not. The Museum was to serve as a great public institution, even as it was governed by the elite of Philadelphia. The Foundation was private, hermetically closed, open only by special permission; yet it was intended to serve the common people; one of its principal officials was a chauffeur, and its instructors included simple women, former employees of Barnes's factory, whose loyalty to Barnes was their prime qualification. The card of admission read: "THE BARNES FOUNDATION is not a public gallery. It is an educational institution with a program for systematic work organized into classes which are held every day, and conducted by a staff of experienced teachers. Admission to the gallery is restricted to students enrolled in the classes."

Barnes thought that the trustees of the Museum allowed that institution to be hardly more than "a pedestal upon which a clique of socialites pose as patrons of art and culture."[18] The stories of how he refused society people (or men and women who he thought were society people) are endless, vulgar, and only occasionally funny. He had requests for admission answered by a stenographer or signed with the name of his dog; on occasion he wrote and signed the answers himself. To the son of a prominent millionaire he scribbled a note: the date suggested was inconvenient, for he, Barnes, was swallowing goldfish that day. To a society woman he wrote that the requested date was inappropriate because on that day debutantes were engaged for a striptease contest. To a respectable Philadelphia lady Barnes wrote: "The last woman I let in gave me the clap."[19] "You will never learn art criticism," he wrote to a

18 Hart, op. cit., p. 163.
19 Burt, op. cit., p. 353. "The outraged lady took the letter to her lawyer who explained how carefully Barnes had avoided legal difficulties: he hadn't said *she* had given him the clap."

woman journalist, "until you have had relations with the ice man."[20] He was supposed to have thrown out a Philadelphia worthy bodily; and when the corpulent Alexander Woollcott (another graduate of Central High School) requested admission by a carefully worded whimsical telegram, Barnes answered that "thousands of birds inhabit our park and swoop down on every visible lump of suet and pick it to pieces."[21] He sent a copy of this letter—as also of many letters—to the newspapers.

In the same year that Barnes's building was completed, the trustees of the Museum, after long searching, chose the man who was to be the Museum's first director and the beneficiary of its burgage for the next thirty years. This was Fiske Kimball, who was principally an architectural historian, and a very different kind of man from Barnes. Kimball was a snob, both in the current and in the original English sense of the word: *s. nob., sine nobilitate*, that is, a man of modest background who is, however, eternally fired with social ambitions. His ability was undeniable, especially when it came to architectural and interior arrangements; and his achievements in adding to the collection of the Museum were considerable. He would flatter and, on occasion, cajole the rich and his social betters, which was perhaps the main reason why Barnes could not stomach him; but Barnes's hostility to the Museum was such that they would have collided in any event, especially after Kimball learned that Barnes was *persona non grata* to many Philadelphians.[22] In 1926 Barnes wrote Kimball:

20 Art Milner in the Travel section of *The New York Times*, 1 March 1974.
21 Schack, *op. cit.*, p. 232.
22 At first Kimball was obsequious. His letter to Barnes, 15 October 1925: "The October *Museum Bulletin* just out prompts me to hope that you will not hold me responsible for everything done here until trains of action that were started before I came have had time to run their course." *Ibid.*, p. 171. Later Kimball turned vindictive: on one occasion (in 1937) he suggested to someone that "he might look into Barnes' importation of some paintings under exhibition bonds which he did not exhibit." He added a P.S.: "One friend of mine, whom Barnes has been baiting, says there is no use going into a pissing contest with a skunk." *Ibid.*, p. 253.

Repeated applications, similar to that which you made this morning, seem to indicate that you share a very prevalent idea that the Foundation is a place for more or less conspicuous Philadelphians to entertain their friends. When you assumed your present position more than a year ago, I told you that the Foundation would cooperate with you as an official in any move that could be intelligently interpreted as educational . . . Not a thing intelligent came of these proposals; what did happen was a series of requests to have your friends and acquaintances use the Foundation as a diversion . . . For casual visitors, whatever their alleged qualifications, or under whatever local prestige they may be proposed, there is absolutely nothing doing. I am writing you frankly so that we shall be spared the further nuisance of further phone calls and arguments.[23]

When Kimball asked for a loan of some of Barnes's paintings, Barnes had his secretary answer that the proposal "would make a horse laugh," as it was full "of the stereotyped blah which comes to us so often from performers who would like to annex us as a sideshow to their circuses."[24] When Henri Marceau, the Museum's curator of painting, asked for another loan of one of Barnes's El Grecos, Barnes refused again to provide "an opportunity for a pretentious parade of 'society' people and *fonctionnaires.*"

In 1927 a suburban developer proposed to build a number of houses next to the Barnes estate in Merion. Barnes printed a notice, which he sent to the Philadelphia newspapers: unless that unscrupulous contractor desisted from his project of creating "a slum " (in reality the houses were to be quite substantial), the Barnes Foundation would transfer its art collection to the Metropolitan Museum in New York and he would "donate the gallery and park to a national center for the development by scientific educational methods of the rare artistic and mental endowments of the Negro." Eventually Barnes had his way: he

[23] Letter of 27 October 1926, cited by Schack, *op. cit.*, pp. 171–72.
[24] Hart, p. 113; Roberts, *op. cit.*, p. 80.

and one of his neighbors agreed to build a ten-foot stone wall to protect themselves and their prospects.[25]

In the summer of 1929 Barnes sold the A. C. Barnes Company for six million dollars in cash. The Foundation was now better off than ever before. The Museum was not. In 1930 he prevailed on Matisse to visit him; he wanted Matisse to paint a mural above the three principal windows of the gallery. The Museum invited Matisse to a splendid luncheon, but Barnes kept talking to him at Merion long enough to prevent Matisse from crossing the Schuylkill in time.

The president of the Museum at the time was J. Stogdell Stokes (*nomen est omen*), an amiable but unimaginative Philadelphian. The most intelligent member on his board was R. Sturgis Ingersoll, who would eventually succeed him as president. Ingersoll was thin, completely bald, with a jaunty mustache; he was both eccentric and aristocratic in his appearance: a complex person, whose attraction to art was at least as sensual as it was intellectual, and whose tastes in painting were similar to those of Barnes. Ingersoll admired Barnes's collection and had considerable appreciation for Barnes's first book. When a Matisse painting (*"Trois Soeurs"*) went on sale in New York for $15,000, Ingersoll asked for Barnes's opinion. Barnes said that it was worth the price. He said that he would take an option on it for a week while Ingersoll and his friends raised the money for the Museum in Philadelphia. This was in February 1931, a deep Depression month. By the time Ingersoll had the money— true, the day after he had told Barnes that he and his trustees had not yet been able to raise it—Barnes told him it was too late, he had bought the picture for himself. Fiske Kimball returned the canceled $15,000 note to one of the trustees: "We always knew that Barnes was a son of a bitch and now we can prove it."[26]

---

[25] Barnes proposed to this neighbor that they toss for the cost of the wall, which was considerable. Barnes won the toss.

[26] There are at least four versions of this story. According to Schack (and of course Roberts), Barnes acted in bad faith. According to Barnes, "Ingersoll's re-

There was every reason in the world why Barnes and Ingersoll should have gotten together on this, as on many other matters; but the heart has reasons which reason knows not; and at heart Barnes, unlike Whistler, was not content to amuse himself with the gentle art of making enemies; he reveled in his own crude versions of that art, if art it was. Three years after the Matisse contretemps he returned to the affair, composing a public letter to Ingersoll, of which he then sent carbon copies to many people, including the Philadelphia newspapers. He wrote that he could have sued Ingersoll for libel; yet he did not, "because I know that in economic, intellectual and aesthetic capital you are what is termed 'a poor fish.' " (Throughout the next seventeen years Barnes kept up his word-play on Ingersoll's name, he would address him: "Dear Sturgeon.") "Before you sent me the telegram . . . asking for my help to keep up your bluff in public as an art connoisseur, I was already familiar with your reputation in Paris as a boob to whom the dealers could sell any worthless picture so long as it bore the name of a well-known artist—a reputation amply corroborated in Philadelphia by the junk you exhibit in public as your collection of modern art. I knew also of your activities among the groups of tea-tasters, morons, and social parasites to whom you purvey piffle in the form of lectures on modern art . . ."[27]

His next public battle with the Museum people came soon enough. Barnes learned that the head of the Federal Arts Project in Philadelphia was a protegée of Kimball, a Miss Mary Curran, whom he had expelled from the Barnes Foundation some time before because of her "incompetence and miscon-

---

quest for advice had been a dodge and that its real purpose, which Ingersoll revealed only later, had been to get him, Barnes, to buy the picture for the Museum." Hart, *op. cit.*, p. 123. According to the dealer (Valentin Dudensing) , he needed the money urgently and sold it to Barnes when he came up with the sum. According to other dealers, Dudensing played Barnes and Ingersoll against each other to make the sale.

27 Schack, *op. cit.*, p 236.

duct." Barnes mounted a public crusade against her.[28] Pamphlets were written; releases were sent to the newspapers; a demonstration by protesting artists was threatened. Meanwhile Kimball was courting Joseph E. Widener, hoping to get for the Museum the collection that Widener's father had begun. He had Widener made a Museum trustee. In 1937 he prevailed on Widener to buy a Cézanne, "The Bathers." In the press release Kimball stated that another version of "The Bathers," "a slightly smaller picture, is in the collection of the Barnes Foundation at Merion." Barnes went into a rage. His "Bathers" was better than Widener's. He demanded a retraction in the Philadelphia newspapers. He called Widener "an ignoramus, an absentee dictator of the local art situation who functions principally at the race tracks of Miami, Saratoga and Deauville"; he said that the Widener Cézanne was "fifth-rate" and that the trustee Carroll Tyson was "half-drunk" when he talked about that picture.[29] A few months later Barnes found Widener in the deck chair next to him on the *Normandie*, bound for Europe, "side by side," Barnes said, "a couple of millionaires on the *Normandie*, just as his old man and my old man once worked side by side in a slaughterhouse."[30] In the end, Kimball failed to charm the sour Widener, whose collection went to the National Gallery in Washington.

When the Second World War came, Barnes moved his office in West Philadelphia to Merion; he also bought a country estate in Chester County, at Rapp's Corner, giving it the Breton name "Ker Feal." His interest in Post-Impressionists and in the twenties' moderns now waned; he began to collect American antiques, particularly Pennsylvania-Dutch ones, and paid more

---

[28] The Roberts comment is inadvertently funny: "Mary Curran was attacked by Barnes. Although Fiske was not now taking an active part in the project, Barnes persisted in coupling him with her." *Op. cit.*, p. 154.

[29] Hart, *op. cit.*, pp. 172–73.

[30] Aline B. Saarinen, *The Proud Possessors* (New York, 1958), p. 200. She took this story, as also others, from the *Saturday Evening Post* article, about which see p. 277.

attention to relatively unknown American painters. He became involved with Bertrand Russell. Russell had come to America with his third wife. In 1940 he was about to be appointed to a chair of philosophy at the City College of New York. Certain people instituted a taxpayer's suit against this appointment because Russell was a self-proclaimed atheist who, among other things, had proposed the salutary effects of masturbation and had ridiculed the institution of marriage. A Tammany judge revoked the Russell appointment. Immediately a committee of cultural freedom, including John Dewey, took up the Russell case. Barnes supported the committee; then he had a brainstorm. He would establish a lectureship in the Barnes Foundation for Russell, with a high salary. He wrote to Henry Hart enthusiastically: "His subject will be the philosophy and culture of Europe from the Greeks to the present day. His lectures will serve as an ideal background for our studies of the traditions in art."[31] He offered Russell a country house, to be furnished with antique pieces.

The educational prospect was splendid; the human prospect was not. Barnes could not stand the third Lady Russell,[32] whose name was Patricia (Barnes said that he preferred to call her Plebeia); among other things, he objected to the clicking of her knitting needles during the lectures of her husband. Russell defended his red-haired Lady, and kept telling people that Barnes had a deep-seated inferiority complex (which may have been true), and that Barnes was comfortable only with dogs and colored people (which was not). Barnes fired Russell, who sued him for $24,000 in back pay; Russell eventually won a verdict for $20,000. By this time Barnes the pamphleteer had the priority over Barnes the collector. He published a pamphlet,

---

[31] Hart, *op. cit.*, p. 191.

[32] Barnes: "She seems to have difficulty swallowing the impressive title of Lady Russell. It evidently gets stuck just below her larynx, for she regurgitates it automatically." Carl W. McCardle in *The Saturday Evening Post*, 4 April 1942. He didn't want her at the lectures at all (she drove her husband to Merion, since the latter did not drive). Barnes "told her to go home and stay there."

"The Case of Bertrand Russell *vs.* Democracy and Education,"[33] and distributed it across the country.

He was now seventy years old. In the same year a series of articles about him appeared in *The Saturday Evening Post,* in the vulgar-breezy style of that magazine, by Carl W. McCardle, with the title "The Terrible-Tempered Dr. Barnes."[34] During the interviews that led to the articles, Barnes cooperated with McCardle, but when the articles appeared he thought that they portrayed him as a genius who was also "a nut." Yet the articles were, by and large, complimentary to him. He went around the Main Line tearing down the cover posters of *The Saturday Evening Post*; he appeared on a local radio station; he made other publicized appearances at certain newsstands of the city and gave out another pamphlet composed by himself. Besides *The Saturday Evening Post* he now attacked one Philadelphia institution after another: the Board of Education, the Pennsylvania Academy of the Fine Arts, and in 1944, Ingersoll again. Ingersoll had made a stab at Barnes in his privately printed memoir of his friend Henry McCarter. ("A patent medicine manufacturer, Albert Barnes, had been accumulating some contemporary paintings under the advice of Mac's friend Glackens.") This may have been incorrect and unwise; Barnes's reply was incorrect and inexcusable. In a multigraphed "Message to Students at the Pennsylvania Academy of the Fine Arts from Albert C. Barnes of Merion, Pa.," he first quoted Ingersoll's erstwhile tribute to him: ("Your contribution to life here is immense"). Then he wrote that Ingersoll "runs true to form in his false statements about me. Ingersoll's book gives the names of rich snobs and bad painters who hang on the coat-tails of

[33] "If the Foundation's students had learned anything whatever of democracy in education from Russell, it was because he presented them with the perfect example of its antithesis." Cited in Hart, *op. cit.*, p. 203.
[34] *The Saturday Evening Post*, 21 March, 28 March, 4 April, 11 April 1942. "Barnes gets his greatest personal satisfaction out of writing poison-pen letters . . . Comprehending the doctor is not easy . . . A combination of Peck's Bad Boy and Donald Duck."

art. His snappy stories of gay drinking parties fail to mention
the sexual orgies which, according to current legends, often
followed these sprees. McCarter was never present at the orgies.
Some years ago Ingersoll tried, by flattery, to entice me into
joining this local band of artistic and mental cripples, and into
allowing them to contaminate our gallery by their presence."[35]

Barnes's last battle with the Museum occurred in 1948. The
Museum was planning a Matisse exhibition. In a polite letter
Henry Clifford, then curator of paintings, tried again: he asked
Barnes to lend. Barnes turned him down rudely; he wrote another pamphlet, referring to the Museum as a place of artistic
prostitution. For once he was not content with the catharsis
of having written. He was fidgety and impatient. Public drama
—which, at short notice, was his specialty—ensued. He learned
that Fiske Kimball was about to give a talk on Matisse; he also
knew that Kimball knew little about Matisse. Having studded
the audience with some of his students, Barnes showed up with
the purpose of showing up Kimball, in which endeavor he, by
and large, succeeded.[36] Kimball was overwrought and left the
room.[37] Barnes issued another pamphlet. The next year he renewed his war with the University of Pennsylvania.[38] In 1950,

[35] Barnes made sure that Ingersoll got his pamphlet. He also added a letter:
"Come on, Sturgeon, you poor fish, toe the scratch by any means you choose—
law, public press or fists. I'm ready to meet any legitimate demands to name the
fake painting, the forger, the fornicators . . ." Schack, pp. 360–61. Barnes and
Ingersoll met a week or so later in a crowded trolley car. Ingersoll remembered
Barnes's face, which "developed literally a demoniac expression, and he hissed,
'You son of a bitch.'" Barnes's version was that Ingersoll "stank of bad whisky"
and that Ingersoll was trying to attract the attention of a woman in the car.

[36] At first Barnes kept interrupting Kimball; after that one of his former
students, Abraham L. Chanin, addressed the director: "You have not made
a single statement that would enable a person of average intelligence to learn
what makes a painting a work of art, or what makes a painting by Matisse
different from the work of any other modern painter." Kimball: "Young man,
art can't be explained like that. The only specific thing about Matisse is
his being Matisse . . ." Thereafter Chanin, encouraged by Barnes, delivered
a twenty-minute lecture of his own.

[37] Hart, *op. cit.*, pp. 225–26. Some time later Barnes told Hart that he was
sorry for Kimball. Hart: "Barnes was not a vindictive man . . . but he believed
that pugnacity contributed to mental health."

[38] About this see pp. 297–99.

in the seventy-ninth year of his life, he had his first serious operation, from which he recovered well. On a hot summer day (24 July) in 1951 he had his usual abstemious lunch in his Chester Springs house with his wife, who noticed that he seemed unusually pensive and absent-minded. Then he stepped in his car, with his dog Fidèle, and drove off to his Foundation in Merion. He sped through a crossing, unobservant of the stop sign. A trailer truck hit him amidships. He died instantly; his dog, badly mangled, was shot by a state trooper.

That was the end of Albert C. Barnes. There was no funeral service. His ashes were buried somewhere in the woods of his Rapp's Corner place. He left a personal estate of about one million dollars to his wife, who survived him by more than a decade, as president of his Foundation. His will provided that after his death "the collection shall be closed, and thereafter no change therein shall be made by the purchase, bequest or otherwise obtaining of additional pictures, or other works of art, or other objects of whatever description"; and that after his death no picture of the collection shall ever be loaned or sold or otherwise disposed of except "if any picture passes into a state of actual decay so that it no longer is of any value, it may be removed from the collection for that reason only."[39] There is a touch of terrible finality in these dispositions. Less than a year before his death Barnes made a change in the bylaws of his Foundation: no trustee of the Foundation "shall be a member of the faculty or Board of Trustees or Directors of the University of Pennsylvania, Temple University, Bryn Mawr, Haverford or Swarthmore Colleges or of the Pennsylvania Academy of the Fine Arts." After his death and the death of his wife, the trustees of the Barnes Foundation were to be nominated by Lincoln University, a Negro institution in Oxford, Pennsylvania.

[39] Hart, *op. cit.*, p. 78.

THE PATRON OF ART out of Argyrol: this is how people remembered Barnes after he died, if they remembered him at all. "Dr. Medici in Merion" would mean nothing to them. This perception has not changed during the last thirty years. In the Uffizi of Merion the paintings are there still; but in the standard, and best, recent history of Pennsylvania, by Klein and Hoogenboom (which contains a longish subchapter on art), there is not a single mention of Barnes or of his Foundation. In Sam Bass Warner's *Philadelphia: The Private City,* the author is obviously unaware of Barnes's existence. In the sensitive and photographic *Philadelphia: The Unexpected City* by Laurence Lafore and Sarah Lee Lippincott, with its multifarious references to art, there is not one word (or picture) wasted on Barnes or his gallery. Nor is there one in Digby Baltzell's serious and encyclopedic *Philadelphia Gentlemen,* a description of Philadelphia's society and of its achievements; in Baltzell's later, more historical elaboration, *Puritan Boston and Quaker Philadelphia,* there is but one reference, a mere listing of Barnes among the alumni of Central High School.[40] All of this is part and parcel of the national habit of shortness of memory, especially when it it not jogged by relentless publicity; but there is also something prototypically Philadelphian about it, typical of the well-mannered but regrettable habit of unwillingness to think about unpleasant matters, unpleasant situations, unpleasant people. In sum, Barnes was forgotten because he had to be forgotten.

This is a pity, because Barnes's achievements, unlike those of many other collectors, did not, and do not, lie merely in the residual matter of his collection: among other things, he was a considerably original thinker, and a considerably interesting writer about art. By "original" I mean that, even though he repeatedly acknowledged his intellectual debts to Dewey and to Santayana (especially to the latter's *The Genteel Tradition At Bay*), very early in Barnes's awakening interest in art he saw

[40] The exception is Burt, *op. cit.*—the title of whose subchapter on Barnes, however, repeats the bromide: "Art and Argyrol."

through much of the pretentious and insubstantial verbiage of art criticism, whereafter he went on, fortified by reading as well as by his powerful insights relating to psychology and perception, to construct his own, and in many ways unique, theories of art and of painting. These cognitive theories may be found in his articles and books; they reflect at times the heavy-handedness of their author, while they also reflect a good deal of common-sense wisdom, detailed factual knowledge, and insight.

The very corpus of Barnes's writings about painting is impressive. There is his *The Art in Painting*, which was published by the Barnes Foundation in 1925, and reissued by reputable New York publishers twice later. The first sentence reads: "The object of this book is to endeavor to correlate in the simplest possible form the main principles that underlie the intelligent appreciation of paintings of all periods of time." This is a formidable proposition, which Barnes succeeds in fulfilling, not only through theoretical prolegomena, but through his almost encyclopedic, and often succinct, exposition of the styles of hundreds of great painters. Yet the preposition in the title is important: *The Art in* [and not *of*] *Painting*, a distinction which may perhaps be compared to the difference between a book about the art of reading and another about the art of writing. This, as well as his later books, dealing with French Primitives, Renoir, Cézanne, Matisse,[41] are massive and scholarly volumes, indispensable for any serious student of these painters, together with an equally indispensable *iconographie raisonnée* of their works extant throughout the world.[42] Among these

---

[41] To *The Art in Painting* we must add *Art and Education* (The Barnes Foundation, 1929) which reproduces many of Barnes's best articles, together with those of others associated with the Foundation. The principal volumes published by the Barnes Foundation are Albert C. Barnes and Violette de Mazia, *The French Primitives and Their Forms: From Their Origin to the End of the Fifteenth Century* (1931), *The Art of Henri-Matisse* (1933), *The Art of Renoir* (1935), *The Art of Cézanne* (1939), *Ancient Chinese and Modern European Paintings* (1943). His pamphlets are too numerous to mention.

[42] The tables of contents of these volumes show not only their seriousness but the varied approaches of their author. The Renoir book begins with an introductory part, of four chapters: I. Method, II. Learning to See, III. Expression

books the Renoir volume is perhaps the best, and the Cézanne perhaps the weakest (Barnes's estimation of Cézanne declined in his later years, though this is not reflected in the book). In 1927 Ezra Pound wrote that Barnes's *The Art in Painting* is "by far the most intelligent book on painting that has ever appeared in America.[43] In 1939 John Sloan, whose relations with Barnes were not good, wrote that Barnes "knows more about art than any artist needs to know"[44]; in 1929 Ingersoll wrote Barnes in a letter that Barnes kept citing in his ugly attacks on Ingersoll: "*The Art in Painting* comes so close to being the only intelligent book on the subject that it should have a wide and useful scope. Your contribution to life here is immense."

The very first published writing by Barnes tells us much about his attitude. The date is significant: it was published in April 1915 in a magazine (*Arts and Decoration*), which means that it was composed only two years after his serious collection of French modern paintings had begun. Yet it is the writing of a mature collector: it shows little of a premature design to rush into print with half-matured ideas, while it is symptomatic of Barnes's method of aesthetic judgment as well as of his, inevit-

---

and Form, IV. Expression and Growth. It follows with the Development of Renoir's Form (typical chapter headings: "Renoir's Fall from Grace in 1879," "Disruption of the 1885–1887 Form," "Color Assumes Supremacy—The Predominance of Rose-Red," etc. The concluding part is the superb exposition of Renoir and his traditions ("I. Renoir and the Venetians, II. Renoir and the Eighteenth Century French, III. Renoir and Cézanne"). There follows an extensive appendix, including a biographical sketch, analyses, and the *catalogue raisonné*. The Matisse book is different: its twenty-two chapters are: Introduction; Method; Plastic Form and Design; The Psychology of Matisse; Decoration and Decorative Design; Transferred Values; Creative Use of Traditions ("Matisse and Impressionism, Matisse and Post-Impressionism, Matisse and the Oriental Traditions, Matisse and His Contemporaries"); Drawing; Color; Light; Space; Composition; Thematic Variation; Portraiture; Black-and-White Work; Development; Matisse's Rank as an Artist; Matisse Compared with His Contemporaries; Matisse and Stravinsky. The appendix is similar to that of the Renoir volume.

[43] Cited in Shaw, *loc. cit.*

[44] *The Gist of Art* (New York, 1939), p. 21.

ably self-centered, exposition of his own convictions. It is entitled "How to Judge a Painting.":

> Every collector who studies his paintings soon learns to accept
> his own discarded pictures as the necessary milestones on his
> way . . . To discard an expensive but bad painting by a famous
> artist hurts me less than to put in the attic a picture by an un-
> known painter that I thought was good when I bought it. But
> mistakes are inevitable and that makes for interest . . .[45]

"Mere possession" is the least of "pleasures" in owning a
painting; but the joy in seeing a great painting is ineffable.
Between these two extremes are pleasures which "like the keys
of a piano" are limited only "by the performer's skill and
knowledge."

There can be no doubt that Barnes taught himself rapidly,
and that his judgment was often excellent. In one instance a
French dealer showed him a Tintoretto—Barnes walked out
without saying a word. "A glance had told him it was a fake,
as it later proved to be."[46] A double portrait he saw was attributed to Veronese; Barnes knew that it was a Titian. He bought
it for $5,200, very cheap even fifty-five years ago. "French paint-
ers," Shaw wrote, "loved the late John Quinn, but feared Barnes.
If so, it is probably because Barnes is more rigidly critical than
Quinn. He is rarely fooled." The famous French dealers knew
Barnes accordingly. The saturnine Vollard as well as the effusive
Guillaume gave him their praise. They had, of course, their own
reasons to praise him, even though Barnes was a tough client
and bargainer.[47]

---

[45] "A man with a house full of good paintings needs no subterfuge or excessive heat or cold to drive him north or south, to get away from his wearying self. Golf, dances, theatres, dinners, traveling get a setback as worthy diver-
sions when the rabies of pursuit of quality in painting, and its enjoyment, gets
into a man's system. And when he has surrounded himself with that quality,
bought with his blood, he is a King . . ."

[46] Shaw, *loc. cit.*

[47] Vollard in his autobiography, *Recollections of a Picture Dealer* (New York,
1936), p. 139 (see also p. 264): "In this expeditious fashion, which only a taste as
sure as his made possible, Mr. Barnes brought together the incomparable col-

Some of Barnes's *obiter dicta* deserve to be better known. For the Impressionists, "technique is strictly subordinate to aesthetic perception." "The artist must open our eyes to what unaided we could not see. In order to do that, the painter often needs to modify the familiar appearance of things and so make something which is, in the photographic sense, a bad likeness. All we can ask of a painter is whether, for example, in a landscape he has caught the spirit of the scene; in a portrait, if he has discovered what is essential or characteristic of the sitter . . . The problem of seeing and the problem of judging, however, are ultimately but one . . . The artist gives us satisfaction by seeing for us more clearly than we could see for ourselves, and showing us what an experience more sensitive and profound than our own has shown him."[48]

Barnes's dissatisfaction with art critics developed early in his career as a collector. He would often relate how, before 1915, he had brought their writings to museums such as the Louvre, reading them and finding that their texts were "word-juggling," obscure and confusing. In this very first article he attacked Berenson, citing Degas (who was not one of Barnes's favorite painters): "Literature has only done harm to art." In "The Aesthetics of Bernard Berenson" he returned to Berenson:

> Mr. Berenson has aided materially in the identification of the works of some of the early Italian painters by means of inves-

---

lection which is the pride of Philadelphia." Vollard in 1937: "With the authority which my age permits me to assume, I assure you that there does not exist and will never exist in the world another collection of masterpieces of the two greatest artists of the nineteenth century, Cézanne and Renoir, comparable to the one assembled by Dr. Barnes." Guillaume in *Les Arts à Paris* (January 1923—it must be said that this shiny magazine was made up by Guillaume himself): "This extraordinary, democratic, ardent, irresistible, unbeatable, charming, impulsive, generous, unique man." *Ibid.*, p. 124. During the thirties Barnes often vacationed in the Breton seaside village of Port-Manech, where he was made honorary mayor, wherefrom he returned with his favorite mutt and with the eventual name of his Chester County house.

[48] "The Problem of Appreciation" and "The Roots of Art" in *Art and Education*, pp. 13, 14, 15, 20.

tigations that are primarily and fundamentally akin to those of handwriting-experts. Interesting as that work has been in itself, it has yielded no data relevant to an appreciation of the values that make paintings works of art. Indeed, the principal effects of the activities of handwriting-experts in the field of art have been bad ones. They have resurrected the names of a number of early, and very bad, Italian painters whose work the picture-dealers sell accompanied by an expert's certificate of authenticity; in other words, antiquity, not aesthetic merit, has become the guide in a traffic in the kind of pictures which George Moore calls "cock-eyed saints painted on gold backgrounds."[49]

"Contrast," wrote Barnes, "is the essence of all drama." In his still controversial but highly interesting chapters on Cézanne and Renoir, he attacked the "Cézanne-cult" in "the present prevailing opinion in the world of art. So great is Cézanne's renown that most contemporary critics and painters regard him as the greatest, if not the only great, artist of modern times . . . Cézanne's influence has been deservedly very great, and when exercised upon artists capable of grasping and assimilating it, it has borne fruit . . . Upon innumerable lesser men . . . it has been a blight."[50] Cézanne "is easy to imitate but Renoir is inimitable."

About Picasso he told Henry Hart—and early in the former's career—"He lacks the *sine qua non* of the true artist—integrity."[51] Barnes would acknowledge that in some of abstract art "forms may be charged with aesthetic feeling even when they represent nothing definite in the real world or when what they

[49] From a subchapter in a chapter entitled "Popular Fallacies in Aesthetics," *Art and Education,* p. 267. Other "popular fallacies" deal with the work of Frank Jewett Mather (written by Barnes) and of Roger Fry (written by Laurence Buermeyer). It is followed by a chapter written by Barnes: "Art Teaching That Obstructs Education."

[50] *The Art of Renoir,* p. 216. Also: "Cézanne and Renoir were alike artists of the first rank." [But] "Cézanne's interests were very much narrower in range than Renoir's, they never displayed any such capacity for growth, and they never had at their service a comparable command of the medium of paint." P. 217.

[51] Hart, *op. cit.*, p. 185.

· 2 8 5 ·

represent is clearly without appeal in itself"; but often such forms are "sterile, and a new kind of pedantry."[52] In his "The Evolution of Contemporary Painting," in 1925, Barnes wrote that Matisse "was never tempted to seek the metaphysical abstract that led Picasso out of the paths of the great traditions of painting." "The very great majority of cubistic paintings have no more aesthetic significance than the pleasing pattern in an Oriental rug."[53]

Many of Barnes's judgments are valid and will remain valid for a long time to come. The fact that *The Art in Painting* as well as the Renoir volume begins with a psychological proposition of perception does him honor; in this sense Barnes anticipated the recognitions of some of the most famous art historians (such as Gombrich and Panofsky) of a later generation. At his best, his ideas rested on a strong foundation of American expressiveness and common sense. "Inspiration," he said, "is being excited about something you have an urge to do something about."[54] The art of life is how to be interested in what we do, no matter what it is. At his worst, he would illustrate his ideas in a populist lingo (the title of that lecture was: "Having a Hell of a Good Time Playing with Art, Education, Science and Philosophy"). He said that Lindbergh was "an artist with guts,"[55] that the greatest artist Philadelphia ever produced was the baseball manager Connie Mack, who "has given honest aesthetic pleasure to more people than anybody I know of in a lifetime spent in Philadelphia."[56] He would elaborate upon the aesthetic character of the Narberth Fire Company, which he generously supported and for which he gave a sumptuous annual dinner, until he chose to quarrel with them too.

[52] *Ibid.*, p. 213.
[53] Reprinted in *Art and Education*, p. 157.
[54] In his lecture at the Rhode Island Philosophical Society at Brown University, January 1943, cited by Hart, *op. cit.*, p. 211.
[55] To Hart as they were crossing on the *Leviathan* to France, May 1927. *Ibid.*, p. 13.
[56] *Ibid.*, p. 161; Ingersoll and Johnson, too, were Philadelphian lovers of baseball.

We shall yet return to other, perhaps more trenchant, examples of this duality of his inclinations between a kind of vulgarity that is almost always (though not necessarily) shallow and a kind of perception that is almost always (though not necessarily) penetrating. But in any event, he know how "to connect": he had an uncanny understanding not only of the value of things but of their relations. His controversial chapters on Cézanne and Renoir are good examples of this; so is his chapter on Matisse and Stravinsky, which begins with the sentence: "The quality of Matisse's form is closely paralleled in the field of music by that of Stravinsky."[57] He had a very perceptive sense of history and of the development of civilization. The first Renoir he bought in 1906 was "The Torso"; he bought it for a good price from a Chicago millionaire whose wife considered it "improper." As his biographer wrote: "Barnes was forty-two when the First World War broke out and his youth and early maturity had been lived in the 'pre-1914' world. But he had never identified with that world, and in fact was in rebellion against many of its values, and the lack of values." And, as Hart put it: "One of the chief reasons Barnes became interested in art, perhaps the major reason, was that in French Impressionism he sensed a release from the pointless strictures of obsolete mores, and an opening of new intellectual vistas the other arts had not yet perceived."[58] Yet his mind was strong enough not to fall prey to the avant-garde temptation of taking comfort in the recognition that one's opinions and preferences are "ahead" of those of the common run of men. His mind was both stronger and better than were the minds of many "advanced" art patrons,

[57] *The Art of Henri-Matisse*, p. 218. Barnes had, as we have seen (p. 264), musical talent, and attended the Philadelphia Orchestra performances regularly for a long time; he also gave musicales of high quality for his guests on occasion. Among his friends was Leopold Stokowski, to whom he once wrote (and showed the letter to McCardle of *The Saturday Evening Post*): "I blush for your hackneyed programs . . . for the surfeit of theatrical claptrap like Rachmaninoff's *Bells* or Mahler's spectacular banalities or Wagner's voluptuous debauches or Weber's inanities." *The Saturday Evening Post*, 4 April 1942.

[58] Hart, *op. cit.*, pp. 59, 48.

of people such as Mabel Dodge Luhan and Nelson Rockefeller. Later in his life he was talking about the painters of the 1913 Armory Show:

> [Barnes] said that its total effect was probably greater than that of the exhibition at the Salon des Refusés in Paris in 1864. When I inquired whether he might not be attributing to the Armory Show effects which were more the result of World War I, he replied: "The war came from the social malaise expressed in the paintings."
> . . . One effect of the Armory Show, however, he never tired of denouncing. This was the servile and superficial imitation of modern European painting by American artists.[59]

We have seen the limits of his appreciation for abstract art. It is significant that during the last dozen years of his life he developed his earnest interest in early American furniture and handicrafts. In the late 1940s, when Cézanne's reputation (and prices) were higher than ever before, he made his last two acquisitions: he traded two of his Cézannes for two Chardins. Had Barnes turned conservative? Yes and no. His appreciation for Post-Impressionists had been lessening; but, then, he had admired Chardin from the earliest of his collecting years.

Unlike many of the patrons of the avant-garde, his political judgments, too, were unusually intelligent. He was liberal throughout his life, in the old and best sense of that now shabbily frayed adjective, meaning that he took his stand for academic, artistic, intellectual freedom; yet long before Stalin, and even Lenin, he saw through the propaganda of Communists. Dialectic materialism was a vicious circle; economic determinism is a "specious oversimplification" and "an idée fixe for the mentally lazy"—an excellent statement.[60] He said that "Lenin had been able to saddle the Russians with 'Soviet tyranny' because the Russian people are several centuries behind the rest of Europe, have never had a non-tyrannical government, and are

---

[59] *Ibid.*, p. 55.
[60] *Ibid.*, p. 155; dialectical materialism was "mechanical and fallacious," " 'men do not live by bread alone,' he said, and *meant it*" (Hart's italics), p. 70.

incapable of appreciating how precious even a faulty democracy is"[61]—another truthful recognition that many intellectuals have been unable to reach even sixty years later. When Stalin started his purges, Barnes told Hart (who had radical sympathies at the time): "I told you so." With all his distaste for Communism and with all his own success in individual enterprise, Barnes thought that the government ought to interfere with rapacious monopolists or monopolies. He respected Franklin Roosevelt (though not Mrs. Roosevelt); he thought that Roosevelt saved much of capitalism and that the New Deal may have prevented a worse kind of dictatorship.[62]

Here was a man with a strong and well-proportioned world view, as well as a strong and perceptive view of art, whose opinions and judgments have stood the test of time very well. Yet it was not only the society of Philadelphia which he succeeded in alienating; the art critics, too, failed to pay him proper attention —with less reason than had the proper Philadelphians, this writer feels compelled to state. His books on Renoir, Matisse, etc., were either neglected or treated evasively. Matisse finished the first mural for the Barnes gallery, which he then had to redo because of his error in the dimensions; but Alfred H. Barr, Jr., the first director of the Museum of Modern Art and the top modern-art panjandrum in New York, in his *Matisse: His Art and His Public*, blamed Matisse's mistake on Barnes. In a later edition of his book Barr corrected this error in an errata slip of which few people were aware. In Aline B. Saarinen's *The Proud Possessors* (the very title would have riled Barnes, who had written, as we have seen, that "mere possession . . . is the least of pleasures in owning a painting"), published seven years after Barnes's death (a best seller alternately fawning and snide, depending on the social standing of the great collectors), Barnes is mentioned in passing, described by a few stock phrases and anecdotes culled by Mrs. Saarinen from elsewhere, and mostly

---

[61] *Ibid.*
[62] Ingersoll thought much the same thing.

of a social nature[63]—all of which have nothing to do with the place of Barnes's collection in the history of American civilization. Yet that place ought to be recognized, quantitatively as well as chronologically. Most of Barnes's collection had been completed before MOMA opened in 1929; and it was after his death that the brummagem era of Hirshhorn's, Annenberg's, Nelson Rockefeller's collections, including the latter's Museum of Primitive Art (a near-contradiction in terms), began.

THERE WAS (at least in this writer's opinion) one basic flaw in Barnes's thought about art. This involved his repeated, and often strained, attempt at "objectivity." We have seen that the qualities of his judgment often reflected his strong sense of historical development. About Cézanne he wrote, for example: "Now that the insurgents of the 1860's and 1870's have made their ways of seeing things a matter of common perception, it is Cabanel, Meissonnier, and Bouguereau—the painters acclaimed in their day as 'sane,' 'normal'—who are felt to be unreal." Yet his next sentence compromises (if not altogether destroys) the essential cogency of this statement and of the entire paragraph of which it forms a part: "The conceptions of the artist, in a word, are verified in the same manner as those of the scientist—by experiment, by the production of *objective* facts which vindicate their standing in the real world."[64] The italics are mine. They indicate that duality in Barnes's vision and in his character. With all of his intelligent perception of modern art and of the evolution of the world in the twentieth century, Barnes (to some extent like his friend Dewey) could not liberate his mind from the solid pragmatism of the nineteenth-century world, a world which he could transcend and yet which he did not quite transcend. He was a scientist as well as a sub-

[63] Examples: "The hot-tempered collector from Philadelphia, Dr. Albert Barnes, the inventor of Argyrol . . . waving his checkbook." [He] "lived in almost pathological isolation in his half-million-dollar limestone palace."
[64] *The Art of Cézanne*, p. 104.

jectivist. He was an aesthete who had been brought up as a Methodist, and the essence of his early education never disappeared from his mind, because he did not wish to suppress it.[65] The shortcomings of his writings and of his theories may be—somewhat coarsely—summed up in one sentence: at times it seems as if Barnes were struggling to establish the *scientific* rules of *art*.

This duality accompanied him throughout his life. His attacks on art critics, including Berenson, are telling; but in the same article Barnes would say that Berenson does not deal "with the objective facts that enter into an appreciation of art-values, but with a form of antiquarianism made up of historical, social, and sentimental interests entirely adventitious to plastic art."[66] Barnes would go to great lengths to analyze paintings, emphasizing their *form* and *plastic content*, sometimes very successfully, positing his analysis against the vagueness and the verbiage of certain art critics; yet on other occasions he himself would use adjectives such as "pervasive," "indefinable," "mysterious," "noble." His unfriendly biographer, Schack, is quite right when he says that the dissection of great paintings, "no matter how skillful or delicate the surgeon, will never give the clue as to why they stir us. The demonstration that the first movement of Beethoven's Fifth Symphony is built up on variations of a four-note motif will not reveal why the music is so poignant at first hearing." He quotes Barnes's own writings against him: he poses Barnes's successful analysis of Giorgione's "Pastoral Concert" against another of Barnes's paragraphs about Rembrandt's portrait of his wife (in the Louvre) where Barnes writes: "We *feel* the wonder and mystery—we only see the objec-

---

[65] In this respect see Hart, *op. cit.*, p. 8: "I came out of a similar background and sensed beneath [Barnes's] intolerances that he espoused the ethics and ideals I too had derived from an enfeebled Protestantism in a shrewdly oligarchic Philadelphia . . . the weltanschauung of pre-World War I Philadelphia, lurking at the bottom of both of us, resulted in an unspoken mutual respect, which survived quarrels and other disillusioning experiences." (This must be set against the other statement by Hart about Barnes and the pre-1914 world, p. 287.)

[66] *Art and Education*, p. 266.

tive fact that calls them up in a way we cannot explain . . .
Rembrandt paints in terms of the broadest universal human
values."[67] If this is not "something close to slush," as Schack
puts it, he is nevertheless correct in saying that "though Barnes
clings with pathetic obstinacy to his 'objective fact,' he has in
reality scrapped [I would say: unconsciously abandoned] his
analytical method."[68]

Barnes was a scientist with great powers of insight and feeling who, at his best, was aware of both the essential presence
and the essential limitations of feeling. In *The Art in Painting*
he rightly said that human beings have preferences "and in
the last analysis these preferences are something behind which
we cannot go. Our feelings, if not irrational, are at least non-
rational."[69] In one instance he criticized Leo Stein for "his ideal
system of aesthetics . . . from which the personal factor is to be
rigidly excluded. He says it is permissible to point out the use
made by a painter of color, light, line, and space, but not to say
that such is good or bad. He asserts that statements of the former
sort belong to science, and have general validity, and that statements of the latter sort reveal something not about the picture
but only about the person who is looking at it." This kind of
"sublime aloofness . . . is a psychological impossibility." All
thought has a subjective element in it; as William James said,
it is "judged true or false according as it satisfies our whole
nature, including our feelings." Stein's "ideal" of objectivity
reminds Barnes of the skeptic who, because all thought may err,
refuses to think at all; Stein's aloofness from reality is the result of "a dread of accepting the responsibilities of action" and
not of "a highly sensitive conscience."[70]

---

[67] Schack, *op. cit.,* p. 200.

[68] *Ibid.,* pp. 200–1.

[69] "The Roots of Art," p. 24.

[70] From "Day-Dreaming in Art Education," April 1926, *The Journal of the Barnes Foundation*. In some ways Barnes's article was an answer to Leo Stein's critique of *The Art in Painting* in *The New Republic*. After Barnes's criticism of Stein, "Stein didn't speak to Barnes for six years. Then, one day in '32, in an art gallery in Paris, he went up to Barnes and offered his hand. They began

This is a very valid criticism, which shows that Barnes's use of the word "objectivity" was not rigid or absolute. In *The Art of Renoir* he wrote that the perceptions of an artist "are never an inventory of objective facts," that aesthetic analysis is not "a dissection," that an intelligent analysis of a work of art produces "the familiar warmth and glow" that pervades "the whole self when a new experience is born."[71] He even says that discrimination may lead to "an ultimate re-synthesis," which is the highest achievement of analysis in aesthetics. The above passages indicate that at times, and often acutely and consciously, Barnes *was* aware of the limitations of objectivity, even though (like most thinkers of the twentieth century) he could not yet liberate his mind from the Cartesian dualism of object/subject; he had not arrived at the recognition that human knowledge is neither objective nor subjective but personal and participant. Aware as Barnes was of the end of the bourgeois-modern world, he was not yet aware of the fatal leak in the Cartesian and Newtonian world-view. But that is another story.

BUT EVEN MORE IMPORTANT, consistent, and enduring than his belief in the "objectivity" of "facts" was Barnes's belief in education. Barnes believed in the educability of the common man. His Foundation was officially dedicated not to "art" but "to the cause of education." This very American conviction accompanied him throughout his life. That loft of a factory where Argyrol was produced he hung with paintings. He had five employees, three white women and five black men, for whom he set up generous pensions and whose mortgages he would often pay. On occasion he got some of them out of trouble

---

corresponding again and when Stein wrote that he was hard up, Barnes several times sent him several thousands of dollars." Hart, pp. 136–37. The dedication of *The Art of Henri-Matisse* reads: "To Leo Stein who was the first to recognize the genius of Matisse and who, more than twenty years ago, inspired the study which has culminated in this book."

[71] Hart about *The Art of Renoir, op. cit.*, p. 143; the original text (*Renoir*, pp. 17 *et seq.* is slightly different) .

(one of the blacks, nicknamed Argyrol Jack, was a prize-
fighter in his spare time). When Barnes later expanded the
factory—he never employed more than twenty people—he paid
the wages of his married black workers to their wives. His workers, in fair exchange, were compelled to attend lectures by
Barnes (and, on occasion, by others) about painting and psychology, for two hours out of the eight-hour working day. Not
all of this effort was wasted. During these long years he taught
the three women (Misses Mullen and Miss Geiger), simple,
homely, unassuming spinsters, about art. Later, when he established his Foundation, he put the Mullen sisters in charge of it,
and not merely of its administration. He published a book by
Mary Mullen; some of her lectures and articles he found worthy
enough to include in his books, and he dedicated *The Art of
Renoir* to her. Here was an engaging element in his character:
Barnes was forever inclined to share his achievements with his
loyal collaborators. This included the three above-mentioned
women, as well as Violette de Mazia, a Belgian immigrant after
World War I and a teacher of French in a local school, a woman
whom Barnes discovered around 1925 and soon made one of the
instructors at the Foundation (after his death she became the
director of the Foundation and a trustee). These people surrounded and protected Barnes's ego with something approaching absolute loyalty. In turn, he was not only munificently
generous to them but he was inspired to list them as co-authors
of some of his books. This was the very opposite of what most
Philadelphians, including those who ought to know better, believed and still believe: that Barnes had other people write his
books and articles for him.

Barnes was the very opposite of an elitist. "To make human
nature intelligible to itself—that is the real purpose of art, that,
and not the construction of some sanctuary for those who find
the real world of practical affairs too much for them."[72] This

---

[72] In Buermeyer, "Art and the Ivory Tower." *Journal of the Barnes Foundation*, May 1925, reprinted in *Art and Education*, p. 41.

was written by Laurence Buermeyer, a young art historian whom Barnes discovered and supported even after Buermeyer could no longer teach or work because of his psychic collapse and dependence on alcohol. It is a fine summary of Barnes's own credo.[73] It is significant that Barnes became a personage in the history of American art in 1915, which was, according to the title of Van Wyck Brooks's important essay-book, the date of *America's Coming of Age.* Yet Barnes would have no understanding of Brooks's fatal distinctions between "lowbrow," "highbrow," "middle-brow." We have seen how Barnes's common sense kept him from falling in with those avant-garde or highbrow temptations which were intellectually endemic to rich American humanists of that period. Thorough democrat as he was, he had scant sympathy for left-wing radicalism, not only because he saw through the fallible nature of utopian ideologies, but because he was aware of the inflated vanities and the weak characters of their supporters. He grew more and more contemptuous of elites, whether social or intellectual: he concluded that they were worthless. During this time—before his first public blast at the Philadelphia elite—he would, on occasion, bring his horse groom, Funk, to the table of the hunting breakfasts of the Rose Tree and of the Pickering Hunt. Later he put his chauffeur, Albert Nulty, in charge of restoration and preservation at the Foundation; he entrusted him with the planning and the positioning of the three Matisse murals above the windows of the central gallery room, a task which Nulty performed well enough to earn Matisse's respect and the right to correct the Frenchman when the latter had made an error in the dimensions. (Nulty, too, became a trustee of the Foundation, by Barnes's will.) Barnes discovered and helped black painters, such as Horace Pippin (in 1940 he bought seven of his paintings

---

[73] Barnes in *The Arts*, January 1923: "Primarily the hope is that every person, of whatever station in life, will be allowed to get his own reactions to whatever the Foundation has to offer; that means that academicism, conformity to worn-out conditions, counterfeits in art, living and thinking, can have no place in the intended scope of the Foundation." Quoted by Schack, *op. cit.*, p. 125.

on the spot), as well as young black doctors (enabling one of them to study in Europe), black organists, choirs, institutions.[74] It is wrong to believe that he used his association with blacks merely to entertain his guests or to threaten his neighbors. People who saw Barnes explain Cézanne to a black hod carrier knew that he was deadly serious about it; he did not do it for show.

When it came to institutionalized education, his experiments and illusions almost always turned to failures. In 1918 John Dewey induced Barnes to finance a study of Polish immigrants in Philadelphia. This "field study" of "acculturation" involved famous researchers, mostly from Columbia University.[75] Nothing came of it. The subjects of the "field study" were either dumbly suspicious or stolidly speechless when the questions were posed to them by the professors and those odd women from New York. This was Barnes's first experience with that kind of "research." He agreed with Dewey that it ought to be suspended. Yet he believed in institutionalized education throughout his life. There was something in his Methodist background that attracted him to the lecture method. At the Foundation the lectures, including his own, went on for three hours, without a break. Soon there was a decline in the number of students. By 1928, when *The New Yorker* published the glowing account of Dr. Medici's collection in Merion, Dewey had already resigned as Educational Director, the two best instructors (Munro and Buermeyer) had departed. "Ironically enough, the courses at

---

[74] On one occasion he led a movement to establish a monument for James G. Bland, the black composer and musician who was buried in a potter's field in Merion. He was, however, doubtful of certain matters in which he saw characteristics of the race: consider his practice of giving the pay to his black workers' wives. Schack quotes him on one occasion: "All Negroes steal" (p. 240). Hart lists his numerous benefices to blacks and to their causes, but adds that "Barnes was not usually sentimental about Negroes, and had few illusion about them. He once said that not one of those to whom he had lent money had repaid it . . . ." Pp. 238–39.

[75] They included Dewey, Francis Bradshaw, Irwin Edman, Anzia Yezierska, Brand, and Paul Blanshard (the last went on to become an intellectual crusader against the Catholic Church).

the Foundation are now almost back to the point where they started, as seminars in Dr. Barnes' factory. The lectures are now given by Dr. Barnes or by his two lady assistants, one of whom is employed at his plant, and the audience usually consists of his employees and a few of his friends who report at the Foundation in the late afternoon after work on Sunday mornings."[76] During the rest of Barnes's life these conditions changed little. The students admitted were of varying caliber; in any event, they found the rigorously monitored attendance at the long lectures difficult. In later years Barnes himself admitted to Hart that he was sometimes jealous of his wife's work in the adjoining Arboretum (established in 1940, and rigidly separated from the Foundation), since he saw that "the students at the Arboretum's courses were, on the average, more intelligent and effective human beings than those at the Foundation's art courses."[77] We have seen how enthusiastic Barnes was in 1940 with the prospect of Bertrand Russell's lecturing at the Foundation; but that experiment failed, too, and not only because of the conflict between Barnes and Lady Russell. Russell's lectures and the attentiveness of the students went downhill soon.

Barnes's relations with the University of Pennsylvania, his alma mater, deserve almost as much attention as his relations with the Art Museum. They show his recurrent, and obsessive, illusions about institutionalized education; they also show that, unlike in his war with the Museum, the blame for the failure to cooperate must not be laid principally on his side. When the Foundation was established in 1925, Barnes's relationship to the Art Museum people was already compromised, while he was full of hopes for a new educational program, to be undertaken jointly with the University of Pennsylvania, whose provost and whose philosophy professors praised Barnes to high heaven at the opening of his gallery. Barnes was ready to underwrite the expenses of a new program at the University of Pennsylvania, including

[76] Shaw, *loc. cit.*
[77] Hart, *op. cit.*, 188–89.

courses in intellectual history, art history, aesthetics, etc., to participants of which he would open all the facilities of the Barnes Foundation. He was ready to offer the university at least partial control of the Foundation. Yet the administrators and faculty of the university were cautious, unimaginative, fearful, and stuffy. They moved—if they moved at all—with turtle-like slowness. They did nothing to publicize the program, little or nothing to direct the students' attention thereto. The few students who showed up were not very good. Barnes saw that they knew little of history or literature; at best they would learn the definitions of certain terms, "but they could not recognize concepts when put before them." "What they went in for was labeling facts and abstract arguments."[78] The classes soon ceased.

This was different from his fights with the Museum. The problem was not the lending of his art for show; it was that his offers of gold were turned to dross. After some years a new dean of the School of Fine Arts of the university approached Barnes again. At first Barnes was very forthcoming, offering to underwrite at least two professorships, including one of music, to be held by Nicholas Nabokov (whom he had invited to the Foundation). The rush was too much for the university people; they tergiversated, hemmed, hawed. Barnes answered their cautious letter instantly: the fine-arts department of the university was an "intellectual, educational and aesthetic sewer." The music department was "lousy." The painting and drawing departments were "decrepit." "This letter concludes my efforts to make our

---

[78] Schack, *op. cit.*, p. 165. In 1926 a committee was formed "to arrange for better cooperation between the [University of Pennsylvania] faculty and the Foundation staff. The committee was formed but never met. Barnes invited its members to visit the Foundation as a group but they never came. Next he invited all the faculty advisors to discuss the work of the Foundation and only two or three attended. In the spring of 1926 Barnes extended the invitation to the entire faculty of the college, graduate and education departments, to consider a far-reaching plan of his. He did not realize that most people, including college teachers, were chiefly concerned with their own subjects, and that most college teachers, like other people, were only casually interested in art. He did not seem to have realized it even when only six persons accepted the invitation." *Ibid.*, pp. 166–67.

resources available to the University of Pennsylvania. In fact, steps have already been taken to make sure that, after my death, the University will have no finger in our pie."[79] Yet fourteen years later the prospect of a Barnes-Penn cooperation arose once more—only to prove the imprecise axiom according to which drama, when repeated, is bound to result in comedy. In 1948 the Republican patricians of Philadelphia had made Harold E. Stassen president of the University of Pennsylvania. (Eisenhower became president of Columbia that year.) A well-meaning intermediary (John M. Fogg, Professor of Botany, who worked with Mrs. Barnes's Arboretum) approached Barnes first (who said, yes, he would listen), then Stassen. Stassen's letter to Barnes revealed the fatuities of this then Boy Wonder from Minnesota. He was "pleased to note the general observation of Professor John Dewey's ninetieth birthday" and expressed his interest in "Prime Minister Nehru's approach to the international situation." In a second letter he made an imbecilic reference to Picasso and the State Department. Barnes immediately concluded that Stassen was a fool. Still, he did address two or three long letters to Stassen, with carbon copies amply distributed among his friends and others.

His last educational experiment was his invitation to a selected group of students from Lincoln University, the black institution. He found that they, too, were woefully ill-prepared. Yet Barnes never abandoned his trust in education. He was on his way to Merion to interview a new instructor when he rushed past that fatal stop sign in July 1951.

On two occasions (in 1925 and in 1945) Barnes attacked the Philadelphia school system because of its inadequate and ineffective programs of art education.[80] He had as much trouble with the public schools as with the educational and social elite at the university, the academies, the museums. Part of this was,

---

[79] *Ibid.*, p. 235.

[80] *Cf.* his "The Shame in the Public Schools of Philadelphia" in the first (April 1925) *Journal of the Barnes Foundation: Sabotage of Public Education in Philadelphia* (1945), a pamphlet.

of course, the result of intemperate attacks on certain persons. But, then, Barnes not only maintained a lifelong belief in education; he believed *"it was his duty* [Hart's italics] to expose intellectual shams."[81] As Barnes wrote in his article "Construction and Controversy," new ideas have to battle old ones "merely for a place to grow." Strong attacks may be in bad taste, but this cannot be helped. "It is impossible to attack institutions," Barnes believed, "without attacking the individuals responsible for what those institutions do or fail to do. All the institutions are directed and utilized by persons," and "if the institutions are noxious that fact is apparent in the effect they have on individuals who profit by the operations of the institutions. This is the ground for the legal maxim that all guilt is personal."[82]

Barnes had plenty of common sense and plenty of guile. For one thing, he refused to insure his collection, for the simple reason that it was invaluable. He, who went to great expense in enriching his books with extensive reproductions, refused to issue an illustrated catalogue of his collection. What for? He did not want to impress people or to invite them. He taught his secretaries to imitate his signature. "The letters he had me sign," one of them reminisced, "were ones he could later deny that he had dictated or sent, and though the recipient would swear that the signature was authentic, if the case reached court—and oh, how Barnes loved his fights to reach court!—the handwriting experts could, of course, testify to forgery."[83] Yet his common sense, his guile, and the vaunted integrity of his privacy deserted him when it came to his public rows and invective letters. He would chuckle over his phrases, which were often brutal rather than witty, carrying copies of his epistles in his pockets to show

[81] Hart, p. 99.

[82] *Ibid.,* p. 101; Barnes's article from the *Journal of the Barnes Foundation,* October 1925.

[83] Cynthia Flannery Stine, "My Private War with Dr. Barnes," *Harper's,* August 1956. Mrs. Stine's employment began with Barnes shouting a dictation to her from his steam bath and ordering her to manipulate the faucets; it ended with mutual disagreements four year later; she was astonished to see that at the moment of parting Barnes reciprocated her tears.

to people. He, who early in his life knew how to use publicity in the successful marketing of Argyrol misused it time after time, at his own expense, in his public crusades in Philadelphia. The owners and the editors of the main newspapers regarded him as a pest or an enemy. He insisted that they print his releases or his letters; he also kept complaining that he was being misquoted. This self-made populist soon found that, when it came to him, the popular columnists of the Philadelphia newspapers would unhesitatingly follow the attitudes of the refined elite of the city. "Get Off Your High Horse, Doc," chuckled the silly old "Horsefeathers" (John W. Cummings) of the *Inquirer*. On another occasion, Paul Jones of *The Bulletin* wrote of "a little picture collection kept by an obscure chemist somewhere on the Main Line."[84] Within a day Barnes addressed a letter to Jones, referring to him as the chemical substance of human ordure, in French.[85] The "letter" was signed by Fidèle de Port-Manech, Barnes's favorite dog, a signatory expedient to which he often resorted during the last dozen years of his life.

The failures of Barnes's life and heritage—the lack of proper recognition of his work, the misunderstandings surrounding and, worse, obscuring his achievements—were, thus, mostly of his own making. And here we come to the essence of the matter—or, more precisely, here we must go as far as we reasonably can in our attempt to understand the strange duality of this man. This granite-faced, strong-willed, often commonsensical and intelligent man who, in addition to his other mental strengths, was aware of his own faults,[86] was obviously not at peace with himself. What was the source of his rages? of his suspicions?[87]

---

[84] 10 May 1950.

[85] The correspondence in Schack, *op. cit.*, pp. 385–86.

[86] To his friend Ralph Evans, a lawyer: "I guess I'm a son of a bitch, but I was born that way." Schack, p. 356. To the widow of his friend Glackens: Her husband he had loved "as I have never loved but half a dozen people in my lifetime. He was so real, and so gentle and of a character that I would have given millions to possess." *Ibid.*, p. 280.

[87] Consider, for example, the procedure for the admission of people who were lucky enough to qualify for a visit to the Gallery during Barnes's lifetime. Applications had to be made; a card was eventually sent. An attendant opened

of his duality, which was psychic and not merely intellectual?
of his often alternating fits of high hope and furious disillu·
sionment? of his pleasure-loving and of his dyspepsia?[88] of the
potent streaks of sadistic cruelty in his expressions, which were
contradicted by his frequent generosities[89] and complemented,
perhaps, by another streak of impotent masochism,[90] expressed

---

the main door a few inches; he collected the card, closed the door again. After
a minute or so the door was opened again a little, just wide enough so that
some of the visitors had to get through it sideways. They entered a darkened
entrance hall, beyond which shone the main room, between whose large French
windows Dr. Barnes sat at a desk, peering at the visitors and looking them
over. —He also had the habit of standing around corners, and eavesdropping
at what some of the visitors would say. —When he started collecting early
American furniture, he had his people take the pieces apart, down to the
smallest wooden screw: if there was any evidence of repairs or substitutions
during the lifetime of the piece, it would be returned to the dealer with a
furious letter.

[88] The dinners he offered his friends were excellent, planned and set out with
great care. (Celebrities among his friends included Albert Einstein, Thomas
Mann, Katharine Cornell, Eva Le Gallienne, Carl Van Vechten, William C.
Bullitt.) His lunches consisted of a bowl of chopped-up dry lettuce and tomatoes.
He had an excellent collection of liquors and wines; he would mix his and his
guests' drinks himself, measuring the amounts carefully, out of chemical beakers.

[89] He would, on occasion, turn on his friends. He once said to Dewey: "Jack,
do you know why I like you? It's because you remind me of a bartender I used
to know." *The Saturday Evening Post*, 29 March 1942. Yet he was munificent
and solicitous to Dewey during the latter's lifetime. —When his friend Glackens
was undergoing an operation, Barnes, on the strength of his M.D. degree, insisted that he be allowed to stay in the operating room; after the operation he
came to see Glackens every day, bringing him homemade soup prepared by
Mrs. Barnes. —His relations with the neighboring Episcopal Academy were
originally good; but soon he would accuse the students of throwing balls over
the high stone wall and destroying things on his property, charges that were
assiduously investigated by the Headmaster and found to have been ground-
less; yet Barnes would think nothing of trespassing on the academy grounds
day after day, when walking his dog.

[90] His enemies accused him of drunkenness and lechery—accusations, it seems,
without substance. He would quarrel with his wife but then write her long,
affectionate letters (especially when he set out on a transatlantic trip, alone);
they were loyal, helpful, and dependent on each other for fifty years. They had
no children. Yet it is not unreasonable to detect an element of sexual frustration
in some of his expressions. He would make such references in all kinds of letters
(to Archibald MacLeish in 1935: a colored reproduction of a painting, even when
it is good, "its analogue is a hearsay version of a honeymoon narrated by an
octogenerian"). His letters of invective often included some kind of cruel sexual

by his fitful show to the world that he was rejected? This writer is not a Freudian, and he does not believe that the source of human failure is the unconscious wish to fail (Barnes himself said once that the Freudians' death wish was "nothing more than a fancy name for . . . lazy, incompetent or ignorant people. 'The secret of life . . . is struggle' ")[91]—and yet there was something self-destructive in the character of Albert Coombs Barnes.

Like another very different Philadelphian, Boies Penrose, Barnes was an unbelieving man. He does not seem to have believed in a world other than this. But this of course was, and remains, a matter between Barnes and God. About this we cannot be sure. What we can ascertain is that Barnes was ridden by a strong sentiment of inferiority, especially toward his "betters" in Philadelphia. His wife recognized this and would mention it to him and to his closest friends on occasion. Here, too, a question remains for a future biographer if—and that is a big if— Barnes's correspondence becomes available to him. The question consists of *when* (rather than *how*, or *why*) his cup was full. There is little that was particularly vindictive in his early career. His furious attacks on the Philadelphia elite did not begin until that celebrated contretemps of the exhibition of his modern paintings in 1923, an experience which, in Hart's words, "affected him more than he admitted."[92] Yet in 1923 he was fifty-one years old. His character had been formed long before. During the previous fifteen years he had attempted to make his own singular impression on the society of the old Philadelphia families, with some of whom he took up the high-horse experience

---

reference—usually near or at the end of the letters. Special examples are his letters to Ingersoll; they may suggest his jealousy of the latter, who was a ladies' man. His sexual references and the illustrations of his arguments with crude sexual examples in his letters increased as he got older; yet relatively early in his manhood (*aetatis* 55) he wistfully pointed out a couple of young lovers in Paris to Hart on one occasion: that was what happiness was all about, he said.

[91] Hart, *op. cit.*, p. 175.
[92] P. 115.

of fox hunting[93]; twenty years later he would issue from his country house with a shotgun to chase the M.F.H. of the Pickering Hunt from his grounds. Undoubtedly 1923 was a turning point in his relationship with Philadelphians; but he had been traveling along his self-made road in that direction for some time, transferring some of his scorn for the elite of art critics to the elite of Philadelphia. He was, and he remained—and he would trumpet this from his housetop—the roughneck poor Philadelphia boy who was every way as good as the refined people of his city and who knew how to tell them the uncouth truth. In this respect he resembled not Boies Penrose but another rebel Philadelphian, William C. Bullitt: impatient, impetuous, Francophile, given to strong hatreds like himself, with whom he struck up a friendship during his later years. Unlike Bullitt, however, whose family connections were certain and uncontestable, Barnes had an attitude toward these Philadelphians in which a fatal kind of oscillation continued to exist.

From time to time his war with Philadelphia was interrupted by signals of truce. We have seen his repeated attempts to establish a close working relationship with the University of Pennsylvania, which, to be sure, failed largely because of the university, rather than because of Barnes; these attempts, however, may be justly ascribed to his unrelenting belief in education. The history of his relationship with the Art Museum people was more complicated. On occasion the curator of paintings would approach Barnes with a request for a loan; Barnes would con-

---

[93] He was not a good rider. Yet Schack is wrong when he writes of the Philadelphians: "If they admired Barnes' courage in coming back after every fall, indulging in a little gentlemanly laughter at his obtuseness in not modifying his style of riding, they could only look askance at his manners. He acquired the reputation of being a thruster, a man who pushed his way in ahead of other people out of turn." *Op. cit.*, p. 66. Surviving members of the hunts do not agree with such a version: according to them the kind of courage exhibited by Barnes was commendable. "His courage may have been admired, but his style and manners were not." Burt, p. 351. After he had given up riding, he explained his decision to Hart in anatomical terms: the frames of large men were not suited to horses. Hart thinks that this was a rationalization.

sider it for a day or so and then, battening on some intellectual error or slight, imagined or real, he would let loose a haymaker and destroy the prospect of their collaboration, at least in that instance. Yet there were occasions when the flag of truce was cautiously hoisted by Barnes himself. In 1936, for example, Barnes wrote to John S. Jenks of the Museum Board, offering to pay for the costs of an exhibit of modern French tapestries. This seemed to be an agreeable prospect, until one day in October when he was visiting the Museum (he would often drop in unannounced), a Museum attendant, a former student who had been expelled from the Foundation, created what Barnes called "a disturbance," interfering with Barnes's contemplation of certain German paintings in a special exhibit. Barnes wrote Kimball, who, true to form, ignored Barnes's letters. Barnes then addressed Jenks: "For more than two years I have been trying my damnedest to keep my public mouth shut about a number of bad things at the . . . Museum," but now he threatened to "blow the lid off." Within a few hours he fired off another letter, containing something of an ultimatum: he requested that all the Museum's employees who had been present in the German exhibition room assemble the following Monday morning "to give evidence . . . Upon that evidence, and other documentary data, I shall ask the Trustees of the Museum to take the necessary action to clean up the moral sewer that has been running through the Museum for a considerable time . . ."[94] It seems that there was some substance to Barnes's complaint; he got a partial vindication; Jenks told Kimball to dismiss the offending employee. Yet a few months later Barnes canceled his offer. He was infuriated by a lecture given at the Museum by E. M. Benson, a second-rate art critic, whom he called a "plagiarist." "The reason for this decision is recent factual corroboration of my previous statement that the Philadelphia Museum of Art is a house of artistic and intellectual prostitu-

[94] Schack, *op. cit.*, pp. 260–61.

tion."[95] "And still," as Schack says, "he did not break off relations with 'the house of artistic and intellectual prostitution.' Where else could he go? It was the only 'brothel' in which he could make the madame listen to him, or failing in that, make tremble."[96]

"I have a big stake in the good name of the city which my ancestors laid out," Barnes wrote the president, J. Stodgell Stokes, around that time.[97] Yet he tried his best—or, rather, worst—to cast aspersions on the "good name" of the city. In this he did not succeed—but, on occasion, he did succeed in making people, if not tremble, at least uncomfortable. That this reaction was subtly transformed into studied neglect and enduring disdain of Barnes the boor was due to Barnes's intemperate acts and words: it was his loss, and he felt it keenly until the very end of his life. Yet wasn't there a loss for Philadelphia too? For we may raise the question: in Barnes's war with Philadelphia, was he the only party troubled with insecurity? Surely his manners were, more than often, reprehensible; but there were certain instances when his judgment (and, when it came to art, his taste) was better than Philadelphia's, when he, the non-patrician, was less of a philistine than the Art Museum crowd[98] (not to

[95] *Ibid.*, p. 264.

[96] P. 266. A year later Barnes made an offering to the Museum, a small (very small) artifact for its Pennsylvania-German room.

[97] *Ibid.* Barnes was proud of the fact that his family on his father's side were the earliest settlers of Philadelphia. In Watson's *Annals of Philadelphia* . . . (Philadelphia, 1899), vol. III, p. 307, I found the name of a Presbyterian minister, the Reverend Albert Barnes, a strong-minded individualist of a preacher, called to the First Presbyterian Church in 1830 and briefly suspended from his preaching in 1837 (one of his main supporters was Joseph R. Ingersoll, a member of the church). Were the two Albert Barneses related? This, too, remains for a future biographer to ascertain.

[98] Frank Crowninshield, the editor of *Vanity Fair*, had come to Philadelphia during the Cézanne fracas in 1937 and wrote Barnes about a lunch with the elite of the University Museum: "I was amused to find at the luncheon they gave me . . . that no one was talking of anything but the Cézanne incident, and all of them talking of the picture in terms of dollars per figure, rather than in terms of art, as if Cézanne had painted with the idea of selling pictures by the figure . . . The main point—quality of content—had apparently escaped them." 5 December 1937, cited by Schack, p. 271.

speak of the university and of what Barnes used to call "the Independence Hall societies").

This is a point that remains to be made, and not only for the purpose of drawing attention to the achievements of Barnes. In one of the few books about Philadelphia, Struthers Burt wrote in 1945: "In all the country, and for that matter in all the world, there are no finer men and women than Philadelphia's best; none more charming, more simple, more dignified, more interesting, more good-looking, more cultivated, and more intelligently liberal . . . In all the world there are no houses where you could find better talk, or better thought, than in certain Philadelphia houses."[99] About half this statement may be true, not more. When Hilaire Belloc visited Philadelphia, he thought that the only thing he could do to enliven a Philadelphia dinner party was to take off his shoes and dance a jig. Philadelphia is a very large provincial town with patrician touches which are real and enduring; yet scratch the Philadelphia patrician and you'll find the philistine sometimes. His social patronage of culture has often a Germanic tinge. From Franklin's scientific-serious societies to the fervor of certain patricians for Science, Anthropology, Excavations, there shows a Germanic respect for Knowledge, immediately beneath the English veneer. It is a culture which patronizes Russian musicians but which is insensitive to irony and is baffled by criticism; a stodgy culture with a radical tinge which would rather pay lip service to Zola than bother with Flaubert, which will hesitatingly follow current reputations elsewhere rather than recognize the best of Philadelphia's own; it happened to Agnes Repplier, to Thomas Eakins, people surely very different from Albert Coombs Barnes. So often has Philadelphia favored the second-, if not the third-rate, due to a sort of provincial suspicion well hidden behind a successfully maintained pose of patrician reserve. It is easy to be deceived by this pose, as if it were the natural reserve of con-

[99] *Philadelphia: Holy Experiment* (Philadelphia, 1945). About the author, see also p. 324; he was the father of Nathaniel Burt (*The Perennial Philadelphians*).

fident and cultured patricians. What lies beneath it is embarrassment, an unwillingness to take risks and, more often, an unwillingness to think.

So far as Barnes's great collection went, Philadelphia got its way. Very soon after his violent demise the first salvo against his will was fired. Harold Wiegand, an editorial writer from *The Philadelphia Inquirer*, whose owner, Walter Annenberg,[100] had often participated in the proper and popular Philadelphian censurings of Barnes, instituted a taxpayers' suit in order to force the opening of the gallery. This vendetta against Barnes's memory was legally indefensible and also unnecessary, since Barnes's dispositions provided that, after Mrs. Barnes's death, her Arboretum as well as her husband's gallery should be open to the public on Saturdays and for students of art during the rest of the working week. The suit was dismissed, but the *Inquirer* (a most dreadful newspaper then) went on, posing as the defender of Philadelphia's right to the contemplation of art. Ten years later it was the State of Pennsylvania that brought suit against Barnes's will, and the Supreme Court of the Commonwealth decided—on a rather questionable legal foundation—that, in order to qualify as a tax-free institution, the gallery should be open to the public even while Mrs. Barnes was still alive. The Foundation now announced that the gallery would be open to the public on Fridays and Saturdays, except in July and August, and that it would now have to charge admission (one dollar) for the expense of additional guards. (Annenberg and the *Inquirer* sought a court injunction against that, too.) There remains, however, a sense of futility and sadness about this—and not only because of the partial dissolution of Barnes's will. The Foundation is now open, and the incomparable collection under one roof may be visited by anyone, yet the number of

---

[100] A communications billionaire whose social ambitions surely eclipsed those of Barnes: eventually he became Nixon's ambassador to the Court of St. James's, whereafter he retired to his estate in Palm Springs, California, friend and confidant of successive Republican Presidents.

Philadelphians who are aware of its existence diminishes year after year.

This is Philadelphia's loss, and also Barnes's, wherever he now dwells: he got what he deserved, in more than one way. Still he deserves respect for his achievements, which sprang from one solitary and enduring strain in his otherwise complex and unpleasant character: from his belief in the perfectibility of man. As his friend Hart wrote: "He believed in it because he was convinced he had proved its possibility in his own life." There is something very American in this, or rather, very typical of Barnes's generation of self-taught and self-made men, when in America so much was possible, when America was the willingness of the heart and, in some cases, of the mind; but, then, there was something non-American in it too. For, after all is said, the American psyche, *mutatis mutandis,* is not a simple matter either, with its superficially optimistic belief, from the beginning of the country, in the perfectibility of society: a belief which, in the last resort, is something quite different—and much less hopeful—than the trust in the improvability of man.

NINE

PHILADELPHIA
1950

REPUBLICAN RULE IN PHILADELPHIA ended in 1951, after sixty-seven years. In the 1940s the mayor was Bernard Samuel, an amiable nonentity, a figurehead among the Republican politicians. There was something typically Philadelphian in the placid indifference with which these politicians padded along on their self-appointed rounds through the corridors of City Hall, even when they heard the snapping noises of investigators gathering behind their tracks. The Republicans took some comfort from the standard figures of the voters' registration: as late as 1950, there were more than two Republicans for every registered Democrat in Philadelphia, 718,000 to 308,000. They also took some comfort from the national political temper that was running anti-Democratic and anti-liberal at the time.[1] Yet in Philadelphia things had begun to change. In 1947 Samuel had defeated Richardson Dilworth in the contest for the mayoralty; but in 1949 Dilworth and Joseph Sill Clark won the offices of city treasurer and controller. Grand juries were investigating various and long-standing practices of corruption in City Hall. Independent Republicans decided to support Clark, even though he was the local leader of Americans for Democratic Action. A new city charter was adopted. *The Philadelphia Inquirer,* daily

[1] They had some reasons for this on the state level: in November 1950 the third-rate Republican machine politician John S. Fine beat Richardson Dilworth, the reformer liberal Democrat, for the governorship; and Senator Francis J. Myers, the Democratic majority Whip in the United States Senate was also defeated by James H. Duff, a pro-Eisenhower Republican.

trumpet for Republicanism, endorsed Clark for mayor. In November 1951 Clark won the race for mayor, and Dilworth the race for district attorney. The Democratic victory was complete.

It was reminiscent of the New Deal; this long-overdue but eventually overwhelming surge of the popular vote for reform (the symbol of the Clark-Dilworth party was a broom), this return of attractive patricians to head a popular government. If the Philadelphia New Deal was twenty years behind the national pattern,[2] so were the Philadelphia Republicans. In 1950 their politics were still a kind of Business-Biblical Americanism of the Old Protectionist Dispensation; their candidates, real-estate men and Masons, brownish men with owlish faces, were politicians out of the twenties. The Republican national committeeman who ran state politics bore the name of G. Mason Owlett: *Nomen est omen*, again. He was the fugleman of Joseph P. Grundy, the latter in his eighties, still sprightly and hale, the boss of the still-powerful Pennsylvania Manufacturers' Association: a Taft Republican, he led the fight in the primary against the more liberal Duff. The Republican candidate for mayor of Philadelphia in 1951 was a clergyman, the Reverend Daniel Poling, known for his pursuit of profitable publicity and for the commercial pieties with which he larded his speeches from the pulpit. He lost.

All of this was reminiscent of something else too: of the reform movements of the early 1880s, before the Republicans established their long hold on the city. Then, too, the reformers were supported by some of the older civic leaders, many of them independent Republicans. Then, too, a new city charter was written, against the low growlings of the ward politicians. Then, too, the final electoral triumph of the reform party came

---

[2] There was an exception to this time-lag on the state level: in 1934 the Democrats won the governorship, losing it again in 1938. The governor of the Pennsylvania New Deal was George H. Earle III, a former independent Republican, friend of Franklin Roosevelt and of William Bullitt, with whom he had much in common, including a flair for foreign policy and high living.

after years of determined work by the mugwumps. So in 1948 the distinguished old Edward Hopkinson, Jr., was raised to the chairmanship of the City Planning Commission; his executive director was Edmund N. Bacon, Dilworth's ally, a sharp-featured modernist city planner (whose favorite of all painters was, as he once told this incredulous writer, Klee). In December 1948 a Greater Philadelphia Movement was founded, studded with patricians and independent Republicans: the chairmen were C. Jared Ingersoll, Robert T. McCracken, and W. Fulton Kurtz; the executive committee chairman was Lewis M. Stevens, a Wilsonian Progressive and lay Presbyterian leader; the executive director was Robert K. Sawyer, a liberal Quaker. The composition of the City Charter Commission, established in 1949, was similar. These were honest people, exercised by the sight of corruption and by the indifference to it of self-satisfied politicians. "In a democracy," Evelyn Waugh wrote in *The Ordeal of Gilbert Pinfold,* "men do not seek authority so that they may impose a policy. They seek a policy so that they may achieve authority." This was not true of these worthies. Their concern with the government and with mismanagement was authentic and sincere.

MOST OF THEM were lawyers. 1950 was the Last Rally of the legal aristocracy of Philadelphia, their last assumption of civic leadership. Very few people were aware of this at the time; yet it was evident that, together with the composition of the city, the structure of its politics was changing—just as the composition of its Bar Association had changed, together with the very practice of the law.

Until about 1890 the education of a lawyer in Philadelphia took place in law offices rather than in law schools. The fundamentals were pleading, equity, trusts, and estates. There were, of course, lawyers on all kinds of levels (what the English called "accident-tout" had become the American "ambulance chaser" well before 1900); but the specialization of corporation lawyers, estate lawyers, divorce lawyers, criminal lawyers had not yet taken place, and the tax lawyer was just about nonexistent. Consequently, large firms were few. Most of the law offices (offices, rather than firms) bore the single name of the distinguished lawyer who headed them. Philadelphia lawyers were not necessarily hardened veterans of litigation, as the cliché suggested, nor were they experts in loopholes of accounting. They were advocates of civic law and civic order. Their offices were small and somber,[3] smaller than the increasingly luxurious and impressive offices of the burgeoning firms in New York; they were bereft of Persian rugs and chandeliers, replete with uncomfortable furniture and books. They had a family touch, which would in time include their clerks and their secretaries, women who were monuments of reliability and rectitude, devoting their lives to their employers. George Wharton Pepper recalled that, in 1939, fifty years after he had bid the Biddle office goodbye,

> I paid a courtesy call on Mr. J. Rodman Paul who, as a partner in the old firm, had fed me my first ration of Blackstone and had conducted many of the office quizzes. There he sat in the modern suite into which in recent years the firm had moved. Around him were the furnishings of half a century before, including a familiar framed facsimile of Magna Carta. "What ever happened to Morris?" I asked, referring to Mr. Biddle's clerk who in student days had seemed to us already an old man. "Nothing has happened to him," was the reply, "you will find him in an adjoining room." I gasped. "There were three stenographers in those days," I said, "Miss Shubert, Miss McGarry and Miss McNutt. Whatever became of them?" They are still with us," he said—and so they were.[4]

---

[3] In the Philadelphia (or, rather, southeastern Pennsylvania) novel of Joseph Hergesheimer, *Three Black Pennys* (New York, 1917), pp. 181–82, a Philadelphia lawyer's office *circa* 1860: "The lawyer's private chamber was bare, with snowy panelling and mahogany, the high sombre shelves of a calf-bound law library, a ponderous cabriolet table, sturdy, rush-seated Dutch chairs, and a Franklin stove with slender brass capitals and shining hod."

[4] *Op. cit.*, p. 54.

Of George W. Biddle (who had been trained by Binney and who, fifty years later, trained Pepper) his grandson Francis Biddle wrote: "He was the last of the old school of Philadelphia lawyers, trained in the classics, a little austere, courteous, artless, with his professional and personal standards."[5] The Lawyers Club of Philadelphia adopted a resolution that spoke of "his mastery of his cause, and his graceful oratory and delightful presence, whilst his spotless integrity and devotion to Christian principles evidenced the purity of his character." Reminiscing about her *fin-de-siècle* Philadelphia, Elizabeth Robins Pennell wrote before the First World War: "The recommendation to Philadelphia of its lawyers was not the high esteem they were held throughout the country, but their social standing at home—family gave distinction to the law, not the law to family."

Her next sentence destroys this truthful impression: "Approved Philadelphia names adorned the signs at almost every office door and not for some years was the evil day to dawn when the well-known Philadelphia families who inherited the right of the law would be forced to fight for it with the alien and the Jew."[6] Whatever "the right of the law" might mean, they did not fight for it. In 1952 the Bar Association for the first time elected as its Chancellor a Jewish lawyer, Bernard Siegel—incidentally, not a descendant of an old Jewish family in Philadelphia—without a murmur.

The devolution that took place between 1899 and 1952, between the era of the Bispham and of the Siegel chancellorships, was of another nature. Throughout the United States the practice of law changed; and Philadelphia moved along with it. It was a devolution of legal practices rather than the result of the transformed ethnic composition of the Bar—a rare instance when the changing character of a practice led to change in the character of the practitioners, rather than the reverse. The in-

[5] *A Casual Past* (New York, 1961), pp. 89–90.
[6] *Our Philadelphia* (London, 1914), pp. 111–12.

creasingly technical training of the law schools, the emphasis
put on the case method, the geometrical growth of legislation
and of regulation on all levels of government, the spreading
intricacies of taxation, the crowding of the courts; in sum, the
bureaucratization of the law amounted to an American devolution during the first half of this century, the consequences of
which abide with us and the end of which is not yet. It developed apace with the bureaucratization of business and industry. As late as the 1920s, the main institutions of industry
and banking in Philadelphia were still governed by men of old
and known families. Corporate managers were to succeed them.
As Edwin Wolf wrote, before 1929:

> Horace P. Liversidge was Philadelphia Electric; his succes-
> sors were merely presidents of the company. Effingham B.
> Morris was Girard Trust and Joseph Wayne, Jr., Philadelphia
> National; those who followed them were but successful and
> competent employees. Nowhere was the change more clearly
> seen than in the legal profession, long the pride of Phila-
> delphia and the reservoir whence many of its leaders came.
> Whereas George Wharton Pepper was recognized as the dean
> of the bar, Morris Wolf as the force behind the fastest growing
> office, and Robert T. McCracken as the most influential lawyer
> in town, it was firms made up of galaxies of specialists which
> emerged as important. By 1940 no Morgan, Lewis, or Bockius
> was known as an individual but the firm was the biggest, rich-
> est, and most active in the city.[7]

This was, I repeat, a national phenomenon, not a Philadelphian one; but what happened in Philadelphia was a gradual
(and, at times astonishing) disinterest in the law among the
Philadelphia Quirites. In many instances disinterest in the law
succeeded disinterest in politics within two generations. During
the nineteenth century there were few prominent men who
abandoned their legal practice after they had been admitted to
the Bar. During the twentieth century disillusionment with the
law became more and more apparent.

[7] *Philadelphia: Portrait of an American City* (Harrisburg, 1975), p. 299.

This disillusionment took different turns. We have seen how in the lives of eminent men, such as Johnson and Ingersoll and Price, interest in art had grown apace with their waning interest in the law. This was not merely the consequence of a broadening view of the world that they acquired through the individual development of their minds. It corresponded with the change of legal practice in the United States; and also with the change—slower and less visible on the surface—in Philadelphia proper. What people would sometimes call "the Web," a close, interlocking relationship of families and boards and directorships, in Philadelphia still existed; but its influence became more restricted, and it was weakening. In 1900 one could detect two governments of Philadelphia side by side, a political and a social one, neatly separated but tolerant—perhaps too tolerant —of each other. It was the legal aristocracy which provided both the inevitable contacts and the relatively trouble-free functions of both. After the Civil War—in Philadelphia a little later than elsewhere—The Best Men No Longer Went into Politics (this was what Lord Bryce, after Tocqueville the most important foreign observer of the American scene, wrote at the head of a famous chapter in his *The American Commonwealth*). After the First World War the best men were less and less interested in the law. This was a gradual development. They did not abandon it altogether; after all, men such as Johnson and Ingersoll and Price went on practicing some kind of law till the end of their active lives, and a career at law was still the expected and preferred occupation for the sons of the Philadelphia patricians until 1950 at least. Moreover, for every Johnson and Ingersoll and Price, there existed a Pepper, a Drinker, a McCracken, a Gates, Proper Philadelphians for whom the practice of the law was eminently satisfactory and who continued to occupy eminent positions in the civic order. Some of them combined their vocations with their avocations, like Henry Drinker, an amateur musician of a high order and an accomplished musicologist. Yet they represented a Philadelphia tradition which, though long-standing, was narrow. They were Republicans, embittered by the New Deal. At least on one occasion Justice Holmes thought that the Philadelphia lawyers were oddly circumscribed: they did not argue well before the Supreme Court. During the first half of the twentieth century, the law school of the University of Pennsylvania was probably the best in the country; yet Philadelphia and Pennsylvania ceased to be the legal Athens and Attica of the United States. During the 1880s John G. Johnson was offered a place on the Supreme Court of the United States on two occasions, but he declined: he'd rather be a lawyer in Philadelphia. In 1912 George Wharton Pepper would have accepted such an august appointment; but we have seen that it was not tendered him. During the entire twentieth century, Philadelphia had but one Justice on the Supreme Court, Owen J. Roberts, a liberal Republican. His career on the Court was undistinguished, his main note of fame being his chairmanship of the investigation which absolved Roosevelt from responsibility for the disaster at Pearl Harbor.

The days of a legal aristocracy were passing. What Tocqueville had written in the 1830s: "The lawyers form the political upper class and the most intellectual section of society," a century later was no longer true. He was "aware of the inherent defects of the legal mind"; nevertheless, he doubted whether democracy could prevail for long "without the mixture of legal and democratic minds, and I hardly believe that nowadays a republic can hope to survive unless the lawyers' influence over its affairs grows in proportion to the power of the people."[8] The lawyers' profession was no longer a counterweight to a democracy, and the liberal lawyer was replacing the conservative one. Instead of the principal task of preserving traditional and private liberties, throughout the Republic the most successful and most renowned lawyers were trying to extend liberties to more and more areas of public life. "Judges," Blackstone had written, "are not delegated to pronounce a new law but to

8 *Democracy in America* (Mayer, ed.) , vol. I., p. 245.

maintain and expound the old law"—and during the nineteenth century, generations of Philadelphia lawyers were
brought up on Blackstone. During the twentieth century, that
"certain scorn for the judgment of the crowd," which Tocqueville noted, was no longer true among American lawyers, including the most conservative Philadelphia ones. Among the
younger ones the bureaucratization of the law resulted in
existential frustrations, involving personal tragedies on occasion. There were a few instances in the 1940s when brilliant
Philadelphia lawyers, full of promise, turned to the practice of
criminal law, a choice previously unheard of—not, as some of
their cluck-clucking colleagues thought, for monetary reasons,
but because they found the standard practice in their large
offices hopelessly dull: the combat in the courts was more interesting, and personally more satisfying. In other instances, the
existential frustrations of young lawyers led to premature resignation, depression, alcoholism, even suicide. In an increasing
number of instances, Philadelphia lawyers were no longer able
to transmit the taste for the law to their sons, and many of the
long ancestral chains of tradition were broken.

Still, in 1950, after nearly a century, the Best Men had returned to politics again. A coalition of patrician lawyers, including Republicans who turned Democrats, of eager young
men, of civic reformers, would sweep the tired and corrupt
Republican government out of City Hall. They elected Clark,
who left the practice of law to enter politics, together with Dilworth, who eventually succeeded Clark as mayor. Many of their
reforms, political or architectural, were long overdue. Yet the
people who congratulated themselves on this failed to notice
that it was but a belated adjustment to a national pattern—and
precisely because of this, no longer particularly Philadelphian.

IN ANY EVENT, the result was a civic renaissance, in more than
one way. The physiognomy of the city, long neglected, was re-

furbished. During and after World War I, the first plans had been made for a grand transformation, for a wide prospect to be cut diagonally athwart the petrified brownstone jungle northwest of City Hall. The Benjamin Franklin Parkway was to be rather magnificent (and, thus, quite un-Philadelphian), with splendid neo-classical buildings flanked by broad green parterres as it swept toward the first damp hillocks rising in Fairmount Park to the north. There was a French inspiration to it; its draftsmen were Paul Cret and Jacques Gréber, two eminent French architects, together with two Francophile architects of great talent, Horace Trumbauer[9] and C. Clark Zantzinger. Their plans matured during World War I, and construction began soon afterward. Along this Champs-Elysées of Philadelphia Logan Circle was the Rond-Point[10]; like the Champs-Elysées, the parkway would slowly and majestically rise to its western culmination, the Philadelphia Museum of Art. Beyond it toward Fairmount Park, Philadelphia's Bois de Boulogne, a few modern apartment houses would rise, not unlike smart buildings in Passy or Auteuil.[11] Toward the end of the 1920s, however, building along the parkway ran out of steam (parts of the parkway remain barren and unfinished even now). Eventually its very name became vulgarized through its slangy abbreviation: it is—officially—the "Ben Franklin Parkway" now.

Around 1950, synchronized with the movement for civic reform, came two great surgical improvements on the face of Philadelphia. The demolition of the so-called Chinese Wall was about to begin. This was a large brick barrier, interrupted only by viscous, dark roadway tunnels forever dripping with black water, built originally to carry the Pennsylvania trains

---

[9] About him see p. 34.

[10] Two squares further on, Paul Cret built the small Rodin Museum, donated by a civic-minded Jewish merchant of great wealth.

[11] They were not built until the late 1930s. Two decades later they—and the Art Museum—were allowed to be overshadowed by two of the most monstrous apartment buildings ever to disfigure the skyline and the physiognomy of Philadelphia—or perhaps of any great city.

into Broad Street Station in the center of town.[12] The Chinese Wall was hideous—and, more important, unprofitable—so that even the lethargic Republican administration decided in 1946 that it had to go; but nothing much was done until the Philadelphia New Deal occupied City Hall, after which the demolition began to proceed. The eventual results were not altogether the best: within a decade Penn Center (an unimaginative name, to start with) consisted of a row of stiff and unimaginative square boxes of skyscrapers, indistinguishable from New York office buildings in the late 1930s, including a parochial imitation of Rockefeller Center, complete with an ice-skating rink and the pathetic possibility of an outdoor café. The café soon closed, the skating rink is sparsely used; it is overshadowed rather than washed by sunlight, the surface of the ice is soiled and gray.[13] When Philadelphia tries to go modern, she merely follows New York; and when she follows New York, the results are usually, and expectably, indifferent.

Still, Penn Center was an improvement over the Chinese Wall. The other great change involved Society Hill. That name, unlike Penn Center, had a snobbish (though, again, somewhat provincial) ring to it, perfect for the appeal of a new urban neighborhood whereto smart young couples would move. The revival of the name included a touch of publicity legerdemain: few people knew, even after 1950, that "society" in Society Hill had nothing to do with Society, that it was named after a Quaker neighborhood in colonial Philadelphia. In 1949 Harold R. Kynett, an eccentric old Philadelphian[14], composed a little book, privately printed, with the title *For Better or Worse? Rambles on Progress and Otherwise*, in which he wrote:

---

[12] Broad Street Station itself, a high-turreted Victorian skyscraper of a terminus, was demolished in 1952; the Philadelphia Orchestra was brought to the platform to play for the last train pulling away, a sentimental and appropriate Philadelphian gesture.

[13] It is to be boarded up, for good (1980).

[14] An old Philadelphian—meaning someone distinct from, but not less respectable than, an Old Philadelphian.

Once, in the flush of newly acquired information I made the statement that the region of Second and Pine Streets was a hill, known as Society Hill and on it, a Friends Meeting House commonly called the Hill Meeting. Polite incredulity greeted the statement and even quotations from the antiquaries could not quite erase the suspicion that I was a monumental liar.

Today's visitor to Second and Pine would find never a trace of hill nor meeting, although traversing the streets in a car might leave the impression of crossing the Alps. Pine Street, between Front and Second, is a disconsolate clutter of wholesale establishments, interlarded with morose dwellings whose entire atmosphere is one of near-collapse. To say the neighborhood breathes a dispirited air is to put it mildly. At Second Street, the tattered remnants of Old Second Street Market, with shuttered windows and abandoned stalls, enhance the feeling of a deserted city.

But after 1950 this would rapidly change. The Philadelphia Redevelopment Authority set to work. Within a decade Society Hill would be in existence. A strict set of architectural regulations forbade the demolition or the transformation of buildings that had been erected before 1840.[15] Gradually this portion of the city emerged from dirt and neglect and obscurity. It became a reconstructed portion of Old America, restored and inhabited by a younger and more transient generation, together with a few Old Philadelphians who moved into small town houses. By 1970 Society Hill had become a tourist attraction.

There were arguments in the 1920s about the site and the shape of the Philadelphia Museum of Art. (Some of its opponents called it a Greek garage.) It dominated the skyline from across the Schuylkill River, the first impressive monument to be

---

[15] There was a loss inherent in the categorical set of regulations. Many of the interesting (and not only the decrepit) Victorian houses and warehouses, built after 1840, were condemned in the redevelopment process. The result was that of attractive rows of buildings with a touch of artificiality in their regimented rows, architectural prospects of unbroken uniformity, often beautifully rebuilt and re-set, but also devoid of the rich variety that marks the prospects of a traditional, as distinct from a reconstructed, town.

glimpsed by people coming by train from New York: the Acropolis of Philadelphia. 1950 was its Golden Age. It was the focus of what was best in Philadelphia, or at least that was what some Philadelphians thought. Membership in the Museum had a social cachet to it. At the Museum parties the social and cultural aristocracy of Philadelphia would gather—often the same people, by and large, who were the leaders of political and civic reform. They took a great deal of pride in this institution. There was a sparkle to this civic renaissance of 1950, at those Museum parties where the handsome men and the attractive women of the older families would mingle, perhaps for the first time in the social history of this city, with the newer patrons and providers of art. A classical-music FM station began to broadcast in Philadelphia, without interruption by commercials. Six theaters were open regularly. The University of Pennsylvania was revitalized. For the first time in thirty-five years the Phillies won the National League pennant.[16] 1950: Philadelphia's New Deal.

THIS CIVIC RENAISSANCE in Philadelphia was, as we have seen, similar in many ways (though unsimilar in others) to the reform movements of earlier times. Like the short-lived provincial reform efforts of the nineteenth century, it did not last. For underneath it all coursed a deeper development that was essentially unbroken: the decline of the power of the erstwhile patricians. In 1950 they still had considerable power—in part because of their material assets; more important, because of their authority. Eventually their authority would erode as fast as their power.

In 1950 this was, as yet, hardly visible at all—save, perhaps, from the odd perspective of an outsider, as this writer then was, and in so many ways still is.

1950 was a milestone in the history of Philadelphia; but it was not a turning point. Around the turn of the century John

16 The New York Yankees blasted them out of the World Series: 4–0.

Jay Chapman (a close friend of Owen Wister) wrote: "We have escaped an age of tyrants, because the eyes of the bosses and their masters were fixed on money. They were not ambitious . . . Mere financial dishonesty is of very little importance in the history of civilization . . . The real evil that follows in the wake of a commercial dishonesty so general as ours is the intellectual dishonesty it generates . . . The literary man is concerned for what 'will go,' like the reformer who is half politician. The attention of everyone in the United States is on someone else's opinion, not on truth."[17] This was as true in 1950 as it was in 1900. There was much in that civic renaissance in Philadelphia that was necessary, useful, perhaps even inspiring. There were attractive men and women who—at times admirably—spent their time, energy, money on causes involved with the improvement of the city and with the patronage of its art collections. Yet a certain cast of conformism went on to prevail everlastingly among most of them. The categories of the conformism had changed, but it was conformism nonetheless. *De rigueur* at those Museum parties (or at the Redevelopment Authority meetings) was the possession of the proper kind of opinions. These opinions in 1950, unlike twenty or thirty years earlier, were politically liberal and artistically avant-garde; but what difference did that make? In November 1950 the Diamond Jubilee of the Museum was celebrated by a glittering party. Fiske Kimball had brought together the One Hundred Greatest Paintings and One Hundred Greatest Drawings in America. It was the moment of his highest glory,[18] though he was already a sick man. He had lately succeeded in persuading some of the richest collectors in the United States to give their possessions to the Museum; he had the Golden Touch, half-Midas, half-Hollywood (his greatest triumph at the time consisted in getting the modernist-abstract collections of Arensberg and of Edward G. Robinson, the ex-Bessarabian movie actor, both from Bev-

[17] From his essay "Society," in *The Selected Writings of John Jay Chapman*, Jacques Barzun, ed. (New York, 1957), pp. 244–46.
[18] He received the Bok Award in 1951.

erly Hills). When the Museum went up, in the 1920s, the philistines of Philadelphia would make self-consciously complacent jokes about it as they drove past the construction. In 1950 many of these philistines were inside, parading past the abstract paintings, no less self-conscious, but also no less complacent. What Saki wrote *circa* 1910 was true of 1950 as well: the sure way of knowing nothing about life is to try to make oneself socially useful.

They surely knew little of the Philadelphia outside their confines. During the 1930s and the 1940s, certain Philadelphia painters painted scenes and vistas of the hilly neighborhood of Manayunk. Often their patronesses failed to recognize the scene, even though Manayunk is less than two miles from Chestnut Hill and clearly visible from across the Schuylkill. Some of them thought that it was an Italian hill town, a kind of Umbria impressionized or ashcanized.[19] As an addition to the Art Museum crowd the University Museum had become a social enclave, with its prehistoric stuffing and archaeological expeditions, replete with Old Philadelphians and their matrons going on the "digs," so very Philadelphian in its Franklinesque mix of Society and Science.[20] So was the American Philosoph-

[19] All respect, therefore, is due to the survivors of the great and old Philadelphia tradition of painter craftsmen, such as Francis Speight, who knew that a painter's paradise consists in his object and not in his subject. "Despite the evident poverty of the working-class neighborhoods he so often depicted, [Francis] Speight's paintings convey little of the sharp social comment characteristic of certain of his contemporaries during the 1930's and 1940's, who saw every factory or shanty as a symbol of the need for social and economic reform. Nevertheless, an exhibition of his work that perhaps made Speight happiest was held in a vacant store on Manayunk's Main Street in the 1930's and attended by the inhabitants of those very houses he loved to paint. Their pleased recognition of their own homes or a neighbor's backyard must have meant as much, if not more to him than the impressive prizes he received in numerous exhibitions at major museums"—except for the syntax of the last sentence, very true. *Philadelphia: Three Centuries of American Art* (Philadelphia, 1976), p. 149.

[20] In Struthers Burt's Philadelphia novel, *Along These Streets* (Philadelphia, 1942), the hero is a young Old Philadelphian archaeologist; his pallid passions and extreme sensitivities are revealing. It is a period illustration, an unwitting representation of how certain parochial attitudes and longings of an earlier generation typical, say, of American gentility around 1910, would survive in their descendants thirty years later.

ical Society (rich beyond the dreams of avarice), where a kind of somnolent philistinism reigned supreme, with measured pinches of incense bowl offered to the cold statuary of the scientific Franklin spirit, the society governed by the safest of professors, usually from the upper reaches of the University of Pennsylvania, descendants of Lancaster County Pennsylvania Dutchmen, thoroughly Philadelphianized, Anglophile, and Republican, having achieved their academic fortunes through passionate subjects such as histories of American medicine.

By 1950 some of the older Philadelphia traits had faded. One of them was the Philadelphia accent. In 1894 Owen Wister, out West, was often taken for an Englishman. As late as the 1940s there survived something like a Philadelphia accent, including a High Episcopalian *a*, its timbre different from the upper class *a* of New York or Boston or their suburbs.[21] More significantly, the Southern touch was fading, too. As late as the early 1940s, few of the girls who graduated from the best Philadelphia private schools would go on to college (they were the "brains," when compared with the debutantes); in this respect Philadelphia was still closer to Baltimore, Richmond, Charleston than to Boston or New York. Ten years later this was no longer true. And while the Southern touch was fading, the Maine attraction was stronger than ever; it survived the disastrous fire that destroyed most of Bar Harbor in 1947; indeed, around 1950 in Northeast Harbor ("Philadelphia on the Rocks"), much of Philadelphia society could be more often "at home" than at home. During the 1950s a painter who attained great national fame was Andrew Wyeth, from a family of talented illustrators. His careful craftsmanship was, however, inspired not so much by the rich Chester County land where he lived as by the climate of Maine; unlike the great traditional Philadelphia painters, Eakins, Cassatt, etc., his themes

---

21 Example: The proverbial *tomahto*, in Philadelphia, less nasal and more throaty than in New York or New England. On a different level, a lower-middle-class Philadelphia diction included a flat, twangy, semi-nasal *a*: "aysk" and "mayd" for *ask* and *mad*.

were, and remained, essentially cold. A painter of stubbled
March fields and of stony textures, his landscapes and barns
(and often even his models) differed from the old warm Philadelphia tradition; he was, in spite of his provenance, a Maine
painter rather than a Philadelphia one.

In 1900 there was in Philadelphia, as we have seen, an appre-
ciable, and often sharply nuanced, distinction between the
older patrician families and the—relatively—new rich. This
distinction did not exactly correspond to the difference of what
sociologists would call the upper and upper-middle classes, even
though it had certain similarities to it. In 1950 many of the
erstwhile new rich of two generations before were, more or less
securely, lodged within society; the old patrician families still
existed, while the new new rich were no longer predominantly
Anglo-Saxon: a more or less normal and expectable development of social acceptance in which the catalyst was no longer
intermarriage or business or church or club membership but,
rather, the patronage—public and social—of certain arts. This
was the Philadelphian pattern of a national devolution, whereby Society had more and more to do with Celebrity. In Philadelphia the two were still far from being equivalent, or even related: but the first was—already—aware of the second. After
all, celebrity means to be publicly known; the bridge between
Society and Celebrity consists of publicity; and publicity will
have its inevitable effect on people whose particular and
discriminating manners are not matched by particular and discriminating mental interests of their own. The charmed pri-
vateness of the Philadelphia patriciandom had begun to erode.
Evidence of this was there, among other things, in the social
columns of the Philadelphia newspapers. In 1900 the social
pages of the Philadelphia newspapers were filled with reports
of all kinds of receptions, dinners, social events, no matter how
inconsequential, item by item, column by column; the newspapers would print the items that had been brought to them,
massive lists representative of the inclination of democracy for

publicity, for people who believed what was printed in news-papers—while many of the events in the social calendars of the older patrician families went unreported. In 1950 much of this distinction between what, on the one hand, was old and private and secure and what, on the other, was self-conscious in its as-piration for publicity had disappeared. The social columns of the Philadelphia newspapers around 1950 were silly beyond caricature. The plainness and the innocence of the endless lists was gone; a kind of adolescent snobbery that is both bristling and unrefined had taken its place. The social columns were now something like gossip columns, but gossip columns that were extremely parochial. Unlike the then national gossip columns composed for people hopelessly distant from Society and Celeb-rity, and therefore prone to take a vicarious interest in the brilliant social lives of legendary men and women, the Phila-delphia newspapers' social columns were now catering ob-viously to the needs of people who thought that the meaning of their membership in society might be further enhanced when that fact was publicly shown.

For one thing, the space given to these columns was enor-mous. In one newspaper alone there were *five* social columns each Sunday, running to as much as ten pages. "The Main Liner," "Jane Wister," "Philadelphia Pepper Pot by 'Frank and Phoebe,' " "Judy Jennings' Notebook," "Deborah Debbie" (the last the most insipid, composed for the younger set). Examples:

> After church this morning we all went over to Uncle Robert's and Aunt Helen's for lunch. The conversation centered on their forthcoming trip to Palm Beach. Aunt Helen was busy debating over the clothes she would take while Uncle Robert and Daddy sorted fishing gear. They plan to stay until March, so perhaps I may go down for awhile. 'T would be divine!
>
> ("Deborah Debbie," 5 February 1950)

> "Susie" La Baw and "Sonny" Knode seen at a party on the Main Line recently . . . "Connie" Lavino riding in Chestnut Hill every day . . . "Noodles" Knode still raving about the party "Eddie" Adams gave recently . . . "B.J." Furley among

the debs of the coming season as are "Zara" Bentley and "Ellie" Drinker . . .

("The Main Liner," ibid.)

A couple we know got a record of the background music of *Lost Weekend*. They put it on the automatic phonograph and it played all night while they slept. Next day the husband joined Alcoholics Anonymous. The same thing happened to them last week—this time with the zither music from the *The Third Man*. Both have applied for permanent reservations at a well-known institution for mental disturbances.

("Philadelphia Pepper Pot," by "Frank and
Phoebe," 21 April 1950—the lead story)

Sorted out my last year's summer clothes this morning to see what was still wearable.

Tonight Steve and I went to see *Battleground* which was one of the best movies I've ever seen.

("Deborah Debbie," 21 April 1950)

In the same number of *The Philadelphia Inquirer* the lead editorial bore the title: "For Vast Truth Drive Against Red Lies." The lead editorial a week later: "Cold War A Task For All Nations."[22]

In 1950 *The Philadelphia Inquirer*, owned and directed by an unscrupulous newspaper magnate, was probably one of the worst morning papers of any great city in the world; it had all the features of cheapness and sensationalism, while preserving the format of a respectable morning newspaper, preaching an Americanism alternately sentimental and strident.[23] Few Philadelphians grumbled about this; they took the *Inquirer* for

---

[22] In a cosseted institution on the Main Line a victim of the Cold War chose to die that day. Biserka Krnjevic, a graduate student at Bryn Mawr College, was the daughter of a father who lived in London, a minister in the former Yugoslav royalist exile government, long abandoned by its Anglo-American allies. On a Sunday afternoon, that cruelest day for lonely people in Philadelphia, on a shiny cold day in April, that proverbially cruelest month of the wasteland years, she found some rat poison, smeared it on her cookies, drank her tea, and died. *The Inquirer* next day: "According to Sgt. James Smyth, of the Lower Merion Township detectives, Miss Krnjevic was suffering from a simple case of homesickness."

[23] Two standard features in its magazine in 1950: *Confident Living* by the Reverend Norman Vincent Peale ("How to Pray about a Problem." "Find

granted, for their reliable morning paper. It supported, as we have seen, the reform mugwumps on the local level—conforming to what seemed to be an irreversible popular movement—but beyond that, its nationalism was indiscriminate, vulgar, harmful. For in 1950 the hitherto last great wave of American extreme nationalism was rising fast: in January Alger Hiss[24] was properly convicted; in February Joe McCarthy fired the first star shell of his improper crusade, with his speech in Wheeling, West Virginia; in June the Korean War burst forth. The editorials, the headlines, the chortling columnists of the *Inquirer* scratched and screeched with the brummagem ideology of the day, elevating the banner and the slogans of anti-Communism as if the latter were simply and squarely identical with American patriotism.

This was not the first time that something like this would occur in Philadelphia; but there was an underlying difference now. There was, for the first time since the 1840s, a swelling undercurrent of distrust between certain classes of people in Philadelphia—or, more precisely, between people of different provenance and background. In 1950 the social leadership in Philadelphia was still predominantly Anglo-Saxon; but numerically the Anglo-Saxon element was a small minority. Many of its members were, as we have seen, active participants in the Philadelphia New Deal; their political convictions were, generally speaking, more liberal than that of the majority of the population. And just as the Cold War had developed out of the Second World War, the second Red Scare in the history of the United States coagulated, in many ways, out of the uncomfortable and undigested memories of the Second World War. In 1950 there were many Americans who saw in the national alert to the Soviet danger a belated vindication of their uneasiness with Roosevelt's foreign policy, with America's alliance with

---

Fellowship and Partnership in Your Prayers"). *FBI Girl* by Rupert Hughes ("A Beautiful FBI Fingerprint Clerk Helps Her Fiancé Uncover a Vicious Plot of International Intrigue").

[24] He had Philadelphia connections: his wife was a Philadelphia Quaker.

the British and Russians earlier in the decade. This was especially true of many Americans of German, Italian, Slovak, Ukrainian[25] and even Irish[26] origin. This—and not some kind of superficial "conservative" political philosophy—was the source, as well as the appeal, of McCarthy's (he was half-Irish, half-German) Wisconsin rhetoric; his anti-Communist crusade was a stick with which to cow American liberals and to humiliate Anglo-Saxons of the Eastern establishment. In Philadelphia Communists were few and far between; but the sentiment of considerable sections of the population followed this transnational pattern.[27] A new kind of American nationalism, anti-Communist and ideological, had risen, in which a genuine concern about the Soviets was commingled with fears of treason, with suspicion, and with envy. I recall how, in 1949, a local post of the American Legion publicly accused the Philadelphia chapter of the World Federalists of anti-Americanism, demanding that the latter be investigated and dissolved. The names of the World Federalists—an innocuous group, with their bland program in pursuit of the illusionary ideal of world government under international law—were, without exception, English, Welsh, or Scottish, some of them bearing the names of the oldest Quaker and patrician families; the names of the people who accused them of anti-Americanism were, without exception, Italian, Ukrainian, and Slovak.[28]

[25] Philadelphia had a larger proportion of Ukrainians than any other large city in the United States.

[26] The Irish in Philadelphia, as also elsewhere, were less anti-British during the Second World War than they had been during the First, but the relentless preoccupation of the Catholic hierarchy with Communism made many of them particularly receptive and attuned to the propaganda of anti-Communism.

[27] Title of an editorial in *The Philadelphia Bulletin*, July 1954, exasperated by the flood of McCarthyite letters to the editor: "What Happened to the People in Philadelphia?" In 1951 the modest and well-known restaurant The Russian Inn, on Locust Street, was renamed The Inn. (In the 1960s its original name was restored. It no longer exists.)

[28] The history of the appeal of militarism and nationalism in Philadelphia—in contrast to the old Quaker traditions of the city—still awaits its historian. In 1915: "Almost everybody who hasn't got a son or brother . . . is lying awake nights for fear peace may break out." Bullitt, *It's Not Done*, p. 223.

In 1950 the ethnic composition—and, more important, the relative strength—of the groups of people living in Philadelphia had changed. The enormous influx of blacks and Puerto Ricans was only beginning; there was, in 1950, still relatively little change in the traditional, and sometimes almost hermetic, national composition of different neighborhoods; but the Americanization of the sons and daughters of earlier immigrations was now nearly complete. The results were not always propitious. It was not only that the "Americanism" with which certain people (often second-generation Americans) identified themselves was both strident and shallow; they were also wont to lose particular features of their popular culture—features which had, after all, enriched the American stew in the melting pot. Among the Catholic working people in the picturesque streets of Manayunk in 1950 the Irish and the Polish and the Italian parishes were still as separate as before, but the monies and the ambitions of their parishioners had been accumulating; and when, in the 1950s, the people of St. Josaphat's decided to build a new church, it was made of steel and concrete and pre-cut stone blocks, modern and oil-heated, indistinguishable from other churches built across the country during the bland and affluent Eisenhower years. The old St. Josaphat's, with its wooden balconies and hand-painted statuaries, a unique piece of nineteenth-century Poland wedged into the streets of an American mill town, was pulled down in no time at all; a few years later something similar happened to St. Rita's, the old gray Italian church around the corner on Green Lane.

Around 1950 the Irish were rising fast; and the Italians would soon follow. We have seen in the first chapter of this book how the peculiar Philadelphia atmosphere of restricted social ambition had affected the Irish in this city: that, despite their increasing numbers, there were no Irish mayors of Philadelphia, and that even the oldest and most distinguished Irish families kept aloof from the social and cultural elite. But by the 1950s the new nationalist tendency, part and parcel of the anti-Communist crusade in accord with which, for the first time in the history of the United States, being a Catholic was no longer a handicap but an advantage, began to be sensed in Philadelphia too: the makers and the managers of the Philadelphia New Deal found that they were very much dependent on certain Irish politicians.[29] The social elite, too, were interested on occasion in such Irish families as the Kellys, whose charming and engagingly modest daughter Grace had risen to cinematic fame and in the 1950s became the reigning Princess of Monaco; yet this kind of interest was not reciprocated by the Irish families themselves.[30]

In South Philadelphia the second and third generation of Italian-Americans, too, became more assertive than they had been before. Their own particular peculiar contribution to American popular culture was beginning. As late as in the 1920s, Christopher Morley recorded the somewhat patronizing but also charmed reaction of certain Philadelphians to the more or less colorful Italian neighborhoods that existed in the otherwise drab industrial climate of the city, including the popular operatic tradition of their people, when organ grinders in the

[29] Until about 1960 real-estate advertisements in Philadelphia newspapers would often indicate the location of houses for sale in certain neighborhoods by printing the name of the parish first.

After the election of the first Irish-American President, much of this particular Irishness began to dissolve. There are no particularly Irish neighborhoods in Philadelphia now. In a middle-class Catholic college, such as Chestnut Hill, the great majority of the students was Irish from its beginning; since 1966 students with Irish or English family names have been in a minority. John Lukacs, *A Sketch of the History of Chestnut Hill College, 1924–1974* (Philadelphia, 1975, privately printed), pp. 24–27. Much more important is Dennis Clark, *The Irish in Philadelphia* (Philadelphia, 1973).

[30] The history of the Kelly family is interesting. John B. Kelly was one of ten children of an immigrant. In 1920 and in 1924 he won gold medals at the Olympic Games; he was the world's undisputed champion oarsman. Yet in 1920 the gentlemen stewards of the Henley Sculls in England had scratched him from the race; his presence was disputable, he had been a bricklayer. He made much money and ran for mayor as a Democrat in 1935; the Republican machine stole the election. His brother George was a fine playwright who had moved to New York. In the 1940s John B. Kelly, Jr., won the Diamond Sculls at Henley twice, sporting his father's old green sculling cap. (Another twenty years later he became a fixture of what passes for café society in Philadelphia.) When Grace Kelly visited her family after her sensational engagement to the Prince-Ruler of Monaco, the Irish of their neighborhood pretended to be uninterested.

streets and Victrolas through the windows and on the back tables of the few and unpretentious Italian restaurants rang with the arias of Verdi, Donizetti, Leoncavallo. The musical ability of the Italian population was indeed such that by the 1940s some of their talented sons and daughters had risen to respectable positions in the Curtis Institute or in the Philadelphia Orchestra and, on occasion, even on the national operatic scene; but soon after 1950 there arose another element. The high schools of South Philadelphia became the breeding grounds of American popular music of a new kind: for 1950 was a milestone not only in the history of Philadelphia but in that of American popular song. The unique half century during which American songwriters, from Berlin and Gershwin to Porter, had made American popular music known and loved and played throughout the civilized world was over. Jazz was being replaced by rock, the lilting tunes and sophisticated harmonies of the former by the crude mechanical tones and adolescent beat of the latter. Many of the performers of this new kind of popular music came from the public high schools of South Philadelphia: "Fabian," Frankie Avalon[31], Bobby Rydell (Ridelli), James Darrin, Buddy Greco, from the Italian-American population of the city.

As almost always, politics would follow. In 1950 an Italian mayor in Philadelphia was still difficult to imagine. The first Irish mayor was elected in 1963, the first Italian mayor in 1971, long after New York; but while James Tate differed from other Irish mayors of American cities perhaps only in his blandness, Frank Rizzo was utterly different, not only from Fiorello La Guardia, but also from Vincent Impellitteri, the first "purely"

---

31 From a television interview: GROUCHO MARX: "Well how do you explain so many singers coming from one section of [Philly]? Is it because they don't produce any ballplayers there? FRANKIE AVALON: "I'll tell you what. Y'know, before, mothers used to meet on the street and they used to say, uh, 'How's your son doin?' and they'd say, 'Fine.' But now they meet on the streets and say, 'How's your son's record doing?' 'Cause everybody's recording in South Philadelphia." GROUCHO: "Well, it was like that where I came from. My mother would say to another, 'How's your son's record?'" *The Secret Word Is Groucho* (New York, 1976), pp. 190–91.

Italian mayor of New York in 1950. Rizzo was not a liberal (and not really a conservative, either) but an Italian-American of a new and assertive breed. His enemies would call him a fascist, which surely he was not; but there was enough of the bully in the character of this uneducated man for us to say that, compared to him, Mussolini was a philosopher and a humanist.

But we are running beyond the confines of our story, which ends, as it must, in 1950. There was something else happening in and around Philadelphia in and around 1950 which was significant. The great estates had closed their gates; they were sold to institutions. We have seen how, around 1900, the then new rich had built their estates on the outskirts of Philadelphia, palatial mansions with turrets and Norman roofs and parterred parks, erected on foundations twenty feet deep and two feet thick, impressive monuments to the founders of family fortunes, to the glory of themselves and to that of their wives and children. Yet their glory lasted nary beyond a generation, and sometimes not even that.[32] By 1950 more than two dozen of these estates, including the magnificent houses of Wideners, Elkins, *et al.*, were empty; they could no longer be kept up. The reasons for this were taxes and the dearth of servants. Their owners could no longer afford them—this is what they said; it seemed reasonable enough then, it seems even more reasonable now. Yet there *was* another reason, on a deeper, more personal level: for when people say that they cannot afford something, this usually means that they don't really want to afford it. Unlike some of the owners of old houses in England who stick it out, if need be in a wing, these owners were unwilling to stay on, at the cost of more expenses or of some cutting back, or of some discomfort. But then they, and their fathers, had not had these houses for long.

I saw some of the houses in 1950 and, again, twenty years later. Most of them were sold to institutions, often to Catholic

[32] The most magnificent of these palaces, the Stotesburys' "Whitemarsh Hall," was occupied by its owners for hardly more than fifteen years. Its ruins still stand, abjectly gutted and thoroughly vandalized.

religious orders. There was something sadly telling in the aspect of these estates, but there was also something in their prospect that was very American and perhaps even inspiring. Here were these palatial houses, these merchants' castles, erected at a time when Protestant financiers and men of business had gathered much wealth and began to live as if they were the Borgias and Medicis of the rising twentieth century, the richest and most powerful representatives of American civilization in the world. Well, it did not happen. After thirty or forty years of opulent (and often uneasy) living, they sold their houses to the grandchildren (and sometimes to the children) of their Irish gardeners and handymen and chauffeurs. And so, around 1950, their estates became the novitiates and the scholasticates and the convents, the training schools of nuns, brothers, priests, of the children of the common Catholic people of America, full of vitality. In occupying these houses the latter would sometimes change things around with a kind of thoughtless vulgarity; still, they brought a new kind of life into these abandoned premises, tending their gardens where elegant thin-stemmed flowers had leaned against the walls, growing thick-stemmed vegetables for their own plastic-sheeted tables, keeping the rose beds, and pointing out to their visitors the rich mullioned windows, the carved moldings, the Renaissance mantels over the fireplaces, with respect and with pride. There was, after all, a strange kind of historical justice in the fact that some of these objects of the old European civilization now reverted to the possession of a new, American, and Catholic people; that the mantel carved by a French *ébéniste* four hundred years before, that the old stained-glass window set by an Irish glazier sixty years before, that the stucco swirls and crenellations on a ceiling kneaded into place by an Italian immigrant plasterer fifty years before now looked down on a crowd of some of *their* descendants, who came to occupy these buildings after the cold men and women who had ordered them to be built had left them for good. The smell of hot dogs, of sweet popcorn, and the sound of television now wafted across these baronial halls—and also the occasional scent of incense, the communal murmurs of the rosary, plainchant, and lusty caroling.

It did not last. Twenty years later many of these houses were abandoned again by their occupants.[33] There is a story, a story with a grave moral, latent in the histories of these houses; it will probably never be written. In any event, it does not belong here: for this story of the estates and the mansions of the new rich, replete with the last transitional chapter, was repeated, *mutatis mutandis*, across the Republic, on the edges of its cities; it was not especially Philadelphian.

The Philadelphia (and Pennsylvania) renaissance of 1950— by now a tenet accepted by historians—is contradicted by certain prosaic figures. During the prosperous wartime decade of the 1940s, the population of the United States grew faster than during any other decade in its history, a fact that is especially remarkable when we consider that almost all this growth was natural increase, since there was very little immigration at the time. Yet Pennsylvania and Philadelphia were declining, dropping behind the national averages. Between 1940 and 1950 the American population increased by 14.5 percent; but the population of Pennsylvania grew by only 6 percent, and that of Philadelphia by 6.9 percent. (The neighboring state of New Jersey had increased its population 16.2 percent during the same decade.) Between 1930 and 1940 Philadelphia had actually lost population. In 1950, for the first time, Pennsylvania slipped

[33] I have seen some of them, with the grass growing rank, the mansions shut down, except perhaps for a gatehouse or a modern refectory and, once more, the wrought-iron gates locked save for a few hours of the day. By 1970 there were few young Catholics who had chosen the life of a religious; the number of vocations dropped precipitously, and the various orders chose to close down large portions of their novitiates or scholasticates. They, too, decided that they could no longer afford this kind of upkeep. With their increasing worldliness, bureaucracy had deeply penetrated into their thinking; they were ready to listen to management "experts" and to consider the offers of "developers." And so, in many instances, the occupation of these once-grand premises by the new Catholic peoples was transitory; the latter, with all of their demonstrable vitality, were not impervious to that strange atrophy of the will, to the fatalism and the impermanence that may be the eternal Indian curse on the American land.

from second to third among the most populous states of the Union; shortly afterward Philadelphia followed suit, she was now fourth-ranked among the largest cities; Chicago had passed her before 1900; now it was Los Angeles's turn.

One of the things that were now happening to Philadelphia was mass suburbanization. The increase of "Greater Philadelphia," meaning the city plus the three suburban counties adjoining it, was 14.1 percent between 1940 and 1950, only slightly below the national average; the population of Montgomery County increased by nearly 22 percent, of Delaware County by nearly 33 percent. But here we run into a geographical problem, since the boundaries of "Greater Philadelphia" defy rational (that is, non-municipal) definition. Not only in 1950, but even now, after more than thirty years of unceasing suburban sprawl, large areas of the surrounding counties have remained rural—meaning that they, unlike the suburbs of New York, for example, have almost nothing to do with Philadelphia: their residents neither live nor work there, and perhaps the majority of them almost never visit the city. Closer to Philadelphia, unsightly suburban developments began to spring up after 1945. (The first large development on the edge of the city was built on the abandoned Stotesbury estate.) We have seen, in the first chapter of this book, how Philadelphia differed from other American cities during the last portion of the nineteenth century: in Philadelphia it was rich people, not the middle-class, who moved out of the city, while within the city rents remained relatively low and the house-owning population remained extraordinarily stable. Shortly after the end of the Second World War, the building boom began: for the first time in the history of Philadelphia, large numbers of middle-class and lower-class families moved out to the suburbs, a movement that is still going on, and the consequences of which on the composition and the character of the city were, and remain to this day, incalculable. In 1950 none of this was yet a response to neighborhood pressures by blacks or Puerto Ricans. Nor was it a result of inflation: the prices of houses in Philadelphia had risen but little, apartments and condominiums were almost nonexistent, real-estate taxes were among the lowest in the great cities of the nation.[34] It was, rather, the result of increasing conformity, propagated by the pictures on television and in the shiny national picture magazines, with their advertisements showing a suburban paradise of togetherness, where happy American families, enviable and respected, would live in their modern houses and spick-and-span gardens in suburban neatery. The massive movement to the suburbs was not yet a flight, not a response to certain economic or social conditions; it was a movement toward the image of a better, more modern kind of life, as well as toward a novel kind of respectability. The result was increasing indistinctiveness, increasing blandness: much that was unique about life in Philadelphia was being washed away; except here and there, conformity to the national pattern became overwhelming.[35] And just as the architecture of the dwellings and the grassy plots of the people in the suburbs conformed to the national pattern, so did the architecture of their minds.

AFTER 1950 much that used to be distinctly Philadelphian— both bad and good—was beginning to crack, melt away, disappear. Cracks appeared everywhere across that proverbially flat, dun, provincial-Sunday dullness. The Blue Laws about which so many comedians made jokes, and which had been

---

[34] Certain indicators of inflation had actually dropped. The expenses of the Philadelphia General Hospital, one of the largest items in the city budget, were lower in 1949 than in 1948 (so was the number of patients admitted: 25,273 in 1948, 23,273 in 1949). The real-estate rates remained constant: $1.70 for the public schools, and $1.27½ per $100 of assessments.

[35] Perhaps some of this was—literally—in the air. Even the weather was changing. Recall (p. 32) the crisp Philadelphia winters during the nineteenth century, when the Schuylkill and even the Delaware often froze over, and were skatable. Now the weather was getting warmer and damper. During the eighty years before 1950, ten of the twelve coldest months occurred between 1871 and 1900, and nine of the twelve hottest months between 1925 and 1950. In 1899 and 1900, 76 inches of snow had fallen on Philadelphia; in 1949 and 1950, 22.8.

imposed on Philadelphia by a coalition of politicians and low-Protestant ministers after the Civil War, began to be eased in the 1920s, though as late as in 1950 some of their curious features prevailed.[36] But ten years later there were restaurants and apartment houses athwart Philadelphia by the dozen, and all vestiges of the Sunday ban on liquor were gone. This was all to the good, except that this abolition was accomplished not so much on its own merits, resting on arguments of common sense, as by the city representatives' insistence on the potential blessings of mass tourism, on the necessity of making Philadelphia conform to whatever was going on in other cities of the nation.

This urge for conformity brought other changes, not all to the good. It was after 1950 that the automobile began to devour the city in earnest. "Suburbanites are traitors to the city," Agnes Repplier wrote with her precise ire around 1920, as we have seen;[37] yet we have seen, too, that for a long time the abandonment of the city for its countrified suburbs remained, by and large, the privilege of the upper classes, at a time when public transportation within Philadelphia was more ample than in many other cities of the nation. As late as 1950, the parking of cars within the city was easy even during business hours, and even in the center of the city. Soon thereafter the construction of the Schuylkill Expressway began at enormous cost, disfiguring, among other things, the entire western bank of the Schuylkill within the city, with the foreseeable result—not, of course, foreseeable to its planners—of creating a traffic problem instead of solving one, of attracting masses of automobiles instead of distributing their movement, of clogging the approach to the city through a hideous coagulation, a crawling flow of colored

---

[36] The sale of ice cream on Sundays was allowed anew in 1922, the sale of gasoline on Sundays in 1926, baseball and football (after 2 p.m.) in 1933, movies in 1935. As late as 1950 there was no midnight Mass on Christmas Eve for the Catholics in Philadelphia; Cardinal Dougherty, a teetotaler, had forbidden it, lest some of the people in Philadelphia be scandalized during Holy Night by the eventual sight of unseemly alcoholic merriment.

[37] See pp. 105–6.

steel. The decline of public transportation and the swelling of the suburbs would inevitably follow; to go downtown became even more difficult; what was more important, it made less and less sense.

It was because of some of their particular qualities, including their financial practices, their investment policies and, first of all, because of the characters of their leading figures, that many traditional Philadelphia institutions and Philadelphia banks weathered the financial crises of 1873 and 1907, and even that of 1929–33, considerably better than had many comparable institutions elsewhere in the nation.[38] Soon after 1950, however, the management of these institutions became indistinguishable from the national corporate pattern. They would abandon many of their traditional and particular procedures, adapting themselves to techniques that were standardized, transnational, and popular at the time. Many of them would select outsiders, men reputed for their management wizardry, to direct and preside over these operations; they would convince themselves of the advantages of merger with large corporations, their former competitors; in some instances they would move their headquarters to New York. There they would dwindle ignominiously and, in some instances, collapse and disappear entirely. This was the destiny—self-chosen destiny, rather than inevitable fate—of such monumental Philadelphia institutions as the Pennsylvania Railroad,[39] the Curtis Publishing Company, Lippincott's (the principal Philadelphia publishing house), Eden Hall (Agnes Repplier's erstwhile forcing school of the madams of the Sacred Heart). Except in the case of the last, these decisions were made by the men of the city, its financial leaders at mid-century. The dénouement of these events occurred in the

---

[38] This is judiciously set forth in Nicholas B. Wainwright, *History of the Philadelphia National Bank: A Century and a Half of Philadelphia Banking* (Philadelphia, 1953), especially pp. 198 ff.

[39] Owen Wister in *Monopolis* (Wister MSS., Box 83, p. 24) : "Allusions to the Railroad were generally made with that bating of the voice observable in the godly as they approach the church-door on the Sabbath." As late as 1950, Fiske Kimball would refer to it as "the Valhalla."

1960s, otherwise a time of national expansion and of—increasingly dubious—prosperity. But they had ripened around 1950, because of the decline of certain convictions and of the belief in the viability of certain traditions in the hearts and minds of men.

Such were some of the results of this inclination to conform to the national pattern of progress. And thus many things in Philadelphia changed; but not everything. Much of the coziness, the slowness, the warmth, the privacy of the Philadelphia spirit continued to prevail. They were not always palpable to visitors: for a visitor in a hotel, bereft of friends or acquaintances in Philadelphia, a weekend in this city remained as dreary as ever. There were, however, things remnant in the Philadelphia nooks and crannies—snowy afternoons in Germantown before Christmas, with yellow lights shining serenely out of the gray-stone Quaker houses, with all of the promises of decency and of the sentimental warmth of an American small town; the coruscating lights through the fog settling on Rittenhouse Square, muffled and elegant, reminiscent of a vanished London; Reading Terminal Market, with a thin coating of sawdust on its floors and its stalls heavy with mountains of produce, sides of meat, shimmering hills of fish equal to the best in the market halls of Europe; the inimitable and irreproducible scent of old Chester County farmhouses inhabited by Philadelphians, a potpourri redundant of furniture polish, mustiness, and freshly dusted carpets; the stores in Chestnut Hill, managed by the descendants of their owners and founders, crisp and straight in their tweeds, knowing everyone, though not all; the flowers in ironstone bowls and vases, everywhere. There was something Philadelphian in the smell of the sea in the remaining oyster houses as well as in the well-lit dining room of the Barclay Hotel, so very different from the rich hotel restaurants of New York even in the 1950s, with its own kind of a smart provinciality, with a dependable majority of recognizable faces all around, something akin to the placid climate of county in England, but in a more comfortable and easy-going American version. If Philadelphia was twenty years behind New York, so be it; and for this writer, coming from Europe and the Second World War, there was something else, too: the utter charm of an American city behind the times, the odd survivals of an earlier and better century as late as 1950; and by these survivals he did not mean artifacts or pieces of overdone Victorian furniture for which he did not care, even when these had become fashionable again, but certain civilities of the heart for which he cared very much indeed. What George Orwell wrote about England during the welter of the last world war applied to Philadelphia perhaps more than to any other city in America: no matter how things would change, it would not lose all its peculiar flavor: the gentleness, the hypocrisy, the thoughtlessness, the respect for law would remain; like England after 1941, Philadelphia during the last half of the American century would still be Philadelphia, "an everlasting animal stretching into the future and the past and, like all living things, having the power to change out of recognition and yet remain the same."[40]

And so Philadelphia did not change beyond recognition; in the private habits of its people it probably has changed less than New York or Boston or Washington, even now. Were Penrose or Miss Repplier or Bok or Bullitt or Pepper or Wister or Barnes to reappear today, they would be surprised by some of the changes and downcast by others; but their city would be as recognizable as ever, and so would many things in the private lives and preferences of the descendants of some of the people they had known. Perhaps Bok would be the only one among them who would be shocked beyond belief by the disappearance of the empire he had built in Philadelphia: but, then, Bok was unlike the others, not only because of his non-Philadelphia provenance, but because of his publicitarian Americanism, which, in spite of the Franklin touch, was not very Philadelphian after all.

[40] *England Your England* (London, 1959), p. 229.

One more thing remains to be said about the biographical subjects of this book and about the spirit of the city where they lived and which they reflected in so many different ways. In 1950 most of them were gone; Agnes Repplier, whose life lasted close to a century, died during that year. What did they have in common? In spite of certain similarities of breeding and education, not much. There was, however, one significant thing. Their mothers, without exception, were stronger than their fathers. These mothers lived during the nineteenth century, when Victorian women are thought to have been subservient, when families were paternalistic, when masculinity was unchallenged and dominant, when not only the orderly hierarchies of domestic and social life but the very appearances and countenances of men were meant to reflect the virile hegemony of the male. Yet, all these appearances and all the accepted clichés about the age notwithstanding, the feminine gender, in these cases, as in many others, was the stronger one. Owen Wister was one of the few people who noticed this. In his unpublished *Monopolis* he wrote about the women of Philadelphia before 1900: "In a few generations they surpassed the men." He was right; but then he was wrong again. "The simplicity of their crystal faith and their unworldliness made them into something spiritually so gentle and serene, that America has seen nothing lovelier in the shape of womankind. When the breath of the cock-tail [sic] and the cigarette blew them away, Monopolis was not a gainer of this change of wind."[41] No: all the latter did not make that much difference, not in Philadelphia. This kind of feminine strength was not dependent on a pristine and Quaker unworldliness; its substance was not that of the more modern version of the sentimentalized (and, in reality, often blue hair-tinted) American grandmother baking the turkey or saying the blessing on the covers of *The Saturday Evening Post*. Nor was it the proverbial strength of the Puritan woman, or of her West-going descendant, a woman with a sunburned face under

[41] Wister MSS. Box 83, p. 21.

her bonnet, peering sternly ahead. The best qualities of American women, as represented in Philadelphia, have always included a fine compound of reticence and understanding: reticence about matters of belief, understanding of matters of the world. They were strong, but they were not assertive. Their strength had much to do with their sense of family and of tribe; and this sense would manifest itself not in an unworldly kind of gentility but in a profoundly female comprehension of the requirements for a decent life. It was not the result of suppressed instincts but of an understanding that was more thorough than mere intellect. I saw, on certain unforgettable occasions, the gently reserved and yet wise and worldly smile of grandmothers among the *grandes dames* of Philadelphia reappear on the faces of old Irish nuns and on those of the two middle-aged Jewish spinsters sewing in a loft where I once ventured in quest of two lampshades of a particular shape and color. The faces were different, but the substance of the smile was the same.

The women were stronger, they were more deeply civilized, than the men. They, not the men, were the true conservatives. So often their domesticity fulfilled the prescription of Dorothy Wordsworth: "It calls home the heart to quietness." There may have been a historical substance to this, relating to the destiny of this country: they were not the Last Best Hope of Mankind (a maudlin phrase, when you think of it); they were, toward the end of the Modern Age, guardians of what remained, and of what still remains, of civilization.

BIBLIOGRAPHICAL NOTES

THE EXCLUSIVE PURPOSE of these bibliographical notes is to aid further research. I shall neither list nor repeat any of the titles of the books and articles cited or quoted in the main text, except when I refer to some of them in the following pages, the main matter of which concerns archives and so-called primary sources. A further limitation: this book consists of descriptions of Philadelphia around 1900 and around 1950, as well as of seven biographical chapters: it is emphatically not a compendium of the history of the city during the first half of the twentieth century.

All students and researchers of the history of Philadelphia, whether amateur or professional, owe a debt to the City Archives of Philadelphia, reorganized during the last fifteen years by an excellent archivist, Allen Weinberg; they are accessible, they have their own guides and their own newsletters, and they include a cross-referenced, rich photographic archive—as does the Historical Society of Pennsylvania and its adjacent Library Company. In addition to the books and articles cited in Chapters I ("Philadelphia, 1900") and IX ("Philadelphia, 1950") here are a few additional items worth consulting: J. T. Scharf and T. Westcott, *History of Philadelphia* (Philadelphia, 1884), to complement Repplier (see p. 108; Thompson Westcott was a distant relation of hers); also the considerably dreary Ellis Paxson Oberholtzer, *Philadelphia: A History of the City and Its People* (Philadelphia, 1912). Joseph Jackson's *Encyclopedia of Philadelphia* (Harrisburg, 1931) and *Literary Landmarks of Philadelphia* (Philadelphia, 1939) are not dreary at all; as a matter of fact, they are invaluable. Poor old Joe Jackson! He loved Philadelphia and worked his history to the bone—with little recognition. Wolf (see p. 39) is concise and occasionally illuminating; Pennell (see p. 12) is disgustingly and self-consciously snobbish, but full of details that would have been otherwise lost; one of its assets is the many drawings by her husband of the city *circa* 1900–10. The literary essays of Christopher Morley and of Cornelius Weygandt (especially the former's *Travels in Philadelphia* [Philadelphia, 1920] and the latter's *Philadelphia Folks* [New York, 1938]) deserve recognition, even though they do not fit into the scope of my two city chapters; they deal mostly with the city after World War I. The two subscription books by Moses King are a mine of oddities: *The City of Philadelphia as it Appears in the Year 1894* and *Philadelphia and Notable Philadelphians* (1902); about the latter see also the amusing but substantial article by "Vincent Wagner" (John Maass) in the 29 August 1977 *Sunday Bulletin*. Concerning the society of Philadelphia, Burt (see p. 15) and Baltzell (p. 280) are near-encyclopedic. The history of cities is a difficult matter; despite the proliferation of urban "studies" and the pretensions of social historians during the last twenty years, no substantial advancements have yet occurred in this field. (There are exceptions to this, of course: see, for example, the numerous articles and books by Maxwell Whiteman, librarian of the Union League of Philadelphia, including Wolf and Whiteman, *The History of the Jews in Philadelphia* [Philadelphia, 1956].) The main problem (though not the only one) of the history of a modern city is that, unlike subjects of earlier times, the material is excessive and ungovernable. (About this historiographical problem in general terms, see pp. 53–58 of my *Historical Consciousness* [New York, 1968] and pp. 528–29 of *The Last European War, 1939–41* [New York, 1976].) I set forth my particular, and perhaps idiosyncratic, desiderata for an eventual history of Philadelphia in Chapter I, pp. 17–18.

The biographer's problem is different: the quantity, and surely the quality, of personal letters during the twentieth century diminishes. This is true of Boies Penrose, who, as we have seen, boasted that he never wrote a letter to a woman one couldn't chill beer on. His correspondence was voluminous; but most of his letters deal with the most routine of matters. *The National Union Catalogue, Manuscript Collections* (Library of Congress) is of little help. Mrs. Frances Penrose Haythe lent me her grand-uncle's black leather Senate trunk, containing many photographs, invitations, ceremonial dinner menus, and a few letters. Its very smell vitalized the imagination; it furnished, however, elements of inspiration rather than muniments of research. Penrose's two biographies (Davenport and Bowden, p. 55) are journalistic but valuable in some of their details. Agnes Repplier was a great correspondent. I estimate the number of letters she wrote as at least ten thousand; a few hundred are extant, scattered throughout the country (see the *Manuscript Collections . . .* supra), the best indexed are in the Rare Books Room of Princeton University. Her two biographers are Stokes (p. 88) and Witmer (p. 87). *Bok* and *Pepper* wrote their own biographies, the first repeatedly (see p. 150 and p. 173). Bok's correspondence was enormous; some of it rests with the remnant of the Curtis Publishing Company files in a warehouse in Indianapolis. Pepper's correspondence resides in the Rare Book Room of the University of Pennsylvania; a small portion in the archives of the university; few of his letters of a personal nature are there. To Orville Bullitt's excellent volume about *William C. Bullitt*'s relationship with Franklin Roosevelt (see p. 184) add Beatrice Farnsworth, *William C. Bullitt and the Soviet Union* (Bloomington, Ind., 1967), and the one-dimensional portrait in Craig and Gilbert, eds., *The Diplomats* (Princeton, 1953). Among all my Philadelphians, Bullitt deserves a biography on a national scale. Unfortunately his papers, which had been deposited in Yale, were withdrawn by his daughter, who lives in Ireland. The two books by *Owen Wister*'s daughter are mentioned on p. 244; to these add *My Dear Wister* (p. 243) and the short monograph by Richard Etulain, *Owen Wister* (Boise, Idaho, 1973), as well as an increasing number of articles in the annual *American Literary Scholarship* (Duke University Press). Wister's papers in the Library of Congress Annex occupy more than eighty large boxes, containing his correspondence with all kinds of people, including Theodore Roosevelt and Ernest Hemingway, as well as portions of at least two of his unfinished novels, *Monopolis* (see p. 255) and *The Star-Gazers*. The two biographies of *Barnes* are Hart (p. 263) and Schack (p. 264). His explosive correspondence is closed to researchers.

Among secondary figures in my biographical chapters, John G. Johnson deserves a biography. His papers exist somewhere in the law office of his successors; his only biography (Barnie F. Winkelman, *John G. Johnson: Lawyer and Art Collector, 1841–1917*, Philadelphia, 1942) is inadequate. Francis Biddle wrote his own biography (*In Brief Authority,* New York, 1962; and *A Casual Past,* New York, 1966, which is indeed casual). See also his novel, *The Llanfair Pattern* (Philadelphia, 1927), more respected but, in reality, inferior to Bullitt's; and Bradley F. Smith, *Reaching Judgment at Nuremberg* (New York, 1975), based largely on Biddle's trial diaries. His papers are in the library of Syracuse University.

HERE MY DEBTS are the opposites of my financial obligations: they are numerous and pleasant. I must record my debts to librarians and archivists: to Miss Helen Hayes, reference librarian in Chestnut Hill College, whose sense of humor and of assistance are instantly fructiferous, a rare combination; to Mrs. Georgette Most and Miss Ellen Wall of La Salle College Library, two ladies who are pert, precise, and unfailing; to Peter Parker of the Manuscripts Division of the Historical Society of Pennsylvania whose advice and help were generous when I was starting out on the track of Penrose as well as when I ended up among the photographic riches of another Penrose; to Francis James Dallett, Archivist of the University of Pennsylvania, with his *esprit de la finesse* when it comes to bibliography and iconography; to the staff of the Manuscript Division of the Library of Congress. Mrs. Frances Penrose Haythe, daughter of the late Boies Penrose (nephew of the Senator and a fine scholar in his own right) let me have the surviving papers of her grand-uncle with instant ease. George W. Pepper III kindly allowed me to consult his grandfather's papers at the University of Pennsylvania. Orville H. Bullitt and George F. Kennan read every word of my Bullitt chapter twice. Professors Fritz Stern of Columbia and J. A. F. de Jongste of Leyden helped me to track down a Bokish matter. My friends Michael von Moschzisker, Lester Conner, and James F. Sullivan read parts of the manuscript; Harry Harris, director of the Woodmere Gallery and former director of the art department of Episcopal Academy, talked to me of the academy's relationship to its neighbor Barnes; and about Barnes I had the good fortune to meet Henry Hart, a *trouvaille* of a man, to whom I was directed by Robert Giroux. My indebtedness to Jacques Barzun is great. He read, and edited, six chapters of this book with the precision that marks the jeweler's eye and, behind it, the presence of a splendid mind. I am inclined to laugh at those fulsome and sentimental acknowledgments that beginning scholars tend to proffer to their wives in the prefaces of their first books. I am not a young scholar and this is my eleventh book and I know without my wife this book would have been written and that she never makes me breakfast or lunch; but she is such a fine reader that I must record my debt to her. This debt consists of the fact that I agreed with, say, 80 percent of her criticisms and suggestions and of the equally important fact that to discuss this book with her was 100 percent pleasure either before, during, or after her dinners that vary from 80 to 120 percent, the latter being a mathematical impossibility but on occasion a culinary fact.

There remains the homage due to the fine memory of two men who died during my writing of this book. How I wished to present it to them; but this was not to be. Joseph P. McLaughlin and Orville H. Bullitt: *fuerant cives Philadelphienses optimi.*

"Old Pickering School House,"
Williams' Corner, near Phoenixville, Pennsylvania
1976–1980

INDEX